D0913839

Frontispiece photo by William Carter

PUBLISHED JUNE 1982
Second printing November 1982

Abridged from *The Journals of A. H. Maslow,* originally published as a two volume
set by the Brooks/Cole Publishing Company, Monterey, California, copyright © 1979.
Edited by Richard J. Lowry (Vassar College) for the International Study Project,
Inc. (Menlo Park, California) in cooperation with Bertha Maslow.

Abridgment copyright © 1982 by The Lewis Publishing Company.

This book is manufactured in the United States of America. It is published
by The Lewis Publishing Company, Fessenden Road, Brattleboro, Vermont.

Library of Congress Cataloging in Publication Data

Maslow, Abraham Harold.
 The journals of Abraham Maslow.

 Abridgment of: The journals of A.H. Maslow.
c1979.
 Includes index.
 1. Maslow, Abraham Harold. 2. Psychologists—
United States—Biography. I. Lowry, Richard,
1940-   II. Maslow, Bertha G. III. Freedman,
Jonathan L. IV. International Study Project.
V. Title.
BF109.M33A342 1982   150'.92'4 [B]   82–15232
ISBN 0–86616–015–9   AACR2
ISBN 0–86616–016–7 (pbk.)

The Journals of Abraham Maslow

Edited by
Richard J. Lowry
Vassar College

For the
International Study Project, Inc.
Menlo Park, California

In cooperation with
Bertha G. Maslow

Abridged by
Jonathan Freedman

The Lewis Publishing Company
Lexington, Massachusetts
Brattleboro, Vermont

Contents

Maslow's journal entries are organized by year following the format of the original edition.

Introduction to the Abridged Edition

In abridging the Journals of Abraham Maslow we have tried to retain all material that is relevant to his views of psychology and to his contributions to the field, as well as material in which he expresses his ideas about politics, university life, sexuality, and the meaning of life. We have also kept his notes on his feelings as he moved from relative anonymity to become one of the most famous psychologists in the world—and on his responses to a field in which many applauded his ideas, bought his books, invited him to give talks, and eventually elected him President of the American Psychological Association—but a field in which at the same time most academic psychologists rejected his ideas, criticized him for not doing research, and did not offer him positions in prestigious universities. This conflict runs through the journals and provides fascinating insights into Maslow as a man.

We are grateful to the original editor, who did such a fine job of producing the complete journals. Although we have attempted to keep all of the most interesting and important passages, we naturally had to make some difficult choices in making this abridgment. We apologize to any readers of the full edition who find their favorite passages cut. But we do believe that this shorter version, with some of the incidental material removed, gives an even clearer view of Maslow's psychology, personality, and ideas.

Bracketed numbers within the text refer to the bibliography of Maslow's works found in Volume II of the original edition.

Original Introduction to the Complete Journals

These are the Journals of Abraham Harold Maslow (1908–1970), who during the last several decades of his life was among the most eminent of American psychologists. Although Maslow had an approach to psychology that was uniquely his own,* the value of these Journals is by no means limited to those who are aficionados of this approach. The aficionados will of course find much to interest them, for it was here that Maslow took his highest and most extended flights into the realm of what he called "B-psychology." But quite apart from this, the preeminent psychological value of these Journals is that they afford an almost unparalleled glimpse into the innermost workings of an extraordinary man.

Maslow began keeping his Journals in 1959, when he was 51 years old, and wrote in them at every opportunity during the remaining years of his life. As it happened, these remaining years were all too few, for he died unexpectedly only 11 years later, in 1970, at the age of 62. Still, even in this relatively brief period, though he was all the while busily engaged with teaching, lecturing, and writing for publication, Maslow was able to fill his Journals with several thousand pages of handwritten notes, records, and reflections. The content of these pages is reproduced here virtually unaltered. Our general editorial policy in preparing these Journals for publication has been to let them speak for themselves. Thus we have tried to leave them as intact, unadorned, and uncluttered as possible. The version presented here departs from the original only in the following ways:

1. A small amount of alteration resulted from the process of transforming the handwritten word into the printed word. In their original physical form, the Journals convey a powerful sense of fluidity and spontaneity. Indeed, the original is a great, beautiful (but very difficult) tangle of main text, marginal notes, submarginal notes, and facing-page additions and commentaries, often connected and reconnected by an intricate latticework

*For a brief general introduction to Maslow and his psychological work, see R. Lowry, A. H. Maslow: An Intellectual Portrait (Monterey, Calif.: Brooks/Cole, 1973).

...es and arrows. Transforming the Journals into hard print required that these ancillary materials be either linearly inserted in brackets and italics else, where appropriate, incorporated into the text. Although we have tried to preserve as much of the "nonlinear" quality of the original as possible, some of it has been unavoidably lost. We have attempted to compensate somewhat by photographically reproducing a number of original Journal pages, so that the reader might approach the printed page with a sense of what the original looked like. Most of the editorial work that falls under this heading was performed by Micky Lawler of Brooks/Cole Publishing Company. I believe she has done a remarkably competent and artful job of it.

2. The autobiographical writings of eminent persons are often marred by literary posturing and artificiality. Maslow, however, managed to avoid these pitfalls almost entirely. I believe this is because he was simply not given to posturing and artificiality—I would almost say not capable of it. Be that as it may, this ingenuous quality of Maslow's Journals also made for certain editorial problems. When Maslow had something to write, he simply wrote it, without stopping to bother with the conventional literary amenities. The result is that much of the Journals in their original form cannot be read without a struggle. Sometimes his sentences would go on for lines and lines, convoluting as they went, so that by the time the reader got to the end he or she could scarcely remember what had stood at the beginning. At other times Maslow wrote in a very abbreviated, cryptic, telegraphic style. And then, to top it all off, there was a tendency throughout toward indefinite reference, omission of grammatical parts, and ambiguous or even inconsistent punctuation. In short, the literary form of the original was rather rough in spots and required a certain amount of editorial polishing. The polish was applied very conservatively, only insofar as it was needed for intelligibility, and never for the sake of mere literary nicety. At all events there have been absolutely no changes in sense or substance.

3. The ingenuous spontaneity and candor of Maslow's Journals gave rise to another editorial problem as well. It is that Maslow sometimes wrote of his students, colleagues, friends, acquaintances, and even family in a rather unflattering way. Those of us involved in preparing the Journals for publication gave the matter very serious thought and at length decided to delete names in extreme cases but otherwise to leave things as intact as possible. The decision was based on two considerations: first, that most of the persons to whom Maslow refers in this manner are strong, intelligent people who are capable of putting the matter in proper perspective; second, that the intelligent general reader will also be able to take such matters with a proper grain of salt. Let it suffice to remind the reader that there are two sides to every story, and in the Journals only one of these sides— Maslow's—is being told.

4. Now and again you will find a brief explanatory editorial comment inserted into the text in brackets and roman type; these have been

kept to an utter minimum. You will also find bracketed numbers (for example, [48]) inserted into the text. These occur when reference is made to one of Maslow's own published works; the numbers correspond to those of the writings listed in the appended Maslow bibliography at the end of Volume II.

There are occasional overlaps in the chronology of the various Journals. This is because Maslow sometimes kept more than one Journal at the same time.

Although I alone am listed as the "editor" of these Journals, the task of bringing them to publication was in fact the work of many. First and foremost among these was Mrs. Bertha G. Maslow, into whose capable hands the late Dr. Maslow wisely entrusted the disposition of his Journals. It is no exaggeration to say that, without Mrs. Maslow, the whole job would have come to nothing. Her contribution was every bit as great as mine, and in many ways far greater.

Also highly deserving of mention are William Price Laughlin, William Crockett, Kay Pontius, and John Wilson, Attorney at Law, of the International Study Project, Inc., Menlo Park, California, which provided the material support for this and other publication projects pertaining to Maslow. I may add that the support these persons provided was by no means limited to the material realm.

Last, but certainly not least, I must mention Micky Lawler, Linda Marcetti, Bill Hicks, and Terry Hendrix of Brooks/Cole Publishing Company. Anyone who has ever worked with publishers—especially editors—will know that they can be either a great help or a great hindrance. The staff at Brooks/Cole has been always the former and never the latter. All in all, it has been a great pleasure to work with them.

For my own part, I am grateful to Vassar College, which provided me with a year's leave during which I was able to work full-time on these and other Maslow materials, and, most of all, to my wife, Marsha, and daughter, Heather, who so patiently bore with me during that intense and strenuous period.

Richard J. Lowry

March 2 1959

I'm reading Kierkegaard's
journals & have recently finished
Ruth Benedict's journal. So I am
thinking of advantages of keeping
one myself. The card system I've been
using is getting to point of breaking
down, what with carbon copies & cross-
indexing and uncountable volumes under
each topic. Have file cabinets
full, so full & so big that things
get lost in them. I've always had
custom of thinking & writing assembled
around 30 or 40 topics at same
time anyway, but now there are very
many - must be 100 or so - & also I can
see that it's all falling together
& interlocking into a single big
job - a philosophy of human nature.
Everything I write seems to be related
& connected with everything else
I'm writing ... that of the ...

1959

March 2

Cuernavaca, June 1958–Sept. 1959. I'm reading Kierkegaard's Journals & have recently finished Ruth Benedict's Journal set & am thinking of the advantages of keeping one myself. Also, the system I've been using is getting to the point of breaking down, what with carbon copies & cross-indexing and numberless headings under which to file. I have file cabinets full—so full & big that things get lost in them. I've always had the custom of thinking & writing simultaneously on 30 or 40 topics at the same time anyway, but now there are even more—must be 100 or so—& also I can see that it's all falling together & interlocking into a single big job, a philosophy of human nature. Everything I write seems to be related & connected with everything else I'm writing, so that often I'm tempted to make 6 carbons for cross-indexing—& it could as easily be 12 carbons. Also, I don't have enough typing help ever. A journal system should help on this score. I can have typed out of it whatever seems useful at its second stage of development. Often for me the first stage is almost free association, not necessary to type.

There are many other advantages, some of which Kierkegaard lists in his journal. For me another one, outside of the personal advantage of helping my thinking—I think so much more clearly on paper—is the sad thought I've so often had: death for an intellectual usually means total loss of everything unfinished, all that is ¼ or ½ or ¾ done. Whenever I die it will be so—many things left half done. The journal system is better for salvaging incomplete stuff for someone else to finish.

I think I'll continue to use my present system of organizing my thinking & writing—3 × 5 cards and 8½ × 11 sheets, topically filed—whenever the topic is clear enough & well enough developed to be singled out & separated for future developing & perfecting, or for classes or lectures, etc. And *until* that point leave it inchoate in a journal, but not lost. A place for the 1st stages of thinking.

Maybe this is also a publishable form—that is, useful for other people as well as for myself. Every intellectual used to keep a journal, and many have been published & are usually more interesting & more instructive than the final formal perfected pages which are so often phony in a way—so certain, so structured, so definite. The *growth* of thought from its beginnings is also instructive—maybe even more so for some rposes. I've been learning to do this in my public lectures a little ore—honestly thinking out loud when I'm not so certain of what I'm saying—show my uncertainty. More honest, more humble, more true. I'm old enough & well enough known so that people in an audience are apt to take as gospel even my uncertainties, my guesses. I feel now the responsibility of not misleading, of not having transference-convictions in my audiences. If I present my conclusions as tentative, I hate for them to be heard as certain! The projects I'm working on now are many, tho they *should* be one—the Psychology of Science that looks very promising & I'm sure I'll work it up formally as articles or as a book. But my long-time interests remain, especially masculinity-femininity, which my mind keeps turning to & which makes me pick things out of whatever I read or hear or see. That too should be a book one day. Psychodynamic theory in general also is an enduring interest & also determines my reading in part. I love trying to formulate into theory the insight of the clinicians like Harry Rand, Walter Toman, Dostoievsky, etc. As a matter of fact I think I'll copy my list of Going Projects in here. I'll enjoy looking back on records of how my interests form, live, & die. Also, it will save some of my forgotten insights, beautiful ones that are lost because I have too many of them to work them all out or even to classify & save efficiently. If one fever is followed too closely by another fever, the first tends to be forgotten. One of my real jobs of self-discipline is controlling & organizing all these intellectual wild horses & trying to keep some sort of order in my intellectual household economy, not to give up a half-finished job in favor of some beautiful inspiration. If I pursued each insight as it came forth, I'd never get any *one* of them done—there are too many. That's one of my sadnesses as I get older—there are so many births from among which I have to choose a few & let the other offspring die. Just not enough time & energy. So it happens that much of what is actually published is not what is most important to me but what is quickest & easiest to do, or what retains its initial inspiration & enthusiasm to get finished before another lovely idea seizes me & organizes me & pulls my energies to it. Like having too many children to feed & bring up. This journal will help in this housekeeping job. A good way of being more anal, controlled, orderly, efficient, workman-like.

March 18

My reading this A.M. set me off again on peak-experiences & B-values. I find it solves or promises to solve many value problems. Wrote a good memo & think of publishing it one day if I have the time to work it up a little. Wish I could just turn it over to a philosopher collaborator to work up. The ideas are all there. Anyway, I will put it down on the project list. Maybe I'll wait for someone to invite me to lecture on it. Might as well get paid for it.

Just got from V. a long & bitter critique of Values book, especially my chapter. Leads me to try to answer or at least explain special aspects of my work which she & others don't understand:

(1) It is empirical rather than philosophical in the traditional sense. It goes step by step, taking one thread at a time out of the whole weave to pay isolated attention to, putting the others aside for the moment. It is not in writing anyway, synoptic even tho I may have this trend in my head. This means also it is more or less operational, not using any words or concepts that are to me not yet meaningful—me as an empiricist—which means operational, researchable. To this extent I am positivistic. The theorizing is only a little way out in front of the knowledge.

(2) It is "philosophical" in the sense that I get most stimulation for my empirical thinking from philosophical writings. It may itself ultimately become "a philosophy," comprehensive, total, etc., in a long lifetime. Meanwhile I do it piece by piece, hoping to weave them all together, eventually & bit by bit (as in the paper for Combs).

Thus it doesn't touch me a bit when they say "You left out this or that." I'll get to it eventually. Or when they say "This is only a partial solution."

Everything I've written so far is researchable, repeatable, validatible.

Also, this means I don't mind too much the inconsistencies that come from different operations. I think of it as growing, just the way science does. An inconsistency or contradiction is a point at which to work, not a reason for rejecting the whole business.

It is naturalistic & antisupernaturalistic. It is not metaphysical. It is pre-science, or the 1st stage of science, *not* these other things.

March 25

1 A. M—can't sleep. Stimulated by Herberg's article in B. Nelson's *Freud & the 20th Century* to work further on relation between self-psychology & society. He contrasts Freud & Fromm—not being really fair to Fromm—& yet he raises plenty of questions that should be straightened out, or let's say, his misunderstandings are typical & should be wiped away. He's a religionist, and there is plenty of crap in it too. Not a good article but set me off anyway. The problem is so big I've been ducking it & postponing it. Also, Maron recently has been bringing up questions of self-actualization *thru the community*—especially now he's

.nterested in the Jewish community. Also Angyal with his autonomy & homonomy as different drives.

How to take into account all stuff on feral children & Goldfarb, Spitz, et al., that shows humanness itself is brought out by people, society. No society, no human—at least in usual sense. Then one of the basic needs—for gregariousness & belongingness & herding—is strictly social, not to mention that most other basic-need gratifications come from other people & that a baby can't even survive without other people. The real self is only partly uncovered. It is also created by the person himself, but he is already enculturated, so *it* (culture) partly creates the real Self. Certainly the culture opens many paths to SA & closes many others; gives a stage for some capacities & not for others—e.g., baseball player, violinist, scientist.

And yet if the Self concept, or SA, has any meaning at all, it is in opposition to culture and emancipation from it. Opposition to culture = Autonomy. This mustn't be lost. And the point I made in the Values paper—that the genes give the possibility of humanness, and culture only brings it out or kills it—is certainly true. All the Ape & the Child stuff of Kellogg, Hayes, & Finch alone prove this. The raw material is given, and the Sullivan kind of crap about Self being what other people think of you is just nonsense. How to put it all together?

Now for Herberg (p. 145). Anthropology has on the whole wound up pointing to a universal human nature. Maybe Freud helped. Maybe not. ". . . Freud who was always striving to discern the contemporary in the archaic and the archaic in the contemporary." I suppose this means seeing both deep & superficial humanness in both primitive & large cultures. ". . . The psychoanalytic penchant for finding the same basic mechanisms and motivation operating in primitive societies as in contemporary ones." But I suspect without Freud they would have come to Kluckhohn's conclusions about universal needs & values.

He regrets Freud's anthropological Totem & Taboo stuff as wrong but says nothing about its rightness as myth, as unconscious, primary-process truth of which it has much. It has the truth of a dream or a poem.

(p. 48) If sex & aggression are instincts, & if they are the only instincts, then Freud is right about the relation between the person & society. The sociologists & ethnologists go sailing smoothly along making a principle of neglect or denial of instinct theory. If they admitted it—or basic need theory—they'd have to change all their theories. Instincts of sex & aggression *are* antisocial if they exist—they must be. And culture would *have* to oppose free play of instincts, and it would *have* to demand instinctional renunciation. "This is so because unrestricted and unregulated instinctoid expression would make social life impossible; it is so for the even more important reason that cultural creativity requires a considerable amount of psychic energy, which can only be obtained by directing it from its primary instinctual aims and using it for cultural purposes."

(This whole idea of sublimation, etc., is nonsense.) So far the assumptions are (1) of sublimation, (2) of instincts, (3) that these instincts are of sex & aggression. These are independent assumptions, not needing each other. (4) The notion of love & friendship as "aim-inhibited libido"—i.e., love is really sex, and so is friendship—is another assumption that, like sublimation, is mostly wrong & certainly not right often enough to serve as a *general* theory, & furthermore which makes it clear that when Freud says sex or libido he means just that, *not* love or Eros as a basic impulse. ". . . its (society's) ideal command to love one's neighbor as oneself, which is really justifiably the fact that nothing is so completely at variance with original human nature as this" (p. 149). I.e., love for neighbor or for children is not an original, underived impulse. But the evidence is now available to indicate or even prove that it *is* a basic impulse, & so Freud is wrong here too, & therefore so is his theory of society. See *Civilization & its Discontents* & *Group Psychology & the Analysis of the Ego*. "Every culture is based on coercion and instinctual renunciation" (p. 151), "so the difficulties inherent in the very nature of culture will not yield to any efforts at reform." No room left for other instincts, especially no inborn social instincts, leaving unsolved the question of why there are societies at all & not just isolated baboon bands.

(p. 151) "Where Freud is dualistic, Fromm is harmonistic." (*Nu*, why not? They're *both* true. In pathology, the person *is* split. But his healthy tendency is toward harmony. And this exists too. And why is it not seen that Freud's philosophy of man contradicts the integrative goals of his therapy, even if *he* didn't see it as integration?)

Where Freud is somber, even pessimistic, Fromm exhibits an amazing confidence in the possibilities of human progress. (Again a false opposition. They're both right. And anyway the question is not one of optimism vs. pessimism but of realism. Just what are the chances of improvement, of good prognosis? How? When? Any chances of any improvement greater than zero are grounds for hope & optimism. And of course psychoanalytic therapy *does* make improvements & *does* show progress.) "Where Freud assumes the posture of a disillusioned observer, Fromm is always the reformer." (Here too the dichotomy is too sharp. Freud is not *always* disillusioned & certainly is rarely so *in his* therapy. Fromm is not always the reformer. [*See review of Schaar book on Fromm, 1962.*] Also, "disillusioned" means there were illusions. Also, what's wrong with reform?) In my theory, I think all of this is integrated, but the hostile critic could still pick out stray sentences to exaggerate & isolate, as Herberg does with Fromm. This suggests to write it more carefully, less enthusiastically & dramatically. The proposition idea of presentation is a good one for this purpose; it can present one thread at a time & yet have all the threads there.

(p. 151) "To Fromm, man is not divided against himself in the very structure of the psyche, but is essentially unified, intact, perfect." No, if one says that the trend to SA (& unity, intactness & perfection) exists, this doesn't mean that's the *only* trend that exists. (See my Defense & Growth [63].) And if one points that out at higher levels of maturity, that doesn't mean it's true at lower levels. Nor does it even mean "essentially"; it means only under different conditions. There is a trend to unity (also there's a trend to split). There is a trend to perfection (which is never perfectly achieved but *is* partially achieved). "The imperfections and distortions of human nature Fromm traces to the corrupting effects of the culture." Partially true. But less so now that Fromm is writing more as an existentialist and less as a Marxist. Anyway the question is "How much is due to culture & how much to the human predicament?" I really should finish up my paper on Evil.

(p. 151) "It is not easy to get a clear picture of man from Fromm's writing because he still wavers between his earlier conception that it is 'The social process which creates men' and his more recent view that there is a normative human nature which is the same for man in all ages and all cultures." Touché. Fromm really can't decide between Marx & Existentialism, SA, Growth, Self, etc. But anyway, again both are true. But how true? And how do the two truths relate to each other? In what sense is man created by culture & society? And in what sense by genes? Which aspects of deeper human nature *are* universal? I think it's largely human motivation. And this Fromm neglects. Throwing out the Freudian instincts, he threw out also basic needs. I think my "Instinctoid" paper [56] makes the necessary corrections.

(p. 151) "He (man) is seen as essentially good and rational; there is practically no vestige in Fromm of the dark Freudian picture of the primordial struggle between ego, superego, and id in the depths of the self." That's because Fromm is writing a philosophy, not a psychopathology. Also, these positive affirmations don't exclude the existence of their opposites. Man *is* good & rational; he's bad & irrational. I think I've made this clear enough in my writings but should stress it even more.

(p. 152) "That is all man wants to be, but society will not let him, at least society hitherto has not let him. The locus of evil and irrationality is thus not in man, but in society." The real conflict, in other words, is between the good healthy human nature, on the one side, and a sick society on the other. It is the evil society that corrupts the perfection of normative man. What dichotomizing! Either-or. The question is "How true is this?" *not* "Is it either true or false?" And I can see again how badly needed is a reinterpretation of "evil."

(p. 153) Herberg talks about Rousseauism. Watch this. Natural man *is* born free & good & also dependent & bad. Or, rather he is born prior to good & evil (which are adult concepts). The evidence *is* that aggression or cruelty is not an instrument but is reactive self-affirmation and is instinctoid.

(p. 155) "The perfect society (which he imagines to be achievable in history) will provide the necessary and sufficient condition for the emergence of the perfect man." Why caricature it so? Undoubtedly a better society is a necessary & sufficient condition for a better man. But why talk about "perfect"? Society *can* improve, & so can man.

(p. 157) "Yet Fromm is surely right in feeling that human aggression and destructiveness are not merely biological, but are somehow emergent out of the human situation, which, however, Fromm wrongly takes to be identical with the social situation. . . . It is not the biological constitution of man that can be held responsible for the human evil we know in history, nor is it the social order, although both are involved. It is out of man's existential situation—out of the tensions between his self-transcending freedom and the inherent limitations of his creatureliness—that are engendered the basic insecurity and anxiety that prompt him to pride." This is not only tragic but also comic. Pride doesn't always come out of anxiety; it can sometimes be quite justified and deserved. The only thing is that it has to live alongside of humility of creatureliness. It always gets taken down by human limitations. It's OK to have it if one is also *quite* aware of these limitations, remains realistic, and is able to be amused by the discrepancy.

April 2

Reading Wheelis and very much impressed. Reminds me of my feeling often that we need not an improved man but an entirely different *kind* of man, the creative & flexible one who, in the midst of rapid and perpetual change, can be a person and not just an adapter. He points out the disappearance of the "eternal" virtues of the last century, of *every* century. The shift of principles, of morals into mores (without necessary "right" behind them), the continually changing view of the universe, the diminution of the superego (with the diminution of institutional force), nothing "to die for," etc. The job of achieving an identity in the middle of a landslide is *the* job and he feels it's too big for psychoanalysis, which can't give values.

"Every man a general."

"What's the use of *facts*? They all become obsolete."

Another good point. (p. 132) He speaks about the mistrust of reason as science failed & as Marxism failed & as progress failed: "Man, having found that he cannot live by reason alone, seems determined that he will not live by reason at all." Helps to explain anti-intellectualism.

But also it means to watch out, as one talks about instincts, impulses, the deep & dark, that reason, even tho limited, is not thrown away. If the ultimate integration is to be between instinct & reason, and i the job right now is to recover our knowledge of our deepest impulse-voices, the way this is to be done is by study, research, theorizing—i.e., by reason!

I think the strong differentiation he makes between instrumental & institutional is better spoken of as means-values & ends-values. After all, tho institutions were the locus of end-values, they no longer are. The end-values are now to be sought in the depths of human nature. This implies also (p. 167) that his deductions about transference need enlarging. There is not only his superego (as repository of parents' institutions, socially given end-values) but also the intrinsic conscience. Conscience will replace superego as a basic concept & also as a concomitant of maturing in the individual. Where superego was, there shall conscience be.

April 8

Reading Whitehead on foresight. He too stresses different social situation of today; i.e., we must learn to live with perpetual change & with practically no stability, tradition, etc., and it must remain so, or even with faster rate of change. Like Wheelis' thesis that with loss of tradition & external stable rules & values to live by, nature of superego changes & also nature of inner topographical dynamics—i.e., between id, ego, & superego.

This is definitely an addition to my thesis in Values book [69] that all value systems have collapsed & we have to look for new ones. True, but *also* add the rapid social changes of the foreseeable future & the need for a new kind of man—flexible, creative, not relying on any traditions, or on routine or habit or any other way of life learned from past & based on assumption of this past continuing on into future. *The future must be unknown*, and the new man would have to stop *needing* stability, order, routine.

My correction is then to remove the implication in my preface that we were *between* value systems, had to look for new ones & *then* could settle down into a pleasant stability, order, continuity, & peace, as of old. Maybe we can *never* settle down. Maybe we simply have to create a new human nature which is happy with perpetual change & can keep identity easily in the middle of change—a human nature that would *prefer* change and be bored with stability.

We *have* no "future" in the old sense of continuation of past & present in a continuous form.

The notion of "progress" is going to get involved here too. There *is* progress in technological change in the same way there is in science. You can't go back, you can't undo knowledge, you can't unsee what you've seen, you can't forget an improved way of doing things, an unforeseen wish-gratification. How are you going to get women to agree to carry water on their heads from the river a mile away? Or how go back to wooden plows? Or cooking with wood in fireplaces?

But on the whole we'd better watch out for the 19th-century implication of the word "progress." Better say "change" or "flux." We don't even know for sure whether it's for better or for worse. *But it's inevitable.* We don't have to favor it or be against it, or at least it makes no difference. Nothin much we can do about it but accept it.

There can be no "preparation" for the unknown future. Not in the old sense anyway. We can't "teach" anything to help (imparting facts, love, skill). Only solution is to make a new kind of person—each one his own general. A new kind of personality. This means a new kind of "preparation" & of "teaching." "Creative Education" *can* prepare people for the unknown. This means also that we must have a new kind of scientist, one "undaunted by the unknown."

May 15

In the middle of Fromm's *Sane Society* (in Spanish) & very much disturbed by it somehow, fighting against it for half-known reasons. Its overstatements irritate me, even tho I think they're mostly correct. Not quite sure why. Anyway it brings up again for me the ever-present warning not to be too intrapsychic, to be aware of economics, history, politics, society—of the social environment external to the Self but always related to it intimately. I've been sort of bypassing all this.

Had long talks with Frank when he was here. They all came down to the question of integrating Freud & Marx, which he considers impossible—a permanent problem. The trouble is that I know so little about Marx—even as a general "environmentalist" symbol.

In any case, Fromm is overdoing the "abstraction" theme & not stressing enough yet (maybe he does later on) the current developments in psychology—finding the Self, turning inward for salvation—and also all the possibilities for the *culture's* helping this Self to appear & grow. Labor union goals. The new executive & administrative efforts to make industry into a basic need & SA gratifier. The new developments in education, art education, creative education, etc. The reforming going on among the serious religionists like Tillich. "Moral economics" of Weisskopf, Hartman, etc. The new-organism philosophers & intrinsic-to-the-self value theorists. Individuality *can* be retained in the industrial society—maybe far more readily than in the primitive, simple, poor society that allows no time for self-development.

If our Values Institute goes through, these are all basic problems to work with. What economic structures are needed to help the real individual to develop, what social theories, politics, education, etc.?

Fromm at various places (see also his quote of Huxley, p. 226) implies that the new effort of industry to "make people happy" when this is good for sales or for profits is just a trick, a fake happiness to make them "love their servitude." But this is silly. The truth probably is that really happy workers & consumers, truly self-actualizing, *are* good for industry, for profits, etc. (As the Research & Development section of industry is now finding out, self-actualizing, creative R & D men are the only ones who discover new products.) Is a slave who has slowly added to his privileges one after another basic need gratifier & self-actualizer still a slave? Even if he keeps the *name* of slave? Does it make any difference that Britons are still called "subjects," "vassals," etc.? The question is: what is the psychic reality? Even now, conditions for creative scientific work are getting better in industry than in the universities. If the boss decides & *orders* you to be your own boss in DuPont or General Electric, are you an industrial slave? And if you get paid twice as much, is this slavery or freedom?

These old socialists are overdoing it. For them industry is still as villainous as it used to be, even tho it's changed its nature entirely.

As I read on in Fromm, now at p. 208, the thought occurs that a fine & basic job for the Institute would be writing on the circumstances of life, on the level of basic-need gratification attained, etc.

May 18

A beautiful thought! From reading science-fiction story by Asimov-Johester. First of all, jokes if they click can be peak-experiences. They *need* not be, but they can be, if they are "high" enough. Lower forms of humor too. (Maybe they too fit. Think about it.) A joke has all the characteristics of peak-experiences: sudden integration; loss of inhibition & defense; "sudden glory"; loss of doubt, fear, anxiety, sadness; intrinsic value, etc. The real point is that it is a solution of the human predicament—it integrates & bridges the discrepancy between hope & actuality, between aspirations & limitations. It is an integrating mechanism very profoundly, & I must add it to love, art, & reason.

It makes it possible for man to be puffed up & humble at the same time, because he can laugh at his bloat—that makes it all right & not paranoia or megalomania. Then it's not a sin. Therefore it *allows* us to retain the pride we need in order to do anything. The self-confidence is really crazy & amusing (in the light of human limitation, death, etc.) & yet permits the godlike quality ("Are you a man or a mouse?"). So we can be small & big simultaneously, since we need to be both. It's OK to reach out to godhood if you do it with a sense of humor, with enough self-depreciation & detachment to know that you're a severely limited human trying to transcend yourself. And because man tries, he succeeds once in a while and also is respectworthy for the very reason that he does try—e.g., David & Goliath. It's a kind of bravery, & it comes very close to tragedy. As a matter of fact, that *is* tragedy: the human trying to be a god & getting slapped down for it by fate. In the comedy, he doesn't get slapped down, because, after all, he's not *really* presuming to be a god—it's all a joke really. Don't take it seriously.

May 31

On gratitude. What do we *know* about it? Practically nothing. But I think that the psychoanalytic transference is, largely & basically, not the sick-sounding stuff Freud makes out of it, but in part & crucially a good human reaction of gratitude.

The examples in which this occurred to me resemble very much theological "grace"—i.e., undeserved, unbought, above-and-beyond-the-line-of-duty kindness. The nurse in the hospital who was so extra kind & motherly, more than I deserved & more than I was paying for, made me feel profound gratitude & touched me very deeply. The male orderly who casually cleaned up the shit I had spilled on the toilet floor and, without disgust or pay, helped me back to my bed in my weakness. The analysts who—it dawned on me when I became aware of something I despised & hated in myself & had denied & repressed for fear of losing my self-esteem—had known it *all the time* & did *not* despise me but went right on helping me.

This grace-gratitude, freely given, whether deserved or not, is what the theologians claim for God's love, & they are grateful & humble.

This can be considered from the value point of view, a validation of the existence of intrinsic values, of B-values, of goodness, love, kindness, beauty, etc. Therefore the world is good & therefore life is worth living, & the person who is grateful changes in his character in some of the same ways that peak-experience brings about. *They* are improved & become better persons—just as in therapy, gratitude of this deep sort also makes the patient a better person. Something is left over in the patient's attitude toward the therapist *after* the transference has been analyzed away. A *good* feeling, a therapeutic feeling.

This can also be seen in sex when it's very good, when the feeling is "this is better than I deserve" & "it's too good for me." Then ensues gratitude, & this too must then be one part of love—mutual basic gratitude & reassurance that the world is good & that B-values exist.

June 15

Thinking about the place of personal or idiosyncratic psychology in my own work & in psychology in general. The study of psychology can be & often is a totally personal search—a person, a *particular* person studying persistently over a long period of time, his own self, his own problems, & writing his own solutions. The deeper he goes, the more universal he gets; the more useful it is for others, for teaching, for theory, etc. I think of the way I got impatient in my Personality course with lectures & words & talk about theories. It seemed to me my students were being deliberately taught to skate on the surface & to use words & glibness & formulas as a way of *avoiding* the depths. To spout Freud & his words & formulas without *feeling* it or in any real sense *knowing* it was worse than nothing in some cases. It made them glib & self-confident when they should have been shaken & humble. So I turned more & more to cases & to personal self-searchings like Marion Milner's & to personal autobiographical accounts of psychoanalysis.

But there's little or no place in the system & structure of official psychology for this stuff. Or for books like Bucke's *Cosmic Consciousness* or for people like Jung, Moustakas, Mooney, & others, big & small! My own work, for that matter, has been a personal search for a personal answer to personally felt problems which I was trying to solve for myself & for the world at the same time. What does "objective" mean, then, for psychology at least? Discussion of this should be added to the Science book.

Official psychology has no place for personal documents & hardly publishes any. But of course it should. Now with the new stress on phenomenology & existentialism & identity & Self, etc., maybe it will change & self-exploration may be admitted to be a core of psychology & a basic method. The thought passed thru my head of a little article on this for *Contemporary Psychology*. [*See Appendix of Being book.*] Or it might do just as well to review some of these books. Maybe in the future—too busy now.

This involves another thought that I have had recently about my style of work & writing, which has really been peculiar in the last years. Tead [Ordway Tead, an editor then with Harper & Row] brought it up sharply a few days ago by refusing to publish a book of my papers unless I rewrote & unified it. He pointed out that it was just a collection of lectures, which of course is true & is partly good & partly bad. Anyway, to me, this is an unsatisfactory way of working & publishing. Practically none of my papers in the last 5 years have been written specifically as scientific papers, for publication in scientific journals or for a scientific audience. They've all been started by a solicitation or call from the outside, not from within me. Practically all have been well paid for. Most of them were for general rather than professional audiences. They all had deadlines & had to be finished by a certain date & *not* when they were really "finished" from within. They were all about an hour long—that is, had an externally & artificially imposed length rather than an intrinsic length. None of them were "scholarly" in the way most of my previous papers were (for instance, "Cognition of General & Particular" [42] & "Method Centering vs. Problem Centering" [39], which I found & find very satisfying, unlike the recent lectures, most of which I find unsatisfying, unfinished, not thorough, not tight & structured & architectonic enough).

This is just what I've been criticizing Margaret Mead for. She's ready to talk on anything. It's true that, even so, she does well & much better than most others can do, but she's not doing as well as she *can* do. I feel uneasy at the comparison even tho it's not quite the same. From among the very many invitations I get, I accept *only* those where I know what I'm talking about, only on subjects I've already been working on, & only on areas I *want* to work up further & say something about. All of them are pieces in the total structures I have at the back of my head & which I'd do as a book, systematic, scholarly, complete, architectonic, if only I had vigor & strength & patience enough & time enough—a systematic Theory of Psychology, the sort of thing I had in mind for the elementary text which I've given up (or postponed). If I get healthy, vigorous, & serene, I'll do it one day. Otherwise not. When I'm under stress, I can do only "pieces," not the whole, even tho I have the whole in mind.

October 13

Started on Science book today. Decided to keep records of its development from beginning—as a careful study of creative process. Also for pleasures of retrospection. Will keep notes and drafts instead of throwing them away.

I am eager to start after so long a hiatus (several months). And yet as soon as I started, I felt certain depression & fear before the task. It's so complicated. How can I structure it? It's always been this way—*until* I get the structure. Then all goes easily, or at least it's then just work, no longer awe, fear, inadequacy, & fatigue before I begin. This is a common phenomenon reported by many. This is the toughest (subjectively) part of the work. Before that it is all insights & inspirations that come all by themselves & without effort & with big or little peak-experiences. Very pleasant, sometimes intensely so. Self-esteem is high then. Feeling of success.

That's what I did all last year—just reading, thinking, being inspired, meditating on the stuff, & writing *only* on impulse or on inspiration. So I came home with a big stack of scattered notes on cards & papers. All sorts of things to read. And *then* the systematic effort begins.

My technique is to browse thru all the cards & notes, one by one, mulling on them. Write down all the categories suggested—i.e., pieces of

ook, possible chapters—one after the other in no order. That's what
i ve been doing all day. Already some of the categories are quite definite,
so I've made index cards for some of them & am already filing the 3 × 5
cards under these headings. Altho most of them are still under Miscellane-
ous. From past experience I know these are tentative and heuristic, a
scaffolding which I'll throw away or reorganize later.

October 28

Going thru a great crisis of self-analysis, especially in relation to
job, school, work, students. There is an interplay between my character,
the external pressures, gratifications, & disappointments, & my strong
wish or need to write the Science book. It's this big job that's precipitated
the whole business, with the necessity for cutting down on involvements,
activities, pleasures, etc. Also the sharp contrast between the freedom of
last year & the 1000 duties & responsibilities. The zest in work of the first
few weeks back is gone.

I am almost 2 months back now & haven't read a book. *Have*
started on Science notes & got some work done, but not much & haven't
enjoyed it. Did a job analysis of where all my time goes & found too much
sociability, too many friends, parties, visits. Too much helping of others.
Too many paper duties. (Have about decided to give up the chairmanship
to improve this.) [*5/20/60: Also, I take on too many "good-citizen" obligations,
like membership committees, president of MPA, APA Council, lecturing as a
duty, getting involved in anthropology department, etc.*] Too much spreading
out in oral style as if the world were a smorgasbord & I had to take a taste
of everything. Too many interests. A definite character weakness also is
my need to do a good job at whatever I've taken on & then taking on too
much. I must be a good teacher, good chairman. good lecturer, good
professor, keep up with everything in literature. I take too seriously every
responsibility, every graduate student, every problem, & then try to solve
it rather than being selfish, shrugging my shoulders over many of these
"responsibilities," & not bothering with them. Only thing to do, then, is
not to take on responsibility in the first place. Not being chairman will
relieve me of many responsibilities which I take too seriously, even tho it
may give me more actual labor. At least then I'll be more detached,
uninvolved, & can be irresponsible & not have dreams that wake me up
during night over departmental agenda or memos or plans, etc. I'm not the
boss or leader type. It's taking too much out of me. Think I do it well, but
at too much cost & not enough pleasure. Have written all sorts of notes on
graduate school & graduate students & my disappointments with them.
Maybe I'll write that out too & try to get it straight & worked out before I
sound off in pique & anger.

I think it mostly comes from the fact that nobody helps me, either in the past or now. But everybody asks me for help with *their* concerns, & I'm tired of it. There is some sexualizing of this—i.e., I feel fucked & taken advantage of. Exploited. Not only by graduate students but by Brandeis & my job in general. A character defect? I feel very sensitive about this, about being exploited. Perhaps I need more display of gratitude & appreciation. Same theme with others always—wife, children, friends.

This overtendency to do a good job, or even a perfect job, also has sexual or phallic parallels. Castration anxieties I suppose. Maybe all precipitated by my fear before the Science book—big job, big pouch, huge orgasm, great admiration from the female. *But* also, will I be able to do it? It is far less strong than in the past but still there in principle —perfectionism & orality & feeling exploited & raped.

Also, I'm getting less & less interested in teaching thru the years. Don't prepare very much; rely on old notes instead. Can't put my heart into it. All my libido is getting down into the Science book. Everything else gets in the way & makes me impatient, rebellious, or even enraged. There is much free-floating anger over all the above, and I am apt to have anger dreams about fighting and being fought. It was like dam bursting a year or two ago & didn't manage it well. Didn't have the right habits & was apt to suppress it. Now I handle it better & more realistically—i.e., my reaction is more suited to the real situation that merits it and less an acting out of past anger long repressed.

It can all be looked at as a growing will to self-affirmation, healthy selfishness, to taking a more dominant position. Maybe it was done not too smoothly & gracefully, but it was essentially necessary & sound, especially for my self-chosen role as iconoclast, revolutionary, & attacker of the old order of science & scientism. Must make myself independent of praise & blame, of pleasing others, of serving others, of being a "nice guy." Have to become a little more of a bastard & let the weak take care of themselves. Must put breast back inside blouse. Also no presenting! Let others present for mounting. If there was an open mouth I *had* to put something into it. Like a reflex. So easily seduced by weakness, helplessness, pathos.

No, better say that I want to be laissez-faire rather than dominant-submissive—to go my own way.

December 30

Dawned on me in middle of night that I've finally solved my 30-year-old question: why do we forget our dreams, our hypnosis, etc.? Because there is no self-observation or detachment; because we experience totally; because there is no self-criticism. As in schizophrenia or mania; *any* psychosis → amnesia because there is no detachment. Hypnosis, childhood, dreams, ecstasy, or peak-experience—any fascination or total absorption → some amnesia, inability to remember the experience (altho can remember *about* it). Anyway, amnesia for surrounding world.

1960

April 11

A little more clear on relation between B-values, self-actualization & goals of education, therapy, etc.—of every social institution.

Goals of good:

education therapy self-improvement growing older child rearing society artist growth	} same as {	more fully human more perfect human being characteristics of SA B-values characteristics of peak-experience

= movement *toward*, as to a limit

Best art moves *toward* B-values, or yearns for them: not only truth, goodness, beauty, but also richness, gaiety, unity, acceptance, etc. Art that simply expresses frustration or nervous age or paranoia or rebellion, etc., is OK but is only step along the path. That is to say, the ideally good painting or novel will have the same ultimate characteristics as the good person. They are isomorphic. But this is also true of the world as seen in the peak-experiences.

April 20

Big decision this A.M. Partly out of persistent depression over Bertha & myself—profound disappointment. Probing down to roots, personal roots, which means also the most profound intellectual problems. Also general disappointment with graduate students who I hoped would do this job I'm setting out to do; because nobody is helping, I must do it myself. Partly my disappointment with EPA meetings of this weekend & the subsequent impulse to teach them. Partly my lunch with Frank Manuel yesterday where we probed the basic life problems. His respect for my solutions encouraged me. Then I met a graduate student with questions about my work, which he clearly had not read carefully even though my grad student, & which I had to answer in a very systematic way. That is,

17

his criticisms could be answered only by the whole system of self-actualization, & I realized I had to do it. Everything in the system depends on everything else. Then this morning I dipped into a book called *The Ultimate Belief,* by Chitton-Brook [*reread*], & realized that he was essentially right about Truth, Goodness, & Beauty, but he couldn't prove it & I could. And therefore I should.

Decided therefore to write a small systemic book for the World Perspective Series by simply expanding my Propositions paper. Have started writing an autobiographical preface. Now I hope the zest will last long enough for me to finish it. I've thought of it often enough, but the job was too big to do just yet & was waiting until a grad student would be grown enough to do it either for me or with me. But if it's a *small* job like the books in this series, I think I might be able to lurch it off fast, by permitting myself to be discursive rather than scholarly and complete. And *then* get back to Science book or let it grow simultaneously. They overlap anyway in the big system I have at the back of my head.

June 13

Very bad money problems for last months. Ann will have cost about $2000 this year. New car will cost $1762 fully paid up. We'll be very badly broke until Fall.

Papers book rejected by Prentice-Hall. Sent it to Beacon Press.

Commencement yesterday & school over. Feel much freer ever since classes ended.

July 30

In the middle of Simone de Beauvoir's *Memories of a Dutiful Daughter.* She talks much of her loneliness, despair, anguish, boredom, etc., etc., & of her friends at college. Why not? That kind of Catholic training & the world it made must inevitably do this for any intelligent person. When she rejected God, etc., a big hole was left in her life, as if a child's parents had died, making not only the self change but also the whole external world. Valuelessness leads to value search, preferably for absolutist values, on the scheme of the religion she had lost. No wonder she became a Communist & swallowed Stalin & now China, Castro, & all. Comes from anhedonia & is an antidote & an escape from it. The taste for violence, the acceptance of killing if only it is done by the Communists, the frantic, anti-intellectual quality of it, even the mistrust & dislike of her *own* intellect, the obsessionals' admiration for the crude, nonabstracting, violent peasant who "really *lives*" because he doesn't seem to have her conflicts (like a longing for her own former violent innocence & lack of ambivalence, thought, & conflict), the underlying reservoir of hostility—all this helps me to understand the French existentialism. It's a reaction after the giving up of reactionary, passive, authoritarian, contemptuous, medieval French Catholicism & then finding it stays in the blood & has to be fought continually. Counterphobic defenses here too. They long to be slaves again & fight the longing, sometimes by being wildly, crazily "free," as she describes. How *could* such a person really enjoy life, be serene, accepting, amused, affectionate? Too much civil war. It can all be seen (partly) as a longing for all the characteristics of SA & authenticity, naturalness, spontaneity, the full enjoyment of the senses & of the body & of the animal, the full enjoyment of thinking & reasoning, the wish to be dedicated wholeheartedly to one's call, to one's "work," & to enjoy it & feel useful, the wish to be serene & whole & uncomplicated, etc.—at the same time that she & her friends were fully equipped with a whole set of permanent conditional reflexes of fears & guilts & disgusts, like Watson's mistrained dog for whom all good things were conditioned to pain & shock. See p. 279, for instance, on boredom. She could be "wholehearted" about nothing. Futility.

The fact that she had mystic experiences, of both depths & heights, anguish & joy, didn't solve her problem—only made it worse by forbidding her to be sunny, "adjusted," adapted, like others. She was too smart & too learned, & with too much drive. She couldn't be an "adaptive, passive character." Strong impulse to autonomy & SA (p. 282).

August 13

Frank Manuel back & spent day with him. Tried out on him my political theory suggested to me by my motivation theory, especially the hierarchy idea. Democracy of Western sort is OK for rich & well-organized, educated society, & capitalism then can work fairly well. For people with lower basic needs satisfied, higher needs emerge & we can talk about freedom for self-fulfillment, autonomy, encouragement of growth, humanitarianism, justice, democracy, etc. The Marxian theory is then transcended, especially where labor unions are strong. But in Mexico I learned that where there is overpopulation & no birth control, venality & bribery, where there is no "patriotism" in sense of rich Mexicans caring for poor Mexicans, no civic feeling, no unselfishness & humanitarianism, where there are the very rich & the very poor & the rich exploit the poor &

have contempt for them, then the Marxian theory *does* apply, & socialism is the answer. And where the democracy is phony, then class struggle of the Communist sort does also apply. Now for places like Cuba & the Congo, Cyprus & Iran, the Arab countries & other "Marxian" countries, then all I can see for the situation is a regime like the Russian or Yugoslavian, a fairly authoritarian-socialist regime. If there were no cold war, & if there were really peaceful coexistence & peaceful competition, then each new, small, poor, uneducated country would probably do best under Russian or, better, Yugoslavian guidance. And wealthier, more developed, better educated countries like Czechoslovakia or Hungary or Germany would probably do better under a democratic socialism, under the guidance of England or Sweden, etc. (Of course, the ultimate answer is a UN; but even under UN different distrusts would have to be treated differently, approximately as above.) The Congo, until it grew up, would have to be administered & "grown" by an elite from above for some time. So for many other underdeveloped countries. And the more they grew into mature countries, the more freedom & the less control they would need, & perhaps also the less socializing & more "free enterprise." As a matter of fact, it might be better, in order to make the point, to consider the whole business from the point of view of an ideal future, when the UN was really strong enough so that no real war was possible. There would *still* have to be a kind of "colonialism" of an educational, benevolent sort. National sovereignty, at least as far as making war was concerned, or other troubles, would be gone. Only internal injustice & exploitation by the rich or powerful would have to be eliminated. This is a sort of utopian or "future UN" politics. And since there would also remain as much local autonomy as possible, Russia might still entrust itself to being ruled by a party of elite priestlike devotees & the U. S. might still prefer to have a democratic-capitalism of the sort it has now.

There is now a hierarchy of societies paralleling the hierarchy of basic needs. Freedom is no freedom when there isn't enough food. This must become a jungle & live by jungle laws. In L. Durrell's *Alexandria Quartet*, one must be either wolf or lamb, hammer or anvil, exploiter or exploitee. What would I do in that situation? Become an exploiter & have to be cruel & selfish or else become an exploited peasant. Nietzschian.

August 26

Bertha had talk with grad student, who's leaving, & it throws a *little* light on the mystery of my relations with my grad students. Not much, because it confirms mostly my opinion of him as orally self-centered, wanting much from me & not wanting to give much unless I made much of him & on his terms. One complaint justified: I have no research going. Usual complaint & fair from their point of view, but I've decided not to do anything about it *just* for their sake. Only if it comes spontaneously out of my goings-on. Second—also justified & frequently reported to me—I repeat too much in my lectures, so it gets irritating & boring. Will *try* to improve this but don't have much hope of doing so. My way of thinking is like a writer seeking for just the right phrase, so I say it in 7 different ways until I'm satisfied. Third, he says I don't listen—I interrupt in the seminars & talk too much. *For him* true—I'm impatient with him & I *do* interrupt to try to teach him. No so much for others— depends on whether it's worth listening to or not. I'm not as tolerant as I used to be. I don't allow myself to be as used as I used to. Less a teacher anyway. They can *learn* from me, if they want to, by helping me, but I'm not especially interested in being student-centered.

September 7

Very disturbed all day & can't sleep now (11:40 P.M.) so will try to write it out.

Partly it's an explosion of anger over my being underpaid. This has been simmering for a long time.

Secondly it's all abursting out of the anger & frustration over a culture that won't pay for pure intellect & won't even understand it. I get paid for teaching kids I care about less & less. Like a composer making a living by giving piano lessons, or a philosopher teaching arithmetic. No one will pay me for being a psychologist, but only for being a *teacher* of psychology. La Jolla finally is willing to pay me purely for being a psychologist. I definitely care less about teaching year by year. The grad teaching has been very little satisfaction to me.

This APA convention touched off & confirmed the whole feeling. I was sounded out about all sorts of jobs. The market is very good for me. I can get lots of jobs. Trouble is they're all jobs so far that I don't want—chairmanships mostly, or places I don't like, like Chicago. Each time I've told them I *am* in the market for a Research Professorship or Distinguished Professorship. And maybe one *will* come soon. Just what S. was perfectly willing to offer Gardner Murphy. I told F. today that if I were given such a Professorship I'd be perfectly willing to stay put forever & not go anyplace.

He agreed with everything & was very soothing & sympathetic & promised to try to get everything I wanted. I can trust him & I do believe him, but what will S. do about it? After all, F. agreed at once to my request for a leave in the spring, & then S. vetoed him.

I guess my own evaluation of my own worth has gone up steadily in the last few years & *very* markedly in the last year. The last two conventions of APA have been triumphal processions, & I've been praised

& flattered to death. Being nominated to the board of directors convinced me that this feeling was universal & not only from "my people"—even the experimentalists. Then being elected one of the 20 most creative U. S. psychologists by the creative ones themselves also raised my market value & bargaining in my own eyes. Not to mention being elected President of everything & nominated about 5 times President of SPSSI etc., etc., etc. These are all external things & represent external applause which I shouldn't allow to influence me too much. I don't think it does, *but* it does mean money value, market value, bargaining power, all things that S. should pay for.

I guess also the confirmation from the outside has also made me more certain & more courageous about accepting my superiority into consciousness. It's hard to realize just how intelligent, original, & creative you are when you're all alone. You must take it for granted & keep quiet about it. But when compared with others! So I must regard my talent as something precious to nurture & care for & protect. I mustn't waste it. And I can use it better at La Jolla than at Brandeis. A talent becomes an obligation. And the question of job security & fear of stepping into financial danger shouldn't weigh as much as if I had no talent to cultivate & with which to bear fruit. I've been entertaining the idea of just quitting my job & maybe the whole academic world. It scares me some & must push this fear aside in order to think clearly about my goals. Fortunately Bertha is fine about such things & will back me up fully in whatever I feel I must do. And yet when I think of giving up the house, & having no salary, & jumping from one place to another! I don't like it. I'm no traveler. And money doesn't mean that much to me. And come to think of it, how good for my work would such a jumpy life be?

September 10

Aggridance. On plane from Chicago had talk with colleague about leaders, dictatorships, aggridants, etc. I suggested we record further discussions & he refused, for fear of possible consequences. Might be "too dangerous." In Eupsychia, the anarchism will certainly have to be supplemented by voluntary admiration & followship which = loss of equality. But how avoid this when in fact there *is* superiority & it's needed? Everybody's afraid of the aggridant possibly because it's been pathologized & criticized in popular imagination—e.g., the dictator, the boss, the general. But it needn't be—e.g., the benevolent father, the older brother, the wise old man, the public servant, "the servant of the servant." A proper picture of healthy & loving aggridance would get rid of the cruel, dominating, raping, selfish picture which inevitably breeds hostility & rebellion in those who respect themselves. Like Nietzsche who himself confused dominating superman with healthy, loving, self-confident superman.

Much will rest on my analysis of the healthy surrender & of the healthy capacity for admiration. Foundation stones because the inferior *must* admire the superior without hostility or else no society. Tie this all up with countermorality or Values. Hostility files. Hatred for excellence, truth, goodness, beauty = all of them in part, hatred & resentment for a superiority which destroys their self-esteem. But superiority needn't destroy self-esteem. For one thing, everybody can be superior at something, so functional leadership rather than general leadership must ensue. That is, you admire me as a psychologist & take my lead & I admire you as a musician & take your lead. Parallel to the ideal relations between a husband & wife. It's true that there is also a general aggridance; i.e., all desirable qualities tend to correlate positively (to him that hath is given), but this is generally small. It's big enough so that in Eupsychia there would be general leaders or rulers of some kind, probably a committee with an executive secretary. That is, general aggridance is never big enough to have just *one* superior ruler. Nobody is *that* generally aggridant, especially in a complex, industrialized society. There *must* be collaborating rulers, maybe like the Russian system of an elite *party* of rulers, or as Hitler planned to do, or as the Catholic Church does. And the committee members must admire each other & therefore trust each other.

Right now in U. S. we have this situation to some extent, but it's hushed up. All insane, feebleminded, disabled, senile, sick, immature, criminal, orphaned, widowed, mothers, etc., are *all* taken care of, which means bossed around to some extent. Also all those reduced to concrete = illiterate, uneducated, diminished.

The one vote/one person system works fairly well where they are persons, where there is a large enough proportion of persons, & where the nonpersons don't vote as *also* in U. S., where there is *supposed* to be universal suffrage but fortunately there isn't. But how to avoid getting Hamiltonian?

One main technique of disenfranchising those who shouldn't vote is to let them not vote.

How get around the Dove experiment. It *proves* aggridance.

Certainly the Congo situation is common. They have not yet developed enough persons to be democratic in the U. S. sense. So also for most of the underdeveloped countries. They have too many underdeveloped persons, even tho in some of them the rich upper class may be very educated & sophisticated. In such a situation this class is usually selfish or exploiting, not patriotic enough, not humanistic enough. Maybe this too is forced & inevitable. I don't know. Too many underdeveloped people in an underdeveloped situation may make patriotism &

humanitarianism so useless that a jungle situation ensues. Vicious circle. What would I do if I were a rich Mexican or Persian or Egyptian? Could I do any differently where desperation & corruption existed all about me & everybody had to be cruelly selfish? And calloused? And doubly so if I were a rich Egyptian brought up in Egypt all my life?

This will soon have to be a problem for the UN. They'll have to govern the various Congos. How? By what principles? And to what goals?

September 25

Shoved a young candidate thru the dept. meeting over their reluctance. Talked with him yesterday, offered him the job, & then was haggled with for 3 hours. After some more time I did a "slow burn" & found myself terribly angry with him by nightfall. Disturbed my sleep. Very arrogant & snotty, making all sorts of demands. Promises to be written out. Complaints & success of all kinds. No thank you or expression of appreciation or gratitude. Without realizing it I spent the time appeasing, coaxing, selling as if to a reluctant customer, making all sorts of promises, etc., as if I were trying to peddle doubtful fish to a careful customer. That's what makes me doubly angry—that I didn't realize what was going on. Only hours later did I get angry as I realized how I, offering him a wonderful job, had unwittingly been maneuvered into the position of the petitioner. The multitude of cracks about Brandeis, with me accepting & apologizing & smiling weakly (because in fact they were all justified even tho trivial), like a guest in my house complaining about the house & its furnishings. He certainly didn't express any eagerness for the job. I felt very foolish after so much insistence on having him & pushing him thru. And he *is* the best possibility, so I'm in real conflict.

October 16

Got over candidate & offered him the job. Figure *I* contributed much to original interview. In later talks he behaved well.

Aldous Huxley lectures were first-rate. Had a very satisfying talk with him. Clearly an SA person for my files. I was very flattered by his attention & praise. Why? Same thing from psychologists pleases but not really as important. It's as if his praise & use of my work *really* validate it—the lesser ones don't matter. I think its because he's of Eupsychia club. I have always written for the judgment of Socrates, Aristotle, Spinoza, James, Bergson, Jefferson. [*Norman Thomas, Upton Sinclair, Lincoln.*] My books & articles were written for their judgment & instruction. That is, if they said it was OK, then it was worth doing. If they were bored or uninstructed, then it wasn't really worth doing. They equal that part of me, ego-ideal, superego, intrinsic conscience, that was formed in me in the libraries early in my life. Their goals & standards are my goals & standards. Huxley is clearly one of the gang. I think this should make my work less ephemeral, give me courage, make me less dependent on local praise & blame. Helps me to understand better the courage, stubbornness, defiance of young, timid, shy man, afraid of fights, who yet stuck his neck out, defied APA, & had courage of convictions. This is what Drevdahl asked me. Also Dorothy Lee for her seminar next week on sources of creativeness, unconventionality, originality.

This is the world of clear-eyed truth, of lack of phoniness, of simple, easy, obvious, effortless truth uncontaminated by fear, work, vanity, striving ambitions; ego = B-truth. Therefore *not* Freud or Hegel or Kant or even Beethoven & *maybe* not Whitman & Thoreau. Maybe not Nietzsche, all tangled up with anger & compensation. Not Kierkegaard with his religious entanglements. No Catholic. No Communist. No precommitted person.

October 29

1:30 A.M. Insomnia again. Last night stayed up all night reading but then got going on Intrinsic Suitability. (Gestalt suitability? Must think of a better name.) Implies justice, etc. See file under Suitability. It got more & more exacting, like a dam bursting, & all sorts of separate problems got solved & many integrated. Real creative frenzy. Wrote steadily for hours until about 3—no food, etc. Very good. Furnishes better explanation of peak-experiences. Toying with idea of reading the whole huge disorganized gush for Horney meeting. It certainly is truer than the final organized, manicured, & varnished version. Much more excitement, more poetic & lush, which usually I edit out. It's wonderful when it writes itself like that & one idea tumbles over another & another. Very exhilarating. But left me exhausted & good for nothing but TV. Talked with Hankses about it this A.M., & more ideas came out along with the words. So excited I lost my breath [82].

One clear trouble with me is that I so much enjoy the inspiration, the frenzied working out of a burst of insight, something new. Everything else is anticlimax, labor, work, dull, & I have to push myself to it. I've got a huge number of first memos. The wonderful insights. Most of them don't go any further because then I have to become the organized, structured, patient, plodding, obsessional workman & editorial assistant—which is not for me, definitely. I *do* hope that Greenway works out with me. [*He didn't.*] I'd get the inspirations, the insights, the beautiful ideas, write them easily & happily in a disorganized gush, hot off the griddle. Then he'd take over. Then all these beautiful ideas would come to pass. There are just too many of them stuck at that stage because I can "write up" like a professor only one thing at a time. If only they could publish my rhapsodic memos, the first drafts. No! Publishing is in the hands of obsessional tightasses, & much of my work will die with me. Or if it does get to the world, it will be ten years later than necessary. They'll still be struggling over publishing my collected papers, & I'm not sure yet that they will be accepted by a commercial publisher.

November 8

Too many ideas to handle. They keep coming & coming, & all I can do is make little notes or memos & file them away. Forever? No, I guess the whole apperceptive mass or knowledge mass shows itself—all of itself—in anything I write thereafter. That big breakthrough—tying together gestalt theory, peak-experiences, suitability, completion, justice, B-values, & I don't know how much else—is still breaking thru. And it's half killed me in the process. I could certainly speak eloquently on the Curse of Creativity. Or what one of the Horney people called my attention to: the negative therapeutic reaction. He had a peak while swimming & it cost him 10 days in bed to recover. The whole Horney meeting & all leading up to it was extremely wearing, even frightening. Reminded me of the frightening exhaustion of the Chicago APA when I gave Peak paper. Don't *quite* know why. Guess I was *really* breaking ground, which is always scary. Also it was too personal & private—like the Dorothy Lee seminar, when I disrobed myself for a bunch of nice kids. The Horney group is just not heavyweight enough to warrant *my* baring my soul. *Es passt nicht!* Not suitable! If it had been a more sensitive group, I think I'd have had no trouble with disrobing.

November 11

6 A.M. Work up clinical personology idea—i.e., the only way not available for psychologists to learn about people is via sickness & psychotherapy, the effort to cure. On model of M.D. This leaves all grad students who are not clinically interacted without access to or experience with human character in depth, ideographically understood. Murray's personology is a step in this direction—i.e., lots & lots of testing. My group therapy experiments in which each one became listener for one & listenee for another. Religious groups sometimes do this uncovering & confessing for each other. How about access to healthy people? My self-actualizers dislike confession & being tested, etc. Private. But cer-

tainly the desire for self-knowledge in young intellectuals is so great that, for this reward, they would let themselves be studied. See also my intense interviews (clinicalizing the experimental method & vice versa) from which I got Dominance data, security, sex, & a lot else. Current stress on assessment implies normal people? Would this help?

This whole recommendation implied by SA psychology, growth psychology, health psychology, etc.—namely, that there is another approach to human beings than this one of diagnosing & curing sickness (*klinikos* = bed, couch). And there is another motivation for the person to bare himself than pain & desire to get rid of symptoms. It can be the desire for self-knowledge or even the unrewarded desire to help psychologists in *their* growth. Just as anyone will help a medical student—e.g., permit him to look down his throat, study his joints, etc.

There's another angle on this too. Freud's discovery, the new dimension in human knowledge that he opened up, is usually phrased as the discovery of "the irrational & emotional depths of the psyche" in addition to the "rational & purposeful surface of the human psyche." This *should* be stated "the unconscious & preconscious depths." This includes not only Freud's id & instincts but also primary processes, which he neglected to exploit in his psychology & which are *not* defined by repression alone—i.e., they could just as easily be called poetic or metaphorical depths. And they are cognitive, even rational, in another sense. To call the unconscious irrational is an iatrogenic theory, a clinical distortion. Furthermore, to identify "irrational" & "emotional" is inaccurate too. Emotions can be quite rational, in the synergic sense found in SA people, & could just as easily be called "intuitive knowledge" or "perception"—i.e., a different *kind* of knowledge, rather than the contradicting of knowledge. What we can study, then, are the unconscious & preconscious depths, rational & irrational, sick & healthy, poetic & mathematical, concrete & abstract, etc. Freud put these medical spectacles on our nose. It's time to take them off.

Furthermore the whole new emphasis on identity, values, life purpose, selflessness is clearly not medical or clinical. It can best be understood & pursued in a different way, for instance on model of the philosopher or the (nonsupernatural) religionist. E.g., Buddha, looking for enlightenment—i.e., to be a good man, fully developed to height of powers, rather than a sick man seeking to get rid of symptoms. Is a new profession called for—personologist? Counselor? Psychologist? Psychoconsultant? Confessor?

November 25

Finally a good solution to the female & male dominance question. Why are U. S. women so dominant, castrating, discontent, lousy wives, etc.? Why are U. S. men so meek, sheepish, dominated? Why so often the marriage of "weak" husband, "strong" wife? Ever since my dominance studies at Wisconsin, have been trying to figure it out, including the clear perception finally of the 2-fold motivation of women (1) to dominate the man, but (2) then to have contempt for him, go frigid, manipulative, castrating, and (3) secretly to keep on yearning for a man stronger than herself to compel her respect, & to be unhappy, & unfulfilled & to feel unfeminine so long as she doesn't have such a man. It is also quite clear that the 1st type of marriage is ultimately no good & that the 2nd type, in which the wife respects or adores or looks up to her stronger husband, so that she feels safe, protected, & can be secure & dependent & lean on him, is sometimes better. Certainly works well not only for mates but also for all their children.

Well, the answer must be a statistical one if (1) the average dominance level of women in U. S. has gone up steadily in last century, & (2) average dominance level of men has either stayed the same or more likely gone down. Lots of historical, socioeconomic, educational, & technological reasons for both changes in average. If this is so, then for any given female there is a lesser number of men who can suit her desire for a strong man, and the probabilities of her finding one such get less decade by decade. A century ago practically any woman could look up to almost any man. The overlap in the sex distributions for dominance level must have been very small, especially within the class & caste boundaries. Lets say the average female was at about the 10th percentile of the dominance distribution for men. That means 9 out of 10 men would be strong enough for the average female. No, there must have been even less overlap. Perhaps 90th-percentile women were at the 10th percentile for men, so that overlap = 10%. Now the distribution must be almost equal or with 80 or 90% overlap, especially for age 20 and even more for age 16 or 18, when most girls are more self-confident than most boys.

So failing to find a real man, since there are so few relatively (& this must be defined relatively, since a "real man" is any man stronger than the woman doing the defining—this is like the definition of an acceptable college freshman for Brandeis: each year the definition gets more stringent & more demanding), she has to settle for a "weak man" (by her relative definition—i.e., relative to her strength), & this never works. At first unconsciously & in later years consciously, the relation becomes one of her dominating him, whether nicely or crudely, & he will unconsciously hate it & her while also wanting it & her, & sooner or later he will revolt one way or another, or become totally crushed & hopeless & give up coping. And she will despise him, covertly at first & perhaps overtly later, be deprived of sexual happiness, & resent & attack her husband, consciously or unconsciously, for failing her. And then we get the total U. S. marriage syndrome of today. She has available only "weak men" & he has available only "strong women."

Of course, a woman's admiration for strong man can be & is defined culturally at least in large part—e.g., wealth, rank, power of any kind, status, good hunter, football hero, etc. Status can be determined arbitrarily by a culture, & whatever determines status attracts admiration of women. Then she can "look up to." But maybe even here there is biological & reproductive sense. If she unconsciously is looking for a strong man to take care of her, protect her & her pregnancies & babies, give her a home, deal with outside world, & let her concentrate on home & uterus, then all these cultural determinants of status do in fact give status to men, do in fact give him power to do all the things a woman wants done for her. Maybe this is more important or as important as the obviously biological determinants of male dominance status—e.g., big muscles, physical strength, fearlessness, ability to overcome & take her, big penis, sexual pleasures. If intercourse is in itself nothing for her but the beginning of a possible baby, then all the above makes more sense. A wealthy old duke could take better care of a female uterus than a poor young athlete, even tho the latter could do better by her vagina than the former. A choice of the former is a vote in favor of the uterus rather than the vagina. And this happens often enough. But then try to figure out Lady Chatterly. There is also often enough a vote for the good biological male as over against cultural status. G. B. Shaw's *Man & Superman* & the vital urge. Ideally, of course, women would want both. Ideally the man who does well for the vagina also does well for the uterus. Probably true. Maybe when a woman has to make a choice between the 2, this is a vital threatening conflict where she must lose something vital whichever she says she chooses.

1961

January 8

Something I should have put in Parallels paper [95]. Why did I overlook it? If what I am talking about there is in general the relations between the strong & the weak, then authoritarian submission fits. So does homonomy, both high & low. See both files. Harry wants to continue with the paper & I'd thought of "masochism." Maybe it should be "authoritarianism." Also fits in with my stuff on will, control, trust, surrender, & that leads over into masculinity-femininity, as everything seems to look as if both femininity & masculinity (dominance & submission, authoritarian dominance & authoritarian submission, autonomy-homonomy, etc.) are present as impulses & satisfactions in everybody, but there are differences in their ratio, so that some turn out to be primarily authoritarian-submitters even tho the other impulse is there too—maybe just because the other impulse is there but unsatisfied (like the sadist-masochist). It's certainly in part the lack of self-esteem (self-confidence, decisiveness, the total-unimpeded-knowing-what-one-wants-without-doubts). With the monkeys [10, 11, 12, 13] (& with humans, too, I guess) the "gaze" settled it immediately. The overlord just looked, & the other one dropped his eyes as if he'd been mastered & admitted it. The gaze is level, unwavering, unyielding, even unself-conscious & spontaneous (as it must be if there really are no doubts; it doesn't even occur to him it could be any other way, like the real aristocrat who is so sure of himself he doesn't have to try to be an aristocrat, is unstriving, "Lord of Command").

Back to the gaze. It's also masculine. The girl drops her eyes before the gaze—it's phallic as in the peeping Tom (there are no peeping Thomasinas). The peeper is screwing the girl he's looking at—with his eyes for lack of a better penis—& she resents being peeped at without her knowledge & consent, even tho she loves being stared at sexually by her husband or even others. Paradox. One is rape under anesthesia; the other is lovemaking. Maybe it's her contempt for the peeper who is a coward & not really a man & therefore disgusting & comtemptible? The gaze is then a kind of strength, an egoless, nonstriving strength (at its best). Such a person gazes out from his castle, feeling safe, secure, unafraid, & no need to defend. He is unaware, unself-conscious, self-forgetful, more the experiencing ego than the self-observing ego. That means he's "interested" totally in what's out there, in the object or the field or the person. He puts his all into this gaze thereby.

Oh, there must be something else too—the X-ray eye before which defenses crumble, as in the eye attributed to the psychoanalyst.

The gaze, without speaking, ferrets out every doubt, every uncertainty, every pretense, every ambivalence in the other. If he drops his eyes, he is protecting himself. The dropped gaze is a screen. Where also does privacy come in here? The dropped window blind is also a defense I guess but not in the same sense always. It may "protect," but it may also be like an exclusive, snobbish club with high entrance requirements. It may also be B-privacy, to be in better company with oneself, to rest, relax, recover from the lesser, dirtier world outside. Like the delicious cave or hideaway, as if all the masks & cloaks & pretenses were useless. There's no use lying to him. He can see the truth anyway. Now the person who is gazing, who is all-there, who is " interested," is perceived as having the X-ray ego by all the uncertain ones, the ones with things to hide, etc. So their eyes drop before the phallic eyes that penetrate & "take" them—almost in a sexual way—as girls recognize by their blush & dropped eyes. This can all be said in the sexual language. Who's the fucker & the fuckee, & who likes which & who doesn't?

But this X-ray eye is not only a projection but also partly a reality because such an interested gazer (just because he's interested & can afford to be thru lack of fear) really does see more & penetrate thru. (I'll bet that part of masculinity is this kind of gaze. I must question women about this. It must be one of the defining characteristics, semiconsciously. It's boldness, sureness.) This could certainly be put on & done consciously & volitionally. How about children before the adult gaze? Must try it.

It's closer to B-cognition, a real looking like Shlien's real listening. And that means also for here-now totally, as in the creative person—i.e., no planning, no future, all there right now with no calculations going on behind the eyes—fascination, absorption, concentration.

The gaze is a sign of strength because it is strength, the real McCoy, in all its implications. It is a sign of integration, of spontaneity, of identity, of boldness & lack of fear, of masculinity, of autonomy & self-sufficiency. [See Grand Inquisitor passage.] And what it all adds up to is real superiority & aggrridance. And that adds up to suitability & justice. The gazer not only is dominant; he should be dominant. It's fitting & proper, fair, right. I guess that's why it so mysteriously arranges itself in the monkeys in the space of a second. And why men & women can recognize each other & size each other up in a second as penetrating or receptive (or, to use Dick Jones' word, the "intensive mode").

January 22

3 A.M. Another offer from University of Southern Florida. No details yet, but, as always with these offers, disturbed me, threw me into conflict, & woke me up. The struggle which has been going on (to drum up courage enough to detach myself from Brandeis) ever since in Mexico I heard of the appointments of J. R. & L., & what with the situation of Manuel, I could see Brandeis going downhill. My irritation & anger, & even fury, have been constant ever since, especially with S. For first time in my life, really angry over salary. I've been screwed on money all my life, & it never really got me angry. But now with all the bargaining power I have, it's different. I feel like an olympian & am not treated that way, & every insult gets me angry. Also the blows from students, undergrad & grad, that I got in the last month made me feel teaching was not for me—feeling unappreciated, unneeded, unvalued. I must admit the adverse criticisms from my psychology class last Xmas really shocked me. Also the fact that so few students registered for my graduate seminar got me. If they didn't want what I had to offer, what the hell was I doing there? Why give up so much of me & my work & my time for unappreciative people? It's quite clear they all (or most) are fond of me, even respectful, but even so, the paternal pleasures & rewards are not great enough to make up for the time taken away from my ideas, my writing, my theories. This is partly hubris & "big prick" reaction because these should be enough kudos for an ordinary mortal, but not enough for me.

I'm having a tough time, however, detaching myself from Brandeis & all that it means for me. Why? It's reasonable here to be selfish about my own call (mission, vocation), & yet I struggle over it. Partly it's the Jewish business. I have been so proud of the great Jewish university—I didn't realize how much—& I feel like a rat deserting the sinking ship, & guilty because of it, just the way I did when I left Brooklyn & abandoned the poor Jewish students whom nobody loved but me. The guilt of upward mobility. As if I belonged in the ghetto. As if I were giving up Jewish identification for bourgeois reasons—like changing my name. The offer from the University of Florida brought this to consciousness—like the Jew who hesitates to leave the sidewalks of NYC to go live among the ignorant peasants. Partly fear too—the fear of leaving home. Like the prosperous Jew who left the East Side to go to Park Ave., where he didn't quite belong. (I was so shocked & disappointed to hear that the Hebrew University was no good in some ways. It should be the best in the world, & I should be there.) I suppose the Negro who moves into a white area feels the same way—a mixture of guilt over leaving the family & of fear —& strangeness. What the hell would I do in Florida with the Southerners?

But Brandeis is driving me out. If I can get a research professor-ship in California, I'll take it. Not Florida—I don't belong there, & neither does Bertha. Not Chicago. Not the various small towns. Charlie Kaufman spoke of a research professorship at medical school in Brooklyn. That probably would be OK, if enough money, partly because I'd be in my proper milieu. Partly because there'd be enough *Yiddishe kopfen* for me, like Frank Manuel. How many Frank Manuels are there in Florida?

I guess one big factor underlying everything is the feeling that I have so much to give to the world—the Great Message—and that this is the big thing. Anything that cuts it or gets in its way is "bad." Before I die, I must say it all. That's what counts most. And I'm so convinced of this that I get contemptuous & angry & hurt if others don't see it & appreciate it enough to help with it. It is a big message. And the world does need it. And I'd be a bastard & selfish if I didn't think first of it! Whatever is best for my work—that is good! Everything else has to be sacrificed. Bertha backs me up on this. Everything else is secondary.

January 29

2:30 A.M. Woke up enraged at House Rules Committee & injustice in general. Must have dreamed about big insight I had this A.M., stimulated by Steve's point on societal SA as distinct from personal SA.

I started out to analyze "functional leadership." This is the kind in which not one man is the leader in all tasks, but each task will have as leader the one person most suited for leadership in that task. So that I might be the leader in a classroom but the follower on a hunting expedition. In each case, & around each task, the whole group along with the leader would reform itself so as to function best for that task. Like the same pool of college boys forming a basketball team, chess team, baseball team, debating team, etc. Would mean shifting, fluctuating re-formation of groups with the one principle of organization being what is best for solving the task.

Immediate trigger for this was science-fiction novel in which wise people function just that way. But it's clear that there are many prerequi-sites before this wise & strong action is possible. It requires real objectiv-ity & detachment, enough to be able to observe oneself & compare objectively with others the true capabilities for the particular task. To be able to admire, surrender, submit to orders, follow the leader without countervaluing or counterhostility, without envy & resentment at the leader or at the others for choosing someone else as leader. This requires that self-esteem not rest on dominance & subordinance status—i.e., to be able to be a follower without loss of self-esteem.

But self-esteem, especially in men in our society, does rest on dominance status. Is it possible to have self-esteem divorced from dominance-submission? But if self-esteem is based on dominance (which is ego-centered & self-ish, rather than truly social or truly task-centered), then this implies that no true social (task-centered, or task-selected-by-the-group-centered) psychology is possible. Because the alternative here is to be centered on the self (dominance) or on the task chosen by the group (& by the self). Each centering point (self or task) will organize the group differently. Dominance will cause everyone to strive to be at the top of every dominance hierarchy; being at the bottom of any will mean being at the top in none, as in the rhesus monkeys. Organizing by the task will permit functional leadership organization.

But this ties in with homonomy-autonomy theory. What I am saying above, then, amounts to saying that autonomy theory can never be a satisfactory basis for a social psychology; it must be homonomy. The task (& its requirement) is outside of & beyond the self. Task centering demands as a prerequisite the ability to transcend the autonomous self & be homonomous. But the true end (final stopping place, finishing, + final goal) of autonomy is homonomy. Autonomy's perfection is for the self to disappear & to be able to be task-absorbed, outside-absorbed, self-transcendent, self-forgetful. Social psychology means high homonomy. It means enlistment in an army & taking an oath to consider the needs of the army's tasks to be more important & prior to the needs of the self. This is no obliteration of the self—only an enlargement of it, if it is voluntary, because in this way the self can take on larger tasks than it could do alone, which can be more satisfying in a strictly selfish way, or at least in a synergic way, like a violinist who plays Beethoven's 9th with 100 others & enjoys it more than playing a sonata alone (because it's bigger, richer), & he chooses a conductor, not to follow or submit to as an end in itself, but in order to get a better performance of the symphony. And if you truly wanted the best possible performance of Beethoven's 9th (if that were the task), then it would have to follow that he would voluntarily & eagerly yield to a better violinist or even seek him out. Because that would do the job better & produce a better product, which then he would enjoy more.

It is clear that a high level of health is a prerequisite for all this. In this sense B-social-psychology rests upon a true individual psychology as a prepotent prerequisite. Social psychology is the matured individual psychology. Homonomous or social ends may be higher in the person's own hierarchy of values & may be more self-fulfilling than strictly "autonomous" ends. Autonomy is prepotent over homonomy in the development & in the motivational economy of the individual. The peaks of high homonomy are "higher" than the peaks of autonomy. The first lowest are the peaks of low homonomy in the child, then higher are the peaks of low autonomy, then come the peaks of high autonomy, & finally highest are the peaks of high homonomy, which anyway are fusions with high autonomy—e.g., the peaks of justice fulfilled, of virtue triumphant, of the truly happy ending. Which reminds me that all of this ties in with completion-of-act stuff, since there seems to be no real completion until justice triumphs, etc. Until the B-values are fulfilled & triumphant there must be a feeling of incompletion, so there can be no peaks. The highest peaks come from triumph of the B-values. Nothing else is "suitable."

April 16

Stimulated by Leytham's reprint "Psychology and the Individual," in which he uses my motivation theory as scheme for a theory of the whole personality, organized in a hierarchical way, in layers. This is possible in a crude way. Each need level is also a level of awareness or style of consciousness (e.g., physical level of awareness = safety; belongingness & love needs = emotional level of awareness; esteem needs = mental level; SA = intuitive level of awareness). This could also be a hierarchy of pleasures, gratifications, or happinesses. Rough parallel with oral, anal, phallic, & genital or with Erikson's crises. Or Jung's sensation, feeling, thinking, & intuition (& then cosmic consciousness). The character types are hierarchically arranged with growth, fixation (freezing), & regression, healthy or unhealthy, being the dynamic operators connecting them. Also the concept of bypassing a basic need.

Contrasts with any dichotomized, mutually exclusive, either/or theory, whether Appolonian or Dionysian, tender- or tough-minded, matrist or patrist (see G. Rattray Taylor's *Sex in History*) or oral vs. anal, or hysterical vs. obsessional, etc. Be careful with the XY theory—it is a dichotomy. Make it an integration. May be good to fold in Jung's shadow concept.

Each of these levels is also a level of cognition—i.e., a style of thinking, as well as of emotion & of conation & of personality. Also as in Taylor, it is a theory of levels of culture & society.

It is a whole organization of partial dialectics & includes within it the defense-growth dialectic, the taking-giving, the dependency-responsibility dialectic, the sickness-health dialectic, the selfish-unselfish (altruistic), the autonomy-homonomy, immaturity-maturity dialectic, even death-life (Thanatos-Eros). Each makes more sense as a local magnification within the totally inclusive map. And each one is also a partial therapy theory, all set against the overall principle of "growth toward SA"—i.e., specific acts within the total drama, the principle of therapy as "regression to the bypassed basic need gratification with symbolic vicarious gratification or catharsis in order to permit regrowth on a firmer basis" is again a local happening that makes real sense only against "growth toward SA" theory. Like building a house, finding that a sill or beam or foundation has not been done well enough, tearing down back to this point, doing it right, & then going on with the building.

What is the place of learning theory here? It must be basically canalization, & other growth-learning processes, & must be based upon prepotent need-gratification theory, & then it can be useful—e.g., acquisition of skills of instrumental techniques toward basic need-grats, choice of specific goals (learning what one's destiny is from among the cultural possibilities), learning all sorts of arbitrary things, like traffic rules, subsidiary.

April 27

Szasz is convinced that my "psychological illness" is an obsolete concept. And now I think "psychological health" is obsolete too, or obsolescent anyway. There are so many puzzles & contradictions in it. For one thing it seems pretty clear that it's not a straight-line development thru life. Benedict & Heider, & I guess Buber & also Goldstein and others too, seem to be neurotic & then in their 40s or 50s have a conversion or cosmic experience & suddenly get "healthy." No sense in it. No predictability. No gradual working up to it. So now I wonder how much good it would be to pick healthy youngsters at age 20. How much predictability to age 60?

When is "authentic" healthy? Can an authentic be neurotic? What is neurosis anyway? Still can't define it well. From the point of view of eternity, how slight the difference in health between analyst & patient? And that's another thing—my slowly growing disrespect for the analysts as people. As a group they just don't amount to much. This makes theoretical difficulties. Then also I seem to have been running across too many cases recently unhelped by analysis or analytic therapy. Is it changing, getting less efficacious? Or are the illnesses changing? Or are we turning to more existential problems and therapies?

As the years go by, my respect for Freudian system gets less, little by little. I think the existentialists mostly did this along with the neo-Freudians & also my own work.

It's funny that I discovered all this, or rather it was precipitated when I heard myself saying it in a lecture on existential psychology to the Harvard Educational Dept. It all rolled out & surprised me. About real human problems being so universal & so shared that therapist & patient "are in the same boat" sharing human problems in an I-Thou way, rather than strong-healthy therapist & weak-sick patient. Both are sick. Or rather human, with shared human problems.

May 1

Past midnight—can't sleep. Insight therapy can be seen from point of view of secrets. They damage. Neuroses are untold secrets often but not always secret to person himself. Therapy (or intimate friendship or love or trust) is a process of getting the patient to tell his secrets by getting him to trust therapist. Just telling them is already, in itself, therapeutic. Expression, catharsis, completion-of-the-act, finishing, getting rid of it. Akin to vomiting, shitting, etc. Relief comes partly just from this, from confession, self-disclosure, being naked, not concealing, hiding. Keeping secrets = lying, not being honest. Therefore not being a nice person. Then other goods come after revealing oneself. Objectification, permitting detached observation of something out there, rather than just expressing. Not needing to control (keeping secrets is effortful & takes control, & therefore tires, like playing a role.) I wonder if the sexual paradigm works here too. Women's secrets can be probed & broken into—they are more "open." The vagina almost invites one into the secrets. Women are more self-disclosing. Men have no opening that isn't shameful & unmasculine. Can ejaculation be a spitting out of secrets? That's straining it too much. No, men have no inviting-in secret parts.

August 9

B-Values

1. *Wholeness:* unity; integration; tendency to oneness; interconnectedness; simplicity; organization; structure; order; not dissociated. [*Fusion of is & "ought."*]
2. *Perfection:* necessity; just-rightness; inevitability; suitability; B-justice; completeness; just-so-ness; oughtness; architectonic quality.
3. *Completion:* ending; finality; B-justice; it's finished; fulfillment, fins & telos: nothing missing; totality; fulfillment of destiny.
4. *Justice:* fairness; orderliness; lawfulness; oughtness; architectonic quality.
5. *Aliveness:* spontaneity; full functioning process; self-regulation; not-deadness; changing & yet remaining the same. [*But how about static character of B?*]
6. *Richness:* differentiation; intricacy; complexity; totality.
7. *Simplicity:* honesty; abstract (essential); nakedness; essentiality; skeletal structure. [*Simplicity? "Love" is not a separate value but an attitude toward reality.*]
8. *Beauty:* rightness; form; orderliness; simplicity; richness; aliveness; wholeness; perfection; completion; uniqueness; honesty.
9. *Goodness:* rightness; desirability; shouldness (it should be that way); justice; benevolence (lack of malevolence). [*See also propositions.*]
10. *Uniqueness:* idiosyncrasy; individuality; total novelty; incomparability; novelty.
11. *Effortlessness:* ease; lack of strain or striving or difficulty; grace; perfect; beautiful; functioning.
12. *Fun:* joy; amusement, gaiety; humor; playfulness; exuberance; effortlessness. [*Add frolicksome, prankish.*]
13. *Truth:* honesty; nakedness; simplicity; richness; oughtness; beauty; pure, clean & unadulterated; essentiality; complete; real.

Why try to make these mutually exclusive? I just can't. They overlap. Ultimately they correlate more & more perfectly & merge into each other. Really, in the B-realm, they are different facets of the same one. Also the whole classification shifts depending on the operation used—e.g., the perfect person, the perfect painting, the perfect group, the perfect society, the perfect psychotherapy, the perfect education, the perfect peaks of sex, of love, of insight, creativeness, of parturition, of sport-athletics, of thought (abstract) of death (?), the goals of growth in person, organism (?), cosmic experience. B-values are the "limits" to which all others approach!

August 12

About time to take up challenge: why are the B-values more right than any other kind? Than neurotic, or "coasting" (or regression or homeostatic) values, or purely selfish ones, etc.? How to validate them? How to answer the accusation: "You like them—that's why you think they're so good. How can you prove they're good?"

1. The main reason I got into them was thru peak-experience work. That's the way the world looks in the peak, in B-cognition. But in itself this proves very little. Extended validation is still necessary, because tho the world may look that way in peaks, this doesn't prove that it is the way it really is.

2. B-values overlap very much with the description of SA people.

But also goals of therapy; characteristics of good paintings (aliveness, wholeness, uniqueness); goals of education, of good child development, of evolution à la Sinnott, Huxley, et al.

Another approach would be to show intercorrelation (positive) between truth, goodness, & beauty. Hypothesis: that those correlations increase as health increases. E.g., the nonrepresentational paintings of schoolchildren all rated for general esthetic value (beauty) & then rated for aliveness, wholeness, uniqueness.If all ratings showed positive intercorrelation, it could then be shown that healthy people are more good, more honest (true), more beautiful, etc. All of Rogers' experiments useful here—i.e., therapeutic improvement → increases in B-values (more perceptive, more honest, more integrated, more just, alive, rich, simple, good, etc.). See also Rudin. (Make point that therapy uncovers or releases all these qualities—that is, that they were "there" all the time as potentialities, hidden & blocked by fear.)

Another line of experimentation would be to show increasing preference (choice) for B-values with increasing health—e.g., choice between honest & phony wine, clothes, painting, music, poetry, food, etc. This would prove that full humanness goes together with B-values; i.e., these are the chosen preferences of the best "specimens," under conditions of really free choice in a good situation (no fear, no reprisals) when they are feeling strong. If they are regarded as biological assays (sensitive versions of ordinary people), then their choices are what other people would also choose under better circumstances.

September 28

Reading S. on Fromm. I find it hard to read. No sense of the empirical whatsoever! As if unwilling to understand. Anyway, one thing he brings up is correct & needs working over. I've done it, but not systematically enough. V. Frankl convinced me that SA had to take account of the "external" duty, task, call, mission, etc. I had this in my empirical description of the SA people, but not really folded into my theory. The Real Self there is too exclusively intrapsychic. The Inner Core in the Propositions book is defined as "intrapsychic"; that is, the intrinsic conscience is inside and is the ultimate Supreme Court. (This is what S. justly criticizes, p. 118ff.) What is the relation of the inner conscience to reality, truth, justice, law, custom, etc.—i.e., the "outer"?

I've already used the concept of the Self enlarging by identification in relation to love objects (e.g., the strawberry example, where it gives me more pleasure when my child eats it than when I eat it). Also in relation to the cause outside, the mission, the duty, the demand-character of reality outside à la Wertheimer (some things just call for doing).

Now, empirically, the intrinsic conscience includes truth & justice perceived as being out there. This is implied as being necessary at many places in Fromm's work (and mine too). I will define it as "not being true to your real self," though I should be explicit, not just implicit, about the meaning of "true" here. Either say "guilt = not being true to your inner self or to the real truth outside" or else leave it as it stood—that is, "guilt = not being true to your inner self," & add definition of inner self to include external truth. But then the distinction between "inner" & "outer" washes out & comes close to being useless. That is, if "inner" includes only as much of the "outer" as has been identified with because it is sympathetic & assimilable to the inner self, then "outer" would include only that portion of the outer world that contradicts truth & is incompatible with the inner self. This gets really complicated. Looks as if I'll have to wind up in Zen position—no difference or gap or opposition between ego & world except in sickness! This cuts at the roots of my whole system. Must clean it up, although it is certainly OK to use "inner-outer" as heuristic devices for the sake of communication, as a kind of lower level of truth which must transcend itself & destroy itself.

October 22

On road to L.A. Working on B-psychology as I drive. "B values" seem to be best described as "characteristics of Reality"—i.e., Being as Cosmos. Then they are just descriptive and are perceived, not invented, like fingerprints. Why did I see them as values, and still do? Because people yearn in their direction. They *want* and *value* these characteristics of Cosmos-Being, and love them too. But also, when I test these characteristics of Reality, I find them also to be characteristics of the highly developed human being of the good painting, etc. They are also the goals of therapy, of education, of "religion," etc. *Maybe Reality is real without any effort; but human beings have to try to be real, and this is difficult.* The more real the Reality is that is being perceived, the more isomorphically real (or valuable) the perceiver becomes. Real reality helps the perceiver get closer to his reality, or Being.

*   *   *

Later. I think my big puzzle has been that the values of Being were first seen and described as "the way the world looks in the peak-experience." But the question of external validity was involved. The world might *look* that way without necessarily *being* that way—e.g., might be a projection of our own feeling good. Just a phenomenological appearance, not necessarily veridical. Only *after* this came one parallel.

I used to stress this too little, & gratification, spontaneity, self-expression too much. But this is so easily misinterpreted to mean self-indulgence, ego-centerism, selfishness, loafing, etc. John has served me as a good example of the way in which SA theory can be misinterpreted in this style. Several other students too. They wait for an impulse to work before getting to work; they *have* to enjoy their work (so they avoid chores which others must then do). They hate or despise authority as an inherent enemy instead of identifying with rational authority, etc., etc.

In conversation yesterday this came up in another form—i.e., the spoiling effect of wealth & luxury. I pointed out that basic need gratifications are *all* easy to get in principle & have little to do with material goods, wealth, etc. As a matter of fact poverty seems a better guarantee of closeness of the family, of inexpensive group activity, of giving something to fight against (poverty) & something to fight for (socialism). Under reasonably decent personal & family conditions all basic needs are very easily satisfied. But wealth gets in the way & makes this *less* likely. Must work this out more. Also must work out new stress on simple life. Must redefine wealth.

October 29

Reading Vance Bourjailys' *Confessions of a Spent Youth*, which I picked up for the sex but then got disgusted with, then confused, then seriously interested. It's a case history in value pathology and in counter-values, full of drugs, whores, delinquency, immaturity, cruelty, self-destruction, stealing—*everything* just like the post-World-War-I "lost generation," the Roman god-emperors, U.S. delinquents with no adult values to live by, etc. At first I was disgusted because I thought the author was showing off. Approving all this & holding it up for praise & emulation. But then it became clear he also knew what a good guy was & was just trying to be honest veridically about what a real shit he had been. Why (mostly lonely, unattached) adolescents need to love & be loved, to belong with some buddy, some gang, & to do *anything* that the gang does. Also, to hell with adult standards because they have really crapped it up with their wars & messes & stupid world—as he says, "putting humanity third after national greeds & tribal prides." I think my Mexican delinquency paper [75] got it pretty well: the absence of adult standards because the adults are (1) shits & *not* admirable; and (2) confused & with no fixed values to offer, only phony ones that they hardly believe in themselves. Why deny ourselves, then? To what purpose patriotism? Nothing is worth dying for. The world is a shit house & an asylum. The only answer is frustration, sensuality, hatred for all authority, discipline, responsibility, self-frustration. The ultimate virtues are a lie. There is no love or truth or justice or goodness —it's all phony & there's nothing to hope for, nothing worth dying for or living for. Nothing worth getting serious about. Cynicism (no trust in any values). Ultimate despair, therefore, because *nothing to live for*. Pessimism. All as if they were *trying* to be psychopaths. (The model they admire is very close to the psychopath!) Why should they admire and emulate the psycho-path? Maybe psychopaths are free of all the things they regard as weak in themselves and are trying to get rid of—values, love, conscience, guilt, regret, shame, sadness, compassion, kindness, embarrassment, homonomy, self-transcendence, unselfishness = drunks, drug addicts, destruction, contemplation, etc., etc.

It's as if every time they got "weak" in any way, this generation got punished for it rather than rewarded. In a cockeyed lunatic world this would happen. If we are to "trust" the world, it must be worthy of trust—i.e., must reward & reinforce the virtues.

November 19

5 A.M.—woke up, can't sleep. Much disturbed in last weeks by the local right-wingers, Birch Society, etc. Dreams of danger, killing, fighting, shouting. Tried to figure out what can be done about those nuts. Usual answer—*nothing* can be done except fight back, be vigilant, etc. They're so certain that talk, evidence don't help. Like paranoiacs. But then the thought: if they're paranoid characters, then that itself explains their attractiveness to so many—which is what's frightening. More people are

uncertain. But they *need* certainty. Therefore they respond to people who are certain & decisive, men of themselves, unwavering. This they interpret as the leader type, the captains. Many people fit in—Hitler, McCarthy, Stalin. The counterattack against such people must be based on their paranoid character as much as on convincing their followers & one's own followers with facts, reason, etc. Try humor—they can't take it.

But of course many leaders who are decisive, unwavering, sure of themselves are not paranoid (e.g., Freud), because of their profound confidence in themselves & in the truth of what they've seen. The good captain, the good father, must be like this so as to reassure the panicky ones, the waverers. When does a good father conceal his fears so as not to panic his family? When does he admit them in order not to be phony?

Kennedy is another type, the one who was so utterly clear about *wanting* what he wanted & was so strong a fighter for what he wanted. (Stevenson half wanted & half didn't want.)

I've been thinking I'd write this up, even tho now it sounds like a commonplace as I write it out. When I first thought of it some days ago, it struck me with great force as an illumination. So *this* was why those lunatics could get loyal followers instead of being laughed at by everyone! Well, maybe I'll let it soak here for a while & see later on how it looks.

1962

February 2

Ran across *Ecstasy*, by Marghanita Laski, an Englishwoman, not a psychologist. Fairly complete corroboration of all my peak-experience material with more details added. Very reassuring, even thrilling. Not much help on the point that worries me most—proof of the poetic quality of the peaks. [*Also greater perception of possibilities & potentialities.*] Probably will have to stress B-cognition rather than just peaks, especially since B-cognition comes in "desolation-experiences" (her good phrase). So far have relied mostly on the improved perceptions in therapy, à la Rudin, etc. But if I'm to speak about the fusion of cognition & valuation, I need more than that. (Also B-love perception-with-care, in which the characteristics of what is perceived are the B-values.) [*Also, if you B-love someone, you can* afford *to see the flaws which illusory love has to repress for fear of destroying this love. Especially since B-love can* love *the flaws as, e.g., cute, or characteristic.*] Also in the isomorphism stuff, i.e., only the integrated person can perceive integration, only the kind man is able to perceive kindness. Therefore, the peak-experience (which is an integration, an SA, etc.) *enables* the person to see what he couldn't before & to retain this perception. Better go thru B-book & thru B-notes to pull together all examples, especially cognition paper (& B-love as a self-fulfilling prophecy, creating what it perceives).

Reading on in Laski reminds me that one of the perpetual changes in peaks & in B-cognition is what I'll call unitive cognition—i.e., seeing under the aspect of eternity, seeing not only the D- but also simultaneously the B-aspect of things. Use example of unitive perception of the B-woman *in* & *thru* the actual woman who might be pretty shitty, at the D-level, or the child in his B-aspect, all possibility of *anything* & at the same time, whining, beshat, stinking, dirty, etc. (Joke: Young Dr. Kildare comes home after weary night & says to his wife: "It was a tough job, but it was worth it. I delivered Victor Hugo!") I think it will be easy enough to make the case that something real is thus perceived as that which is *there* & which is ordinarily not seen, & which thereafter *stays* perceived = revelation experiences.

Use also example of high-maternal woman to whom babies look beautiful. This *could* be taken as purely subjective phenomenon, like beauty of food to hungry man, with beauty disappearing after satiation. But stress that it can *also* be taken as objective, as the *perception* of the beauty & structure of a symphony, in contrast to its noise to tone-deaf person or to uneducated man. Something real is perceived which could be tested in various ways, but *not* in the ordinary public, objective, machine-recorded perception of an apple on a table. Mustn't permit this latter to be *only* contention of poetic quality of peaks, of B-cognition, & of veridical quality of B-percepts. Otherwise couldn't say gods perceive more than worms. [*Gods also see timelessly & from* above *time—i.e., see past, present, & future simultaneously.*] Gods don't see more in a sense of seeing more objects (the objects can be seen by anyone) but of seeing *thru* them, into them, into their essence. Give also Kirkendall example of lower-class perceiving of girls & boys (i.e., exploitee, don't even know their name). See also example of dalliance in the *Chapman Report* novel. [*Also Spinley.*]

This is also the difference between deep & superficial or shallow perception. Take D. A. Richards' lecture on man's loneliness (the isolation of the human situation). The facts of birth and death, in their inexplicable oddity: the inconceivable immensity of the universe. Man's place in the perspective of time, the enormity of his ignorance. The more stupid, afraid, defensive, shallow, & "busy" you are, the less you will see of this.

Treat also the difference in perceiving between the clear-eyed, unafraid man without illusions & the hysterical Pollyanna who doesn't *dare* to see what is except thru rose-colored glasses = before & after therapy. Perception *with* repressions, denials, projections, etc., vs. perception *without* such defenses. Might use as an example the evolution of an insight in therapy (e.g., of a penis envy, or masculine protest, in a woman). First refuses to see it, resistance, etc. Long work to get her to see it. Catastrophic, crushing depression, loss of self-esteem. Danger of suicide or panic, as with homosexual panic. If she is strong enough, she will bear it & be sad. Slowly it gets to be accepted. ("So I *am* a shit. So what. I'll live!") Then slowly it doesn't sadden anymore. It is fully accepted, like the color of one's eyes, which *might* have been prettier, but they aren't—so what? It becomes neutral & unemotional. But finally it gets to be positively evaluated & *liked*, even enjoyed. Its value can be seen & used. It's not just a fault; it's also a virtue, an asset. The dichotomies are transcended; e.g., the woman's strength & forcefulness are quite compatible with being a good wife, even a *better* wife than otherwise.

Verification of a kind of peak-knowledge *is* possible, even tho *camera eye* verification is *not*. Also, one *can* specify the (rare) conditions under which a nonpeaker *could* peak, which is as legitimate as specifying the long training, special talents, & character necessary before being able to understand higher math or to be a tea-taster. All tea-tasters agree, which means they're responding to something real, just as all peakers & mystics & ecstatics agree. Use example of the sensitive smellers & how to know that they're responding to something real (to them I smelled faintly fruity). In other words, the fact that nonpeakers can't perceive the B-values or their identity with B-characteristics is no proof against them.

Stress that the fusion between value & fact occurs "under the best conditions"; i.e., good choosers' (healthy, aggridants) wide range of choice = good person + good situation. Use appetite examples; that is, "What is desirable is desired," and "The organism desires (values, chooses) just that which is good for it (biologically)." The 2 statements ("That is the case" & "That ought to be the case") become synonymous. The facts become desirable (from anthropocentric point of view). What is desirable & ideal becomes a fact.

Certainly this can be confirmed or disconfirmed by all the appetite & self-choice stuff. Also the contention that B-cognition takes place in peaks, which equal deeper, more intuitive perception of certain aspects of interpersonal reality. The test would be to check the external validity of descriptions & predictions made during peaks (by comparison with nonpeaks); also compare validity of cognitions of peakers & nonpeakers.

February 13

Can put together completion theory with SA & growth & perfection theory, etc. Reading about Adler: "He came to interpret feelings of inferiority [not as negative states which must be overcome by compensations but] as states of imperfection or incompletion." (That is, not "bad" so much as "not good enough.") "He came to see man's restlessness & incessant striving not so much as a desire to rid himself of deficiencies but as a more positive process in which the individual seeks to grow & to move forward to higher things" (p. 321, Chaplin & Krawiec). Thus this striving (all striving, any striving) is the same as the urge to complete onself, to be, to become fully human, to be a whole, satisfied, unitary, complete, final, perfect thing rather than just an incomplete, unfinished piece or part of something. This is to be fulfilled, actualized, instead of potential or a promise. This is the contrast between motivated (stirring, restless, incomplete, unsatisfied, becoming, trying, effortful, unsatisfactory, imperfect) & unmotivated (metamotivated, resting, satisfied, fulfilled, perfect, final, complete, etc.).

Cessation of striving (i.e., incompleteness trying to be completed). Striving is the restlessness of imperfection & incompleteness, dissatisfied with itself (= tension of a poor gestalt "trying" to become a good gestalt).

To say that everything strives to complete itself is the same as saying that everything strives to be itself, to be fully itself, to purify itself (to purge itself of all not-self contaminants), to be perfect. It is to say that everything endures its own nature, or *affirms* itself in its own nature, or strives to continue, strives to be (rather than not-be).

February 18

The whole generation is without dedication or excitement or hope, priests who don't really believe in the church, value-deficient, value-neurotic. They are unable to work, to renounce, to be frustrated, to be strong, to help, to devote themselves to a cause. Essentially selfish, self-centered, privatistic.

March 19

Reminded of my conversation with Rogers in Madison about Skinner. I was making my old point that all these arbitrary connections were stupid & not to be taken seriously because they could *all* be eliminated by truth, insight, facts, as is the Baker-Metzner experiment. Apparently Rogers had never thought of this & was much impressed. I pointed out that this was true for *all* the controls that did not rest on truth & honesty & openness—the subliminal conditioning. Verplanck's operant conditioning of a speaker's gestures, propaganda, false advertising in *all* of these are destroyed by the truth! Now what kind of "stamping in" is *that*? Only "intrinsic connections" are stamped in truly—that is, learnings which are suitable to the nature of reality & of the organism & of the commerce between them (e.g., learning not to touch hot radiators). The Skinner box teaches only what is in the experimenter's mind, his whims & wills.

I pointed out that two Skinner teaching machines could be set up to teach opposites; e.g., one would teach that Jackson Pollock was the end of art, the other would teach that Andrew Wyeth was. (Here taste is arbitrary. But one could also teach an arbitrary language or math this way;

i.e., the reinforcers are passed out by the arbitrary experimenter, not by the truth of reality.) (Contrast authoritarian hypnosis with democratic hypnosis. Rogers' therapy—*all* good therapy—is truth therapy, honesty, uncovering, insight, etc.) What truth strengthens—that is intrinsic to the organism. What truth destroys is *not* intrinsic to the organism.

Therefore the only real learning is *not* arbitrary association! The only real learning is of the truth, of reality, of the facts, of Being, of the way things are. The only real medium of learning is honesty, & helping the person on in his self-discovery (which usually calls for a concerned-loving-Taoistic attitude).

The gestalters of all the academies were closest to this notion, & they don't bother using the word "reinforcement" at all, or "reward," etc. Anything worth learning is its own reward.

April 1

(54th Birthday) 3 A.M.—can't sleep. Read James V. Clark thesis on worker motivation & got all sorts of ideas from it. Very good job. My motivation theory has really been tested & confirmed in life situations rather than the lab.

Set me off on metamotivation theory & it went well. Put the whole structure on top of basic-need motivation structure & it goes well. Quote 1 is talking of SA motivation, or unmotivated, or pure expression, or search for B-values. Metamotivation covers all of these very nicely. The whole business can be conceived of as the psychology of good conditions, or even of perfect conditions of good SA—that is to say, of lucky or fortunate people, which means people with a life history of orderly basic-need gratification, so that all basic needs can become inactive as organizers of activity (i.e., can be taken for granted). Then the higher nature (or the higher life-spiritual life) emerges to be seen clearly. Was it there all the time? Yes, as a universal potentiality. That is, every human being has within his nature a yearning for truth, beauty, goodness, justice, order, humor, completion, etc. (or a preference for the true rather than the false, or to see rather than to be blind, etc.), but this emerges only as lower basic needs are satisfied—i.e., under the very best conditions. Are they in a minor degree *always* active, even while basic needs are not satisfied? Yes, I guess so, especially in those with strong constitutional leanings or talent in this direction. But very weak, subtle, easily obscured by their opposites, etc. Or, to say it in another way: Under what conditions are the metamotivations *not* preferred? Under *bad* conditions!

Oh, yes—differentiate basic need gratifications—i.e., the psychological goods from economic riches, objects, things, luxuries, which are mostly gratifications at the psychological level, not really needs at all. They almost can be seen as avoidances of the real needs, or as defenses against them, decoys & confusers. Or put it this way: the basic needs can be satisfied in an economically poor society as well as, & maybe better than, in a rich country. *But* this isn't all there is to it. The higher life of movement toward the B-values is probably a little bit better available with more leisure time, which means more wealth. Self-actualization of many of the special talents means a rich society, which can afford research, education, music & art, & can support all these people. Certainly the school system & higher education can be a precondition or at least make possible SA for many people, & this is *very* expensive. Needs wealth. Looks like a good apothegm: wealth is not necessary for the basic needs, but it is necessary for the higher life, at least for many people who otherwise would be grubbing for a living full time & not actualizing all sorts of capacities. Think about this further.

April 8

Just finished Sykes' *Hidden Remnant*, & it brought all sorts of things to consciousness & to crystallization that I've been coming to slowly over the last couple of years—e.g., with students, teaching job, my place in the world, etc. In effect, I must accept the necessity in middle age of changing *Weltanschauung* about beneficence of freedom & Taoistic laissez-faire. The clearer recognition of distance between my values & the absence of values in an indulged, over-rich, spoiled, blasé generation of college students, oral types who expect *me* to stir them up, to entertain them, to inspire them, to take responsibility for them, run after them, & worry about them, etc. (We fired 4 grad students finally & flunked all 6 people taking a major exam. Turn of the tide. Moving into new era.) Have to become the stern, distant, disapproving, punishing father. Another thing I remember from the dozens of talks I've been having: students helping a professor seem to think they are working *for* him, being exploited, having their blood sucked. They just don't "admire-identify" with their elders. The older ones are "over there on the other side" with antagonistic interests. Hence also the lack of communication, the silences, my feeling that they are a lot of Sphinxes, my feeling of puzzlement & confusion as if I didn't know what was going on, my feeling that they simply didn't understand. (Mike said that this was due to fear of the elders, fear of vengeance, retaliation, etc.; therefore "they don't stick their necks out"—like delinquents with cops, or like prisoners with jailers. This is true in a way. It must be. No student has *ever* disagreed with me openly, altho I know they disagree behind my back. They must therefore think, as Mike said, that it could be dangerous for them to disagree with me—that I would destroy them for it.) Part of it also was that the younger students are indoctrinated by the older students, rather than by the faculty, not to take notes, exams, papers, seminars seriously. Must get rid of older ones in future—or else brief younger ones against their influence. It occurs to me that we can't really break thru to them. So far, of the discharged ones who spoke with me, only one took any blame on himself. A. & B. were incredulous. C. absolutely overrates his competence. D. was tolerant about being flunked—almost condescending & good humored. E. still sphinxlike, etc.

The whole change in view is more toward greater "pessimism," which I have to build into my psychology. Much greater attention necessary to bad influences of wealth & indulgence, need for discipline, frustration, etc., the stern father, not motherly father, modification of Taoistic theory to be somewhat more skeptical about *inevitability* of good results of let-be. Same for *inevitability* of self-actualization. Even under good conditions, as in U.S., it doesn't come as often as I would have thought 10 years ago. More attention to laziness, inertia, etc., as block to SA, to orality & dependence of the Nero-Caligula-psychopath type as result of complete indulgence in the child-centered family. [*Overindulgence makes children useless—i.e., castrates them, enfeebles them, lowers their self-esteem, which is based on real achievements & real skills & capacities. Makes them useless → they feel useless & worthless, not necessary. They are treated like toys or dolls.*] More attention to the value-abdication of the elders (as in my Mexican paper [75]), so that the youngsters use them & despise them (the way John D. Levy's indulged overprotecteds did). Along with this contempt goes anger & even hatred for failing them (they blame the parents for their own sickness & lack of fiber). On the whole, this means in my Propositions book much more attention to all the aspects of evil, to value pathologies, to destruction of character by indulgence. (In middle of night, my impulse was to jump up & start on this book. Maybe that's what I'll do this summer *along with* or *instead of* the B-stuff. I'll see.)

April 15

Reading *Summerhill*. Extremely interesting. And extremely extreme in extreme freedom, extreme trust in child nature. No question that he's far more correct than his opposite numbers. The real question here, or at least the real difference between him & others, is his profound acceptance of & liking for human nature, even love & admiration for it. He trusts it more radically than anyone in history—& with open eyes too. No denials of what kids are like under noninterference. He just likes it that way, or at least trusts it to eventuate in good adults. Most people would be scared & would lose their nerve—I know I would—at the temporarily bad results of noninterference. He isn't.

Important point: he's not close to the children, or an indulger or overprotector. Noninterference for them also goes with noninterference for himself, at least in the ultimate questions. He protects his *own* freedom. Noninterference doesn't mean "everything for the children," indulgence & self-sacrifice. It can go with healthy selfishness. Be sure to stress this in propositions book.

But even more important is his ultimate remedy & ultimate diagnosis. I think the deepest & first point is his philosophy of human nature—he thinks it's fundamentally good, at least in the long run. [*But kids have no sense of future. He says they can always learn later on whatever life demands. But sometimes there may not be enough time to do so—i.e., reading, writing, or arithmetic. Piano practice? How about impulsiveness of children? And need to learn controls? And to have controls? Are all our beliefs here erroneous? They could be, but I'd sure be cautious about evidence, checking, testing.*] Therefore it should be given freedom & let-be to let it emerge. But he thinks of it as love & hate (rather than let-be respect). *Or*, freedom is not so much per se, sacred in itself, but only because it is the best way to get out of the way of the good, self-forming, trustworthy, self-choosing child nature. That is, if human nature were not good, then freedom would not be good. Unfreedom is *not* necessarily out of hate; it can be out of fear that the child's nature is not altogether "good" or that it is not altogether wise, or social, or loving.

Therefore a mother may love her child & in general respect child nature, & yet be so afraid that he'll hurt himself, or his little sister, or be hurt by autos, or bigger kids, or perverts, or open wells, etc., that she will interfere & guide & punish. Also, parents' healthy selfishness normally will go further, *much* further, than Neill's, who was perfectly patient and could stand noise, interruptions, questions, etc. Most parents are not nearly as patient. Also, many have their own work, which excludes the child (Neill's work included the child because it *was* the child). I, as a scholar, couldn't possibly tolerate all the interference with my papers, books, quiet, & talk that he did. The truth is, Summerhill *is* child-centered. The interests of the adults, even tho not obliterated, are certainly secondary.

On page 95 Neill assumes much unfreedom to be antipleasure. Not necessarily so. Too strong a statement. I fear that the pleasure may be damaging, as much pleasure *is* in truth. He forgets that he, too, reflexly forbids all sorts of pleasures—e.g., heroin, pornographic movies, nudism, homosexuality (not a word about this in his book). If his school were in a NYC slum, I wonder what would happen.

Then also the ordinary stress on discipline can *also* come out of love rather than hate—i.e., preparing child for a cockeyed world where he dare not be innocent. He must be prepared for the evil outside the family circle, the crooks, the lions, the bullies.

Also, we need empirical *study* & *research* on what happens in a complex civilization to kids who were *not* forced to calculate, to read, & to write. Is it true that they will pick this up very quickly as soon as they need it & want it? It's possible, but should be proven. And *not* with only one case.

Also, empirical phrasing = what limitations or inefficiencies upon wise choice are dictated by limitations of youth (e.g., inability to abstract). Of course, the burden of proof should be clearly on the one who wants to *limit* freedom of choice. (Just read review of Muller's *Freedom in Ancient World*. Looks apropos. Should read that too before writing propositions on freedom, choice, permissiveness, discipline, indulgence, etc. I keep thinking of my college students, here & all over U.S., who *were* indulged, free, undisciplined, etc., & who are *not* lovable & respectworthy, but rather are bored, blasé, selfish, & without values except selfish ones.)

But must remember that Neill *accepts* child as dirty, noisy, masturbating, greedy, selfish, apolitical, authority-rebellious, gangster-loving, work-hating, play-loving, disobedient, unmannered, impolite, undocile, self-indulgent, forgetful, vengeful, stealing, destructive of property, disrespectful.

Maybe best way to say it is *not* "Child nature is basically 'good.'" Best to be descriptive & empirical; e.g., "This is the way kids are under these conditions." It's not so terrible after all, in terms of later results.

In a sense, it is not that they are "good" but that Neill has redefined "good," just the way I have sometimes, & the way any patient in psychoanalysis does. Best to say it this way in the proposition on evil & the one on maligned human nature.

Another thought about "trust." Best way of producing it is via knowledge of what's going to happen as consequence of trust. The more I know about kids, the more I can "trust," let-be, take it easy, not get worried, etc., about most things. But the more worried I get about *some* consequences, (e.g., of giving too many gifts to children). This is a parallel with my mistrust of psychopaths because I know what to expect. Maybe the nominative word "trust" will give way to neutral word "prediction" or "knowledge of consequences" or "expectations."

Since most of my doubt about *Summerhill* freedom comes from observation of indulged & spoiled kids, I'd better figure out more intensively just what the differences are between this & healthy gratification, freedom, free choice, etc. Just exactly what is done & not done to produce an overindulged kid or college student. Just what should have been done differently. What would Neill say about this? How prophylactic is healthy selfishness in the adults? Will this alone do the trick? How much training in frustration, delay, wanting-because-of-not-having? How much physical punishment? When, at what age, is the critical period of irreversibility? As in authoritarian kids? Real bullies? Broken spirits, hopeless, crushed, defeated kids? Which kids will freedom alone *not* cure?

May 19

Rogers—I accept basic Freudian concepts & he doesn't. Viz.: repression; defense & defense mechanisms; resistance; transference; dream analysis; neurosis as a compromise between fear & persistent desire; getting *some* gratification in a sneaky way, under cover; the phallic-symbolic language; repetition of earlier states, especially traumatic or deprivation states, probably as a dynamic effort to water down or solve or detoxify these earlier frustrations & traumata. I accept an instinct theory, or, anyway, make much of biological basis of self, instinctoid needs, etc., & Rogers doesn't (altho when I tried to start a debate with him on this in Florida, he said he didn't disagree). I will lay much greater stress (à la Freud) on analysis of earlier life history in order to understand present personality. Also on stages of development, perhaps *rightly*, like oral, anal, phallic, genital—altho I don't take this libido-theory language very seriously, & *not at all* the theory which it implies about the origin of character traits. That is, I'm pretty sure there's something in the schema & in the approach, but the specific content of the model is partly wrong, mostly wrong, or almost entirely wrong.

That is, Rogers & Adler are too ahistorical for me, altho Freud is *over*historical for me.

Rogers doesn't have enough sin, evil, & psychopathology in his system. He speaks of the only drive as self-actualization, which is to imply there is only a tendency to health. Then where does all the sickness come from? He needs more theory of psychopathogenesis, of fear, of resentment, of countervalues, of hostility.

On the whole, he also seems not deep enough, too superficial, not enough primary process in archetype or metaphysical kind of thinking that comes from the depths. Not enough unconscious, or dream psychology, or symbolic activity. In this respect he's like Adler. Also I'd say not esthetic enough in my particular sense. (Even tho he does paint, not badly, in a naturalistic way, makes mobiles, etc., he *himself* is not an esthetic person as, e.g., Norman Brown or James Joyce is.)

Not enough sociology, history, politics, economics, etc. Social determinants not important for him. No ethnology. No notion of society as itself necessarily, intrinsically bringing power, problems, evil, dominance, into intrapsychic situation. Of the Frank Manuel, Herbert Marcuse, Norman Brown sort—the "tough" sort of thing. The harshness & cruelty & Nazism are missing. How could Rogers figure out those French villains in Algeria? Where is anti-Semitism, anti-Negroism in Rogers' theory? Where is murder? Death? Destruction? Why do people go insane? Neurotic?

Perhaps it's unfair to expect all of these. After all, I'm not sure Rogers is trying to construct a general, comprehensive psychology as I am, or as Freud tried (& Jung, Goldstein, Fromm, etc.).

I think today, now that my B-psychology notes are out, I'd have to add more on "ultimate concerns" à la religion. How "religious" in this sense is Rogers? That is, is he grappling with the old religious question? To some extent, yes. To some extent, no! I *think* he's trying to incorporate peak-experiences & all that they imply about mystic knowledge, but I'm not sure; certainly, compared with Huxley, it's weak, or compared with Jung. In this respect he's more like Adler: rationalistic, socialistic, superficial, conscious, phenomenological (i.e., no unconscious).

Freud—no peak-experiences or mystic knowledge, no higher needs. Assumption of destructive instinct unfounded. Libidinal origins of everything proven wrong, & the enlarged meanings of libido, sex, Eros, etc., just breed confusion. That needs throwing out & then reconstructing from the ground up, probably something like Jungian picture. Too much reductionism: all the "high" things (curiosity, love, creativeness, fun, joy, peaks, etc.) turn out to be "low" after all, in a disguised form. Psychoanalysis is a huge effort at debunking. Really a debunking psychology. (See my article on personality in Helson book [48].) Not holistic enough. Too deterministic of the helpless type—i.e., not enough self-determination, will, autonomy, strength to fight against or to reject the determinants. (Here I like Adler better.) No place for creativeness. No esthetics. Plenty of evil, but where is the good? Virtue? Nobility? Love? Altruism? Truth? Unselfishness? Also, where are the purposes of life à la Adler? Freud not purposive (teleological) enough.

On the whole, I can accept en masse all his clinical observations with only minor corrections. Also, his system of psychotherapy has not been much improved on. But his abstract "system," his concepts, vocabulary, theories, his philosophy of man—all have to be overhauled & much of it thrown out. So also his *stated* conception of science (which he constructed unconsciously by his practice & procedures) is too physical-chemical-mechanistic, à la 1880. No answer to the legitimate religious questions. Female psychology needs redoing. So also psychology of creativeness; so also his social psychology. Must extend to the B-values his theory of superego & of guilt, transference & countertransference, anxiety. The clinical truths in his death-instinct theory must be salvaged & the rest thrown out. (For more criticisms, many of which I agree with, see Adler & masthead of *Journal of Individual Psychology*. Fromm, Horney, Jung, Rank, existentialists. Also cull out of all my writings agreements & disagreements.) Maybe in propositions book I should make a list of things I agree & disagree with at beginning or end of book—in all of these people & in behaviorism as well. This would help make it comprehensive & also would obviate repetitions & explanations. But stress primary loyalty to the corpus of scientific data in the journals. These data come first in principle. Also must make peace with science & make explicit my philosophy of science.

So also stress that main point of difference with Fromm is his lack of empiricism. I consider myself a scientist & I consider him *not* a scientist. I consider as scientists: Goldstein especially, perhaps Freud, Rogers, Allport, Murphy, Murray. Others are clinicians & philosophers, not to mention exhorters.

By the way, I should mention how much I've learned from all of these people, who were all my teachers. Also stress that I was first a philosophy student in CCNY & Cornell, or anyway wanted to be, thought myself to be that, & then got impatient with just talking & wanted to *do* something about all these philosophical questions, solve them & move forward, & so turned to psychology as a kind of empirical or scientific philosophy. (I remember that my *main* interest was *social* philosophy, to improve the world. It went along with my socialism & do-goodism & utopianism & "idealism.")

It was John B. Watson in *Psychologies of 1925* that converted me to psychology in the year 1927–28 (after I had tried Titchener's psychology at Cornell in the spring of 1927 & thought "Phooey!"). Then went back to CCNY for a year, took philosophy & literature courses mostly, and asked John P. Turner about psychology. He recommended I look up Watson's & also Woodworth's text. The latter was uninspiring, but Watson's—wow! I remember reading it as a great peak-experience & turning point of my life. I read it at 42nd St. Library & then met Bertha &, in high excitement & exhilaration, danced down 5th Ave., jumping & shouting & gesturing, trying to explain to her what it meant. Then in September 1928 to Wisconsin & took mostly psychology courses with some philosophy & some biology. (Latter partly because preparing for medical school, since I never expected to get an academic job, partly for intrinsic interest & out of love for the subject, & partly because it fitted into the prevailing conception of psychology as a biological science). Later at Wisconsin discovered anthropology in Malinowski, Mead, Benedict. But we were all behavioristic psychologists there: Hall, Cameron, Sheldon, Husband, Harlow. Also all "scientists"—me too. No thought of criticizing it as a way of life.

But in first year there & before Bertha came, I roomed with Manny Piore, physicist, who sneezed at psychology as unscientific. He irritated me, & I think I started working up a paper later published as "Means-Centering & Problem-Centering in Science." This was as much a rebuttal of Manny Piore as anything else.

First seminar in Freud with Kimball Young of sociology department.

I wrote paper on Adler. My Ph.D. thesis on monkey dominance really was an effort to see who was more correct, Freud or Adler, sex or dominance. Then to NYC & many teachers. See prefaces to *Abnormal Psychology* book [22] & to *Motivation & Personality* book [57]. Should stress Wertheimer more as an influence & especially his lecture on Being & Doing in his seminar, which influenced me so much & turned me in a different direction, where I still am. I think I still have the notes on that someplace. It was very much like an introduction to Zen & to Taoism & to unmotivated behavior.

*   *   *

Well, to go back, where do I agree & where differ with Fromm? In addition to his nonscientific approach, I'd add his rejection of instinct theory. He throws it *all* out just because Freud's theory was no good. Of course, he drags it all back thru the back door by talking here and there about "essential nature of man," etc., but it's not explicitly biological. As a whole, biology is missing from Fromm. Otherwise I like most of what he says, agree with it. I was taught & led by it. It seemed that every time I was working up to write something, he got there ahead of me. But this also meant speaking *for* me as well. I certainly was a Frommian & cannot understand why he arouses so much hatred & antagonism & why he is not more honored as a leader & innovator. Of course, it's hard for me, too, to like him as an individual. He's been too distant, not friendly enough, not colleague & collaborative enough. Fromm was far nicer to me when I was filial on Central Park West. He doesn't seem to want to learn from me.

Fromm is Freudian enough for me, & I agree with most of his criticisms, corrections, & acceptances of Freud—*except* for instinct theory.

Who else? Allport and Murray I don't consider to be innovators or creative men. Good professors & organizers & systematizers. Each has contributed some specific notions, & these are acceptable: functional autonomy and ideographic psychology from Allport, needs from Murray. Beyond that a lot of intelligent & interesting & ad hoc empirical stuff. No system-builders. Murphy an excellent systematizer, historian. His canalization a real contribution.

Goldstein is different. I agree with his work & system in practically everything. I thought of calling my work a synthesis of Freud & Goldstein, & this wouldn't be *too* far off. It's empirical, holistic, vectoral, dynamic, high as well as low, biological, genetic, historical, etc.

I like Horney as far as she goes, but I don't think of her as a systematic thinker. She was a clinician primarily, & a woman too. Excellent clinical & therapeutic writings, basic psychology, real self, self-realization, etc.—all OK.

The behaviorists bore me. I don't even bother reading them. Started Dollard & Miller book & never finished it. Childish translations. Cattell too bores me, even tho his work will one day be useful. I guess any non-Freudian looks pale & watery to me.

Existential psychology & psychiatry is now having—or recently has had—a huge effect on me. Not so much out of teaching me new things (which it *did* some) but rather of making me realize that's where I belong. Have enjoyed their meetings more than any other, & I feel most at home with them. I've been writing existential psychology all the time & didn't know it. Same with Taoism & Zen. Of course I knew about them as far back as 1935–36 with Wertheimer, but in its fitting together with existential or Being-psychology it clicks & I can use it to build into my synthesis.

Also, in last couple of years I've gotten more stimulation out of religious & theological & mystical writings than out of psychology. Must check thru my reading record if I ever do this job carefully. For instance, I think I read very little psychology in La Jolla period—mostly philosophy, mysticism, & religion.

By the way, the tape recording of my Brandeis religion record is very poor in many places. Can't get it typed and published as I had planned. Must sweat it out & write it, so I guess *that's* what I'll be doing in Del Mar this summer. Which means also that most of my reading will be on B-psychology & on religion.

No sense trying to be systematic now. I'll add to this, whenever something occurs to me, on opposite pages. Think I'll leave several pages blank as space to add. Sometime I'll go thru Ruth Munroe book, Lindzey & Hall, Thompson, & other such books on theories of personality & test my own work systematically in relation to these books.

My new B-psychology or unitive psychology is going to gum up the works so far as theory is concerned, at least for anyone trying to describe it, place it, compare it. For instance it's *absolute,* like Plato. But that's been impossible for a whole century. I talk also about finality, completion, value, ends. But science is supposed to have nothing to do with ends & goals & ethics. Also conceptual knowledge (B-knowledge) is supposed to be the *opposite,* the antithesis, of scientific knowledge. And science is supposed to be the antithesis of religion. Etc. Etc. I seem to have all the polar opposites in the same group. Well, that's tough for the commentators. I'm trying to be comprehensive, to include everything, even the contradictions, just to be totally true & rich, to omit nothing. When I write my propositions book, I'm going to include everything, even if it contradicts something else. I'll just point to the contradiction as a problem. It certainly will be a new & different kind of system, one that wouldn't have been possible before Freud, Jung, Goldstein, et al. Systems have always tried to be architectonic (maybe this will be, in part at least, but it certainly isn't *all*—& I won't worry about it), rational (I'll include the irrational), logical (ditto). A system is supposed to exclude (mine won't). It doesn't even have to be consistent.

May 21

2:30 A.M.—sleepless again & reading the freshman papers. Some of them are very affecting & rewarding. The kids seem to have been "touched" & affected & made thoughtful—some of them at least. Also, I got fonder of them as I got to know them better. I could feel some affection, even paternal love, for some of them. I guess that's the justification & the reward of teaching, if there *is* any intrinsic reward: to enjoy watching *them* grow, to enjoy being effective as a stimulus to growth.

Happy day today. Visited new house & sat & watched the river & the lake. It was *so* beautiful & peaceful & woodsy that it got into my bones. I'm sure I'll love it there. Pity we have to leave for the summer.

May 31

Better sleep last 2 nights.

Fine peak-insight this A.M. Bertha telling me about her socialist-party-meeting peak back in Madison around 1930. Everybody concerned over her, patting her, touching her, warmed, etc., & she had peak, one of two most memorable in her life, she says. (The other, age 5, nature, in the rain. She speaks of "rightness": everything was right—the wind was right, the flowers were right, the rain was right.)

Socialist-party-meeting peak: "Completeness & fulfillment; it couldn't be better." (The hope fulfilled, which, after all, might *not* have been fulfilled.) She speaks of this as just right for counteracting & to some extent destroying her feeling of abandonment & isolation. After all, she was *not* alone; she *was* accepted; she *was* part of a group & did belong: "Everyone thought I was wonderful . . . feeling of gratitude . . . life is good, life is wonderful . . . produced feelings of guilt for a little while." (Because tho she worked for the group, she refused to join it officially.) [*Killed my doubts. Everyone thought I was wonderful.*] Then she had impulse to join the Party group, to take full standing in it: "I felt finally self-acceptance. This made me feel worthy. And then I saw my failings & shortcomings. The glow has lasted to this day. It's been an antidote to my feelings of abandonment. This started the change in my feelings of total shyness, & I've never been as shy since. Slowly losing it thru the years ever since then."

This peak was therapeutic. It also was an insight in a certain sense. Also it was indicative. Life taught her something that contradicted the *Weltanschauung* built by her early experiences. This was also a yearning fulfilled, hope fulfilled, need-wish fulfilled. She speaks of completion. Something missing was supplied, something needed that was missing. It was unexpected. (Walter Toman speaks of the element of gratuitous luck in addition to the element of need-gratification. Doubt was lost: i.e., it might *not* have been fulfilled. It wasn't calmly & surely predicted & waited for as we wait for sun to rise. Rather like a long shot coming in.)

Now in relation to the therapist's eternal question: when is an insight therapeutic and when is it not? The possible answer may be: when it is peaky, it is therapeutic; when it is *not* peaky, it is not therapeutic—i.e., merely intellectual, merely verbal, not deeply felt, not lived thru, not experienced in the guts, etc. (Sometimes an insight is spoken of as a perception, seeing something always there before but not seen. Sometimes it is spoken of as a lesson, learning something, educational. This peak is both a perception & a lesson & an insight.) Must an insight also be a missing basic-need gratification, as this was? No, I don't think so. Work it out. When yes, & when not?

Also observe that her glow & happiness, etc., made it possible for her to see her faults. She says it was a kind of B-cognition. Seeing her worth made her able to see her failings. This, too, follows the Rogers schema.

I suppose, in a certain sense, all pure knowledge is growth-fostering, psychogenic, whether need-gratifying or not, whether peaky or not, whether conscious or unconscious. (By the way, the peak seems to be *conscious* always. No unconscious peaks! Never thought of this! What does it mean?) A peak seems to be an eruption *into* consciousness. Bertha's peak certainly was. All of this concern must have been there before. Resistance, denial, fear of disappointment & hopes-dashed-yet-again must have kept it unconscious. But now it was so obvious, so added up, so unmistakable that she could no longer resist it & didn't *have* to. Fears allayed, it *was* the fulfillment of the hope rather than just the *raising* of the hope; thus no need to defend against it. So she could let it come into consciousness & then of course be overwhelmed by it. This was the breaking of a repression, of resistance, of blindness (because of childhood expectation).

So add to *sheer* pure cognition: insight, the element of peakiness (true basic need gratification) + unexpectedness & luck + eruption into consciousness & breaking of defenses + a lesson (perception learned) = a change in the *Weltanschauung* + a proving false of childhood mis-generalizations + the deficiency fulfilled & growth made possible + the greater identity (list all the identity changes) + the changes in the world (life is after all good rather than bad; life is validated; it is worthwhile to live). Talk here also about biopleasure & zest in life as sheer prevention of suicide.

Therapy is all of these things (at least). Question: how exactly does & does not the description of peaks overlap with the description of therapy (insight, uncovering, etc.)?

Add: the encounter kind of therapy tries to *give* the peak-experience (insight, experiencing, living thru contradiction of the child's misinterpretation) *in* the office. In principle this can be done. But in principle the noninvolved therapist can also help to bring insight-peaks. Look up the notes on anaclitic therapy (Sechehaye style, existentialist, Buber style). See Austin Wood's "But he did love me after all!" In the basic-need-gratification kind of therapy (giving love, giving respect, giving safety), the patient *can* be taught by *actually experiencing* a good interpersonal relationship one hour a day or a week until he gets the feel of it, possibly in a peak-experience. ("So, he really *does* think of me as worth something." "He really *is* worried about me." "How terribly patient he is. Am I worth it? Must be worth it if he thinks I am.")

July 7

In Fran's apt. in L.A. Spoke with Huxley. Date tonight. Then thinking about how he has changed in his life & how nicely he takes the criticism & keeps on changing, deserving, & getting new enthusiasms, & being eternally curious & open to new things. Always renouncing a past career & past success to go on to new discovery. Raises an old question about creativeness, about this going on to one new plateau after another, one peak after another, instead of resting content in success & resting on laurels, cashing in chips, collecting rewards & just *staying* there, devoting old age to defending what was done earlier—like Alfred Adler a little. (?) (No, he changed to social interest.) Well, plenty of others—I guess the 2nd-rate ones I can't think of now, who build a castle early in life, plant their flag there & protect it, get associated with one idea, like Hulsey Cason or Gordon Allport. (?) Was the one discovery an accident? Or *felt* to be unrepeatable? Does this person feel empty, drained, unable to do it again? No trust in self. (Good parallel I was suggesting to Kay—of making a million, fixing up a successful enterprise, & then giving it all up for the sake of the fun & challenge of doing it all over again.) This *really* means self-confidence. Also = love of the process itself rather than of the final rewards. Making means into ends. Being able to throw away the product, as in creative art education, where we must teach kids to love "arting" for its own sake by freely throwing away or giving away their paintings. The spirit must be "There's plenty more where that came from." Like the lesson I learned from someone's stealing my idea at the University of Wisconsin—i.e., to give my ideas away freely because "there's plenty more where that came from." Not to mention that a crook will so often choose to steal the worst rather than the best (if he had taste, he wouldn't have to steal). Also, the cost of protecting against crooks is higher than the cost of *letting* the crooks steal a few things—as in Kay's businessmen who had no secrets (look up notes on this). I was very impressed that Kay showed no fear of losing his money = zeal, creativeness, & self-confidence. What can you steal from a creative person? His creativeness is his precious secret, & this can't be stolen. If one idea is stolen, so what? What harm does it do a bird to have one song stolen? Not being willing to give up success in order to start all over again is sign of basic lack of self-confidence—just that self-confidence that I get more & more impressed with as necessary, sine qua non, of real, here-now, flexible, naked creativeness, of the Taoistic unstriving sort.

Therefore, just this change in the life career—as in Steichen in his interview, giving up photography 2 times (he had 3 careers) when he found he was repeating himself, repeating what had been successful, making his "success" over & over again. (Plagiarizing from himself?) Yes, that's it—it means not being original, repeating the same joke again & again; at first it was very funny, but it quickly gets unfunny. Or like Chaim Gross repeating his acrobats & clowns again & again. Or for that matter like *most* artists who find a style early, one that they get applauded for, & then repeat themselves, looking for the same applause forever. It worked once; why shouldn't it work again? "They loved me in Scranton!"

The Huxley who went from one triumph to another—each different & each one uncomfortable to others—this is just like a wealthy man giving up all his wealth to start again, like the Blackfoot Indian giveaway (that was the realest, most profound affirmation of self-confidence, of courage, of lack of fear). [*That's what you call a game! A real game. The acceptance of & enjoyment of challenge. Real risk, gambling, thrill.*] It's just that fear that forces most people in the face of a problem to look frantically through the file cabinets of the past for something that once worked & could be used now, rather than trusting themselves right here and now to see the solution *within* the problem itself (as with Wertheimer & Katona—look up Katona again). Stress this *trust*. That's one aspect of courage, or, better, I think, it's lack of fear—not the same thing. The child may trust, may lack fear, & therefore may be ideally creative in improvising on the spur of the moment, because he doesn't yet know fear out of ignorance. Relate this to the trust, the Taoistic waiting in, e.g., childbirth & in pregnancy, which also makes a nice parallel to *any* kind of creativeness: you just *can't* push too hard, or strive too much—that may kill it. Have to wait, & be patient, & trust processes of nature which in their own good time & at the right moment will let things happen.

Another thing: the trusting child also expects to be loved & applauded; it doesn't yet have the dark fears of being laughed *at* (laughing means for the trusting child as yet *only* laughing *with*, not yet ridicule or hostility or condescension). Such a child delights in making people laugh. It doesn't yet have suspicions or paranoia; the world is still perfectly good, reliable, loving, caring, etc.

This is all part of it, I see now. Thus I am now able, as I wasn't years ago, to trust myself to improvise in some situations & before some audiences; but I must feel sympathy & friendliness from the audience, or at least an openness, real curiosity. If there's antagonism, then I just can't improvise in a good way. Then I must be carefully prepared in advance, written out, cautious, defensive, or defiant.

Thus, it seems to me, this improvising & making people laugh is the B-play, the B-joking = *easy* creativeness that's casual & without striving or effort. Must add: this "delight," this laughing-with, this communion which is then formed where there is trust & lack of fear & when laughing means delight & happiness rather than hostility or being ridiculed, enmity. Only among friends, then, can you be really creative in this Taoistic style of B-showing-off, of being amusing as virtuosi must be when they play with each other or talk with each other. I guess there's a great delight in fully functioning here, in being at one's best easily, playing together. This is a kind of communication which hasn't yet been described. (Maybe I'll try it; e.g., listen to Frank Manuel & Herb Marcuse talk with each other & take notes.) They quickly commune (i.e., "understand each other") & then very soon talk in a kind of shorthand, short-cuts, anticipate each other, get all excited at the dyadic thinking & discoveries, & practically always then start with this B-humor, gay superman play, & Olympian jokes which themselves are creative.

Come to think of it, this fits in too. This kind of virtuoso play on Mt. Olympus occurs only in a good, sympathetic, friendly atmosphere, best of all in private & with no one around to criticize. (This is like brainstorming in this respect, I guess—*no criticism until later*. I think Olympians know how not to criticize. B-play is a kind of not-criticizing— to hell with all the trammel; let's roar off the face of the earth for a while. Let's play total acceptance.)

Is this showing off, fully functioning, a kind of creative activity itself? Isn't this kind of a retention of the child's innocence? You say to the trusting child "jump," & he jumps without a second thought. (Daddy will be there to catch me!) But the creative adult is not childishly innocent. Huxley knows very well that Daddy won't always be there. But he doesn't need catching. He's not afraid. Even when he's wrong, he's not hurt. The metaphor fails here. It's not like jumping off the mantelpiece into Daddy's arms. I guess it's a kind of realistic recognition that, in truth, one doesn't have to be afraid when one makes a mistake. All you have to do is wave it aside later on, or just be amused by it. (Why should people be so damned afraid to make a mistake?) It dawns on me that the metaphor of jumping, & maybe getting hurt, is totally wrong & that I've been using it too. But why? Anyway it's clear we don't have to. I can say, in truth, you can't really be hurt. Be crazy. Play. Make mistakes. (But you can say this only if you can supply a friendly atmosphere. As in therapy, where I guess just this happens—we learn to open up, to not fear being laughed at, scolded, punished. We learn to be naked and to show the secret scars we've been hiding all along. We discover from the true friend, or from the accepting therapist, that we can jump & we positively will not be hurt. We will not be laughed at, punished, etc.)

August 18

Talked last night with A., all starry-eyed, devoted & worshipful, wants to come to Brandeis to work with me. I talked tough instead of encouraging & supporting. Realized this A.M. how tired I am of the big starry-eyed talkers who never *do* anything but talk. Reminded me of B. & my sharp disappointment with him—and lots of others who wanted to "work with me" & then pooped out. This boy may or may not come thru. Can't tell. But I certainly made it very clear to him about my wishes & demands & expectations. I spoke about dilettantes (vs. workers & doers) & indicated my contempt for them. Someone brought up C., & I told how I had tested her (by giving her some work to do) & how she had failed the test—& how I then brushed her off completely. "Did you want to be a psychologist?" I asked, as I closed off his flow of flossy words. Then *be* one! By working! Start writing book reviews. Take on responsibilities (Sutich for instance). Join the League of Responsible Citizens. Down with freeloaders, hangers-on, nice talkers, permanent passers, students who study forever with no results. The test was: would he bear fruit? That's the way you tell the difference between fruitfulness & sterility.

He talked much about personal salvation, & I remembered D. I indicated my disrespect for such people. They were selfish, did nothing for others. Besides, they were stupid & incorrect, because seeking for personal salvation is *anyway* the wrong road to salvation. The *only* path was the *Ikiru* path—salvation via hard work & total commitment to doing well the job fate or personal task destiny called you to—an important job that "called for" doing. This speech I had made several times at Santa Rosa & elsewhere too. I cited the savior heroes (Sutich, Geiger, et al.)—*all* of them good workers & responsible people, & all of them happy. The other way just doesn't work for anybody I had ever seen—introspection full-time in a cave.

August 30

This A.M. finally dictated a little bit about being cautious with the overextensive use in business of my theories & findings. They're being taken as gospel truth, without any real examination of their reliability, validity. The carry-over from clinic to industry is really a huge & shaky step, but they're going ahead enthusiastically & optimistically, like Andy Kay, as if all the facts were in & it was all proven scientific truth. I *must* publish the critiques of SA & also of my motivation theory. Even so, I must expect to be blamed for all the mistakes of these enthusiasts if any real discrepancy or contradiction turns up. Then I'll really get hopped on as an unscientific optimist. Oh, well! There's no avoiding that. All I can do is to stress caution more & more. Anyway, I'm glad I finally remembered to include these warnings in my notes on management theory.

Then the question comes up again: why *don't* people replicate, e.g., the SA research? They spend so much time on so much crap. Why not some time on something critically important? I just don't understand it. My motivation theory was published 20 years ago, & in all that time nobody repeated it, or tested it, or really analyzed it or criticized it. They just used it, swallowed it whole with only the most minor modifications.

September 2

Have been asked over & over again what got me to go to Non-Linear Systems. What was so interesting? Why did I change my plans? I'd better start working it out & collecting together all the remembered bits of influence. True, I came at first mostly for money, $1000 per month + all expenses, which finally wound up $2000 per month for 3½ months. But the deal was, I made very clear, to support *my* work & to give Non-Linear 2–3 hours per week to talk with Kay, give my ideas, & see what would turn up. I brought all my papers, cards, & books for completing my writings on B-psychology. But soon after I came I got all fascinated with Kay & Non-Linear & gave up all my plans. I never looked at any of the books or papers I'd brought, but turned full-time to studying management literature, talking with Andy dozens of hours, dictating huge amounts to the tape recorder, listening to Kuriloff's classes, talking with consultants, etc., & I've worked very hard at this & nothing else all summer.

One thing was the slow realization that my theories, especially of motivation, were being used & put to the test in the industrial lab rather than the experimental lab (e.g., Clark, McGregor, Roethlisberger, et al.). I've felt guilty because I couldn't figure out how to test motivation theory & SA theory in the lab. This relieved me of this guilt & freed me forever from the lab. Life-situation testing is what's needed. How could it be otherwise? Non-Linear is one big lab & one big experiment.

I gave up my simple notion that management psychology was simply the application of pure psychology. Pure psychology could learn more from real-life work-research than vice versa. Life psychology had better be tested in life-labs. The chemistry lab & the test-tube experiment are lousy models for human-life research.

I get interested in Kay as an SA person & very curious about tracing back the origins of his novel & daring ideas, his boldness & decisiveness, & his social service & do-good impulses.

I think very important was the realization that here I could study Eupsychia. Non-Linear was an effort to be Eupsychian. I realized that most Utopian thinking had been a flight *from* industry to, e.g., the farm. Since I knew so little about economics, I'd simply omitted it from all my thinking about Eupsychia. Now I got all excited about this huge gap being filled in. This is like actual observation of Eupsychia, manipulation, experimentation, as if it were existing today before my eyes.

There was also a big shift-over because of my interest in mass therapy. Individual therapy is useless for masses. I had thought of education as the best bet for changing the society. But now the work situation seems even better, especially since there's so much experimental data available. (Why *not* in education? If it's possible in one, why not in the other?)

The experiments themselves were so frequently fascinating & supported so definitely everything I believed in. I loved the way the experiments came out on the side of virtue practically always.

Also, they bore in a surprising way on psychology in general, all branches of it. This is real social psychology. Also interpersonal relations, growth-fostering conditions, the nature of growth & SA, creativeness, synergy, etc. B-psychology in general proved very useful & very powerful in analyzing & predicting for these new industrial situations.

I remember now hearing George Katona lecture at MIT on consumer psychology, & I was astonished at the lessons I learned about psychological theory in general.

The first book I read was Peter Drucker's *Principles of Management*, & I was bowled over by its brilliance &, for me, novelty. I enjoyed the sheer virtuosity & intelligence & common sense of it. That won me over. The 2nd book read was McGregor's *Human Side of Enterprise*. Also effective in different way—Eupsychian, ethical, democratic. Maybe my old socialist hopes came back.

Non-Linear is a good lab—good conditions for watching good growth & SA or, if not, then why not? Some are doing well there, some not. Why?

September 3

Want to start formulating the ideal let-be, nondemanding, non-evaluating college (nonrewarding) that I've discussed with Kay. He & some others are thinking of setting up a college in Del Mar, & he asked me if I'd be interested in being president. I said NO, but that I'd be delighted to be involved & to be a helper, consultant, etc. Then we talked about it, & I've been thinking of it ever since. I suggested for Item #1: no degrees. Therefore no grades, no requirements (altho there would sometimes have to be prerequisites, or maybe not even *that*). The full responsibility for self-education would lie on the student's shoulders. He would also be free to noneducate himself, just as he is free to commit suicide.

To enhance this feeling of responsibility, I proposed that the student pay for his own education *entirely*. No endowments, no fundraising, etc., in order to make lower tuition. Just a revolving loan fund from which each student would borrow full cost of his education to be paid back out of his own earnings later on. This would permit faculty salaries to be set at sensible levels, which would guarantee a fine faculty.

[*Have whole range of ages, up to & including the really aged. Education is & should be continuous thru life.*

Leave of absence at any time on student's own cognizance.

Not necessary to take full-time program.

Much of "faculty" should be non-Ph.D.s (e.g., local engineers, bankers, physicians, etc.) Many people should be teaching part-time. It's good for them & for society.

Much of the wall between "students" & "teachers" should be broken down. The two concepts should shade into each other. Most teachers should be studying at same time; many students can teach or tutor.]

College size to be 600–800.

Quarter system to make it more convenient for adults to take some time off from work for a chunk of education, & to permit students to take off & earn money when necessary. (No necessity for continuous education. Leaves of absence should be automatic upon request.)

Whole business to be pragmatic & experimental because no precedents. No rules or laws until their necessity demonstrated. All tentative. Change & decision to emerge from testing of experience, feedback, etc. Each law or rule is really a tentative proposal that really means "Let's try this & see how it works." [*Feedback from* students.]

I think faculty would probably offer one course of traditional sort (so that college would have some resemblance to conventional education) & for the rest of the time be available for having research assistants & for stated office hours—to be available to students on their own initiative. (Since no degrees & no credits, therefore no bookkeeping requirements of who does what, when, & how much. Or whether they finish or not.) One big requirement must be that students not interfere with the onward march of knowledge, art, science, etc. That is, they mustn't take professors away from their proper work, but rather must be willing to learn by helping & being apprentices.

Scholarships for adults & part-time adults.

Special provisions for mothers of children à la Brandeis.

Must have unitary faculty, eating together & living nearby if possible. Faculty housing provided by college will do it.

Must have fine library for scholarly work.

No fraternities or sororities.

Small dorms, self-governed.

As much self-instruction as possible—e.g., guided reading, papers, research apprenticeships, older teaching younger, student-run seminars & debates. Magazine to publish student papers.

All lectures & courses available to anyone in residence, except where specifically forbidden by instructor. (Don? Adviser? Seniors? What name to give them that doesn't imply active teaching & passive learning? Consultants? Experts? Resource persons?) [*Professors?*] Anyway, no hierarchy of ranks. All same rank.

September 20

Reading Colin Wilson's *Religion & the Rebel* &, as usual, impressed & stimulated. "The poet must be a visionary—& makes himself one by deliberate derangement of the senses." (p. 73). "The enemy was boredom & unfulfillment. The incentive was a feeling that *there should be some way of living life to the full*," (p. 72). They got bored, irritated, defiant, nose-thumbing with everyday society—which irritates and even sickens them. (Why have I always called this the merry-go-round—with easy salvation available simply by getting off the merry-go-round?) [*"Stop the World—I Want to Get Off."*] The really perceptive man who sees thru all the pretenses, the phoniness, the stupidity & short sightedness—if he is also sensitive & easily hurt, if he is very esthetic. (Like Bertha & Ann, who can't stand ugliness that I can tolerate easily or not even notice—they are *both* acutely perceptive *plus* acutely demanding of perfection, even tho in a priori principle the two need not go together.)

I guess I'm sensitive too, *very* sensitive, even tho not as much as Ann & Bertha. I'm writing on my beautiful brick terrace for the first time, overlooking the Charles River; the sun is out; all is green & rustly. Watching a little group of yellow warblers feeding on *my* property, my trees, my river, my world, my birds. They're so beautiful—it's all such a miracle, & suddenly tears come to my eyes. I feel so fortunate. This river is such a fulfillment, such a hopeless hope come true unexpectedly. And then the thought of all the Jews starved & gassed & burned, who don't have all of this. I could so easily have been one of them. Certainly it's none of my doing that I wasn't one of them. I feel grace—as the Catholics say—undeserved good fortune.

Well, certainly I have that kind of positive sensitivity & do get tears in my eyes from a novel or a movie where justice triumphs or beauty is poignant, etc. But I seem to be able to shrug my shoulders during the ordinary course of life with its mixture of truth & falsity, of beauty & ugliness, of goodness & evil. Now I remember that I was the same way about food—able to appreciate good food intensely, but not really minding mediocre food or even bad food.

The sensitivity & the negative emotional reactions are separable.

But Colin Wilson talks as if they were not—as if the sensitive perceivers also had to be the sensitive emoters, who had to become outsiders & anti-merry-go-round.

But what started me off writing was the thought that all this tied in with my metamotivation & *metapathology*. (That's a good word I just coined; it covers the psychological pathology resulting from deprivations of the B-values. Or maybe I should call it metapsychopathology?) Rimbaud could be said to be sick because of his ugly environment, as Wilson claims—or at least there's a certain partial truth here. He's sick of the countervalues. [*The countervalues sicken. Deficiency of B-values sickens. I.e., it can be expressed either as a poisoning or as a deficiency disease.*] Just as ugliness can make Bertha & Ann sick, & as evil & injustice & phoniness can make me feel angry, depressed, hopeless, & give me insomnia, rage, constipation, loss of appetite, & all sorts of other tangible symptoms, leading me to drink more & smoke more (used to) & not to be able to work, etc. All of Colin Wilson's writings are about metapathology coming from B-value deprivation. This I think now is what he's been trying to express. My vocabulary & concepts can make it quite simple & clear.

An experimental paradigm for all this exists in the beautiful-room experiments. Beauty in the environment has a tangible, pragmatic, measurable effect. (So does ugliness.) Helps also to explain our fondness for children: they represent B-values & have not yet developed counter-values.

Metapathology. This is the general name for the unknown (as yet) diseases I predicted someplace (where? I think in motivation theory article) where I called it "value pathology." This is a triumph of predict-ing & therefore is a kind of validation of the whole theoretical system of B-psychology—just like finding the hitherto-unknown planet by deduc-ing that it must exist or else the system would make not enough sense. Start collecting instances. [*I think I'll make this the Horney lecture. "The Fusion of Fact & Value" is the announced title. I'll add metamotivation, countervalues, & metapathology.*]

Talked a little with Bertha & Ann. Seems necessary not only to make separate variables of degrees of perceptiveness and degrees of emotional reaction but also to separate positive emotional reaction from negative emotional reaction. I think the best way is to be highly percep-tive and highly reactive to positive B-values and relatively unreactive to countervalues. This latter is a kind of strength which could usefully be separated out: Ego-strength? Toughness? Countervalue tolerance?

Start differentiating out metapathology from neurosis, psychosis, character defects, sociopathology, etc. Much of this must be the disap-proving labels put upon the rebels by the conventional, middle-class psychiatrists, especially the climbers & strainers. Compare with middle-class values forced on school kids by their teachers as if they were eternal principles. How often is a "neurosis" iatrogenic? A gift from the people on the merry-go-round.

Part of Wilson's implied thesis: only peak-experiences are worthwhile. Only they are truly life. Anything short of that is death. Peak-experiences or nothing! The fact is, we know now, that they can come only occasionally at best, & for some only once or twice in a lifetime. This is then a kind of unrealistic perfectionism, possibly out of an ability to enjoy life only at its highest levels—i.e., lack of biopleasure in, e.g., just walking, eating, sitting, chatting, getting jobs done, feeling emotions, etc. This might be one aspect of the arrogance of the gifted—"art for art's sake." Only perfect beauty is worthwhile. Also characteristic of adolescent & young adult—impatient, idealistic, perfec-tionistic, uncompromising.

I guess *all* neurosis must be partly metapathology—everything beyond basic-need frustration & beyond historically based inabilities to use basic-need gratifications, & the cognitive & attitudinal changes created by these. The presently existing countervalues had better be differentiated from past experiences of countervalues. These may have been traumatizing, & anyway prove the possibility of their perhaps occurring again.

All this probably makes possible a better & neater conception of illness. Today it's still impossible to define neurosis fully. Maybe because the metareality element is missing. (Being can be called metareality, I think, since it includes the ends, the goals, the limits to which we approach, the ideals, the perfect. Calling it metareality might be better than calling it Being.)

I suppose this all ties in with all the talk about the "need" for meaning, for significance, for values, for understanding. The religious urges & questions. Also the whole area of the "sacred" & its separation off, its difference from, the ordinary, the profane, the secular, the everyday, all-that-doesn't-matter-much, the routine.

The B-values are instinctoid like the basic needs. So only these satisfactions are self-validating. The basic-need hierarchy is prepotent to the set of B-values, all of which are equally potent with each other.

In Rimbaud there was very clearly a whole mixture of forces & counterforces. Among them, include the kind of dissociation that Deutsch speaks of + the internal civil war of one part of the self against another part of the self (that is, whenever the integrative forces are not strong enough to fuse them gracefully, forces that seemed to have been very weak in Rimbaud). Then there is the arrogance of the talented, of the superman (every genius sees himself now & then as a superman), who defies all the laws because they are for lesser people (of whom he is contemptuous because they are too blind to see the B-values that the superman-genius can see). Then there is also the fear of & struggle against one's own greatness & godlikeness, as in Frank Manuel. (This is a defense against paranoia.) Also there is a resentment against it, because of the special duties, obligations, & pains that it places on one's shoulders. It can therefore be seen as a curse to be talented. In fact, it *is* partly a curse; it means permanent isolation (like the albino crow), & it means *hostility* from all, along with admiration & applause, resentment. "By this sign shall ye know the great man—that all the mongrels are leagued against him," (Swift). Page 80 in Wilson on Rimbaud & his satanic pride: "Ancient Egyptian noblemen boasted of being related to the gods; Rimbaud, too, began to create with this certainty, refusing to accept the lot of common humanity." He began by thinking of himself as a god (Nero? Caligula?); he ended by thinking of himself as (merely) human. He said "One makes oneself a visionary."

September 30

Much emotional turmoil & some depression ever since I returned to Boston. Trying to figure it out amounts to an attempt to see the isomorphism of my intellectual tasks & my personal problems & also the general task of integrating good & evil.

Many evil, bad, depressing, & disappointing happenings. The trouble in Mississippi, other Negro troubles (or rather white troubles). The defection of the Rands, the falling apart of the psych dept., my feeling of distance & even loneliness & strangeness from all my dept. colleagues & almost all grad students, reading the Wilson book on the relation of the sensitive outsider to the insensitive low-level average of society, disappointment with the new house (*not* with its location) because it's costing so much to bring it up to adequacy, Ann's situation—God knows what else—have made me sad. (It's lucky Bertha has been such a comfort—the river, too.)

Also long talk with Dick Lowry—I guess I identify with him some—in which he asked me to explain myself & my work. I guess sometime when life & humanity look like a big pile of shit & when evil seems to be inevitable & seems to be overcoming the world, I have to turn back to the bases of my work to reassure myself again that it is not Pollyanna, unrealistic optimism, not denial, etc. Well it *isn't!* Then comes the task of being sure it won't be *misunderstood* as being Pollyanna & denial of evil.

Far from being unrealistically optimistic, I told Lowry that my tragic sense of life & evil, etc., can sometimes be so overwhelming that all I can do is to fight against it the best way I can, so as to remind people—& myself—that it's not necessary to be overwhelmed & to give up, that there *is* a counterforce in truth. That there *are* some hopeful possibilities. That fighting back and working as I am doing *is* realistic, effective, & fruitful—especially because there are so few doing it. So many of the Third-Force people are deniers, over-optimists, not able to assimilate evil to their systems. Very dangerous therefore. Always the possibility of disillusionment & disappointment after shock. Like Voltaire, whose optimism & rationalism were shaken by the Lisbon earthquake. "What kind of philosophy can it be that has no room for earthquakes?"

One thing I've been doing for the sake of better communication is stressing my Freudianism, & that my whole system is built upon this foundation (as well as others) & that it is *not* a contradiction of the Freudian clinical findings but assimilates them, builds upon them, sometimes transforming them (by assimilation into larger structure with higher ceilings). I'm looking for a Greek or Latin word for "upon" so as to coin the word "upon-Freudian."

Anyway, when Lowry talked about his sense of loneliness (because of his high intelligence & I think good taste), I could say that I felt that way too much of the time, in a certain sense, because I really *am*. Whom do I have in the world to discuss my work with? Some strangers at a distance—Huxley, maybe June Hanks, a few young people, Andy Kay, I think (of all people!), a few of my students. No wonder I miss Frank Manuel so. Even tho he disagrees with my work almost entirely, at least he understands it & takes it seriously. If Bertha weren't so patient about being talked at, I'd hardly ever have a chance to talk it out. Angyal did, come to think of it, but I hardly ever saw him, & he couldn't chat. Nor can I chat with my peers—Rogers, Fromm, or Allport, for instance. Not Sutich either. Oh, yes, Henry Geiger—he really knows well what's going on.

My work certainly is written about & quoted often enough. But I have yet to see a really satisfying (to me) account of it all as a system, as a revolution, as a general theory of human nature, as a philosophy.

October 3

Thought while walking & meditating. I changed my mind about my summer plans when I realized that Non-Linear Systems (& others like it) was the equivalent of the dream come true, the hope fulfilled, the potentiality actualized. Then I saw the theoretical possibilities of this for social psychology. *But this* is exactly parallel to my absorption long ago with self-actualizing, fulfilled, people-living-as-well-as-people-can-live. I think I saw half-consciously that the psychology of the time just simply didn't cover Ruth Benedict & Max Wertheimer & others like them (not Freudian psychology either), & that a *different* & new psychology was necessary, & that if I could get to understand them, I could understand what *everybody* might be.

Same for factories or organizations or departments of psychology, or managers, families, friendships, teams, etc.

October 9

[*H. Bergson birthday 1859.*]
New thoughts on emotion this A.M. as I realized that we've been annoyed for 10 years—*actively* irritated—by the lack of a second toilet. One of the reasons we wanted to move was this. Now we have a 2nd toilet, and it dawned on me that after the 1st or 2nd use of it I forgot all about it. It's totally taken for granted now, not actively, consciously enjoyed or appreciated. These gratifications-pleasures adapt out or extinguish very quickly, especially for things or objects. (For people too? We also take our friends & family for granted.) The only thing that brings these gratifications to mind again is threat or frustration. This does *not* extinguish so easily. Real pains hardly extinguish at all. In this sense, pains far outnumber pleasures, & we are far more often aware of nuisances (deprivations & frustrations & threats) than we are of gratifications, & the frustration-angers last much longer too, each one of them.

The tendency, then, is to seek more gratification-pleasures, but on the whole this won't work unless they are "higher pleasures." More of the same won't do the trick—2 cars instead of 1, 2 houses instead of 1, 2 girls instead of 1, 2 million dollars instead of 1 million, etc. For example, see self-indulgence, without limits on the "pleasures," which means ultimately almost the same as no pleasures. For instance, the sexual pleasures. This means that the best way to maximize gratifications-pleasures is to seek higher & higher ones rather than staying on the same level—more & more complex, more difficult, more challenging, more straining & stretching.

Somehow I get the feeling that this truth is less true for the *basic*-need gratifications themselves. The pleasures of being loved, of being admired, of respecting oneself, of feeling capable, of belongingness are more lasting & recur more often, even tho they too tend to get taken for granted (not consciously enjoyed). Perhaps the paradigm above holds *much* more for things, for means & instruments & exchange-values, than I thought at first. Of course this is easily researchable. It is a simple quantity measure: How often? How long-lasting? Also, I think these latter basic-need gratifications *feel* more solid, more deep, more satisfying, not so fleeting, & certainly with no after-depression or after-disappointment of the kind that comes often with object-gratifications.

I think this after-depression is a kind of disappointment of unconscious expectations. We must have unconsciously expected that this (money, house, power, auto, sex) was a means to some deeper end—e.g., that the money would bring admiration, respect, love. So that what looks like a search for money or power is more deeply & truly seen as a search for basic-need gratifications. Since this is a neurotic confusion of ends, disillusion & disappointment & therefore sadness *must* come after the "gratification." But for *zeal* gratifications (i.e., basic-need gratifications), no such disappointment need be expected (altho here too it may come where the expectation of ecstasies has been too great).

But the pleasures that last best of all, that recur again & again, that are most easily & often resuscitated into freshness & aliveness, & that last longest in each episode are the metaneed-gratification pleasures ("meta-pleasures"?). I noticed the contrast between the 2nd toilet & the river. The beauty of the river hits me each time I look at it. It fluctuates up & down in pleasure level to some extent, but not very much yet after 3 weeks of living here. Also, it *is* already possible for me to look through the river when I'm distracted or thinking of something else. And yet, on the whole, the pleasure—or rather the thrill—remains fresh & easily available & often recurring. I already seek it out. My favorite spot for reading is sitting in front of the river view. Of course this is no longer the gasp, the total autonomic reaction, the esthetic shock of surprise, disbelief, & peak-experience, as when I saw it first, when I first owned it & sat quietly to drink it all in. Just like my experience with music where the great thrills & peaks that came at first experiencing them came no longer. What I get now from the Firebird or Brahms 1st or Forellen Quartet, etc., is a very solid pleasure. The first time I really heard these pieces they half killed me with delight, ecstasy, etc. So with the river & the trees & the beautiful street. So also with my great insights—the quality & intensity of the pleasure *do* change from a great peak to a pleasure. I *do* after all get used to my most beautiful & satisfying conceptions. The peaks don't recur.

But even so, these metapleasures, not only from beauty & the perception of new truth, but almost surely from the other metavalues as well, are more solid, more deep, more recurrent, more reviving & therapeutic (e.g., produce hope, biopleasure, etc.), last longer, validate life more, are more easily obtained, etc. The B-values can be enjoyed again & again. They don't extinguish ever, even tho some qualitative adaptation takes place. (They go from peak-experience to pleasure, from shock-pleasure to serene-pleasure. After all, we couldn't stand many peak-experiences.)

Think how different this phrasing could be made! *Seek the Life of Pleasure! Seek Happiness! Be Selfish! Be a Hedonist!* (All you'd have to do, then, is redefine B-pleasure, B-happiness, B-selfishness, B-hedonism, etc. At this level, the opposition is resolved & the life of pleasure tends to be the same as the life of duty. The life of unselfishness (altruism, service, philanthropy) becomes very much the same as the life of selfishness (true, real, sensible selfishness). Self-seeking becomes the same as serving others. Etc.

November 10

Part of this probably is the first experience of dropping the mask & being naked & honest. To "rush" a person, as with one's first sweetheart or sexual partner, must develop a special kind of relationship, a special kind of intimacy, as with the M.D. who sees me naked, weak, sick, frightened, who sticks his finger up my ass, who examines my scars. I can thereafter feel easier with him, more relaxed, less vigilant or defensive, as with one's wife or brother or close friend. ("I can take my shoes off there.") No persona is necessary (because he's already been permitted to see thru it), no makeup, no dressing up, no telephone voice, no polite-ness. This feels good with friends; why should it not also feel good with therapist? Isn't this more than an illusion, a strict & literal "transference"? *Keeping up the front* is fatiguing; taking off the girdle is relaxing.

This ties in with the persona as (possibly) rejection of real self = keeping up the front (the persona) = against intimacy (or inability to be intimate, to be naked, to drop the defenses) = ability to surrender, to give up well. Control, pride = resistance to B-transference.

It is necessary for B-transference that we be able to be humble, to be able to respond to the other in his B-aspect, in a unitive fashion to his symbolic, metaphoric aspect, to his "uniform" & to what he stands for. Of course this is easier the closer his D comes to his B, the closer his actuality comes to the true symbol—i.e., if he is older, wiser, better, etc. But it is still true that this is not in principle necessary. Any person can be seen in his B-aspect. Therefore B-transference can take place in theory even to a baby. (And babies *have* been worshiped, as in Tibet.)

Just as transference is considered an almost *sine qua non* prerequisite for psychoanalytic cure, so also in real growth toward SA is B-transference probably a necessity. One must be able to be humble, to receive help, to be weak & low & subordinate, to oblate, even to worship, to look up with awe, gratitude (as with religious conversion, with Alcoholics Anonymous, with love-surrender & frigidity, with fear of loss of control vs. need to be able to give up controls & to "trust" in a Taoistic way). As a matter of fact, B-transference is an example of Taoism & Taoistic science. But to be able to surrender & trust Taoistically, one must be anxiety-free. Preliminary to health is clearing away illness.

This can all be tied in with love theory too. Prerequisite to ability to love & be loved is ability to trust, to surrender, to B-love the other, to be Taoistic toward the other, to let-be & *also* to enjoy the SA of the other. B-transference is a form of love.

November 27

The notion of what "theoretical psychology" is has been crystallizing more & more in my mind [ScI]. I think I'll liken it most to "intuitive mathematics." The mathematicians, of all people, know & accept intuition (correct conclusion leaped to with inadequate data & short-circuiting all the processes in between, coming to correct conclusion without knowing why) as *the* hallmark of the born mathematician—i.e., desirable & admirable. So also I think theoretical physicists. *Proof* comes later, *after* the intuitive leap into a hypothesis.

This is what I do: come to tentative conclusions on the basis of inadequate data. It's like predicting the future, or like betting on a horse race. To criticize my kind of theorizing because I don't have enough data is to criticize *any* theorist.

This kind of theorizing is different from pure speculation because it is under the flag of science; it *is* based on data, even tho not adequate; it *does* yield to contradictory data & throw itself away; it *does* try to phrase itself in a testable way; it *is* frankly tentative.

The so-called "hard-nosed" & "rigorous" experimental psychologists & psychonomists are simply naive & self-conscious "scientists" à la 19th century. To give up intuition is to give up science.

December 18

The thing I've been mulling over for last week or so is that authenticity is not enough. It is a necessary but not sufficient condition for, e.g., the therapist (who must be honest *before* he gets therapeutic, permissive, accepting, etc.). Also, for morality, being honest & spontaneous & expressive is not enough (honesty can *kill* other people too). The "inner core" of personality gives only the most general guidelines & directions—it does not give specific & detailed instructions for every situation. The necessity for making ethical decisions, decisions to *withhold* expression, to renounce gratification, to control one's impulses—all these are in addition to authenticity, succeed upon its achievement, & are different from honesty. One can be an honest fool, for instance. Also, even honest, authentic, spontaneous, correct anger & indignation may be dangerous & therefore should be controlled in order to make any society work, i.e., even justified murder must be renounced.

This all has nothing directly to do with the most common objection to SA theory of spontaneous expression of inner core—i.e., "why shouldn't the rapist or the pyromaniac express himself too & be spontaneous?" These neuroses are not part of the inner core, but neither are defenses against them.

I think I was so much impressed by reading about therapeutic interviews with prostitute in *In The Life*, by Rubin, that it led me in this direction. Here is a woman—typical also of drug addicts, of immature & self-indulging persons in general—who lives in the moment only, here-now, who is completely impulsive (van Kaam differentiated this from spontaneity), who lives for kicks (peak-experiences?), etc. What's lacking here is control, delay of gratification, discipline of self, planning into future; it is just pure self-indulgence without regard for anyone else. Clearly "spontaneity" or impulse expression is not a cure-all. It's true that an honest (authentic?) unphony prostitute is somehow more appealing & respectworthy than a phony, false, pompous do-gooder. And yet unphoniness is not enough. It is a necessary first step, a prerequisite condition for any higher development. But it just clears the way for higher decisions which need data (over & above just honesty) in order to be made well.

1963

January 8

Read Betty Friedan's *Feminine Mystique* right thru, finished at 5 A.M. A passionate book, — I was swept along unintentionally. (This seems to be my usual way of reading. I criticize it & judge it. I have to go over it a second time. Reminds me of brainstorming.) It's very impressive & I'm glad I helped her. Now I'll have to look it thru to see where she exaggerated, overstated the case. One thing I'm sure of: she *tends* to dichotomize being a female only from being a general human being. Often she disavows this & criticizes others for doing it, & yet she falls into it herself. Or, better said, she doesn't really think hierarchically. Instead of attacking the feminine mystique ("reproduction is enough"), she should approve of it & then build upon it. She should be "epifeminine" (good word—just like epi-Freudian). That is, accept it, need it, demand it as a prepotent requirement which must be respected. Then, after it's satisfied, build upon it. Humanness is postpotent to femaleness. (*I think!* Now, after reading her book, I'm less sure of this. Maybe that's too local & ethnocentric a conclusion? But no! It works in Mexico too.) If this is correct, then many of her arguments, especially about education, are vitiated at least in part. Because of her own good experience at Smith, she's accepted the "degree mystique" instead of demanding a different *system* of education for women (e.g., something like what I've done at Brandeis with the married women in the graduate school).

The fact is that these are more sober second thoughts. I identified with the book completely while I was reading. Just like a convincing novel. So often I realize something was wrong with the play after I leave the theater & become sober. Like the uncriticalness of the dream.

January 16

1:45 A.M.—still can't sleep. Even more disturbed over grad students & my feeling of defeat & helplessness & anger. I just don't know what to do with them except to stand firm. But how can I work with people whom I don't respect? And that's about ½ to ¾ of them. The feelings seem to go deep—of a whole culture breaking down, of my whole way of thinking, my whole philosophy of psychology shaking on its foundations & needing revision (Frank would snicker at *that*), of having less hope for human nature because here is an instance of "good conditions" of a kind I myself have prescribed, of people with capacity, of a first-rate faculty, a fascinating subject, chosen by the people themselves, & yet *not* growing, *not* self-actualizing, but instead cowardly, anxious, flabby, unambitious, undedicated, very few catching fire, etc. Lowry looks very good. A few others. Then of course there's the disappointment of personal rejection. Hardly any one of them has been inspired to pick up my brand of psychology. For instance I don't think any *one* of them subscribes to *Journal of Humanistic Psychology*, or to *Manas*, even tho I tout them all over the place. I don't have a single friend among all of them past & present. Again I have to remind myself that it may take a long time for them to develop. Our past Ph.D.s have done OK in a fair proportion. Maybe these will too, but I just don't think so.

January 28

9 P.M. Stumbled across a most unexpected publication today, in Dec. 1962 issue of *Perceptual & Motor Skills*, of Clark Hull's "idea books"—rather like my journals. Wonderful way of seeing a man & his system from inside. Makes the whole stuff of neobehaviorism—which I've never been able to read since 1935 or so—more human & less like the product of perversion or blindness or pathology, etc. I've always thought all these boys were half nuts, or at least obsessional, mechanistic, bloodless, unemotional, certainly adolescent rather than grown-up. Well, now I know that Hull was sincere, authentic in his beliefs—at least honest. And he sincerely thought the Gestalt psychologists & other "mentalists" to be "obscurantists" (his own word). Not that that makes it any more correct or inclusive—it doesn't. He's still an oversimplifier in the name of science. But I can identify a little with it & recall how I felt thrilled when I first ran across Watson's chapter in *Psychologies of 1925* & had a peak-experience in the 42nd St. library & danced down 5th Ave. with Bertha trying to communicate to her my vision of—by gosh & by golly, maybe, possibly—a *science* of psychology, a program, a road map, plans ahead all laid out, with a clear promise of progress. This was after I had lost all taste for psychology, with Titchener's stuff at Cornell. Then I went

to the University of Wisconsin & they were all behaviorists & I was too—until I discovered its limitations & how many things it couldn't do.

Well, that was the young man's faith, & that's what Hull had to the end of his days. He was simply an uneducated, nice, ambitious, scientist, an intelligent, hard-working, leader-type, system-building kind of a nice man. I remember how much I liked his lectures at Wisconsin—but *not* his lab.

Hull gives me a much better insight into the simplistic, scientistic way of thinking. He can't stand vagueness, looks for certainty & exactness. Anyway he stimulated me to reactions & comparisons, especially where he made me realize how different I am from him in so many fundamental ways. For instance, throughout he is so purposeful, ambitious, planned, grim, teeth set in a kind of competition to be king of the hill, to be famous, to be in history books, striving, driving. Something like a young business-man working to build up a big organization which will be his monument. I know & remember that he enjoyed his work—he *must* have—& yet it doesn't show in his notes. All grim, as if everything was a means to some *future* end. I have some of that, but far, far less. My work has been far more fortuitous, unplanned, unpersistent. Rather it's been one lightning stroke of insight ("good ideas") after another, many with a very peaky quality. A whole series of excitements, emotions, and inspirations rather than sober, logical, patient plugging, persistent building up & working out. It's been fun, & I wonder if his was. I never seem to know what will happen next! And it seems to happen to me, rather than my deciding by an act of will what I am going to do (even tho there has to be some of that whenever I make a promise to give a lecture, etc.). Anyway, the times I enjoy most, & have done my best work in, are when I have no commitments or plans or promises, or at least as few as life permits as at Pleasanton, as at Cuernavaca, as at La Jolla). That's all the freedom I'd ever hope for.

My ambition is more for the world (Utopian, do-gooder, Mes-sianic) than for myself, or for fame or glory (even as much as I now have of fame is pleasant, but it is also a burden). And if I had to publish anonymously, or under someone else's name, I'd write exactly as many words. He seemed to be running for political office. I've *avoided* like the plague being a leader-of-the-school type.

Hull talks about his ingenuity in devising experiments & ap-paratus. I envy him this. *Just* what I lack. I'm sure this made a difference in the direction of my work. Same for his skill with numbers, statistics, exactness.

Often he speaks about machines, & he built some fancy ones. His whole outlook is mechanistic. He was proud of it & thought any other way was crazy.

He collected disciples, formed groups, etc. Maybe more impor-tant, he *attracted* bright young mechanists. Partly, I think, going to Yale did it—top students, good labs, research time, etc. But I'm *sure* it was largely because he had research assistants. I've never had a successful official research assistant where I was boss. *Never.* I always had to coax, or yield, etc. Bertha's been closest to it, but she just doesn't have training enough. I must *insist* on an assistant next year. I can take advantage of Sachar's sweet talk in pushing me to be chairman during Ric's absence.

February 8

Thought to play with & maybe work out further: to what extent is the "good man," or the fine man or strong man, constitutionally determined? To what extent does the SA person parallel the "good choosers" in Dove's experiment with chickens? The superior organism? The good specimen? [*2/16/64: Must add zest (or will to live, gusto, "good biological specimen") as a precondition for all this system to work. Add to propositions.*] The animal breeders & zoo collectors (and it used to be human parents, e.g., Spartans) could examine the babies at birth & choose the healthy ones & kill off the others. Was their confidence in their own judgment illusory? Read Sheldon's stuff, which makes a similar implication. Stress again the positive intercorrelation of all describable traits. I've got relevant materials scattered thru a dozen files. The suspicion has been slowly getting stronger & stronger thru all the years since grad school at Madison when I first read Terman. And more recently my uneasiness about the Negro has precipitated it. Is Garrett right, perhaps, & the liberal wrong about Negro intelligence capacity & forcefulness? Is there possibly a true racial difference? Everyone I know—all the liberals—would think the question itself reactionary.

February 14

Have been tense for weeks & weeks—bad sleep, fatigue, preoccupation, etc. Partly due, according to dreams, to getting all wound up & a little awed & scared by tremendous implications of work I'm doing contrasted with very shaky foundations it's all based on. So get scary dreams; also dreams of fighting, singlehandedly, against evil, ignorant, & stupid hordes of people, sometimes outwitting them, sometimes not. Ties in with the rages I get into when anyone resists logic, data, facts, science, etc. My psychoanalysis showed isomorphism with little Jewish boy among the crowds of anti-Semitic people, whose reactions couldn't be understood, & who seemed uncontrollable, cryptic, mysterious, weird.

Also Oberholzer's comment long ago in psychoanalysis that I was born an anti-Fascist, with no mother & fighting her as the incarnation of stupidity, antirationalism, evil, selfishness. In the dreams, I'm always fighting alone, against stronger forces. My anger expresses itself in some violence, which then, in the dream, brings too-great retaliation from the more powerful opposition, & I back up in the dream & start all over again with some other alternative, usually less violent, until winding up with intellect, demonstration, patience, understanding, etc., as the only realistic possibilities (which in fact is just about true in real life). So it's as if I were trying in the dream itself to reconcile myself to reality & therefore to the impossibility of winning by violence. That is, I come to the same conclusion in the dream as I come to when fully intelligent. And it's all so isomorphic with my work, & my relationships to the APA opposition, & to my resisting, passive, valueless students who get me so angry (just like that vegetarian nut, 20 years ago, who calmly rejected all facts, knowledge, logic, authority, etc., etc., insisting that raw cabbage had mystic powers of some sort, while I got more & more angry, finally winding up in a yelling rage, frustrated, baffled, beaten, & angry).

February 19

I've been fighting off people who want me to get involved in consequences of *my* own work (of the past). For instance, Tannenbaum invited me to Bethel this summer, where they're trying self-actualization via sensitivity-training group. After much wavering & guilt & fighting off the attractiveness of it, I finally refused. Have also refused all sorts of other things like this which essentially involve exploiting ideas of *mine* that I threw out & then walked away from, e.g., my motivation theory, peak-experiences, enlightened-management theory, etc. People get all excited about things *I'm* finished with. By the time they catch on, *I'm* on something else.

But now I think this is right & sensible. It is my job to go ahead & break ground. (I refused to help Shostrom work up his test for SA & felt a little guilty about it. *He* can make good tests—better than I can—but he can't pioneer & have new ideas.) OK then, that's my duty, my job, mission, call, vocation, obligation, fate, destiny. I can't duck it. And anyway I don't want to duck it—I love it. That's when I feel most alive, even tho I'm also suffering. Anyway, I feel *compelled*. Everything else bores me & sooner or later irritates me. So that's it—much better cyrstallized in my mind. I should feel guilty rather if I *don't* do this. After all, who else can? It's my job—uniquely. If I die, it just won't get done for a good long while. I think that makes a good criterion: if someone else can do it as well as I could, then I shouldn't do it.

April 6

To continue with epi-Freudian, epi-scientific point of view, stimulated by question from Frederick Weiss in NYC about relations between
Freudian psychodynamics & existentialism. I reacted, in a very strong &
decided way, that I thought the latter without the former could be a real
danger, a superstructure without a foundation, a Pollyanna theology
without end, a loss of depth & roots. Same for Tao, Zen, & other "merely
hopeful" psychologies. They are "high psychology" without the "lower
psychology." When hierarchically integrated with their lower foundations, which make them possible, they are the highest ceiling; without the
foundation, they are illusions & fantasies.

Something of the sort is also true for the attitude toward science.
These flossy, high psychologies can become antirational, antiscience, &
are therefore a great danger. *Or,* they can serve as critical tools to make us
realize how limited orthodox science is & so can stimulate science to
enlarge itself, & to raise its ceilings. The 3rd-Force psychology is scientific,
but in an enlarged sense. Jim Klee asked "Why fuss about the word
science?" I think it makes many big differences, & I'm going to try to keep
the word & redefine it.

April 8

Something else to work up: "Authenticity Is Not Enough." I find
this sticking in consciousness for the last few weeks. I think this goes all
the way back to discussions with Steve two years ago (I'd better reread his
papers) in which he laid bare the difference in opinion about this. I was
assuming, implying (without being really conscious of it), the Socratic
equation: to know = to do automatically. Steve spoke of the obsessional
gap here. Slowly I've come to agree with him (& with Bertocci too); & then
it came up at the Weiss party with the question that Arieti brought up
about neurotics & psychopaths actualizing themselves. It helped, I found,
to solve these problems well (& others, too, about the nature of ethics, of
choice, etc.), to say "Truth-honesty-authenticity is a necessary but *not*
sufficient condition for solving ethical problems." Certainly it gets rid of
lots of pseudo-problems; most "moral problems" are in this sense
pseudo-problems. But there still remain the *real* existential problems of
life, some of them insoluble, where arbitrary personal choice is necessary
even for the saint or the hero or the self-actualizing person. E.g., "Shall I
live out the cancer or commit suicide?" or "Which of my children shall I

choose to keep alive & which to hand over to the executioner?" Or as in Shaw's doctor's dilemma, etc.

The whole thing was precipitated this morning by rereading Chapter 3, "Tyranny of the Should," in Horney's *Neurosis & Human Growth*. *This* was precipitated by Lyon's novel in which a character admires De Sade for getting rid of what man is *supposed* to be. See value-fact file for this stuff. Now going off to office to add a footnote on this to Horney paper. But it's quite clear to me that I want to make something more of it than Horney did. I think that's a good title—"Authenticity Is Not Enough"—to attract careful attention, not be forgotten.

Another good discovery on masculinity-femininity. Found I had $1500 to give Bertha for her kitchen after taxes. More than I expected & felt very good about it. The big breadwinner & gift-giver, etc. Presented it to Bertha as a gift of violets, only to have it rejected with disappointment & disgust. "It's not enough. I can't do the kitchen with that." I got quite angry & withdrew the money, as if it were useless unless appreciated. Being the breadwinner & money bringer is a big & basic point of pride with me—*and* I imagine with most men. It's a very basic version of adequacy, of masculine power & strength. It's very satisfying to be able to overcome & master problems of living with money. Very isomorphic with the good hunter, the good warrior, the one who can take care of his family, i.e., the one who does not fail. It equals a basic masculine success.

But it looks as if it has to be appreciated or not undervalued. It's impossible to fill up a bottomless hole, to try to turn each defeat into a victory. No matter *what* I do, I can never be an adequate breadwinner, let alone a successful one, an admirable one, a worthy one. It contradicts my being pleased with myself if what *I* consider a victory is automatically & inevitably turned into a defeat. Reminds me of the kids who finally give up trying to please their parents who are never satisfied (e.g., "You got a 98% average? Why not 100%?"). Same with the nymphomaniacs; their men finally may give up screwing *altogether* because their achievements are never enough. Or, parallel, going impotent with the frigid woman who *never* reaches orgasm & who then blames her husband for not being adequate.

Looks as if masculine victories (what *men* value as victories) must be validated by the females to be fully satisfactory. Just as female victories (defined by women) must also be valued by their men in order to be fully enjoyed by women.

April 10

Discussion with Art Combs & Bertha at APGA conference, & it got personal. B. complained that I was a demander, a pusher upon her &

Angyal, etc., that I kept pressing people to work & achieve & that this produced the opposite effect. I was a one-man pressure group. I had the effect of making people feel guilty (& therefore resentful?) for not working & achieving. Combs agreed that this might be so, & that he had the same effects upon people maybe, & the same accusations. He said I looked warm, relaxed, & accepting on the outside but was more driving & demanding underneath. (Hand of steel in glove of velvet?) I said maybe yes, but that, as in the case of Bertha, it is not my demands, but simply my ever-present example of hard work & total commitment. Never have I had any doubt about the worthwhileness of what I am doing. I am a confrontation, a guilt-producer, whether I want to be or not, whether I *say* anything or not. Bertha claims I keep on pushing & being demanding of her about sculpture. Not so. It's her inner self speaking to herself & projecting it upon me. Use this as a dynamic in countervalues. Speak of the necessity for admiration & looking-up-to in an Adlerian & dominance way, & of the discomfort thus produced. If the person is a projector, then this discomfort will produce hostility toward the Billy Budd or toward the aggridant person. If he's a *non*projector, an extrapunitive person, then no overt hostility; perhaps the acceptance of the passive, the admiring position, looking-up-to, & perhaps erotization lead toward masochism & "homosexual" fantasies. Where, oh 'where, are the ones who don't sexualize or dominatize these admiration situations? Why can't we *simply* love & admire superiority, or, rather, competence, adequacy to the task? Maybe *that's* the trouble—that instead of seeing the beautiful adequacy to the task of, e.g., the tennis champion (& *love* it as an example of fully functioning, of suitability, of B-justice; be happier for it as before an esthetic experience), we *see* it as a superiority, i.e., as a comparison, as "better-than-I," as "he is above me & makes me feel below him." That is, we *see* it as an interpersonal relation, in which my self-esteem is called into question. Why? We don't do this comparing-with-self when we look at birds, or at animals, or even at men who are very good at something we haven't pinned our self-esteem on.

Why did I make Ann—maybe Bertha & Ellen too—feel inadequate intellectually? Could I have avoided this in *any* way? I don't think so. Simply just being there myself did the trick. Nothing to do about it. What could I have done better with Angyal? Nothing that I can think of. He must have avoided me as a guilt-producer, a reminder of all he had left undone, of all his self-castigations. But, on the other hand, I was not only an uncomfortable reminder; I was also his respected & admired friend, I think, because I was also his best self speaking to himself & saying "Fulfill yourself (do your duty) before you die." In fact, he was a bit feeble, ineffectual, leaving it to his friends to finish up *his* job. Such a fizz of a firecracker way to die. And, by gosh, I'm certain he must have known it & felt it consciously, full of regret, wishing he could have done it otherwise.

Well, OK, if I am the fortunate man, the rich man, the beloved of the gods, the one man in a thousand who knows exactly what he wants to do & who lives in a world that rewards him for doing it (which makes it one man in a *million*), & who was born to do just that, & prepared himself perfectly in a long-time plan, & who then is so convinced, so unambivalent, about his destiny that it enables him to have all the courage he needs to be his own fate, & to do what is just right for him to do, to do his unique duty, that which no one else in the world would or could do (it enables a timid man to be courageous & brave), so that I can be as unconventional as necessary, so that when I am blue, I can enjoy reading my published works (*that's* a real blessing), and then also to be rewarded & praised & honored & applauded even before I die—well, then, if I am so rich, so favored, so lucky, how could I possibly expect the poor, the less favored, the unlucky ones to avoid envy, guilt, threat, conflict, confusion, & ambivalence? It's just asking too much of human nature to hope that homely girls will calmly & peacefully love & enjoy pretty girls, for cripples to admire athletes without resentment, for the untalented artist to admire the talented one. [*The composer vs. the music critic; the poet vs. the literary critic.*] It just hurts too much. This is *part* of self-actualization, of the trend toward perfection, of our universal admiration for the great, for the beautiful, for the fully functioning. Why should we expect people to admire the good & to yearn for it, to love truth & simplicity, elegance, virtue, etc., & then not be hurt when they themselves are lacking in these values? If I didn't resent ugliness in myself, this would be at the cost of not admiring beauty in others. This likelihood of self-denigration is one existential price we pay for our version of perfection & yearning for it. It's a *sign* that we still admire perfection, & that therefore the world may yet improve.

Perhaps the great intellect *must* bear the resentment of the morons, as inevitable, as the other side of the admiration-coin, as a necessary call to humility, as a reminder of the B-injustice which made him more perfect than the others.

April 14

Nobody *really* deserves *anything*. The circumstances into which we are born are an accident. The small difference in deserts earned & deserts deserved is infinitesimal by comparison with the shared background of B-injustice. That is, the difference in virtue-rewarded between a good American & a bad American is nothing beside the undeserved rewards to *any* American by contrast with any poor Arab. (The ground is luck; the figure is earned & deserved justice.)

If the unlucky one attacks, the lucky one should feel: "Yes, I should apologize. I understand your bitterness. It is justified. You are right. It is unfair; it is unjust. It's true. I don't deserve. It's not my own worth that made me rich (or intelligent or an inheritor of the earth). It was a throw of the dice that permitted me an education & deprived you of one." *This* is the kindness & the B-humility of the aggridant. Aggridance is unearned mostly, at least in its ground, or beginning. But, of course, beyond the beginning it can be lost or gained, used or evaded. *Then* we can certainly talk of deserts & earned income.

And then comes the difficult problem of kindness, the B-kind, the sloppy & dangerous kind (à la Ayn Rand), which comes out of guilt for being lucky & aggridant & out of inability to enjoy it & use it, as if spoiling it were somehow a good answer to B-injustice. The sensible kind of B-kindness recognizes B-injustice & therefore is a kind of humility, an absence of the feeling that one deserves one's good fortune, e.g., in being a rich American in Mexico.

What is dangerous kindness in this kind of situation? Much that passes for kindness here is really weakness that brings bad results, indecisiveness, etc. The fact remains that a moron is still a moron, even if it is genetically unjust; a crook is a crook; a cripple is a cripple. Denial, evasion, self-castration, fear of standing upright because one might thereby hurt the cripple—these are all dangerous to everybody & certainly to the society, which needs the aggridants. It is best for efficiency & productivity, etc., for the aggridants to be unleashed—for them not to conceal & camouflage themselves. Also, they ought to be favored as much as is necessary for their growth & for full functioning, in education, etc.; even if this looks like privilege; that is, they ought to have & use & enjoy guiltlessly whatever advantages are actually functional. The writer must get a typewriter, etc., because it helps him to fulfill his function—even tho other people *don't* get typewriters. Bright boys ought to get a far more expensive education than average boys because it is just & sensible = functional. (Of course, they shouldn't get snotty about these privileges.)

Much that passes for humanitarianism is the kind of guilt that the superiors have simply *because* they are superior & somehow feel the biological injustice of it. But this helps nobody & wastes our natural resources.

Of course, this need not mean a privileged class; it could as easily be a *responsible* (& therefore less privileged) class, like nuns or soldiers or monks. I suppose this would partly solve the problem of resentment & of envy, etc. If the aggridants become a *generally* privileged class (more privileges than are functionally necessary) instead of a functionally privileged class only (only that which is good for the development & use of their specific talents), then there is the danger of class & caste splitting. I don't see what harm it would do to the aggridants to live a more simple & even spartan life. Maybe this would mean that they needn't feel guilty & undeservedly fortunate. Then they could be treated like the elite they are (e.g., special education, homogeneous groupings, etc.). No need to get confused about what democracy means, as is true now, when some demand equal educational opportunities for the intelligent & the stupid.

Then "kindness" needn't be lying or denial of the harsh truth. Good treatment of inferiors can then be good treatment of their deepest & best selves, *not* their neurotic & fearful overlay. Can treat them candidly & honestly (which is a compliment) instead of falsely, as if they were brittle, nasty, envious (which is an insult). Theory-X treatment is Theory Y.

April 18

One of the points I made to the guidance & counseling people was that ultimately they and the therapists were doing value counseling or therapy—that this is the far goal of all their efforts: to move people toward growth, toward SA, toward metamotives = B-values. This is a very simple & blunt & unmistakable way to deal with the confusions of therapy, & also with its relations to medicine, to scientific psychology, to the local culture, to cultural relatives & absolutes, etc. I think this could clear up the Szasz confusion & also clarify existential therapy & *its* goals. Also the relation between therapy (for illness) & psychology (for health). This all needs working out, but in outline it looks unmistakably true.

Also solved the active-vs.-passive problem that they're all confused about. For instance, they at once understood me to mean that they should just *give* them values, like the priest of a church. Then I had to correct & say "no!" No propaganda or indoctrination! *Just* helping them to deserve their own values within themselves—both the species-values & the idiosyncratic ones. This *assumes* inner, biologically determined, intrinsic values. No confusion with external locus of values. *Therefore* nondirective, democratic, client-centered therapy à la Rogers *and* Freud is best suited to avoid *imposing* values & to helping person find his *own*.

This all fits in nicely with our agreement on the panel (with van Kaam) that the main present problem was a result of *lack* of values, i.e., boredom, apathy, looking for kicks, anhedonia, etc. Nothing to die for, to sacrifice for, to work for. Nothing to *live* for.

July 1

All plans changed. X rays show gallstones, which must be removed surgically. And one hour later I'm in the Faulkner Hospital getting ready for an operation in a few days. If only all those vague & idiotic symptoms that have taken so much fun out of life—the gas, the indigestion, the pains, maybe also the sensitivities that recently developed to coffee, to alcohol, etc.—if only these will go, I'll be very happy about this—*retrospectively* of course.

Anyway, trip to Bethel called off; we were supposed to leave tomorrow.

Even tho it's a routine operation, the thoughts of possible death do come, & also the thoughts of 8 days of pain after the operation. I'm not very good at taking pain. During the gall-bladder attack a few nights ago, 4–5 hours of pain seemed endless.

July 3

Set myself the problems of working at metapsychology & thought of a simple way to begin investigating it: use technique I started to use in interviewing scientists. "What are the biggest kicks & rewards & high moments you get out of your work? When do you feel best & happiest about it?" And then I'd add the opposite. "When do you feel *worst* about it? What are the moments of depression, of failure, when you wish you were in some other work, when you feel like giving it up?" This would certainly give rich details of a more concrete kind than I dreamed up from the peak-experiences, in which a good part of it must have been *my* organizing contribution & classification.

August 11

Brain beginning to function. Convalescence about over. And yet *still* tense and worried over promised lectures & papers, as I've been all this year. The year has been a procession of "obligations" I got myself into, so that no pleasure & gaiety & relaxation were possible for me of, e.g., the Cuernavaca style. Of course, the operation had much to do with this. It threw me way out of schedule, & now I'm in a rush. And *when* I get into this kind of rush to finish by a certain date, then all sorts of resistances to the work come up, & my impulse is to rebel against the "assignment" & to prefer to do everything & anything else. Finally I have to force myself by sheer willpower to do what I promised. If I had not signed a contract to do the Healthy Personality record by Aug. 15, I'd be relaxed about a delay. Now I realize there was no *need* to sign a contract, to make a promise of a date.

November 14

Much more shaken by Frank Beach's attack than I expected. Has taken since then to work thru. I'll have to get used to this sort of thing. I *managed* it well, but it perseverated & cost me a lot in sleep, fatigue, etc. Discussing it with Harry & Ric helped.

Good thoughts on paranoia & ego. The paranoid mistake is to swell the ego until it becomes the only thing over against the whole world. Then everything that happens in the world is "on purpose" to help or to hurt. Self-reference means unbridled grandiosity. Does this come from alienation from all else? No identification of the person with anybody or anything? As if a person were all alone, no ties, no merging or melting? All else strange, not belonging to self in any way. This cut-offness, like a spy in a foreign land → suspicion, as in the deaf person. Deafness → suspicion via cut-offness, isolation, alienation, aloneness ("you can't really trust anyone else").

"You Are Not the Target" = ability to allow other people or things an independent life of their own, without self-reference. It is paranoid to wail in midst of an earthquake or a war "Who is doing this to me? What did I do to deserve this?" As if all the other deaths were of no account, as if the only target in the world was the self. Nobody else is or could be a target. (Why not?)

No wonder it is a symptom of "eyes all around," all looking at the self, even objects looking (as with George Klein under LSD, "The clock on the wall was watching me"). Since these "eyes" are always perceived as hostile, I suppose the inner isomorphism is with fear, panic, feeling alone & threatened with no friendliness in the world = plots = no trust. "Nobody (nothing) loves me." Why should one feel that? It must come originally from a feeling of weakness, aloneness, powerlessness à la "basic anxiety" of Horney or Adler. And I suppose such a feeling is an easy consequence of bad experiences in the child, of being frightened, abandoned, alone, betrayed, helpless, with no one to counterbalance this by protection, mothering, reassurance, being cared for. I guess mostly feeling *alone,* which in a child must breed a feeling of (a) helplessness, (b) worthlessness, and therefore (c) hostile world with which no trust relation can be formed (*should* not be formed because that would tempt one to drop the defenses & then be even *more* frightened & endangered).

It is self-identification with one's "skin-ego" (that is, no identification beyond the skin) which is broken up suddenly in the cosmic-consciousness type of peak-experience. Two of my SA subjects cured their neuroses in such a moment, as they expressed it, by suddenly getting a view of the Whole of Being, *with themselves included* in it. They suddenly realized that they were in truth small, *but* they *belonged within* the world, were part of it. (Not outside of it looking in, like the orphan looking in the window at the happy family within, & therefore feeling doubly alone, cold, unloved, *or* like the frightened little Jewish boy in a wholly anti-Jewish [= non-Jewish] world, not understanding why, only feeling miserable, & since the child "accepts what is," not feeling strong enough to change it, he must feel this aloneness as permanent & eternal.)

Any B-cognition (of the Being of the other) must help, because paranoia can be defined as lack of ability to B-cognize anything, i.e., to be independent of the paranoid's skin-self, to be not purposefully hurting. Once a paranoid can accept the impersonality of an earthquake, or of the stranger's laugh, or the curious look, or being given an order by the boss, then to that extent he's *not* paranoid.

Somehow I feel this has something to do with the "Gaze". The "look of command" is found in primates, maybe also lower than that. *All* people tend to fall into place in the dominance hierarchy according to the Gaze, given & received. This seems to parallel the paranoid's obsession with "eyes" looking at him (always in a threatening, hostile way).

Checked this with Harry. Fits with Freudian statement about reduction to secondary narcissism in which only the self is libidinized, becoming the only reality, with external world becoming shadowy, & with the dialogue going on with the inner representation of figures in the world. The whole thing is an internal dialogue. I expanded my notions, or rather regressed them to their precursors, to infancy. Tried to imagine myself: (a) a beloved baby & (b) a not-loved baby (not-love need not be active—just an absence, or a distance). The baby develops a picture of his own worth in the mirror of his mother's (et al.) eyes. He must think of himself as either (a) beautiful, edible, something that is able to arouse the light of love in mother's eyes (compare the girl who can produce desire in the male with the girl who can't—obviously she comes to conclusions about her stimulus power; so must also the baby get some vague notion of its own stimulus power), or (b) repulsive, ugly ("ugly" seems common to the unloved; does feeling of being beautiful = lovability in the child?). Look up old notes on "edibility," which is also a characteristic of femininity, but not of masculinity. The latter is produced—at least the "command," high self-confidence, unquestioned worth-feeling—by being treated with respect & getting wanted things from mother, à la "golden boy" like Freud or Andy Kay. As if his wishes & needs mattered. Respect more than love. Femininity is a product of love more than respect; masculinity is a product of respect more than love.

Also, Harry pointed out that shame is involved here; it is the precursor to superego formation. But I'm interested in going further back, to the precursor of shame, which is the expression of the feeling of worthlessness, of not measuring up to the expectations of the spectator, of being exposed as a fake behind the ripped-away defenses. This shame is different from the delicious embarrassment of having one's treasures taken out of hiding, or of having dignity taken away, etc. The difference is: Is what is exposed bad or good? To be ashamed because one is ugly or fat or has no muscles or no erection or feels disgusting or nauseating—this is different from the embarrassment a pretty girl might feel on being seen naked.

Maybe worth, or some version of it, like edibility is the earliest concept; but anyway one's stimulus power is what is basically involved. The mother's gaze is the mirror in which one's self is born. The gaze *creates* the self & its worth, just as the bid to the auctioneer creates the value of the painting bid for.

Harry thinks it better not to call all this paranoia. Must make up some word for these universal dynamics—against which B-humor & the ability to self-observe are the antidotes—& then use paranoia for this when it is compulsive & has gotten out of control, & also I think where humorous detachment & self-observing-self are unavailable for decontamination.

But what has all this to do with the Gaze? And its power? And who gazes & who doesn't gaze? In the dominance situation? And why does "delicious embarrassment" (pleasant shyness before compliments, etc.) cause a dropping of the Gaze?

The strong-weak, dominant-submissive dimension is easier to make sense out of with respect to the Gaze & to suitability; but why should the Gaze & the dropped gaze & blush also be "nice" like courting and wooing? It's true here, too, that the Gaze is bold in a sexy or in a loving or ardent way. Maybe the dropped gaze is a kind of acceptance of the Gaze—with delight or pleasant confusion or modesty or humility = "I'm pleased that you find me worthy of being penetrated by your gaze, but I don't know what to say or do & I am disorganized a little bit in a nice way = be gentle with me, but don't stop = I love it but I mustn't agree with your estimate of me because that would be grandiose & paranoid; i.e., I must say 'I am not worthy of such adoration.'" This is just the way I am supposed to react in our culture if someone estimates my brains high, at the worth which I also secretly consider true worth. I am supposed to be modest. Why? I think it's cultural; in the marquesses, for example, there are no maidenly blushes & dropped eyes. Doesn't go here with the part of the definition of phallic masculinity of producing fear that I see in adolescent males & females; i.e., the females are attracted to the someone "who looks as if he could be cruel," as in my dominance test.

[*Generalization: Male would rather be respected (feared) than loved. Lack of respect will destroy his self-esteem more than lack of love. Female would rather be loved (than respected or feared). Lack of love will destroy her self-esteem. Female is not destroyed by being raped; the male is. (Because it represents weakness, being conquered, fear, but also being desirable & having stimulus power, for after all the rapist has an erection which her power has produced. This same stimulus power in the male is actually threatening to his masculinity.) The female doesn't mind being afraid (it is compatible with femininity). The male cannot be afraid (it is contradictory of masculinity). Fear makes her (& him) more feminine; it makes him feel less masculine.*]

The erect penis is *supposed* to produce a little fear, a little awe, a little respect—or, rather, a *lot* of fear, etc. It must be admired in this way—in our culture at least. Therefore the young man, identifying with his penis, *also* likes to be feared, respected, looked up to. Perhaps *this* ties in with the old cultural tradition of wanting a virgin female—because he's so big & she's so small & her pain is a tribute to his bigness, & also her fear before the huge thing which will hurt her. (But see also Helene Deutsch & others on the female's agreement with all of this; she *wants* to be a little afraid in this way.) She also wants all the dynamics of being small, fragile, & pained by the big penis for which she's too dainty, too doll-like, too little & cuddly to have room. She's not *that* gross, that huge. She's delicately small & therefore is worthy of being protected, of arousing the chivalry reaction. She's so timid, so like a beautiful but fragile flower which can be crushed or destroyed easily. So she wants her tough-strong-fearful man to be also tender & gentle with her. (This is what interviews always elicited for the ideal man: I want him to be (1) "strong" but (2) gentle & capable of tenderness.)

OK, this in our culture seems to be what *both* young males & females want. The emphasis is on the adolescent-phallic-swagger conception of strength & of masculinity & femininity & therefore of dominance-subordinance. Feminine "strength", or, better, "power", consists of being edible, desirable, irresistible, beautiful, & therefore having teasing & erection-producing stimulus power just by *being* (not having to do anything). Well, maybe this too follows, then: that the *stronger* & bigger the male she can lay low in her feminine way—to make him desire her & willingly lay aside his strength & become tender & greedy—this is a bigger feather in her headdress. She's *more* female & feminine, the bigger the man she can "conquer." No, who conquers himself *or* who gives up his strength to her, or dedicates it to her & puts it in her service, in her hands, in her vagina, where she can incorporate it, & identify with it in this particular incorporating way, & then it is "hers," it belongs to her. *He* belongs to her. She has the penis & the strength & the use of it, in the same way that she queens it over the powerful horse that she rides. It's delicious to own this power between her legs. (Are they saying the same things metaphorically? Is the horsepower between her legs "like" the penispower between her legs?)

Eventually she becomes *not* afraid (at least in the good case) of the penis either before her eyes, in her hands, or within her vagina. What does this mean? Well, if the *possibility* of fear is gone, then only contempt & domination remain (?). Anyway, this is so in the average situation; it may be different in Eupsychia & in mature females and males. The horse that can no longer run away, or be wild, or be frightening is no longer really a horse. Also, the male who won't get frightening if she dominates him (if she *only*-dominates him without sometimes surrendering also—that is, if she destroys the mutuality & equality by making it one way, taking advantage without giving advantage) then becomes a slave &

she a slave owner, rather than *both* of them being slaves to each other *and* slave owners to each other. Lovers *can* & *do* take "delicious advantage" of each other, dominate each other, surrender totally to each other, delight in using *and* in being used; that is, there is no dominant-submissive hierarchy. But the moment this is not mutual, when the favors are not returned, when, for instance, she demands cunnilingus but refuses fellatio, when she serves him & he never serves her, etc., then it becomes a dominance situation & synergy is lost (along with identification-love), & their interests become mutually exclusive.

No, it is better for them both if she retains the possibility of awe before the penis, before male strength, wildness, & bull-stallion, wild-undomesticated-animal quality—and if he retains the possibility of awe before her B-female qualities & powers, but even more if he retains the awe before the beauty, the ability to be aroused by her, the impulse to protect & be responsible. But I suppose what she would prefer above all else to the day she dies is to be desirable, beautiful, doll-like, edible, flower-like, that he is helpless & *must* have erection, *must* want to kiss & hug her; i.e., she must be lovable & loved, she must be seen as loveworthy.

December 31 (35th anniversary)

A good development I want to catch—a combination of creativeness theory & isomorphism. Treat the creative encounter (between the sculptor & his wood, the musician & his violin, the painter & his materials) as an I-Thou relationship, like an interpersonal relation, with mutual respect, courtest, deference. One *must* be Taoistic, not only in the sense of pure receptiveness, but in a more active sense of living-harmoniously-with, of actively feeling out the nature of the other & molding it & oneself to each other, with fusion & obliteration-of-separateness as the final goal or telos. I've been taking Taoism too exclusively in my recent writings as a passive receptiveness or surrender. It is *also* like a love or, better, sex relationship between 2 equals, as well as an all-giving/all-taking relationship of surrender as in the mother-child relation. *Listening* to music is *only* surrender; *composing* music is surrender + Taoistic-respectful-of-the-materials "activity."

This sex-intercourse model, with its equal flow back in *both* directions, can be used for creativeness model too; i.e., they create each other (Diaz-Guerrero interprets the therapeutic relation as creating an interpersonal relationship, à la encounter, as a work of art). The big point is that the artist has to prepare himself, be ready for, be isomorphically "high level"—he has to deserve a high experience, be worthy of it.

   If creativeness is ultimately generalizable as a search for B-values, or a reaching up toward them, then it is obvious that one must be "high" oneself in order to perceive the "high" or be I-Thou with the "higher levels."

   The greater possibility of perceiving the solution *within* the problem itself (à la Katona or Wertheimer) means surrender-receptivity-perception of the problem (materials, situation, person, etc.) = Taoistic attitude = lack of anxiety = lack of defensiveness = innocence & loss of self-consciousness so that total curiosity is possible = psychological health. The "healthier" one can make oneself before the experience, the likelier it is to happen, & the higher the level it will happen at. This is a kind of purifying oneself before the experience. To perceive integration or to make it happen, one must *be* integrated. See creativeness file, isomorphism file.

   The Gestalt psychologists are mainly interested in the field, in the percepts rather than the "within" of the perceiver. It's as if the person were just one passive element *in* the field, as with Lewin sometimes. (Of course, they'd all deny this.) The Goldsteinian holists, like me & Genia Hanfmann, were more interested in the *within* of the person, & in *his* hanging-togetherness, & in his creation of the field. Partly it's a matter of personal interest. I, for instance, wasn't much interested in Arnheim's evening of minute analysis of the perceived interaction within the Yin-Yang figure. Shlaym Asch was fascinated, & so was Ric Morant.

1964

January 20

Wrote letter to Kai Nielsen about his article in *Social Research*, Summer 1962, "On Taking Human Nature as the Basis for Morality." Very critical of my values chapter [69] & Fromm's in the MIT Values book—even snotty. I had intended to write an answer to it & then never bothered because I kept writing answers in my articles, one after another—or at least part of the answer, as much of it as I can make now. I think tomorrow I'll copy out of my letter to him & work it up some more. As I lay in bed ready to fall off to sleep, I realized that I had better be even *more* cautious & modest than I was in my letter to him.

My work is essentially theoretical—that is, it's based on insufficient evidence. So I'd better not get too snotty about it. It's OK for me to feel very confident about it, but I can't demand that others should share my confidence until the evidence is more impressive.

Also, it's true that the whole business remains shaky until I can clearly phrase it all in a non-normative way. *Not* in terms of high & low, good & bad, healthy or unhealthy, desirable or undesirable. He says "But to pick out these particular potentialities as those that are peculiarly human is in effect to apply a moral rule to human nature, rather than to determine what is moral by finding out what is distinctively human" (p. 173). Is one potentiality "more human" than some other one? In what sense are "higher values" more human than "lower values"?

It would clearly be cooler to be able to specify what behaviors would emerge under such and such conditions. As he says, ". . . all we can say from a scientific point of view is that there are many different human potentialities, & that given different environmental, cultural, psychological, & physiological conditions, different potentialities will be realized." Of course, that's what I'm working toward, all the time. But the truth is that I'm relying less on answering specific questions or difficulties than I am on sweeping onward, paying little attention to the difficulties but rather building a bigger & bigger, more & more inclusive & comprehensive system of interlocking facts & concepts. The whole big system is getting to be so impressive that the questions fade away or become obsolete—let's say, as they did with Freud & his system. He never proved much directly in answer to a posed difficulty. He *couldn't* because any one part of the system rested on other parts of the system rather than on separate, teased-out facts independent of the system. It was the system as a whole which "answered" each of the hundreds of questions—really, by not bothering to answer them individually but just by building an awe-inspiring structure.

For instance, I've never really proven well that a neurosis is *not* just another human potential like the ability to speak or to walk. I call it a defense against "real intrinsic human potentials." It's devoid of human-ness rather than partaking of humanness. Well, how in God's name to *prove* that? Impossible to do this ad hoc. It takes faith in the whole history of therapy & pathology to do the trick. I have to appeal to "general clinical experience" & to "therapeutic experience." And whoever wants to reject this as valid data has a perfect right to.

February 4

A long talk with Murray about D. R. generalized into his & my relations as teacher, as authority, as father, with students, assistants, etc. B. B. some days ago was trying to explain his failures, spoke of having to be individual, creative, autonomous. *That's* why he could do nothing for me. I pointed out to him that he thereby had cut himself off from ever learning from anyone older than himself. That he was all crapped up about his relations with authority, with father, masters, teachers.

With Murray I generalized this. The young men of the U.S. (the girls have no such problems; nor do the foreigners or, Murray added, the Catholics), having had weak, wobbly fathers who couldn't be identified with, who couldn't serve as a model, long perpetually for the missing father. When they need a "big prick," decisive, strong, smart, capable, masterful, knowing what he wants, one-pointed, they fall in love with him & eroticize, in a sadistic-masochistic & paranoid way, the whole relationship. The sex part is massively repressed & defended against by hostility, contempt, etc., against the father. The sex is projected onto the father—he's a big penis & wants to sodomize the young man—so the father is called seductive, erotic, sexy. The young man is then in the position of protecting his asshole from the big prick. And to get mad at the big prick for having such awful desires. And at himself for secretly *wanting* the big prick up his ass—he might enjoy it. So he has to defend strongly against it.

February 8

More thinking about my place in psychology & APA & my con-flicts about it. What started me off this time was *Contemporary Psychology's* current issue, which depressed me some, & then I realized it practically

always does. So does *American Psychologist*. The APA is closing me out &
rejecting me. And I realistically get farther & farther away from the central
APA norm. I couldn't pass the exams we give our grads. My statistics &
experimental design are obsolete. I don't read the experimental stuff
anymore. Fall farther & farther behind, & less & less interested in all these
things. Even the vocabulary in many areas is getting beyond me. I
couldn't do the elementary psychology book that I'd been working on all
my life—since 1931. It's just too big for me to encompass well. Like math,
chemistry, physics, even biology—psychology & the APA are a federation
of specialties that don't & can't know each other well. Just too much
knowledge explosion.

   And yet in spite of the realities of this situation, it hurts me a little
when I get rejected, or attacked, or, worst of all, sneered at. So have to
keep working it out. Of course, the ultimate answer is to go my own way,
decide by my own guts, & be my own self in my own style. Which is what
I'm doing—only I'm still vulnerable underneath.

March 10

   Yesterday had dyad therapy with Neisser. Told him I disagreed
profoundly with him on educational policy & on taste in people, grads, etc.,
& that since I no longer had to integrate the dept. & pour oil on troubled
waters & hold my own opinions in abeyance, I could now forcefully present
my personal point of view & push it hard. And that I wanted him not to feel
this was enmity. I'd push hard but impersonally. I told him I thought of his
interpretation of firmness of standards with grads as "harassment" & that
cruelty was the equivalent of overindulgence. He told me that he thought
my irritation & anger & disgust with grads were irrational & arbitrary
prejudice & dislike. That is, that I was being stern & tough with people I
disliked just because & only because I disliked them. And that I was
renouncing all the standards by which I had built the dept. & that I was
belying my own philosophy. I told him that my philosophy remained
exactly the same for those who could & did work, & who were eager to
become psychologists, & that once I was convinced they'd proven themselves, I'd give them complete freedom. But as for the others who begged to
become plumbers & then refused to touch pipes, those who wouldn't work
or learn, who showed little sign of involvement & dedication—yes, I *did*
have contempt & anger for them & wanted to cut them off & throw them out,
that I didn't want the dept. to become a sanitarium for therapy for wounded
& delicate souls who couldn't work & study, an academy for cripples, for
turning out union-card psychologists, whom I never see in the library, at
lectures, at conventions, who never discuss psychology, who miss the

colloquia. This is not a Summerhill school & shouldn't be. Professional training is a matter of acquiring knowledge, skills, confidence, professional attitudes. I'm irritated by such things as going to live in Cambridge & then not showing up *because* one lives far away.

March 25

On the decisive leader—or, rather, on the guy who becomes a leader & attracts followers just *because* he is decisive, for *whatever* reasons, good or bad—an additional thought. My original thesis was that most people are so uncertain about their wishes, judgments, etc., that they follow anyone who is decisive, sure of himself. And since this decisiveness can come from paranoia, that's why Hitler, Stalin, McCarthy, et al. were followed. (*It's not a taste for evil; it's a taste for certainty.*) Well, I started with an additional understanding of why the "arty art critics" exert so much influence. It started with looking at a pretty little dish Bertha had bought. As I looked at it, I remembered that I hadn't wanted to get it. But she *knew* that she wanted it, & I had learned to defer to her opinions in art. They mostly turn out better than mine—at least in the sense that eventually I get to agree with them. It's as if her vision (of something real—not *just* "taste") were sharp & mine dim. She can see the esthetic truth faster than I can, just as I have better distance vision than she has & can see stop lights & road signs before she does. Same with Ann, who just looks scornfully at the tie I've chosen, which is not *quite* right for the shirt—she is *certain.* So they are the leaders & taste-setters for me; I defer to them.

So it may be with, e.g., the 57th St. crowd. They seem confident that they are *perceiving* something, that they have vision. They are decisive, authoritative, confident. Then all the 99% who are dim, unsure, uncertain, will follow along, defer, accept the opinion, even when it's crazy or distorted. So the homosexuals can set taste in art, fashions, music, & God knows what else. Because they are decisive, the undecisive ones will accept their visions; *but* these are the authentic, real perceptions of *homosexuals*! And therefore quite unsuitable for nonhomosexuals. Also, just as homosexuals are fickle & have whims & changeable tastes, so is fashion changeable & fickle. The homosexual falls in "love" for sure, but it doesn't last long.

Why they are sure & decisive about pushing their tastes I don't know. But they may very well start with clear, sensitive vision, like Leo Bronstein, & like Bertha & Ann. In addition to this there is another variable: no blocking shyness or inhibition. Then comes the separable variable of decisiveness of behavior. This covers the final variable of "taste," which is partly idiosyncratic & characterological & local-cultural (i.e., the sharpvisioned, perspicuous Chinese), but they'll still differ in tastes. In a word, fashions (in art, politics, etc.) come because some people see clearly & are decisive & unequivocal; most people are not, & uncertain people follow certain people.

April 13

Want to write more on paranoia (as a universal human tendency) & our defenses against it in ourselves & in others. Stimulated not only by N.'s grandiosity, which looks to me more & more like a kind of noncertifiable paranoia, but also by hearing John Rosen speak yesterday at psychiatric meetings in his unbridled way. It all relates to aggridance & *its* problems, to factual superiority, to our fear of the superior (countervalues). How about President Kennedy? De Gaulle? The strong man in general? The necessity to encourage within ourselves the heroic element? In our society one *must* be modest or everybody bristles, as they did with John Rosen's simple self-congratulation. But I was comparing with simple Blackfoot boasting of same kind, upon which the society is based & no harm done, i.e., no need to be modest. I suppose, in our society, when one loses recognition of bad effects upon others of boasting, this is a loss of reality-testing & may in fact be sick, a failure to understand feelings of other people.

Also, the question comes up of the universal (or almost so) fact that superiors, geniuses, talented people, have thru history occasionally been (openly & publicly) aware of their superiority & have reacted to it with awe, pride, etc., in a peculiarly impersonal way, as if their talent was not quite part of the self but rather like something they were carrying, something that had been entrusted to them. But even in the obvious genius we can't stand his admission of genius. We bristle. We demand that he, too, be modest & humble—& usually he plays the game & *is*. They know damn well they are superiors, but they don't boast about it usually.

How will it be in Eupsychia? I think there must be more room for acknowledgment of factual superiority—more in the Blackfoot style, or perhaps in the military style, where one's medals boast for one. And then the task of preventing it from going over into hubris?

Funny how our whole political system is built upon self-choice & self-congratulation—instead of being picked by others & praised by others. Our would-be leaders "throw their hats in the ring," "run" for office, i.e., choose themselves, praise themselves, boast of themselves, and then sneer at the ones who don't "run" but who wait to be drafted instead.

Write also about knowledge, truth, honesty as a defense against & cure of paranoid suspicions, hypotheses, guesses—as nudism is a cure for scopophilia. (Is it in fact? Anyway, it *should* be.) John Rosen in his peasant, earthy, primitively direct way dictates notes on a patient in the presence of the patient after a session. (I vaguely recall others who take notes, permitting the notes to be seen by the interviewee.) My own long-time feeling is that knowledge of self via tests or anything else *should* be given to people. We shouldn't be so afraid of hurting them. They are not that hurtable. And in any case their own secret suspicions often are worse than the truth. It will hurt the homely girl to be told that others consider her homely. But she already "knows" this anyway. Reminds me of my talk with Shelton in La Jolla of his open mutual ratings. Also, I think of Abell & his *Road to Reality* TV program, in which actual patients were helped by seeing the actors impersonating them &, peculiarly, in which the actors *themselves* stick together as a therapy group.

April 18

This semester as chairman has been a very unpleasant & wearing one. Disappointing. The nice family-type department that I constructed & led is gone. Post-Oedipal? I feel distance from most people in the department. Perhaps from G. too, about whom I dream as an opponent. Loss of pleasure in teaching & disappointment in students. Harry, in my analytic discussions with him, has made this disappointment more conscious. It's as if my whole philosophy and psychology were being proven false, or at least faulty or limited. Carl Rogers' paper on graduate education in psychology had a considerable effect on me because it reflected perfectly my opinions of 10 years ago, & the basis on which I set up the grad program. Since then "I have known evil" & while it's still all true for some people, it's *not* true for the weak, the inferior, the frightened, the passive & dependent, the psychopath-type wise guy, the countervaluer. There are *many* who can't use freedom & trust well á la Theory Y. Maybe that's why my seminar last Tuesday P.M. depressed & angered me so. When I turned responsibility over to them, they went passive & wanted a lot of big-shot visitors in to debate with me, instead of relying on themselves & "using" me, & then they wanted term papers made easier & played mock-stupid about not understanding that I *also* wanted a research paper. I treated them á la Theory Y, & they behaved like Theory X.

But then Harry asks: Why do I take it so personally? Why do I over-react? That's clearly irrational. Well, it belies everything I've believed in; it attacks my *Weltanschauung*. (And my anger & disappointment, & my consequent temptation to punish & attack, teach me where the reaction comes from. It's important to remember that not *all* are Theory X.) My associations have been back to childhood & the puzzlement, hurt, & repressed anger of the little Jewish boy who can't fight in the midst of a hostile Gentile world (but not *predictably* hostile, & not *everyone* was hostile, so that the end effect was puzzlement, as if there was no lawfulness or predictability in the world). Anyway, my passion for a better world & better people via understanding, knowledge, science, etc., has deep personal roots. Maybe that's why Jews were so often prophets, ethical thinkers, Utopians (every Jew I knew when I was a kid was either a socialist or a communist or a selfish bastard). That's why I'll identify so strongly with the persecuted Negroes in the movie tonight. Injustice or meanness or sadism *anyplace* in the world gets me down.

April 27

12:45—can't sleep. Disturbed & apprehensive over fight to come. So, I'm eager for Ric to come back and inherit the whole business. But then, also, I'm impelled to keep the department going in the path I set. It's getting more & more experimentalist & conventional. So I do what I can—& *that* keeps me awake. Also, some sadness when I got Cofer & Appley text on motivation. Skimmed thru chapter on my stuff. Fair, respectful, gentlemanly, but rejected it on grounds mostly, I gather, of lack of good definitions & of rigorous data & proof. They have little conception of a place for the theoretical psychologist, the one who deliberately works with inadequate data. I must read it more carefully & write my reactions, if only to justify myself & my place & usefulness in the world. Same reaction when I read what Rokeach & McClelland said about me in Larry Gross' study. Too loose, not rigorous enough, etc. Very true, but I am *still* the generator of ideas which *others* can test, including both of them, who are not aware that my ideas helped to generate their researches. I guess that's part of my reputation—loose, not rigorous, "unscientific," etc. Well, for one thing, I'm just not able to change. It's no longer controllable. I must go the way I must go. Secondly, I like & approve of the work I do and the way I go. I'm contributing what no one else can & what I rationally believe *ought* to be written about. Most important thing I can do is to write my ideas about science, about B-psychology, about metamotivation, etc. If there were an all-wise dictator someplace, that's what he'd order me to do. So I'll have to assimilate the criticism & what I've noticed recently as rejection or implied criticism. I've never been invited over to Harvard by *any* of my friends in Social Relations, *or* by the grad-student seminar—not by Murray or Allport or

McClelland or *anyone* else, even tho everyone in the world is invited. Yet they quote me, use my work, & are friendly with me, even affectionate. That means, I guess, affection but not scientific approval. That *kind* of thing is common among my friends.

May 21

Need level (which = frustration level) determines which are the most pressing values, what is yearned for, definition of Utopia, etc. For the one who needs safety or love, that is the most important thing in the world & SA is *not* important. But need level is to a large extent (*how* large?) determined by culture (certainly true anyway for lower needs & in another way for higher needs, SA, & metaneeds as well). The higher the culture, the more "secure" or healthy it is, and the higher the need level. Thus the satisfaction or frustration of "instinctoid needs" rests on level of culture, on other people, on status of parents, etc. To this extent, ideologies, philosophies, yearnings, Utopias, rest on level of the culture.

But this is very far from "materialistic," certainly a stupid word under the circumstances. Consciousness *is* a product of social forces which exist prior to the individual & help to shape him *and* his consciousness. Instead of using the word "materialistic," we *could* say "socially determined," which means to some extent "economically determined." But physical & economic wealth, tho they can *help* higher-need gratifications & make them more possible, do not inevitably get used for higher-need gratifications. And also higher needs can be gratified under poverty (it's harder, but it's possible if we remember what needs we're dealing with—respect, love, SA, etc., *not* autos, money, bathtubs). Marx seemed. to think *only* of material needs—for objects, things, money, food. No place for higher needs (except in early Marx, according to Fromm).

May 26

In middle of Colin Wilson's *Sex Diary of Gerard Sorme*, &, as usual with his books, stimulated intensely to all sorts of thoughts which I've been writing down. So far this book is a *perfect* expression of the sex attitudes, reactions, philosophies of a male (*not* a female) who can't love but who is "oversexed." A perfect projection, & helps me to understand the absolutely essential place of love, or at *least* affection and/or respect, in sex satisfaction. If no love, then sex act becomes a repetitive acting-out, a looking for a secret, unknown gratification which never comes—as with the traditional frigid nymphomaniac. This explains why, throughout history, there has usually been sadness after sex. That is, there was no love, because love was impossible without the female's growth to selfhood: she has rarely deserved to be loved-respected; at best she was paternally loved for the cute little doll-girl, whom, however, one could not respect. *But* love is a need, an instinctoid need, & has always been looked for whether people knew it or not. So they got it with friends, with children, with religion. But the sex way to love-gratification has been missing (see also Kirkendall), & perhaps it's the best way, most complete, etc.—for men, anyway, who can't go into convulsions of passionate love for the baby that are possible for a mother.

Now we are *able* to live at a higher level. Even tho it's not guaranteed, it's more *possible*. Real love-sex gratifications should lift people to a higher level. It's perhaps the easiest trigger for peak-experiences—for males at least. For fusion-experience, transcendence of ego, experience of altruism, unselfishness, dedication, etc. Also of tenderness, dropping of masculine defenses, etc. It's the easiest religious-transcendent experience for men—with *every single thing* that religion has always implied! Also, as Wilson says, it's the easiest way for a male to feel *alive* (zest, biopleasure, not dying, vital, etc.); like pain, perhaps, it equals undoubted aliveness (it is perhaps most basic of identity-experiences, along with animal-need gratification after long frustration).

Yesterday after Polly & Ellen came, crapped up the place, & then went, B. got into rage-depression & started scratching, scowling, etc. So I dropped what I was doing & took her out for therapy, i.e., driving in the country & letting her talk everything off her chest while I listened silently & sympathetically. It worked, as it usually does. In the past I would simply have gotten angry myself for the attack upon me, not seeing that I was not really the target. From Colin Wilson's point of view—or, rather, Gerard Sorme's—I was wasting my time, being exploited, etc. But as I read on & on in his book, I thought of my therapying as a great privilege, really. He didn't really care for any of his many women & therefore was alone, bored, anhedonic. An act of love is not only altruistic, it is a privilege, & even in a selfish way, it is "good for a person" because it makes him feel needed, useful, powerful, thanked, etc.

All this brings up also many questions in motivation theory, e.g., bypassing, repetitive acting-out as criticism of behavioristic theory, because it's a motivated art which doesn't gratify. Also because it deals with sexual compliance of the various females, even tho they get nothing out of it, & because their wills disappear like the girls Kirkendall writes about in the lower-class "gang-bangs," the girls who permit *anything* to be done to them by anybody who is persistent enough. That's always been so hard for me to understand. But Wilson's theory to explain it (p. 104ff & many other passages) is so much like mine about the subordinate-authoritarians, the

John Birchers, the followers of paranoid leaders. I felt that: (1) most people don't have a will, an identity, a self; (2) they are therefore uncertain about everything—they have no real opinions or judgments; (3) therefore they are easily convinced by *anyone* who is decisive, sure of himself, without doubt; (4) anyway, all people, especially uncertain ones, are looking for certainty, & since they can't get it from within, they'll get it from without (like the obsessionals Harry & I talked about); (5) they will follow any decisive leader, true or false, & feel better thereby; (6) paranoids (obsessionals) are "certain" for safety-need reasons & therefore *look* decisive, strong-willed, etc., in their behavior (even tho this is a defense against its opposite & a coping mechanism to make do in the world in the absence of inner impulse-voices).

Cunningham in Wilson's book had *real* will, strength, selfishness, self-confidence, & desire. Before this the female will—which is anyway low, in this book at least—disappears or melts away, & especially in the passive ones (will-less?). It's as if the willer is perceived as fear-inspiring, timidity-producing, and "unstoppable," as if he *must* have his way & it's no use fighting it, even as if one *shouldn't* fight it, as if it's "suitable," appropriate, B-justice in the world, as if such a person *deserves*, as if it's *right* in a deep Gestalt sense, in the same way that men will see the stronger one, the aggridant, the superior, as *deserving* the girl more than the weaker one, as if that's the way a God would arrange it.

Cunningham says (p. 104): "People can be hypnotized by conviction or purpose. They possess none themselves and the idea of coming into contact with it excites them." And then he gives examples of all sorts of immediate sexual conquests in this way. Additional question is: Why does it excite (if indeed it does)? It can all happen *without* excitement, even with fear & loathing, as the traditional bird is helplessly fascinated by the snake, & can't run away even tho in mortal terror (maybe *because* of the terror?). Men too *can* be excited in this way, so that they can *want* sex & *enjoy* it even—at least some can. Not enough data here. To yield to strength is clearly thrilling to some (many? all?) women by their own reports. And it certainly is openly evident in *juvenile* males at least (their open admiration & eager yielding to the strong, tough, fearless "leader"). Is it there in adult men but simply repressed? Is it a potential in *all* human beings at any time, coming out even in the most powerful & successful males when they meet a superior? But, again, why does male self-esteem crack under such a rape & yielding, & the female's self-esteem not? Is this biologically inherent? Instinctoid? I think so. But this then means that the instinctoid tendency to yield is stronger & also less ambivalent & conflicted in the female. I also think this is so. Homosexuals (& maybe also Wilson's sex criminals) should teach us much here. Also if we could only get good female introspectors to give phenomenological sexual reports! Practically nothing available.

June 7

Bert Gross brings up again the problem of parallel between need level in individual & development level in nations. Seems clear there's *some* relationship. Anyway, there ought to be. It makes sense. Safety-level society in e.g., Tanganyika? Mentioned Oron South's writing. Or I can say that U.S. Negroes are at pride/dignity/self-esteem level. Same for poor people in slums being paternalistically "helped," i.e., treated like helpless Theory-X children, instead of like Theory-Y, improvable, potentially proud & dignified self-helpers. (See motivation & society file.)

Also talked with 2 alumni now in grad school & felt very alien, distant—as if I were in the next century. One is an "experimentalist" at University of Pennsylvania & thinks it's marvelous! What could I say? The other boy, in clinical psychology at NYU, & I got started talking, & as the words came out & I listened to myself talking, what I heard unexpectedly was: "I'm trying to shake the ground beneath clinical psychology. It's too confident, too technological, too proud. But all its concepts are moot. What is 'cure'? 'Illness'? 'Health'? There should be more humility, more fear and trembling. Just as no human being is fit to condemn a man to die, or to judge and condemn anything, just so *in principle* is no human being capable or worthy of 'curing' another person."

And yet, since we *do* need hangmen, judges, policemen, & therapists, OK. *But* if they feel confident, then they are lost. Like someone who feels "confident" about atom bombs. There should be some kind of prayer or ceremony before a therapeutic hour; one must say the equivalent of "Lord, I am not worthy" & *feel* it, *mean* it.

And then I talked to him about the existential view of illness & health (as in my summer notes), or how we're *all* almost equally sick or condemned to death ("in adjoining cells in Death Row; in adjoining beds in the terminal ward of the hospital").

All the boy could say was to quote a recent study that showed therapists with self-confidence could cure more people than therapists without self-confidence.

June 25

Little item in magazine about Swedenborg. He didn't believe in salvation by good works or by faith alone but "by seeking natural perfection through service to the world." It clicks—with some changes. It implies self-actualization or full-humanness (as an ideal) being sought *via* good works. That is, good works are "good" because they conduce to SA. It's almost, tho not quite, like saying they are a means to an end, collecting gold stars in heaven. It could also imply more subtly that the good works are themselves intrinsically good. One could say this: SA is defined as good works; i.e., ultimately it has a behavioral & social definition as well as an experiential one. But even this statement, tho it's at a higher level, can be transcended. Good works can give peaks & B-cognitions & in this sense become self-validating. They *are* heaven. Also, they are epiphenomena of SA which prove it to exist, & which can be enjoyed & contemplated in themselves, as we enjoy & contemplate flowers. And this can be a kind of self-enjoyment & self-contemplation, a kind of B-narcissism, an aspect of godlikeness, self-approval, & self-love at the highest level. If a God were to be perfect, omniscient, etc., the necessary implication is that *he* knows that he is, & likes it.

I'll have to make something more of this feeling of virtue, as I've usually called it. It's good to be virtuous because it makes you *feel* virtuous, & this is such a nice feeling, an intrinsic reward. It's nice to be wise [*& enjoy one's self*], not only because of applause & love from others, but, more importantly, because one can then feel wise, experience wisdom, & like oneself for it. Self-approval is certainly "higher" than approval-by-others. As a matter of fact, any complete definitions (or cataloguing of attributes) of SA, or full-functioning, or full-humanness, *must* include self-approval, self-love, "feeling virtuous," feeling godlike, etc., even tho our culture would find this repugnant, & even tho this necessarily is structured with humbleness of a B-sort (which is just part of realism, e.g., knowing in fact how little one knows even tho one were the wisest & most knowledgeable man alive, of intrinsic human limitations, etc.). That is, B-wisdom *includes* humility.

But I prefer to go still "higher" to a B-psychology phrasing. Salvation comes, is approached & experienced, as we approach the ideal limit of total identification with the B-values. This includes (1) fusion of self with the world, (2) identification with the best, (3) love for and contemplation of the best, which means also (4) love for & contemplation of the best as internalized in us (in the individual, the person, the me) = self-love of the B-narcissistic sort of the pregnant woman, or the talented genius, or of the only doctor on the island who must selfishly and unselfishly value himself & protect himself more than he values & protects others because he is so much more important to others, or like the parent of children. This is the final fusion of selfishness & unselfishness. It also springs beyond the personal implications of the word "salvation," since personal salvation & salvation for the world are not differentiated (synergy). It solves the dichotomy of Bodhisattva & Pratychabuddha, since helping oneself toward perfect Being automatically helps the B-values toward full actualization, which is good for everyone, as a flower is good for itself & for everyone simultaneously. And devoting oneself to B-values "out there" helps *oneself* toward Being & toward B-actualizing & B-exemplification. No inner-outer difference here.

July 2

In my discussion of Mrs. Roosevelt with the girl from Israel, I stressed the "normality" & usualness of Mrs. R., because she had no special talent or genius or gift. She had nothing *but* universal human qualities—nothing unusual or strange or esoteric. What was remarkable was that there were no losses or diminution or inhibitions. Nothing normally human had been taken away from her. She retained the usual normal human qualities & could therefore be called "normal," even tho she was so unusual. In this way I made my point that SA is—or should be—the norm, the average, the expectable, nothing special or unusual. [*Unleashed. No brakes. Free. "Innocence #2." Fully human. Altogether human. Unspoiled.*] It is just full, unhampered, undestroyed human growth. Anybody & everybody could & should be that way. The question really is: why is anyone *not* self-actualizing?

Mrs. R. didn't possess *a single unusual* quality, & yet just possessing all the *usual* human qualities was enough to make her self-actualizing; & in the past she would have been canonized. Can be called simply the "lack of error," avoidance of mistakes or harms.

August 1

Much impressed by reading about a tough criminal who reformed thru the love of a "good girl." This apparently is the usual way in which most juvenile delinquents are cured. Fascinating research problem.

But most interested in the research possibilities of using criminals & reformed criminals to try to throw additional light on the meaning of dominance in relation to self-esteem, in relation to the authority problem. Why is the rebel, the tough guy, the fearless, reckless (& therefore stupid) fighter against fathers, authorities, policemen, teachers, etc., admired by tʰe others instead of being sneered at for his stupid self-destructiveness? The other boys (not girls?) would like to be like him but dare not. But this is adolescent stuff. The really adult male finally gets around to identifying with authority, & even to *being* authority. How does this transaction take place (when it does)? How about the perpetual adolescents like Herbert Marcuse who react to authority as convicts do to wardens?

I had thought of using prostitutes & homosexuals to throw light on dominance-subdominance, but now I think I'd add all criminals & delinquents. This will, all of it (as with the parallels paper), throw light on self-esteem, identity, mature masculinity & femininity (in contrast with adolescent masculinity and femininity), on homosexuality in all its forms, overt & covert, on class & caste relations, religion (prostration, reverence, "God-man" relations), etc. The "leader" must often have some of this "toughness" against authority (even when he himself *is* or is seeking to be the authority).

August 19

Another beautiful thought (I think I dreamed it & suddenly recalled it in the tub—yelled out to Bertha & she came running with a pad to write it down, without blinking an eyelash): the goals of self-knowledge, a perfectly legitimate form of knowledge, are the exact opposites of prediction, control, exactness! Not only the methods but also the mode of approach of orthodox science are less useful here than personal-science methods. But also the goals themselves have to be renounced in favor of the new ones of fusion, identification, experiencing from within, of Being, of B-knowing, of SA, of contemplation of eternal B-values, of peak-experiences, etc. The new science. (What the hell *will* I call it? Personal science? Interpersonal science? Humanistic Science?)

I see that my phrasings are changing away from stigmatizing cool knowledge & more toward balancing its advantages & disadvantages with those of warm people & warm knowledge. Clearly they must be integrated & allied with each other (*within* each person, too) rather than being set *against* each other. Not war but collaboration.

Same for the relation between idiographic knowledge & nomothetic knowledge. True, the former is of final importance in facing *any* particular situation, & yet the latter can keep on improving the former. General, lawful knowledge, if it is merged with idiographic knowledge, improves it greatly. Knowledge can help love. Also, knowledge in this sense can help innocence too. The innocence based on wisdom is certainly better than the innocence based on ignorance. Also, it's true in the same way that "knowledge" can be shown to interfere with perception & indeed to substitute for it. And yet when they are in a good relationship—merging—then obviously knowledge can improve perceptiveness. Knowledge of art history, etc., *can* improve our pleasure & sensitivity & appreciation, even tho it *need* not & even tho it may replace real looking. See art-test data.

This is all an intrapersonal problem for me. How to put together the artist in me & the scientist? The mystical with the sober? Somebody wrote me recently admiring me for managing to live simultaneously in the conventional world & in the far-out, unconventional world. So I can be in the D-realm, with good reality-testing, *and* in the B-realm, contemplating eternal B-values. In & out of the world. Matter-of-fact & also awed by sacredness & mystery. (Orthodox science has desacralized everything —one reason I don't like it. They're never awed by anything. They acknowledge no mystery. All this means is that they're not humble enough—hubris. Scientific pride = technology that expects to be able to do *anything* & keeps up this illusion by denying & repressing anything that they cannot do, or by laughing at it as if it were not worthy of attention.) "The difficult we do right away; the impossible takes a little longer." The Sea-Bee attitude. Phallic adolescence.

September 4

On terrace overlooking my river. Everything *very* beautiful! A thought is: Why go away from here?

I made a good decision to come home. Felt happy, relaxed, validated. Just talked with Frank about his Utopian paper & my place in it. He was very approving also, as Bertha was, when I indicated my refusal to be the leader of a church or of a value group. Of course, they both disapprove of the whole group & all the people in it & their needs, goals, motives. I approve—but for *them*! I think humanistic psychology is far better for them than any alternatives I know as a way of life. It's better than any known religion or "rationalist"-atheist humanistic association. It's better than any political movement. It's better than any other psychology. And it's better than *merely* social action. It gives them something to hope for, to do, to work at, to use their energies productively & synergically for (selfishly good for the world). It's a new educational movement & new philosophy; it makes growth toward greater personal happiness possible. And, besides, it's all intellectually fascinating! It makes it possible to be ethical & therefore to feel like a good guy (rationally).

September 10

4 A.M. Since I started with Harry I sleep somewhat better, but not well. While in Del Mar & Los Angeles, sleep was good. My psychoanalysis

is full of insights, exciting, disturbing, sometimes depressing. But I'm still only in the middle of it I guess. Will have to publish it as an extremely important experiment. The science book [115] is a kind of isomorphic acting-out of all sorts of unsolved problems, conflicts, & dissociations from the past, from childhood. It parallels in intellectual terms my emotional development. It tries to solve in the world what needs solving in it. It's an expression & also a coping, an effort at personal integration of all sorts of warring elements, even of different kinds—or at least aspects—of personality insufficiently fused & blended. It's an effort at self-therapy. It's an effort to bring about the kind of world (Eupsychian) that I longed for as a child—the big family that gets along well together. It's an effort to solve the mysterious problems of people in the world who made me unhappy as a child & whom I couldn't understand. Partly it started out to be a counterattack, a revenge on the kinds of people who hurt me as a child, people I feared & also hated. But this attack is changing into an integration, an effort to understand them & therefore to forgive them & make friends with them. And of course all of this "them" is internal as well—elements of my own personality that I repressed or rejected or feared or hated. The management of anger is the main problem of the last year or two. My guess is that that's what's keeping me from sleeping. I caught myself grinding my teeth in anger over grad students & colleagues whom I disliked or who disliked me. When I leave town, I seem more able to leave them behind.

September 14

Hypomanic day yesterday. All excited from morning on, when Bertha came with tears in her eyes about her "problems," which really are privileges. How wonderful to have lovely daughters to worry about! I somehow thought of all her troubles as superficial even tho real; deep down she's lucky & might even call herself happy. Same for me. *Very* paradoxical. With my troubles about insomnia & bad back & conflict over my role in psychology & fear & awe before my science book &, in a certain sense, *needing* psychoanalysis, if anyone were to ask me "Are you a happy man?" I'd say "yes, yes!" Am I lucky? Yes. Fortunate? Privileged? The darling of fortune? Sitting as high up as a human being ever has? Yes! Fulfilling myself? Yes.

Then it dawned on me that what this meant was a redefinition of happiness & of the good life. All of my conflicts & emotions & bad dreams over my book are not the opposite of happiness—they *are* happiness! Happiness will have to be defined as being pained & troubled in a good cause! The good life is to have good-real-worthwhile worries & anxieties.

Took notes all day long. Continued with Harry in P.M. Will dictate it all tomorrow. It's all an extension of my hierarchy of grumbles. The good life is to have metagrumbles instead of low grumbles. Also extension of peak-experience stuff—the discovery that joy comes in short spurts rather than continuously, at least most of the time. (The long spells are possible & do happen but not very often.)

It all reminds me of Goldstein's (Wertheimer's also?) renouncing happiness as the goal & end of life. Freud too. Self-actualization, self-forgetting-in-the-service-of-good-cause, being in the correct army (even if you're getting shot at). This is the best life has to offer from day to day, & for this you get rewarded with an occasional glimpse of heaven, or one can have, when things are going well, lots of wild, peaky happinesses.

All this is especially true the older I get. It's as if all the body pains & troubles & nuisances are at a level altogether different (& less important) than the level of B-values, of whether one's life is basically worthwhile or B-valuable or not. If not, then *that* is the *real* misery. People at Los Angeles & here have been sympathizing with me over my painful back, & I tell them usually "It's a nuisance, but not a tragedy. It doesn't touch me deeply. My thinking & discovery go on, & life is good." (Of course, if the goddam stupid, silly body kicks up a *big* fuss, then all higher life stops, & life is essentially meaningless in itself—only something to endure until real living starts again.)

So my problems with the science book must be seen as a privilege, as real living, as partly real existential fear & awe before the sacredness & enormity of seeing something for the first time that any human ever has. That's what a good idea is—like Balboa first seeing the Pacific. If you get cold shivers under *such* circumstances, *that's* high living.

September 20

Various thoughts coming together: reading Polanyi on confrontation of 2 "languages" or systems of thought & how hard it is to change from one to another, because the systems are life-views, like total perceiving outfits (maybe like our eyes). A language is self-protecting, self-proving, & it rejects what opposes it or doesn't fit.

Seems to me to come down mostly to characterology. Like last night, arguing over Utopian thinking with Frank & Lew Coser, or the night before, arguing with Ric & Frank over authoritarian attitudes to grad students, or fighting with Marianne Simmel or Dick Neisser last week over accepting E. S. or how much freedom to give students vs. how many requirements. They all seem like confrontations of character-types, of life-outlooks. Ric has steadily been changing the whole department toward a standard APA, conventional, experimentally based Ph.D. factory, away from any stress on freedom for growth of uniqueness, acceptance, & openness for the far-out, etc. This in spite of the fact that Ric is a gentleman, decent, honorable, intelligent, & a good friend, etc. Also in spite of the hundred talks we've had about policy. Ric just can't help being an experimentalist because that's what he *is*, in his soul. Even if he were to try to please me, he wouldn't know how. How can I get mad about it? We're all different-type souls, & that's the end of it. The data that convinced me about Theory-Y management & against Theory-X management which most of my colleagues favor—are not powerful enough to shake up a whole belief system except where it's ready to be shook up or where the belief is not characterologically determined.

Anyway science education, the whole intellectual life, philosophy, politics, can be understood partly as the confrontation of diverse characters. Ought then to work out a strategy for getting along, for marrying, for being friends with or partners with different characters. Polanyi is certainly partly right, at least, that to rely only on an objectivist conception of impersonal truth, facts, logic, data, will not be very effective, e.g., with Goldwater or Birchites. There should be more knowledge & appreciation of (even love for) the differences. Put this in last chapter of science book, but also work it up for interpersonal relations file, social psychology, etc.

This would certainly be one of the lessons in any value-education or humanistic religion test: how to get along with different kinds of character & *Weltanschauung*, i.e., different biologically based value systems. I can see this in myself reading Polanyi, for instance; I just can't understand the details & the intricate engraving-on-head-of-a-pin kind of thing. Well, my Rorschach test long ago, & my whole life since then, showed very low Dd score. I'm just not good on small details & at my age never will be. Same for his huge architectonic book. That's what I planned to write as my science book & kept postponing it for ten years or more. Same with elementary text—worked at it ever since I was a grad student, & it got bigger & bigger & overwhelmed me, so I just did chunks out of it & now will never do it. Doing the abnormal psychology book almost killed me. So I'm not good on big, architectonic wholes or systems. My Rorschach also showed this years ago—there were very few W's, considering. Most of my responses were D, & that's the way I've been ever since. Then with my horrible memory. I've about accepted it.

September 22

Maybe the *best* example to illustrate the possibility of self-love *and* other-love is to use the male-female example. This is simple. Certainly my self-acceptance as a man does *not* mean snottiness about women. I can *like* it that there are 2 sexes & not just one. And maybe life would be even *more* interesting if there were 3 sexes, or 6, or 8. Point out that ultimately no male can ever fully understand any woman, & no woman can ever fully understand any man. Yet the degree of increased understanding of each other's quirks can help them to get along together. Yet the *definition* of a quirk is something you accept tolerantly even tho not really understanding or sharing it. Ultimately, I could say, don't try to understand your wife altogether; you can enjoy her without understanding. Enjoyment can come first, to say it in another way, & meanwhile perhaps understanding can go on improving, as in scientific advance, & hopefully can improve the enjoyment also.

October 2

Colloquium last night. Frank gave his paper on 3 eras (or levels, or types) of Utopia, Euchronia, & Eupsychia. Very good in his style. I pointed out parallel to the 3 need-levels (safety, esteem, & metamotives), but I don't think he got it—or he got it & didn't accept it. He was very perceptive on my Eupsychia & pointed out things I hadn't noticed such as that its source is ethnology, synergy, good & secure primitive societies á la Benedict (*not* Marx). This is in itself true but not all the truth. It also comes out of the prophetic Jewish tradition of improving people & making a good world. Also parallels closely the Jewish tradition of the few just men (lamed-vavniks) who live among the lesser people in the world, for whose sake God allows the world to exist in spite of its evil. The parallel with my thinking is that even the existence of a very few SA people gives us hope & makes living & society worthwhile. If there were none at all (no Lincolns, Jeffersons, etc.), we might as well give up & let the world end, & who would give a damn? This tradition was not a source or a motivation for me, at least not consciously. The tradition may have formed my soul in a tacit way. Fits in with the Protestant good-works (Paul-Settlage type) & liberal tradition. And with the Norman Thomas, Upton Sinclair, Eugene Debs type socialism of my youth. (I wrote to Upton Sinclair & got an answer. Will also write to Norman Thomas. And how old was I when I started reading & subscribing to the *Nation*? A kid. That must have formed my Utopian motives & goals.)

Also, it's quite clear from my work with Harry that the anti-Semitism I met when I was a child left very deep effects on me & made it extremely important for me to understand why people were so nasty for no reason, & how this could be helped, & how to improve the society to avoid this kind of viciousness. Retroactive self-reparation, self-comforting & soothing, self-therapy, trying to understand & to prevent this from happening to other little underdogs—like the Negro kids, for instance. Utopianism can be retrospective therapy.

So also is the loving-family aspect of it retrospective therapy for the lonely kid without a family. Frank had it right by stressing the aspect of implied disappearance of cruelty & hostility, noninstinctive & therefore improvable by lessening frustrations, etc. This aspect is character-based.

But most important of all was Frank's missing the big point—that my Eupsychia is an empirical Utopia, perhaps the *only* empirical one (Fromm is not, or only partly). [*And a reasonable extrapolation into future from present empirical data. A penetration now of future possibilities now existing in* Anlage.] The others are all wish-fulfillment dreams, as he claimed, but Eupsychia is not, even tho it was instigated by wishes & dreams (like *any* empirical theory). He declares it a personal wish-fulfillment dream of mine & has never conceded that a scientist could test his *own* works & even prove them wrong. He just waves this contention of mine aside, & pays no attention to it, & treats it like all the others, as a pure product, or a by-product solely of character, of *Weltanschauung*, of wishes & fantasies. A theory is as much a pure creation of the person as a painting or a dream would be.

October 4

Just spoke with Frank over phone. His point about the dualism of Utopias finally broke thru, & I could translate it into the dichotomizing of rationality vs. instinct. So that some (especially the older) Utopias are Utopias of reason, calm, common sense (let us say like the Utopias that Unitarians & humanists would construct), & others are Utopias of nonrepression, of full freedom for the instincts à la D. H. Lawrence or Marcuse or Brown. (But then, come to think of it, Aldous Huxley's *Island* is an attempt at *my* notion, or Fromm's or Rogers', that the "instinctoid" or deeper real-self impulses are "nice" & "good," while Marcuse is talking of Freud's instinct theory.)

What I said to Frank was that I was trying to integrate the higher & the lower, the bowels with transcendence. The Eupsychian man *does* express his instinctoid impulses—partly because they are good, partly because he doesn't make moral issues out of shitting or pissing or, for that matter, out of screwing, partly also because he tends to structure the expression of his instincts in a somewhat Apollonian way (essen, *not* fressen). He enjoys them more that way, is able to delay gratification, is more able to choose a gratification object which is just right for him.

For Marcuse & Brown, instincts mean all the pregenital "privileges" of shitting on the floor & then genitality & aggression. But the higher needs & metaneeds are also instinctoid, even tho weaker; i.e., they are of the deepest, realest, animal self. They are *not* dichotomized against each other à la Freud (individual instinct gratifications vs. civilization).

They are not mutually exclusive & incompatible. A higher synthesis (synergy & B-psychology) *is* possible, not only to conceive, but even to describe with the proper selecting out of samples & groups. Frank spoke of maybe some big prospect in the future of getting money & working up all this Utopia stuff. Some day I'd *like* to work up my Eupsychia. And this would be one of the lines, of integrating the animal & the transcendent, the instincts & the rational. It will be difficult because of the basic problem of integrating also impulse & control. Eupsychia is not, like Marcuse & Brown, nonrepressive. Control & selection *are* there. More specifically, the difficulty is in documenting & working out a system which speaks of spontaneity & expressiveness (but only for the healthy & real self) & also of rejection & control of neurosis & of symptoms. Neurotic, acute, rational impulses are *not* to be accepted in the fullest sense; sometimes they are to be rejected, controlled, punished, etc. Phenomenologically it's practically impossible to discriminate a healthy impulse from an unhealthy one. They both feel the same at the moment, or, at least I, from the outside, cannot help anyone else to discriminate right now. Only in *time* do the results work out differently for the person, & he can *learn* which impulses make trouble & regret & which bring happiness. I can tell from the outside about *other* people's impulses, but, if I am mistrusted, I am not permitted to help.

Only trust, transference, assurance of benevolent neutrality will permit unpleasant truth to be swallowed.

If someone says to me "You talk a lot about acceptance; well, accept me as I am," then I must say that acceptance applies to deepest, realest, authentic self, which I do accept. But if I accept that, then I must reject that in you which is the opposite. The denial of your true self. That's ultimately acceptance in the fullest, deepest sense of the word. For example, if I punish my child for stealing, then this can be called my acceptance of his deepest honesty. It means ordinarily that I assume he is essentially an honest person & I want to teach him *not* to give up his authentic self. (This is proven partly by the different feelings & spirit in which one punishes a deeply dishonest person or a professional criminal or a psychopath.) Acceptance of & love for truth mean anger over untruth. One implies the other.

The psychotherapeutic situation is very special: here there *is* an acceptance of everything, at least in the superficial sense of not scolding & punishing & also of letting a transference form, of proving neutrality & benevolence. But even here, it is only the deepest self which is accepted in the full sense; neurosis is tolerated but disapproved of, & the constant effort is to get rid of it. "Acceptance" of the overt kind is here a *strategy*. Maybe I'd better redefine several levels or types of acceptance: Godlike acceptance, B-love acceptance, D-love acceptance, acceptance of children, weak, sick, etc. Therapeutic strategic acceptance is the basic irreducible amount of unconditional positive regard (which is like saying no cruelty even for the worst bastard in the world, etc.). The deepest acceptance is to actually love the difference or the symptoms or anyway to be amused by it, think it cute. Next deepest is to be able to tolerate it, to forgive it, to "buy it" as a necessary part of a package deal, & never again to make any fuss or complaint about it—or else simply to regard it as a "defining idiosyncrasy," that which gives character & makes the person unique & different from others. No, I think this latter is the 2nd layer & the "tolerance for" is the 3rd layer, because here the disapproval or dislike for the trait doesn't change to love or amusement or fascination or cuteness, as it does at the 1st & 2nd layers, but is simply controlled & swallowed for larger, more inclusive reasons. (As aspirin is bitter, & you don't like bitter, but it's a small price to pay for health. And this is different from *liking* bitter aspirins, as Ellen did.) I guess a 4th layer is to keep your mouth shut about unchanging disapproval but also to keep on trying in a nice way to change it if possible, as one might with a friend's alcoholism, or as I feel about Ann's smoking.

All of these layers of acceptance I think also apply to one's own acceptance of one's own nature. Layer 1 for me would be my IQ. Layer 2 is my enthusiasm & quick interest in practically anything & anybody & then losing interest often & getting out. It would be more strategic if I waited & contemplated for a while, but then I wouldn't be me. I'd be somebody else. That's a defining characteristic & is extremely deep, going along with creativeness, high IQ, emotionality, peak-experiences, great love for music, & being able to have a good time. It makes trouble, but I wouldn't really change it. Layer 3 is my bad memory, which I disapprove of & dislike & used to be very ashamed of, but have finally "accepted" because I can't do a thing about it—I'm stuck with it. And now I can tolerate it without feeling guilty or disliking myself for it. The 4th layer is trying to be more obsessional, orderly, planned, responsible, to keep dates & to get places on time, to do my professional work well, duty, etc. I'm really not enough like that & keep trying to change & improve it (as I've given up trying to improve my memory). Same for smoking. I struggled to give it up. It had a strong hold on me, but I so disapproved of it & felt I could & should give it up. And finally did. But it was a long war. I certainly "accept" this character defect in the sense of permitting it to come into consciousness, of not repressing, denying, etc. That's what the analyst means when his patient finally gets to be conscious of, e.g., his denied sadism; the analyst says "He has accepted it" (i.e., has permitted it to come into consciousness), like admitting "OK, I'm a liar" or "I'm stingy, I now realize." Something that makes you depressed to think about & that lowers your self-esteem. Here acceptance *at least* means "accepting the truth of" or "not denying the truth of" about oneself. At this level, I suppose, "acceptance of the other person" means, at the very least, perceiving & apprehending the truth about him & then at one level or another trying & succeeding to get along with the perceived but disapproved-of characteristics.

October 8

My self-absorption makes trouble all around me. I get bored listening to anything or anybody not useful to my work, & I come to life & enjoy myself only when I am respectfully asked questions about my work. (Like last night at Newton College, where 100 girls & professors had obviously studied my books line by line & knew them well & understood them thoroughly. So I felt as if I were precious & important & useful & respected, & as if I were bringing water to the thirsty & as if they smacked their lips over it. Reminds me of Bertha, who felt so good when Ellen was just born & latched onto the nipple at once, while Ann just born didn't care for the nipple & the milk, & Bertha felt insulted & rejected.) So it looks like megalomania & grandiosity, & of course in a way it is—not in a psychotic or unreal sense but in a very real, functional, & necessary sense. I agree with Kuhn, Polanyi, Watson, and all the other writers on the creative thinker, that no creativeness of the breakthru type is possible *unless* a man can be "selfish" about his "work." Of course, it means fighting everybody—the scientific community (my APA), one's colleagues, one's students, one's family & friends (they'll all worry over his swelled head & self-importance—& thus being all alone (except for seeking out once in a while his audience of respectful listeners & disciples in order to get a little refreshing applause & reassurance, to get bucked up again after living in the midst of rejection & neglect & misunderstanding & not being taken seriously). Colin Wilson had it right in his *Stature of Man:* to do godlike things, you must have godlike aspirations & therefore must have pride, arrogance, hubris. You can choose feeling like a hero or a worm (best if you can integrate them, of course). If the latter, you'll never get anything done.

November 12

Seminar at home yesterday, & the eternal question comes up again of the balance between discipline & freedom in education—in this case in science education. My question was: what changes & improvements in science education are generated by this rehumanization of the philosophy of science and the scientific *Weltanschauung*? How can we teach *everyone* to have the "scientific" or empirical attitude about *everything*? How to take it away from the professional scientist & give it to everyone? How take it out of the lab & bring it everyplace? How break away from cookbook science courses? How break away from conceiving of science only as a body of methods? How teach 4–5-year-old children the empirical attitude? What does this attitude mean in a child, a housewife, etc.?

It seems clear to me (I said) that the regime of freedom and self-choice which is desirable for innovating-creative people (& which they desire) can be ruinous for noncreative people who are too authoritarian, too passive, too authority-ambivalent, too noncommitted, etc.—ruinous at least in the sense that this regime permits them to fail, since it assumes resources which are not there. If we leave plenty of time for self-chosen reading, meditations, etc., this time *may* be used badly by some. They feel they are fooling the profs. The profs get mad at this & won't want such students to think they are fooling anyone, & are therefore likely to get "tough" & demand *so much* work that there won't be any time to loaf for these loafers. But of course, for *non*loafers, this is bad because it leaves them no time for self-chosen work.

So I vote in favor of making life better for the ones I call "good students,"—those who are autonomous, committed, dedicated, hard-working, etc.—& letting the others go hang. Actually, I pointed out, such a permission to fail is *good* for the loafer rather than bad. It may confront him with insight & shocks which *may* set self-improvement into motion.

After the seminar it occurred to me to phrase it so: how much unstructure (chaos, disorganization, anarchy) is the person strong enough to take? It ties in with the child's *need* (not wish) for discipline, limits, for a firm leader who "knows," who is decisive, sure, certain. Relate this to the tendency of nonselfs to follow the paranoid leader because he's so sure of himself. *Every* child is not sure of himself. Practically *no* child has a strong identity. He is not yet Self enough to get guidance from his own impulse-voices. In this sense, he may be expected to go into anxiety if no leader is available to structure life & reality for him. If the child must be the captain of the ship, he'll get scared. Of course, since the adult leader is always available, children can afford themselves the luxury of fake calls for a freedom, which they don't really want & which they would be punished with if they got.

The eternal cry of the adolescent as he behaves like a child is "Stop treating me like a child." It's a paradox & can be solved *only* by helping him to grow up, & best way is to stop treating him like a child. Apparently, the solution is a *graded* giving of freedom & responsibility, bit by bit, as fast as possible, but no faster than is assimilable & usable. It will vary a great deal from individual to individual & from subculture to subculture. In general, it implies that *adults* keep the reins in their hands, keep power & structure values, à la Mexican paper [75]. But unlike Mexicans, we must loosen reins bit by bit, try out the consequences of giving the adolescent a little more freedom, a little more, a little more, each time testing the consequences to see how well it works. Pull back when it doesn't work well or when it's dangerous. The whole situation is helped by full communication & feedback, by explanations to avoid misunderstandings, & by insight confrontations, etc.

November 22

I was writing and thought to list here some of the "mysteries," unanswered questions, that I've been struggling with.

Why do children like dolls, puppies, etc.?

Why do we love children? Or, rather, which children do we love?

Why do paranoid people collect a following? Hitler, Stalin, McCarthy, Welch? Or grandiose people like General MacArthur? Blusterers like Herbert Marcuse?

All the questions of masculinity & femininity. My files are full of questions & puzzles. Big mystery. Today I wrote a memo on definition of beauty. For males it is females; but for females it is *not* males. Differences in female & male cognition? Differences in reaction to babies?

Why can't we remember dreams? And why can't we use them for growth or therapy *unless* we can remember? Why don't dreams or psychoses help us? Why is self-observing necessary? Why does *pure* experiencing mean not self-observing or remembering?

Why does progressively higher need gratification produce in some SA plus B-values, *but* in others just selfishness, snottiness, feeling deserving à la Republicans, Americans, etc.? Why does it make some *more* greedy, others less greedy? Lower need gratification is a necessary but not a sufficient precondition of higher, spiritual life, altruism, love, etc.

How do we explain the evolution of *unused* capacities? Poetry, math, philosophy, science—all are possible for *anybody* today & for *any* baby going back to the first caves. They have always had the *possibilities*, even tho they were not used (therefore not rewarded, therefore not involved in natural selection?). Or could they all meld together into aggridance, which *is* a basis for natural selection? Or what?

Why is sex so important for men *beyond* the usual explanations, in itself, as one of the validations of life, as a pleasure that defines living?

How to reconcile ideal SA (fullest humanness) with the best that a particular handicapped person can do?

The "need" for limits? For punishment? Discipline? Is it a need in the same sense as other needs?

These are just the mysteries that I have thought of today. I guess it's silly. Anyway, a complete list would be endless.

November 24

Bill Bruce told me yesterday that kids don't report peak-experiences. True in my experience too. But they *do* have them. Any adult can report peaks retrospectively. I had lots of them. I remember, I think I used to call it "exultation" to myself, with lump in throat, tears in eyes, chills, prickles, slight feeling of (pleasant) nausea, & all sorts of other autonomic reactions plus impulse to shout & yell, etc. Question is, why did I keep it to myself, absolutely secret?

Also reminds me of data collected so far on nonpeakers, one by one. It is certainly a suppression or repression process. I *still* find myself somewhat embarrassed to talk about my own experiences & rarely do. Why? Why did that woman bawl the hell out of me for publishing—anonymously—her peak-experience in *Journal of Humanistic Psychology*? Why need to keep it so private?

Maybe the fear of being flooded & overcome by emotion—even the most joyous—is the negative side of the positive *need* for integration, to hold oneself together, to be in control, not to lose the reins of self-control. Fear of passivity, of receptivity. In this sense, to have peaks willingly is an act of courage for some, a sign of health. Nonpeaking = *fear* of losing control. Harry Golden's candor & openness about his sentiments are, I think, also signs of health. (Embarrassment about such things is an inhibition, the loss of a human capacity.)

Bertha suggests that I talk about happy grumbles & unhappy grumbles. Not a bad idea. It's true that we'll have to define happiness often as specifically *not* conscious. Awareness of being happy sometimes seems to mean less happiness. Often it is a condition of being happy not to be aware that you are. Then it is known retrospectively (Golden remembering his childhood & realizing that the hardships, etc., were really happiness) or thru the eyes of an observer who can understand even when it's covered over by "happy grumbles." Maybe we can't *stand* too much happiness.

Certainly I know this now about the peaks, the great joys. They would kill us if they lasted too long or came too often. (Supposing a great orgasm lasted for 15 minutes instead of 10 or 15 seconds! The organism couldn't stand it. Surely the heart would collapse.) Same for love. Or for any other ecstasy. Maybe all these defenses against joy are based on a reality. Maybe we'd damn well *better* be afraid of ecstasy, or at least very respectful, & take it in graded, assimilable doses. The definition of Heaven or of happiness as constant & permanent is wrong & unreal. Must redefine it more realistically.

To have a peak means *not* to fear flooding. One can "take it." One can give up control, self-consciousness.

But this also means not being aware, not remembering, at least to some extent. It tends to be *total* experiencing to the exclusion of self-observing. Have to work this out better. The *total* experiencing without *any* self-observing, or editorial criticism, that comes in dreams, deliria, psychoses, hallucinations, etc., means complete or near-complete amnesia, & therefore not being able to make any growth-or-therapy use of it. (Psychoses & dreams teach us or improve us little? Nothing?) Peaks are not so extreme; they can be remembered to some extent, more or less.

December 26

More thoughts on grumble-joy ratio & on the parallel charactero-logy. Certainly part of it is a kind of obsessional defense against emotions of any kind, but especially positive ones of joy, pleasure, happiness, apprecia-tion, gratitude, good fortune, esthetic reactions. So I thought of calling them *sobers* & their opposite numbers *drunks*. This is not a bad way of paralleling the hysteria-obsessional split. Complainers (nay-sayers, peak-fearers, emotion-avoiders) don't like the loss of sobriety, don't know how to handle it, but also don't like it in others. For instance, B. doesn't like me to say anything about the beauty of the river, or of anything else, it I say it more than once or twice. Mustn't react too openly to music. Mustn't get too gay at parties. Mustn't enjoy applause, admiration, etc., at conventions or lectures. Because my head will get swelled? Because I get "high"? Exhila-rated? Happy? B. gets uneasy then & has finally decided to stay away from meetings of this sort altogether. Nor can one get too affectionate or "crazy" or wild. Is it fear of "loss of control" in oneself or in the other? Apollonian distaste for the Dionysian? Suddenly reminded of Emerson's Theory of Compensation—that you must pay for any happiness. Sooner or later, a bill will be presented. Pleasure now means tragedy later? I guess we have to talk of *fear* as one of the ultimates here. (Reminds me that Freud was the *first* to make anxiety a basic psychodynamic in his system. Must give him credit for this.) Another angle was suggested by Frank, who said to me "I am a skeptic & you are not." What does this mean? That he is loathe to trust, to believe? I'll discuss it with him.

1965

February 9

Question: why do so many of the poor, new countries, especially the socialist & communist ones, have to spend the little money they have on spreading revolutions, military manipulations, etc.? However poor they are, they spend huge sums in this stupid way. Question: is this part of being at lowest need-levels? China, Egypt, Cuba, for instance. Is this dichotomizing of "us good ones" vs. "them lousy enemies" a by-product of poverty? Is it a necessary political trick by prosperous leaders of poor people to keep the poor people working, patriotic, etc.? Is it necessary for the poor countries, e.g., Tanzania, to cut their throats by attacking the U.S., which wants to help them? That is, *must* they hate the U.S. for being wealthy, or what? It's all so illogical, stupid, self-defeating. Egypt, for instance, could use every penny it's got to improve itself & *thus* grow *really* strong, serve as an example, etc. Same for Algeria, on the edge of bankruptcy, East Germany, half-starving, giving huge credits to Egypt, bleeding its own blood away. Meanwhile plenty of examples of Switzerland, Scandinavia, etc., which get on fine by minding their own business. The richer Russia got, the less belligerent it got. Will same be true for China? Perhaps poverty breeds hate, & this must be channeled someplace—so better outside the society?

February 13

So glad to see X & other old friends & acquaintances. I get very sentimental about it, but long discussion at bkfst reminded me of old incompatibilities & is relevant to what I wrote on plane & also to my long discussion with Walter Weisskopf. X simply isn't *awfully* bright, & since he's also very obsessional, neat, orderly, & has-to-compete, it's almost torture to *have* to hear him out as he gives an ordered, laborious, repetitive exposition on some truism or some obvious point, & he simply can't be headed off, directed, or interrupted. He climbs his way, step by step, laboriously, up the wrong hill, & it's impossible to break in & correct him. At first I had thought I'd be sure to look him up when in N. J. Now I'm not sure. We're too different in intelligence & *also* in character type. If I'm always in the B-realm (at the back of my head, anyway, & in a unitive way) & he's always in the D-realm (even tho he's got *all* the B-words), how does one communicate? Certainly no easy play is possible, of tossing the ball back & forth. He reads my writings & is very careful. I'm sure that he understands them at some level—but not at the transcendent level. Verbally, all we could arrange, I think, is an exchange of lectures (he is polite & listens when I lecture at him.)

But it *was* useful to hear his meticulous, logical, tight-ass critique of the Jackson & Getzel study. He was absolutely right, & yet it was useless mostly, because it was a critique of a beginning from the point of view of the ending. The innovator being criticized by the military policeman. About this he was quite intelligent, & it was useful to *me* in a way that I suppose he didn't intend. I tried to explain to him that the study was a beginning research & was therefore fated to be clumsy & mistaken (I quoted him Jung's "I dare to make mistakes"), & yet it was important because research progress comes from discovering *which* mistakes were unforeseeable; i.e., one learns from the beginning venture how to do it better the next time (like the Nebraska farm which could support a family only after 4 previous bankrupt farmers had poured their lives into it & failed, or like the ants which climb over the barrier, over the platform, formed by the previously killed ants).

Also I pointed out to him that, peculiarly, 4 or 5 such clumsy initial ventures (no one of which could be trusted for policy-implementation in the classroom) *yet* could support each other & add up to an advance in knowledge or at least the reliability of this "knowledge," i.e., that creative children have a pixie, fantasy humor. Noplace in the textbooks is such a thing mentioned.

Then I tried to tell him that, whenever I started something, I gave up the inhibiting effects of logic, proof, reliability, etc., & all the cautions & criticisms of my careful & critical friends, & dashed on ahead into the wilderness, trusting myself & my intuitions. Otherwise I'd never do anything (except criticize the doers—just as X has done; he's so aware of the possible mistakes that he's paralyzed & has never fulfilled his capacities & been fruitful like others who are more dashing & daring & no more intelligent). I remember the letter I wrote once to Eliseo Vivas, replying in the only way possible to his very just & sound criticisms & cautions about tangling experimentally with the philosophical questions & difficulties— that it would take 2 lifetimes to study everything & be perfectly scholarly before beginning the research. I told him I understood what he was saying but that "I would be determinedly naive," i.e., not get immobilized by the philosophical difficulties, but just go ahead & get wet by plunging into the water, even if it wasn't lighted & I might crack my skull. Can a cautious man attack an unexplored wilderness or swamp? In research training, I told X, we all act on this by urging our students to plunge *in* & get wet with actual research. The criticism from within the circle of researchers who have gotten wet is so different from the criticisms of the spectators in the stands.

What I kept trying to tell Walter Weisskopf was that he was too vulnerable & too responsive to the applause & criticism from below his level. To be on top of Mt. Olympus *means* loneliness, very few people to talk with. But one has to be lofty & compassionate & can also be affectionate & friendly—let's say, as I can be with P., whom I'm very fond of—with infra-Olympians, below the B-realm. But one mustn't be touched or affected by their lack of understanding, applause, etc., *nor* by their criticism & punishment. Walter is a great & creative intellect, & X is not. And yet Walter keeps seeking for the Xs to love him & respect him, & is *very* hurt when this is not forthcoming. But this is silly, since they're living at different levels of life.

The terrible thing here again is not neglect, misunderstanding, etc., but rather hubris & also the terrible hurt that this attitude can cause. Supposing X were to read what I have written! Could he possibly believe that I'm fond of him, feel friendly & respectful in a particular way, which carries goodwill & *not* contempt? I suppose he'd be very hurt & very angry, & would have to try to hurt me back. And yet what to do? The fact is that X's IQ is around 130 & mine & Walter's & Frank's, etc., are around 180 or 190. Again that old Utopian problem of what to do with factual superiority—how to unleash it & use it without producing an arrogant monster & a resentful countervaluing hostility & hurt.

February 20

What you are fitted for—that is your destiny, which you must accept & give yourself to wholly, & train yourself for in the best way possible. All this then reads at the highest level: which of the B-values (which, of course, are your ultimate destiny) are you going to specialize in? Because you detect in yourself specialized capacities or possibilities or because some B-value tasks "call for" you more strongly; i.e., they need you, so you respond. Which of them "calls" you most? What is your calling? What do you hear in your own deepest recesses, your deepest impulse-voices, & what do you read in your B-cognition of the demand-character of reality? In other words, what needs you most? Your kind of you, that is? (I could call this the "ought of one's destiny," constitutional & environmental.) [*League of Responsible Citizens. The Just Men. The Saving Remnant. The Hidden Remnant. The lamed-vavniks. All the people who take the cosmic responsibilities on their own shoulders voluntarily, partly because they have broad shoulders & partly because, by one accident or another, they happen to see the fire burning & so it becomes their job to put it out.*]

Becoming less than you were capable of becoming = voluntary self-diminution = voluntary "castration" = voluntary suicide & renunciation or wasting of life = you are not a good member of the species, like a tiger who loses his appetite for meat = misery—the intrinsic guilt of evading growth & SA & therefore misery, self-punishment, & sense of having failed, regret, etc. This is what we can *now* add to Plato—this oughtiness of the facts of inner potential & the dynamics & psychosomatic consequences of not living up to potential = illness of mind & body & an Ivan Ilyitch end.

February 23

Last night I tried out my argument on Will Maslow, Arnie Gurin, & Jerry Berlin—on the necessity of a redefinition of liberalism, progressivism, etc., to *include* realistically the new data on compensation neuroses, welfare neuroses, states' rights, "understanding" criminals, discipline, individuation, etc. Didn't get across. It was misunderstood as an *attack* on the unconscious rather than as demand for re-evaluation, bringing up-to-date, etc. I pointed out that Goldwater, Ayn Rand, et al., were not read carefully by the liberals or listened to even when they had a legitimate point. I can foresee that what I will one day *write* (no use talking) will be misunderstood by many. Writing therefore had better be done at length, in full, not in small isolated pieces which can then be more easily misunderstood as, e.g., anti-union, anti-Negro, etc.

But one thing I generated out of the discussions of yesterday was the new & necessary profession of the social therapist (or psychosocial therapist?). Suppose I recommended that discipline problems in Harlem schools be taken out of the class at once (well-meaning but wishy-washy adults are helpless before a few disrupting kids who defy them) & recommended whatever punishment turned out empirically to work well, however harsh it might have to be, in order that education for others might go forward. Then, since you can't dump these kids on the street, you must turn them over for remedial & therapeutic treatment to someone? To whom? Must be people trained as teachers *and* social workers *and* psychotherapists *and* punishers. Well, such workers would be needed & useful also for delinquents, adult criminals, psychopaths, immatures, welfare neuroses, etc. Society could refer each *individual* who makes trouble for it for whatever treatment would be indicated. Pure psychotherapists are often useless because of their tradition of no punishing. Must have socially realistic & tough-as-necessary people who, if necessary, would be able to strike *fear* into, e.g., the criminal tough, & *then* treat him kindly. [*Put under "revolution."*]

It's a question of dealing with people fixated at lower-need levels & in a jungle world-view. It's useless to deal with them as if they lived in a higher-need-level world.

This is a level of thought & of treatment prepotent to normal insight therapy. Lowest comes social therapy for social pathology. Then comes psychotherapy for social pathology. Then comes psychotherapy for individual sickness within a better society. Then comes psychogogy (outogogy, orthopsychology) for helping not-sick people to fulfill potentialities & achieve identity—real self *and* personal value system. And finally transcendent philosophy (?) with a guide (?) for achieving mystic fusion, peak-experience, B-cognition, platonic contemplation of B-values.

Everything is different at lowest (Congo) level—politics, economics, work, art, poetry, everything.

March 2

(Still sick at home with flu, etc.) Reading *Republic*. Socrates in Book IX talking about "the lawless, wild-beast nature, which peers out in sleep." "Then the wild beast within us—goes forth to satisfy his desires, & there is no conceivable folly or crime . . . not excepting incest, or any other unnatural union, or parricide, or the eating of forbidden food . . . which at such a time, when he has parted company with all shame & sense, a man may not be ready to commit." Reminds me that I've never really worked up the relations of the Freudian id & the real self. It's OK to reject neurosis on grounds that it is the rejection of real self. But this can't be true for our wishes of sleep. My assumption is that these lawless wishes (absolutely selfish & undesirable in any society, especially since they include whatever happens to be locally forbidden too, like the "forbidden food" above) exist in the healthiest people too, & that therefore they are *part* of the real self, not external to it. They're just controlled, or laughed at, or shrugged away, & don't constitute a serious temptation to the matured person.

Part of the solution must be that the real self is itself a very complex organization & hierarchical integration of lower & higher, of younger & older, immature & mature, babyish, childish, adolescentish, & adult. Like the hierarchy of pleasures: the one who can experience the highest pleasures is certainly not tempted to go in for the lowest "kicks" & thrills, except maybe while asleep, when the upper layers of the hierarchy disappear or get weak. In a hierarchy, as in the central nervous system, the lower layers always keep on existing in various special senses, like the Babinsky reflex, *in potentia*.

One would then have to make a sharp distinction between these unconscious (or forgotten, or better, "overlaid," as the vice-president is by the president) impulses &, on the other hand, the defensive, Freudian-type repression (that which is feared) & that which you fight with, struggle with, *keep* down & under by force). The overlaid impulses are not like that at all, any more than I have a temptation to piss in bed (altho I might with senility, or in a dream, or in some other regression, in which the "overlay" is weakened or lost). The overlaid unconscious (which is certainly a biological part of the core self) ≠ the repressed, feared unconscious (which I guess is *not* part of the biological core self or real self, almost by definition). In Socrates' examples, the Oedipal impulses probably *are* part of the overlaid impulses, low in the hierarchy & unpreferred as long as the higher layers are in charge & the forbidden food *is* repressed & *not* part of the biological self.

March 28

Reread Huxley's *Island* for Utopian seminar & *very* much impressed—much more so than first reading, when it looked far out, eccentric, & hysterical. It takes a little getting used to & familiarizing. A manual of theory & practice of SA, experiencing, transcendence, etc. I doubt that any better could be done today by anyone, altho I think I'd re-phrase much of it to make an easier bridge between today & the quite possible tomorrow—make it more plausible, acceptable, as I try to do in my teaching. I had the vague thought that, if I live long enough, this would be a pleasant pastime for an old man, to construct a Utopia. Maybe it could take the form simply of re-evaluating & rewriting *Island* in a more sober way. [*How to listen to inner voices & to what you hear.*]

Had a group over to the house & tried to put SA into terms they could use, & much of it came from Huxley.

1.   Experiencing fully, vividly, selflessly, with full concentration, total absorption, without self-consciousness = to be whole = SA. [*Stop running & busy-ness each day & contemplate. Stop "behaving" as substitute for feeling, experiencing. Behaving drowns out, deadens, & dulls the inner voices & can be a flight from self-knowledge. "Noise" drowns out inner voices. Become (openly, expressively, integratedly, monistically) what you (intrinsic core, real self, biological core, deepest & hidden self) really (congruently, honestly, authentically, deeply, covertly, unconsciously & preconsciously, basically, intrinsically) are (at the moment in a dissociated fashion) = give up being a split, dissociated, multiple personality with different levels or selves in*

conflict, with impulses warring with repressive controls (instead of Apollonizing controls) = get unified, organized, harmonious; pull yourself together; get your selves together; become One.]

2.   Making the growth-choice instead of the defense-&-fear-choice a dozen times a day = moving *toward* SA.

3.   Listening to one's own impulse-voices within means being *able* to experience. This is the basic operation for discovering identity. Self *equals* these thousands of little real experiences which add up to "I am this kind of guy" = self-knowledge. [*All the trivial choices and decisions add up to real self. Body awareness, consciousness of emotions, anxiety, consciousness of dreams and fantasies, consciousness of needs, wants, desires.*]

4.   When in doubt, be honest rather than not, with both yourself & others, in both speech & action. (They worried a lot about the *hurting* powers of truth. They think people are more brittle than they really are. Also, they're not aware that the hurt may be worthwhile for long-run benefits. Being hurt is not the worst thing in the world. Paranoid suspicion is worse, I told them, i.e., not to know what's going on & to have worse suspicions.) [*We know the purely selfish life doesn't work out. The thing is ultimately to forget yourself.*]

5.   Looking within yourself for many of the answers implies taking responsibility, which itself is a great step toward SA = to become a self-mover, an authentic person, a man instead of a boy. Master of your own fate. [*Intrinsic core = if the job is to find out what your potentials are, the delicate, subtle, overlooked whisperings from within, that tell you what you like & dislike, what you want & don't want, what gives you joys & what bores or pains you, what you believe, what your tastes are, what your style is, your pace, your mode of apperception, your (Sheldonian) temperament, what you admire, when you feel happiest, peakiest, fully functioning, preferred behavior, what suits you, what sits well in your stomach & what doesn't, adrenalin-nonadrenalin, active-passive, warm-cool, knowledge about yourself, self-confrontation, fitting in shoes or clothes, free association—then you'll know better what to do about it, which direction to go in, what compromises are necessary.*]

6.   All this guarantees better life choices. "Better" = what's constitutionally right for you, what your destiny is, who your wife or husband will be, what your mission will be.

7.   Dare to be different, unpopular, nonconforming.

8.   Be courageous rather than afraid.

9.   SA is not only an end-state; it is also the process of actualizing your potentialities at *any* time & in *any* amount. Becoming smarter by studying = SA. Practicing piano or surgery or glass-blowing or whatever your potentialities are = SA.

10.   *Any* moment of authenticity, congruence, honesty = SA.

11.   Peaks are transcendent self-actualizations.

12.   Trying things out in school & discovering that you *don't* like

chemistry or psychology or art is an advance & is valuable. [*An explorer cannot fail. Everything he finds is helpful.*]

13.   Don't worry too much about staying selfish. Compassion & love & kindness are also in the real self that you will discover within yourself.

14.   Even if all this process shows up psychopathology instead, this, too, is worthwhile, because then you can seek help instead of covering it up.

15.   One way to *become* yourself is to reveal yourself = to be yourself. Let yourself be yourself. Self-disclosure. Don't fear revealment. It also helps *you* to perceive yourself if you disclose to others. No false public selves. No "roles." No acting. All of these are like self-rejections, & therefore are splittings & dissociations. No "telephone voices."

16.   Dissociation is the splitting of inner from outer, of preconscious from conscious, of one aspect from another. ("Sociation"? "Monizing"?) Integrating puts them together into one & heals the splitting. ["*Holizing*"?]

17.   But add the moot question of *trusting* your impulses. Very difficult question, because there are people who *shouldn't* trust their impulses (the sick ones), & there are times when *none* of us should. How to tell the difference? Certainly it's safe to say: "*Know* your impulses. Be aware of them." Even in the strict, limited sense of "Accept your impulses." But, after all, impulses are not all there is to the person. To let them rule is also a splitting. The job is to meld the impulses with reality testing (sometimes it's dangerous to go to sleep even when you have impulse to sleep), with feelings for others (sometimes sex impulse has to be stepped on because not good for partner or for one's child), with knowledge (diabetic shouldn't yield to impulse for sugar), with reason, logic, etc. Not to mention that Apollonian organizing & integrating & harmonizing the multitudes of impulses mean postponing or forbidding some. The question is *when* to trust one's impulses. How much? Under what conditions? *Who* should & who should not? To be able to trust your impulses validly is already evidence of having attained the high-health state (like Reich's perfect orgasm).

18.   Add also "Man becomes truly human only at the moment of decision" (Tillich). But make sure that this means *authentic*, congruent, honestly expressive, from-within-out decision or choice. (It *can* be otherwise. Choice-*behavior*, like any behavior, is doubtful as diagnostic of the inner state.)

19.   I suppose I will have to add in to this system the problem of the good death, either symbolic or actual, the death before rebirth, the good closure, completion, ending of perseveration.

20.   What to do with pain, illness, etc.? This system says "Let yourself be overwhelmed by it; surrender to it; be passive before it; don't fight it; experience this too; reconcile, not *deny*."

21.   Whole problem of surrender. Taoistic receptivity. As a matter of fact, no real listening to impulse-voices (or reality-voices) is possible without this surrender, noninterfering, nonfighting the experience. [*Try things out. Go places. Have experiences. Each one will teach you something of your tastes & capacities.*]

22.   Look deliberately for ethical & moral principles. What is right & wrong for you? Think about it; examine it; get righteously indignant. Scorn what is rotten. Fight it if you can. Is this moralistic—or moral?

23.   Help yourself to become selfless by being philanthropic and helping in a good cause. Be good for others.

April 15

Plane back (from Minneapolis). In order to do big things & tackle big problems, a certain grandiosity & self-trust is absolutely essential. It can easily shade over into hubris with all the applause, the honors, the adulation, & even near-worship that is easy to get, willy-nilly. The task, then, is to retain equilibrium, "modesty" & humility of a particular kind. (That is quite compatible with the necessary heroic & grandiose quality.) Someone was saying "That must be good for your ego" as I was congratulated for the hundredth time. I told him that the very same technique for protecting yourself against criticism & attack, disapproval or ridicule—that is, to be your *own* judge, your own self-critic & rewarder—also protects against praise & honors & permits you to take it objectively, not to overvalue it, not to need it, not to be willing to buy it at a ruinous price—that is, to march to your own inner music toward your own inner goals, doing what your destiny is to do, & all without reference to what happens outside, whether praise or blame.

It was my impression this trip that it's possible to get too big, to look too big, too overwhelming & awe-inspiring, no longer human. And I went out of my way to be "just folks," *not* to be austere, distant, & untouchable. This is good for *them*.

I refused the honorary degree. Must try to keep these "honors" to a minimum.

April 18

I am a new breed—a theoretical psychologist parallel to theoretical physicists or, even better, to theoretical biologists (because the latter actually *do* lab work, or *did*). In one way this is different from the example of Wm. James & John Dewey, who turned to philosophy from psychology, because they were never researchers, & I was (I am). I think of myself as a scientist rather than as an essayist or philosopher. I feel myself very bound to & by the facts which I am trying to *perceive*—not to create. My creations are structures or organizations of facts. I do not feel free, nor do I ever *want* to in any way, to leave them. I want to describe them & organize & communicate what I see.

May 1

Irritated by several intellectuals & writers, & also Ellen. She asks how I can be so benign in a dehumanizing society. Or from a review: "Granted the absurdities of our economic system, the incoherence & irrationality of our social & political system, the qualities that lead to success in either & the value that we place on success, integrity is bound to be problematic. It rarely occurs naturally or flourishes in our social climate," etc. So *many* people write with this total blindness to any goodness or virtue (or even *despise* it for existing & contradicting their generalization). The whole attitude of degree & of quantification is lacking. It's all terrible! There are *no* redeeming features! It's a total evil!

This is *one* other aspect of a particular kind of liberation: that it must reject the U.S. altogether because of its imperfections (seen as total evils), & so many of them are perfectly happy with China or Cuba or Russia—who aren't even trying. I must try to understand this better. Also, why does this rejection of democracy, of the Bill of Rights, of political parliamentary improvement, this contempt for social improvements, sweep the intellectuals so often? They were the only ones who swallowed Stalinism & sneered at English Socialism or Scandinavia. Now they're all unanimous on Vietnam & can see no *bit* of virtue in fighting aggressive imperialism—as in Korea also. They somehow are against the reformers & the improvers & yet swallow authoritarians. Mao is treated with respect in these circles, as Stalin was.

Well, anyway, the original thought was: is it not likely that the sheer fact of great numbers in a large & complex society must breed evils of all sorts—or are very likely to, quite apart from the character of individuals? That is, *any* large economic system must be absurd. Any political system *must* be irrational & incoherent, etc. Maybe it's *better* for it to be irrational (like Mel Dalton's "informal organization"). That is, maybe they're not evils, or at least not all evil.

A good way to counter all this rejection of the U.S., which is *relatively* one of the best societies in existence, is to ask the question "Which nations do you think are better?" This would show up the perfectionistic nature of the criticism or the rejection.

May 15

Flexibility is health—maybe *the* basic characteristic of health (the way inflexibility & rigidity, confusion of past with present, of one person with another = neurosis). The healthy person responds to affluence by being generous & to poverty by being stingy. Good conditions = good human nature, & bad conditions = bad human nature *in the flexible, healthy person!* [*But why the exceptions?*] In the neurotic, or the one with too good & vivid a memory (the one who can't forget, the traumatized one for whom the trauma remains alive & present forever), it is just the opposite. Therefore we might guess that it is precisely the SA person who would be the best survivor in the jungle, adapting to *its* laws more quickly & with less lag than others.

Again I suppose health or fullest-humanness or SA would probably mean flexibility, i.e., the ability to enjoy when conditions are good, & without denying the real existence of pain. Also the confrontation of pain & suffering without automatically having to devalue happiness. No either/or, dichotomizing, mutual exclusiveness.

May 31

Reading MacInness' *Affair in Venice* (all played out after editing summer notes). Spies, Communists, American patriots, etc. But it hit at the discussion of American patriotism. That's what I am, but for B-reasons, far more universal, species-wide, B-value-fostering reasons. So I will try to say it to myself because it's not time yet to say it to anyone else—except Bertha, who knows how I feel & who approves insofar as a "non-do-gooder" is able to. But pretty soon, I think, I'll be forced from within or from without to speak up, so I better think it thru carefully. I may be on the edge of a break with many (all? most?) of my friends. Maybe that's part of what's been worrying & depressing & keeping me up nights occasionally. Maybe it's been especially difficult with Frank, but also with most others who absolutely reject the policy in Vietnam & in Santo Domingo, who think of Johnson as an imperialist, who reject the U.S. in general, the absolute pacifists like Henry Geiger & my own Ellen too, with whom I disagree about most things (at least with her there's no unpleasant quarreling). The faculty at Brandeis & elsewhere & the brighter, more active students have all formed a kind of united point on these matters that reminds me very much of the Communists in the 1930s. It's funny that it goes together with a complete skepticism, cynicism, ridicule, & hostility toward American policy, as in Frank, at the same time being very understanding, charitable, forgiving, & permissive with the Chinese, with Castro, with the Vietcong, with the Russians. Reminds me of the Spit-on-Daddy Club I talked about at Brandeis when I got mad at the *Justice*, the militants & the so-called "liberals" who follow like sheep, in flocks.

Meanwhile they all go on creating chaos by destroying the police, by pulling the rug out from under law & stability with sit-downs that goad the police & make them look either cruel or ridiculous & that make them wary of "sticking their necks out" by arresting Negroes or even criminals. (The judges don't back them up; nor do the liberals; nor does the ADA or ACLU who reflexly think of them as Cossacks—I may quit these organizations.) I keep telling the students this is all pre-Fascist; this all helps the next Goldwater or McCarthy (& sooner or later a really smart one will come along). Mussolini & Hitler & de Gaulle, & I imagine many other dictators (good & bad) were preceded by waves of strikes, the breakdown of law, police, government, democratic politics.

One real & true source of honest conflict & confusion is the outworn concept of natural sovereignty. Is this sacred (& therefore U.S. should never go into Santo Domingo, etc.), or is it nonsense? Well, at the moment it's not settled, & isn't even recognized as an inconsistency, which makes sensible & real solutions quite impossible. *One* thing that's needed is the transcendence of nationalism, regarding it as a transitional problem, which has very different importance for various peoples, & for the less mature & more mature people. Anyway, I've decided to get into the World Federalists, become pro-UN, & the like.

The whole discussion becomes species-wide, One World, at least so far as the guiding goal is concerned. To get to that goal is politics & is in time & space & will take a long time & cost much blood. (I'm not certain that it *will* come, but I am certain that it *must* come or *else* there will be WW III—& after *that* there may be nothing much left.) That's maneuvering, compromising, spying, fighting, bargaining—all in the D-realm. But the description of the far goals & of the principles & values involved—that's the platonic, Eupsychian, B-realm job. And that's what's missing still. All the "freedoms" talked about in the UN are either "freedom from" (rather than positive goals) or else refer mostly to lower-need gratifications or to preconditions for growth (like freedom of information). But what to *love*, to *worship*, to be dedicated to, to get religious about? To struggle *toward* rather than away from?

I wish we could manage something like a UN trusteeship-caretaker-educational government for primitive nations, or for those that are just post-Fascist, like the Dominican Republic or Cuba, or like Haiti, Guatemala, Ghana, when *they* break their dictatorships. Such a caretaker government could immediately start training for democracy & self-government & give it little by little, as deserved. This is a realistic combination of the Marxian version & the humanistic. (Better add to definition of "humanistic" that it also means one species, One World.) The hierarchical nature of human motivations & of social development is also taken care of this way. (We don't apply the same laws, duties, privileges, and rights to mature & immature individuals or societies, to adults & children, to SA persons & to crippled, stunted, diminished individuals or societies, to brain injured, to those reduced to the concrete, to feebleminded, to seniles. They all have the same *rights eventually* or in principle—or, better said, every newborn baby does in principle. But we know that humanness can get diminished or lost altogether.)

Only a world government with world-shared values could be trusted or permitted to take such powers. If *only* for such a reason (which includes avoidance of wars à la Congo) a world government is necessary. It too would have to evolve. I suppose it would be weak or lousy or even corrupt at first—it certainly doesn't amount to much now & won't until sovereignty is given up little by little by "nations."

Also, I keep wondering about the necessity of "philosopher-kings." I suppose not. It's probably better to have philosophers *without* power, like a high-IQ Peace Corps, sages, wise men, advisers, teachers, atheistic priests & ministers. [*I must look up what the Quakers mean by "having a concern." Is this the same as "ultimate or universal patriotism"? Or anything like it?*]

As for U.S. policy, I believe that on the whole it *has* been guided by good ultimate values, altho sometimes in a bumbling, confused, & conflicted way. (We too have plenty of Fascists to be heard from, & with lots of power, so we get into internal conflicts & mistakes à la Eisenhower, Goldwater, & now quite possibly in Santo Domingo, altho there too I'm not sure.) I think principles of this sort have also been mostly guiding the British, the Scandinavians, the Dutch & Belgians, & a few others here & there. And so I'm on their side, politically, i.e., in the D-realm, without attributing or expecting perfection. So I'm—in this world—pleased with the U.S., proud & devoted & *quite* grateful (supposing my father had stayed in Kiev?) for my good fortune. I am *within* the culture, part of it, identified with it, a reformer trying to improve it, rather than one who is outside it, rejects it altogether & despises & hates it!

June 9

Much troubled for a long time by the political problem in my theory—that is, the relationship between a beautiful ideal & practical politics in the D-realm.

And I think slowly it's been crystallizing for me into the difference between being a father, a responsible boss, an authority, an executive or administrator charged with actually constructing something real from the ideal blueprint. I think I despise these jerks because I know so well that they can play the adolescent game by avoiding authority and responsibility. (Or, if they *get* authority, then they become "fathers" & *tougher* ones than usual.)

Partly it's like the Beckett story—the role shapes *you* into its shape. Just as the presidency improved Truman, Kennedy, Johnson—they grew up *into* its responsibilities. So does bosshood & being a chairman, etc., *force* D-politics. There are no ideal bricks, nails, planks for the builder—only actual ones which must be imperfect.

Every son fights his father. And then he himself becomes a father & changes into a repressive force necessarily, a controller, the policeman, judge, punisher, a stabilizer, a restrainer of impulse freedom. And he learns the advantages of stability, order, politeness, reciprocity, etc. I guess the only way to discover fatherhood and its conservations is by experiencing fatherhood. Until I became chairman, I too could play adolescent at Brooklyn College and be against committees, dates, schedules, organizations, laws, rules, etc. But the intrinsic necessities of the role of chairman taught me much.

June 29

What is the good friendship? No one has ever described it. I want to eventually, I told Harry, partly for personal reasons (my shock & depression over Frank's leave-taking, my failure to *recognize* Charlie Kaufman in the hotel lobby, & I could have mentioned many other disappointing friendships). "What is a real friend?" I asked. And I told him about my confusing Ellen when she was in her teens because I loved her & accepted her totally but she thought I was blind & she was fooling me; i.e., she was a faker & I was a blind man. I tried to tell her that I did in fact see her realistically & was aware of every one of her faults, but that I accepted them & made no fuss over them & didn't care about her having faults. (I wrote about this—the B-perfection & the D-perfection—in my book in the chapter on dangers of B-cognition.) To see someone with absolute realism & then to swallow the whole package deal—that is love & that is friendship. It's a kind of total commitment or "being hooked" or buying the whole package deal or imprinting. It's to be totally involved, crap & all. This is like our attitude toward our relatives & toward the nondivorcible partner—you just make the best of it without even *thinking* that way (because that pleasing implies the possibility of nontotal responsibility). As in the Italian picture of the Sicilian father. His daughter was forever his daughter, fully, completely, irrevocably, irreversibly. He could never cast her off—that's not possible whatever sin or crime she might commit. My brothers are my brothers, no matter what.

All these love & friendship relationships are possible without any idealization of any unrealistic kind. I could know Frank well in all his nooks & crannies & then buy the whole package. We must remove the taint of unrealism, distortion, blindness, denial, from the definition of the true friendship or love. It accepts the real & is perfectly aware of it. No halos necessary.

There is an additional quality of indulgence (which is a little different from acceptance), of forgiving, of understanding instead of scolding or disapproving. Joy, or at least pleasure, in the company of. To be with a friend is intrinsically & finally enjoyable & worthwhile, per se, & not as a means to any end. Even eagerness to be with. Missing him when he's not around. A goal object toward which to strive.

(This is getting peculiar! What's the difference between this & love? Is friendship love without sex? Is there any other difference? Also, the same question comes up with B-love & how to differentiate it from respect, from admiration. I can say equally well that I love or respect or admire Abraham Lincoln or Wm. James. It's possible for sex to be there without anything else, neither love nor friendship, respect nor admiration. I remember one subject who hung on to her insane and despicable husband just because she needed his excellent penis very badly. There was no substitute available.)

July 16

On plane to Washington, D.C. Strange coincidence. The Ethics Committee of APA has Dick Alpert up on charges. He asked for me & in a weak, dutiful moment I consented. Feeling badly (virus?) last 3-4 days, so had half decided not to go, with illness as excuse, until this A.M. when I read the transcript, documents, etc., & it suddenly dawned on me that part of this affair is a struggle over the nature of science, & partly Alpert & Leary are being charged with "not being scientific," i.e., in the orthodox mode. I think, in part, the question is of freedom to change the *definition* of science and scientific method. Just what I'm doing in my science book! So then I felt I had to go, partly because few people would understand this point (so it's not likely that there would be easily found a good substitute for me as I had first thought). Second, it will be useful & interesting & maybe very instructive for me & my book. I have 2 hours flying time, so thought I'd use it to comment on the documents & see what reactions they raise in me. Partly, this would also be good preparation for tomorrow's hearing.

1. Part of the trouble was dealing with subjects' experiences, rather than behavior. Naturalistic observation rather than "research design."

2. p. 9 of Exhibit H: "I think both of us had done good research, & if someone disagreed with our research strategy, it seemed inappropriate to attack us as being inconsistent rather than questioning whether or not we had moved to another kind of strategy. . . . We needed unique methods to handle the data (& to elicit them too)."

3. Difficulty with languages to describe the subjective experiences.

4. p. 26; McClelland said "The more Leary & Alpert took the drug, the less scientific they became."

5. p. 28: "Keeping a clean shop." "Transcendental notions may produce" behavior laxity, i.e., change him away from being a good scientist who keeps a clean shop. Alpert replies (p. 29) that this is like psychoanalysis in that it involves the "way of approaching research." "It's conceivable that this research has, indeed, changed our perspective about which is suitable human research. . . . what we do is humane & moral in the broader sense. If we ask now, does it conform to research methodology [of the normal sort], is it acceptable?" "The unique problems of dealing with experimental data demand unique research methods." "Insight . . . which has led us to develop new models for doing research." "I'm interested in how it's changed my philosophy, my orientation, my way of proceeding with research." "The public concern is primarily motivated by fear."

One main charge against Alpert is violation of the APA Code of Ethics, & as I examine it I see that the prevailing outlook on science has even been built into the Code of Ethics. Never noticed this before. For instance, "modesty, scientific caution, & due regard for the limits of present knowledge." The committee agreed that "exaggeration, sensationalism, & dogmatism are more accurate terms to describe Alpert's statements." [*This applies to public statements, I see. Makes a difference.*] Of course, that's just what I also accused them of & got angry about. If I'd been in McClelland's place, I'd probably have done what he did.

August 1

Ann said a few days ago that Jerry Kaplan was a wonderful teacher, Socratic in style, & could get her to understand something without offending her. That I, on the other hand, was "of the podium." I thought about it, & it seems correct, & explains a lot, e.g., huge successes with my lecturing but *not* with small classes or seminars. One reason I gave up doing therapy—I couldn't be patient & wait for the patient to see it for himself. I had to tell him. I suppose this too is a reflection of the arrogance of a smart & creative man. I just can't suffer fools gladly, & "fools" means *too many* people who bore me after a while, so that it irritates me to listen. Also, besides not being the Socratic type, except with very intelligent people or people I have affection for there is the very high level of aspiration or ambition, or whatever it could be called. It takes the form of being impatient with the one-by-one approach—I must affect thousands or millions or the whole human species.

That, too, I guess, was a reason for not being a therapist: I've got big plans for the whole world, so I can't spend too much time on individuals—& certainly not on cripples & inferiors—& most certainly not if I don't even like them. Guess I like to spread my message around.

In a hurry also because I have more to write than I'll have years for writing. Life-span too short for my plans. I'll die not completed. So can't "waste" time. Also, easily bored with stupid or even average people, even when I like them.

Same example I've used before, often: "Supposing you suspected you had a possible cure for cancer. Think how your life would change & your values & tactics & strategy." Well, I think I have *better* than that. I'm working on war & peace, on Utopia, on revolution, on changing the world & improving the human race. That explains a lot. (And my job is a hell of a lot more urgent too.)

August 3

Holiday Inn. Good fruitful conversation over breakfast with Bertha about science & the clinician, much of which I think I can use in the science book [115]. We were talking about Harry Harlow's remarkable films of the relation between monkey babies & their nonmaternal mothers. These caused a great shock of discovery as I realized how profound the clinging to & the need for the mother are. No matter what cruelty or neglect from the mother, the baby ceaselessly tries to cling to the mother, almost like a leech. Well, this has been overlooked in human babies because they can't cling & grasp & follow. They're physically unable to. But it certainly set off in me & in Bertha an identical reaction. I remembered my clinging to my rather casual-tho-kind father, very much like the monkeys. (I have no memory of expecting anything from my mother. *This* tie must have been broken early, so that I don't remember *ever* expecting anything from her, & not trying to get it.) B. remembered vividly what it was like not to have parents around.

Well, this great, stumbled-across discovery of Harlow's: I now remember, years ago at the American Academy of Sciences conference on progress, how enraged & bitter & condemning Erik Erikson was over Harlow's "cruelty" to animals. He thought of it as all useless because "we know all that already," meaning we clinicians. He acted like one of the outraged ASPCA people, at *any* researching with animals that might hurt them. Harlow doesn't really "know" anything until he's demonstrated it, & was awfully hurt by Erikson's personal attacks & simply couldn't understand them. He felt virtuous & deserving (look what he had discovered or demonstrated). That's a good question, too, to use for the science book for Erikson: his intuitive "knowledge" felt so firm that he needs nothing further, & science for him is really meaningless, a way in which blind men get to see the truth indirectly [& *prove the obvious*]. His "findings" & writings are all intuitive, global reports of his personal impressions (like much of *my* work of the last 15 years); he needs to go no further. But his work is in a cul-de-sac unless someone else experiments & researches. In his own style, no real progress is possible, maybe not even great "discoveries" (because at best his "discoveries" are really affirmations of personal belief, further unsupported). They are hypotheses with very low status as fact. But he could look at human babies experimentally & not see what Harlow, tho less intuitive, was able to discover by comparing monkey babies with human babies.

Another question was raised by the Harlow experiments. Erikson thought them cruel & therefore unethical. Attitude of the clinician = the patient first, absolutely, & to hell with the advancement of knowledge. Because of this, Genia stopped my insurance research. She was so afraid that there was the *slightest* possibility of harm to the Brandeis students, if they found out some were pushed as healthy & some not, that she refused to cooperate & I gave up. Such a loss. This experiment would by now have been finished, & we'd *know* if healthier students had more efficient perception. This crucial experiment was thrown away. The advancement of knowledge was given zero weight against the far possibility of hurt to a student. This is almost an absolute.

August 8

It is quite possible to love *without* overestimation. I think healthier people would. They can love actual human nature as it is, just as they can love nature as it *is*, without prettying it up, or dogs (without making them cute or anthropomorphizing or without proof or pedigree), or babies (even tho they're *not* bright & can't be shown off). I think that all the prettifying of human nature (to make it conform to our a priori essence) indicates an inability to accept human nature as it is, with all the "evil" too. (This is a tricky thing to say, because much of human nature e.g., sex, sibling rivalry, etc., has been arbitrarily defined as evil. This is part of the nature of the word "evil" itself.) And also the "instincts" have been arbitrarily assumed to be evil—that's part of the *Weltanschauung*. Part of therapy is getting to *like* human nature in ourself & in others & to accept it & finally wonder "Why did people think this—sex, etc.—was evil?" As with Ellen, I loved her almost, it could be said, *because* of what *she* considered flaws; that is, for me they weren't flaws anyway. Just in the same way as, so often in therapy, we find that it is *exactly* what is *most* charming and lovable & characteristic that he's been repressing & trying to hide from us in order to keep our love = the patient's assumption "If the therapist knew what I was really, secretly, like, he would despise me," while the therapist sees it all the time & waits patiently for the patient to let it out bravely & in order to be honest with the therapist, bravely taking a chance on a full confession driving the therapist into fleeing in disgust. That's a sign of real love for the therapist, i.e., of being unwilling to fool him & to take his punishment rather than to continue fooling him.

Human nature (taken raw & without being cooked in order to be edible, or taken naked without the necessity to clothe & hide the nakedness) is & can be lovable! Isn't psychotherapy a kind of nakedness, & doesn't the therapist get to *like* the person better as he unclothes himself? So I think the more we know about actual human nature, the more we are going to like human nature. Men will be able to take it straight, like whisky without water, or oysters without cooking, or like being able to look at the sun directly without sunglasses.

August 13

Plane to Newark. Going to visit Synanon outfit on Staten Island. Figure out why? I've had a feeling for some time, ever since *Manas* first told me about it, that there's something *generally* important here & that it is for more than curing drug addicts. (1) First of all, it raises for me the question of the "dark night of the soul," of symbolic death before rebirth. These people have hit the bottom of the barrel. Is this a necessary prerequisite to rebirth, to real honesty & bluntness? (I've often wondered if SA is really found only in older people just *because* they're old enough to have made their peace with death.) Some of the existential philosophers are saying just this. Is real maturity or real living possible only after one has died in some fashion, or is it *one* path only to illumination, B-cognition, dropping of defenses & "games" & planning into the future (instead of living in the present), ambitions, etc.? (2) My guess from what I've read is that real, blunt, tough candor is *the* leading thing in Synanon, & maybe that's what we can learn from it. Also that people can take it under the right conditions. (3) Part of "the right conditions" is experiential-knowledge of the cures. They've gone thru the same mill, & the patients know it. Why should this be so effective, or maybe even necessary? That's to be worked out. *Very important!* Same for Alcoholics Anonymous.

August 14

Plane back. *Very* remarkable experience—much learned, many questions. Probably would have stayed on if I had the free time. Like learning something about the whole invisible underworld I've never seen.

I was astonished by the rough, direct bluntness, the "no-shit therapy" attitude of the leaders (former addicts), ripping away defenses, scornfully pulling away pretenses, politeness, formulas, evasion, & lies. Like punching everybody in the belly. But it's *honest,* & they all seem able to take it & even to like it. The truth gets shoved down their throats instead of the Freudian waiting for people themselves to discover the insights in their own time. Psychoanalysis seems to assume that people are brittle & sensitive, while Synanon assumes they're tough & prefer straight, tough honesty. The scorn for social workers & psychiatrists is thick.

It's a kind of educational institution, maybe a *model* for the colleges. Supplies all basic-need gratifications, enculturation training, training in mature responsibility, a ready-made group of friends, a set of "square" values, good leaders. An oasis maybe, rather than a backwater.

August 15

More thoughts. I was told that in drug addicts the father is usually missing, actually or psychologically. No model. It is a failure primarily of masculinity? Only 10% or so are girls. Do they suffer less from absence of the father? And therefore from the mother who is also father—and who thereby easily becomes a castrator or treats her son almost like a lover, as a girl loves her doll? The mother I saw yesterday was beautifully evasive about her son & clearly was indulging him, rather than sternly educating him. (You can give heroin thru the tit also.) They told her bluntly that there was no hope for her son unless she threw him out & got stern. And then she commented on the beautiful view from the window. Castration is not exactly the right word here; it's more like "infantilization" or "keeping her child" & fearing that if he got strong & adult, he would not need her, love her, cling to her—that he might then go away and she wouldn't be a mother anymore. So, in effect, she supports his habit in order not to become the obsolete, useless, unneeded woman. I was told many such stories there, but *seeing* her & her son evading cure, lying, resisting, was something else again. Same for all of it. I've read enough about Synanon & its ways. But seeing & experiencing? No substitute for that.

I thought also of my value-fact paper [95], with the sure & decisive & uncomplicated perception of oughtness that is intrinsic to the sure certainty about the facts. The leaders were like dentists or surgeons in their drawing out of pain, ridicule, contempt—even shouting down the resident's efforts to talk, etc., because they themselves had been addicts, they could *experientially know* & be certain & therefore decisive & harsh & pitiless. In a peculiar way, this must have been what Socrates meant when he said "evil comes only from ignorance." I could say it the other way about: "From the sureness of knowledge—& ultimately only experiential knowledge can be certain, and sure—come swift decisions, stern, strong, unambivalent action."

The leaders are decisive because they really *know*, they're sure, like the dentist & the surgeon (but the latter not from experiential knowledge). Easy competence & "right" action out of knowledge. Factiness tells them exactly what to do, so they can exert full force, without fear or holding back, when the pain is necessary, intense, fruitful.

These are the answers to questions I came with: (1) Yes on "dark night of the soul" stuff. Both residents & leaders said it. You have to hit bottom before you really commit yourself & before will is broken, etc. The applicant had some inheritance money; they simply assumed he wouldn't commit himself until this money was all spent & until his mother threw him out. I was told to call this "hitting the bottom of the barrel" rather than "dark night of the soul," which means something else.

(2) As for the "death & rebirth" idea—yes! Their ceremonies & tough hazing & initiation ceremonies are very much like initiation into manhood in a separate culture or fraternity. Ethnologists should be interested.

(3) Is real honesty of this kind possible *only* after the bottom of the barrel, death & rebirth? Why is honesty so difficult & so infrequent? It seems to me to be very easy. Am I fooling myself? On reflecting, I don't think so. But then, how about others? Why do I *get* this kind of honesty from so few, even tho I think I'm prepared to give it & to take it? This would be one good reason for returning to Daytop & being a member of a group. Then I'd really find out. Individual analysis is not the same. I've thought also about joining a T-group when I can. I got the feeling that the residents were not afraid of me in any way, not deferent, etc. I think they could very easily be blunt with me as with each other. In the discussion, they seemed to me to speak very directly & bluntly, altho without pugnacity.

August 27

"Finished" 1st draft of science book [115] today. Actually achieved this by shaking myself loose from my original outline, which would have taken me another year or two. I was trying to write the book I had planned, & then it occurred to me I didn't have to write *that* book. So I shifted the whole "plan" around to fit with the pieces I had actually gotten written. I looked them over & made a "plan" after the fact. I can understand better now how I've gotten stymied before & how many others must have too. Once you've made a plan, *that's* the book. It's hard to see it as heuristic, as a temporary scaffold to throw away very soon.

This is part of the urge to completeness, comprehensiveness, all-inclusiveness. My files got bigger & bigger & finally overwhelmed me. The upshot was that I haven't even *looked* at the thousands of notes I have, & instead of being architectonic, like Kant, etc., I just wrote one scattered piece after another as the ideas hit me, jumping around all over the outline. These added up to more & more pages. A few weeks ago, I saw that I had enough words to fulfill the requirement of 25,000, so I started dropping chapters out of the plan one after the other. In other words, I "wrote" the book by progressively lowering my aspiration level, which was too damn compulsive & obsessional. I put all the scattered pieces together & with correcting, editing, & smoothing the transitions, which will take me another week or two, I'll have a very different kind of book than I had planned—a discursive, contributions-toward, lecture-type book. Changing name from "Psychology of Science" to "*Toward* a Psychology of Science." Preface will explain & apologize. It will be *samples* of a point of view, not a complete structure. But that can be just as good. It was the same with the religion book [102]. Also piled up huge bibliography which I never got read, huge piles of notes, etc. *Had* to meet a deadline, so overrode all the obsessional tendencies, & now when I look at it, I think it's fine & can't even remember what kind of book I had *planned* to write.

A psychodynamics of intellectual life ought to stress *this* aspect of perfectionism, which has lost us much good work, I'm sure. Fight against urge to cover everything, to be complete, to cover every single good idea you ever had, or good quote. Don't try to answer every question or solve every problem. We must free ourselves from the encyclopedia picture of a good book.

September 12

Keep running across one misconception of SA that I can correct & will. It could have been stated less dramatically as a real respect for individual differences. Good Society = permission for full development of individual differences. The woman problem is easy: individual differences is the answer. Some women will self-actualize via maternity, others via business, others via science. Why not leave them *all* alone? The thing is to be able to do as you wish (covers both females & males). Be what it is in you to be = express your real self = respect & accept your own instinctoid nature = actualize yourself. (But be careful not to obliterate commonalities, specieswide similarities; e.g., *everyone* needs to be loved, & here the individual differences are far less important than the similarities.)

But then the question comes up today: but supposing you don't want anything. Supposing you are bored & played out. Do what you wish to do = you want to do something. Wantlessness (valuelessness) of course is at the conscious level & covers over deeper basic needs which are really *not* fulfilled. Why then are they repressed or rejected, especially in the overindulged (commonly called overloved)? But the love has to come from a respected one (& these parents are despised, so their love doesn't mean anything). The elders must be respected. If not—at least this *seems* to be true for the youngsters I know—then the gratification which must come from elders & from them only is not forthcoming. A nongratification of needs. See Mexican paper [75]. Elders mistrusted means real trouble for the young.

October 17

Utica. Have been saving all sorts of notes to write up, but just haven't felt like writing for weeks, nor like reading anything taxing at all. Played out. But when I mailed off the science book ms., I started feeling better, more relaxed, better sleep, feeling gayer & happier, etc. So far, enjoying trip.

Saw good movie tonight (*Darling*) & want to save thoughts. One was the need for a concept of levels of love (rather than either/or & rather than just much or little). The girl in the film *really* loved, but it was immature, lower-level. She got bored easily. But it was sincere, low-grade. Wouldn't last. Not deep. Not B-love, etc.

Other thought is: we need a concept of "levels of sickness" too (rather than just sick or healthy & rather than much or little). The girl in the movie (Julie Christie?) was not very sick, but yet sick. Also add discussion of boredom, need for stimulation & kicks (*any* kicks rather than *no* kicks). Boredom in this case is a lack of inner resources & a need for outer stimulation. The inability to withstand this lack of "something to do" for any length of time. Means also some redefining of "impulsivity," *away* from the implication of strong impulses & toward psychopathic *lack* of impulses. This girl in *Darling* is sleeping around but says explicitly that she's not interested in sex.

Add *restlessness* (inability to sit quietly or just do nothing for any length of time); childish & immature, starting & not finishing if there are any difficulties or blocks, i.e., very quick losing of drive & impetus; shallowness; easily satisfied, i.e., with less than the best; lack of depth, i.e., superficial. (In the movie, excellent example. Now she is rich, married to a prince, & on impulse starts redecorating rooms & leaves it all in the middle, loses interest in it.)

October 24

Saw drunk on street of Grand Rapids, looking cold, lonely, & going no place, rootless. Reminded me of my feelings after Daytop Lodge, that long addiction was a flight from a kind of depression (boredom, anhedonic, lack of zest or interest in life, going no place, having no place to go, no feelings, peaks, emotional climaxes). If depression is described as endlessness, an empty plain, nothing to look forward to, a flatness without hills, no ups & downs, then this sounds horrible & practically anything would be better. What *would* one do if faced with endless boredom? One would do *anything*—anything at all that would break up the monotony, make a change, give some differentiation to endless time.

Therefore *any* excitement, any thrill, any emotion would be a welcome change, or any forgetfulness of the horror of endless nothingness. Hence the barbiturates on the one hand (forget, sleep, be unconscious) *or* dexedrines (stimulation, excitement) on the other. Also LSD, alcohol, morphine, marijuana—these give an improvement of consciousness (over boredom, grayness, & emptiness), & I can understand why they would be taken no matter *what* the future cost to be paid for the present surcease or lifting of consciousness, because what's so good about the future in such people? Their state can be defined as "having nothing to look forward to," so unconscious consciousness *now* is free, so to speak, without cost (since there's no loss in giving up a future zero). If *I*, having a rich future, something to look forward to, am told that smoking or drinking will bust me in the future, then of course I'll give up pleasures today for the sake of greater & safer pleasures later on. But supposing I'm to die within a year. Why give up smoking or drinking?

Add to this discussion the constitutional factors of the baby born cheerful (I think this is the greatest single blessing I could wish for a baby). The Eupeptic. Contrast with the colicky baby, or the sick one ₐho cries all the time, or pukes up his food, or can't sleep. Hard to love, a la David M. Levy, who points out that a cheerful, smiling, clean, good-eating baby is very easily loved even by low-maternal women.

What are the constitutional factors that encourage the im-poverished conscious? The lack of zest, enjoyment, cheerfulness? The easy-to-grumble & slow-to-enjoy syndrome, the St. Neot margin, the nay-sayers? It must be pluralistic & complicated, with the time dimension involved, & all sorts of feedback circuits. This is another way of asking about nonpeakers— anyway, it overlaps. Understanding nonpeakers would help to understand the impoverished conscious. How about the IQ? This must help. High IQ means curiosity in everything = interest = caring (in contrast with the not-caring of the impoverished consciousness or the low-grade anhedonic, who is hard to stimulate, who is stimulated by almost nothing. Everything & anything can stimulate the high IQ. (Is he then less susceptible to depressions of the clinical sort? As I remember, IQ makes no difference in psychotic depression.

The alcoholic (or addict type, or bored kid, or immature type without "inner resources"), so bored & empty that he must *be* stimulated, must look for "something to do," *anything* to do, some action. He must look for excitement, thrills, kicks, risks. Even to the point of courting pain or death.

Often it looks as if this kind of recklessness & taking of suicidal risks seems to make the equation: having strong emotion of *any* kind = feeling alive & "nonbored." Perhaps even strong fear is better than no emotion (apathy). Perhaps this is like the sadist-masochist for whom ordinary life, ordinary sex, ordinary meat & potatoes are not stimulating enough to prevent his slipping into boredom, impotence, loss of appetite, loss of pleasure.

November 4

Waiting outside a junk shop in Mo. More notes on the weakness of the liberal. As we talked about Lindsay's election in N.Y.C., the question is "Could he be tough & strong?" For instance, if I were in charge of education there, the obvious thing to do is first to clean out the bums & restore order & discipline in the classroom. In order to avoid "hurting" 3 or 4 bums in each class, the other 35 kids are deprived of education. Everybody's afraid of "hurting" the crooks, the delinquents & so give up *all* law & order. Actually, of course, the most educational & therapeutic thing one could do for these nuisances is to be tough with them (in a discriminating & effective way). The thought came to me that I could parallel all this with Synanon "toughness," which really is a refusal to be conned & which therefore is appreciated by the addicts (because it is a form of being understood & cared for & worried about). It's a frightening mistake for the liberals to allow this kind of toughness & firmness & sticking to limits to be monopolized by the rightists & fascists. Buckley in N.Y.C. election, a very bright guy, made a big point of this & got a lot of votes because of it, I think.

The liberal is weak & ineffective often because he is afraid to use force, to punish, etc. They identify strength with fascism—as if democratic people couldn't be strong. This in spite of the obvious lessons about the awful things that happen to the kids of weak or indulgent parents, or parents who are afraid to be unpopular momentarily with their children; they are then conned & manipulated by sulking, whining, weeping, complaining, & therefore earn the contempt of their children.

December 4

In his speech, Jerry Bruner says "Learning has always been at the heart of psychology." Not so, & explain why in "system." The needs of the organism, its directions, vectors, goals, desires, and ends, are far more basic and explain more. Without a self to be discovered & shaped & enculturated, learning would be a shaping from nothing of a tabula rasa (as indeed the behaviorists imply) & then *would* be the heart of psychology. But if there is a self to be discovered & actualized, then learning is an auxiliary, secondary, helping process, & not de novo, but always is or should be Taoistic (yielding, sensitive, adapting itself to the material to be shaped rather than arbitrarily shaping by fiat). If there is a self, then learning & teaching can be a *danger* to the delicate self-*Anlage*, by forcing it out of shape, by shaping it in violation of its own nature (aptitudes, needs, capacities, interests, genius, different constitutional forms). It can twist & distort. It can be an enemy to the biological self.

Contrast them as arbitrary (willful, fiat, overactive, shaping, interfering) learnings vs. Taoistic learning. List all the different kinds of learning, starting with the most important ones of discovering the self & actualizing it, including learning the skills it is best suited for (like practicing to become a good musician), learning to hear the inner impulse-voices, & learning to differentiate them from the integrated voices of authority. Learning to hear the voices of real reality in its own nature, e.g., a sculptor "learning" how to be respectful of the grain of the wood or of the stone. Or of learning to listen to the voices of other people, i.e., to let their unconscious speak to our unconscious, or even to learn how to be receptive, how to be a good, noninterfering listener. How to adjust & adapt in a harmony with nature, with animals, with people, with one's own self. [Calling this "learning to be human beings"—since all the potentialities are there, learning how to actualize them.]

December 25

All excited again about Synanon, kicked off by letters from Dederich & Quinn inviting me to visit their homes in Calif.—which I'll try to do. Also reading Yablonsky book, & the thoughts keep tumbling about in my head. It's all so revolutionary in so many ways; I want to save the ideas, maybe to use in some way.

One is that the complete paraphernalia of science & of scientific medicine & psychiatry all failed with drug addicts while Dederich succeeded. The implications for philosophy of science are very profound. I have some of them in my science book, for which I'm very glad (been glad I had the courage to write the Synanon section even tho I had no real "knowledge" & wasn't "sure" about anything). I think a study of this case history & others like it should be put into the science books, to teach how courage, bullheadedness, fight, trust in one's own beliefs, faith in one's intuitions, the ability to fight off the whole world of authorities—how these can succeed where the orthodox physicalistic model totally fails. Dederich is the great discoverer, the inventor, the hero—not the timid ones who wouldn't stick their necks out.

1966

January 7

A lunch (Palace) yesterday started question with Mike Murphy of privacy at Esalen. I'd be too shy or reserved or inhibited or whatever to go thru the "happenings" & the expressive dancing, & acting out my dreams à la Perls, or experiencing my emotions. I couldn't do it & neither, I told him, could the elders, Murphy, Rogers, Allport, et al. Is this a matter of taste? Reserve? Privacy? Or an inhibition to get rid of? This question then led to: Must I love *everyone?* I don't! Or be friendly with everyone or be "free" under *any* circumstances? Be intimate with anyone? It was my thought that this just can't happen if a person has taste, & if he chooses & discriminates. The person who can screw with *anyone* is proven thereby probably to be not able to give himself totally to sex with one intimate person. If you're friends with everyone, you probably can't be a really deep & good friend to anyone. Really good friendship takes all you've got—lots of emotion, involvement, time.

This all ties in some with conversation last night with the 2 (Episcopal) priests on celibacy. I remembered how, lying all alone on the work table at Italian Frame Co. when I was a sophomore at C.C.N.Y., reading Sumner's *Folkways*, I had a great feeling of dedication and oblation. This was what I wanted to be & to do, I sort of swore that I was going to. Something like the religious ceremonies of vowing & of offering oneself on the altar. And then I wanted to do it totally. I remembered how I had tried to get a job as night watchman so as to be alone for my studies. And the repeated fantasy of getting locked in a jail & working there where nobody could bother me. This was a total dedication, & it turned out to be mutually incompatible with total love for a woman. I didn't feel it at the time, but in retrospect I could see last night how 2 total-love commitments could clash. If I had not been so in love with Bertha, I *might* have been a celibate, or at least not totally committed to a person, or at least I can understand why so many of the great philosophers chose not to get married. To love a woman totally *and* to love your vocation totally is a kind of bigamy.

I don't think this ever bothered me. I could manage the double loyalty, but I was hard on Bertha. Maybe only the German *Hausfrau*, like

Freud's, who specifically subordinated herself to her husband's work, could really manage this. And every time I got into a fight with Bertha, as I protected my work against her incursions, in the ensuing coldness, split, & depression, I couldn't work very well anyway. Have finally worked out the pattern of double loyalty which works pretty well. If Bertha really needs me, then I'll drop my work. And also, there are plenty of times when I'm not working or can't work, & then I'll put myself at her disposal. Meanwhile all efforts to fuse the 2 worlds have failed, & it's best to keep them separate. I go off to my "work" alone. And when we go off on vacation, then I give it all to Bertha & keep my work out of it altogether.

January 10

Weekend very enjoyable. Lecture in Grace Cathedral OK. But B-language workshop was a fantastic & insane failure. Taught me several things en passant. (In this P.M. session I simply withdrew altogether & said not one single word.) (1) My values & interests & methods—as a producing & creative writer & thinker—are quite different from those of every single one in the whole group. They don't know how to work, how to progress, how to collaborate. They quibble & change the subject & get no place & blocked me off entirely without any better alternative, & the whole business came to nothing. My fury has been mounting & mounting to the point where I don't dare open my mouth for fear of the violence that would come out. (2) Simple, plain, old-fashioned IQ is a wonderful thing, & there wasn't much of it there. (3) What there was was frustrated by the obsession with here-now experiencing (which most of them can't do anyway)—"What are you feeling now?" Which naturally got no place. Especially since the few who *could* talk about their experiencing were also blocked off & interrupted. This gets close to anti-intellectual resentment of concepts, words, labels. (4) Must have a strong chairman or else an old fool like Fritz Perls takes over. He interrupted not only me from the very beginning but everybody else, & nobody was willing to shut him up. Mike Murphy should have done it as the host, but didn't. Perhaps what I should have done when my lecture was interrupted & rejected for another plan was to leave the meeting altogether.

For another, I'm getting more & more to acquire Bertha's taste for privacy, for selectiveness among "friends," for a little more formality & politeness. I enjoyed Esalen at first—very much—but the last few days I find distasteful, too far-out in procedures, to the point of self-paralysis. I'm less enthusiastic & less attracted (of course, by now I'm extremely tired & want to go home to a cleaner, more sensible world). If I could call off the rest of it, I would, & leave for home at once.

Another thing: these people, supposed to be psychologists, are *against* science, rationality, & language. (If they say they are against language, why did they come?) They have *no* idea of research or interest in it.

One good thing anyway was the B-massage I got from Mollie Day & Storm Wilkerson & the body awareness from Bernie Gunther & Gia Fu. They say I'm very good at it except for stiff neck, unable to relax properly.

January 14

Flying home. Great turmoil of impressions & no chance to write them down. Will take time to sort them out. Think about these:

(1) The B-massages, especially, the first one, led to profound passivity, feeling like baby in hands of mother, timelessness. Compare with passivity after gall-bladder operation; quick adaptation to naked-ness; different kind of eroticism, serene & slow & mild (suggested these techniques be taught to all husbands & wives & that sex come after long period of B-massage; also for obsessionals, frigid & impotent men & women; as B-technique for getting passive, timeless, ego-abdicating "delicious helplessness," etc.). Also the body-awareness stuff which I'd better fold into my proposition 1 somehow. This is part of finding the real self, the biological core, identity, etc. Discovering one's body, or being helped to become aware of all its parts and articulations to make it more intricately & completely structured, & to become more aware of the stream of impulses which we ordinarily pay no attention to.

(2) I enjoyed the "weekend" format, & apparently it was a huge success, but I hated the "workshop," which was a complete failure so far as its stated purpose was concerned—altho it had many useful, fruitful by-products. The scolding, denunciation, & "lecture" I gave them the last A.M. before leaving is to be transcribed & published by Tony Sutich. The big lesson I learned was how difficult it is to work with professors & intellectuals. Essentially I'll have to do it alone. Very few people are able to play intellectual basketball of this kind. They tend to jockey for domi-nance, etc. Also, I've just learned from Dederich that it's very difficult to discuss with a "strongman," & I don't really like fighting my way into the conversation with the loudest voice winning. It was just like a faculty meet-ing with nothing getting done. But also I wasn't used very well at the Synanon evenings. Chuck was too driving & dominating & not really able to listen. IQ not high enough, as also with the others—Yablonsky, Garrett, et al. Henry certainly higher—much higher—& even so I often felt not quite understood & rephrased things more simply. Henry seems to do better when we're alone. The audience lowers his intelligence. My 180-195

is just too high, & I keep forgetting it. Must have no illusions about "working with" people, or discussing, collaborating, etc., for real high-level work. Best for me to be alone. All I really get from audiences & discussions is an insight into their misunderstandings so that I can communicate better in the future. Sometimes, as during the weekend, they *do* pick a real hole in my thinking. But this is rare. It's mostly consumer-satisfaction & understanding surveys.

As for Synanon, also a turmoil of impressions. Most important one was meeting Chuck Dederich. He *is* Synanon, & everybody else takes orders. He's the most powerful human being I have ever met personally—dominating, absolutely overwhelming, driving. A force of nature like an earthquake. A 5-star general. He could very easily be president of the U.S. & do a good job. Or, better said, a general of the armies (he's no politician). I never heard him say "thank you," or express gratitude or humility. He's certainly a "great man" in the sense that Napoleon was, or de Gaulle. He's like Lyndon Johnson. Absolutely blunt, candid, uncompromising. Completely self-confident and impersonal. Yes. I felt that I had to go along with him & his opinions or else make war. So I probably will disengage myself from Synanon, or else go to one of the other houses. I don't want to make war. Neither do I want to be one of his stooges. It was funny that, as he gave me the Synanon Club gold buttonhole pin, I was reminded of the woman who gave a souvenir to each of her "tricks," or of the man who kept a snapshot of each of the women he had screwed. Like a badge of ownership. Also, I was conscious of having been finagled & shanghaied into testifying at the trial. In effect I saluted & said, "Oui, mon general" because I was happy to do it—even honored. But it rankled that he might think he had forced me to.

February 11

Gallup, N.M. Start new file on vulgarity. TV & radio thru most of country have irritated me more & more. Why not approach this as a scientific problem? Perhaps define it, dismember it, & maybe eventually work with it in some fruitful way. Maybe we could teach people how to recognize it, & maybe then they'd avoid it.

First thoughts: call it a value pathology, a muddling & confusion of values, loss of hierarchy of higher & lower values, basic & expendable, or important & unimportant. Radio newscaster (Paul Harvey—he's one of the worst) in one item reports deaths in Vietnam & in next a boxing kangaroo. The one desacralizes the other. That too is part of it: desacralizing can be a form of vulgarization, like using Lincoln in a brassiere commercial. Also, what is lack of taste? Looks as if there are different kinds of vulgarity. Eventually these would have to be called by a specific name.

Vulgarization of word "love" on the radio, with all the idiotic songs by people who obviously have no idea what it means. It's like a moron playing with a Stradivarius. It's too good for him.

February 16

Parked at International Bridge, Del Rio, Tex. See B-language file for "killing time." Bertha feels guilty for "wasting time" & "holding us up" as I urge her to shop to her heart's content. I gave her my little lecture, repeated for the thousandth time (& not listened to for the thousandth time), about "richly-filled-with-pleasure-time" is *not* wasted time, because that's the point of the whole trip. If no pleasure, then the whole trip was senseless.

February 24

Perry, Fla. Set thinking last night by TV show of N.Y.C. Vietniks, peaceniks, etc. Reminded me of the Marxian days in the 1930s. Same people, same types, & I think also very much the same psychodynamics. On my mind all day while driving. I think I'll label the file "anti-authority," altho it's much more & much else than that: immaturity, child-adult war à la adolescence, a stupid way of growing up to be a man or a woman. The adults are identifying with the youngsters instead of with other adults. Like Jim Klee & Dick Neisser & Ken Feigenbaum, who felt closer to students than to professors, i.e., really feel like kids rather than like grown-ups—like so many of the patients Harry told me about, who dream of being small among the giants, or little pricks among the big ones, who look out at the world like Saul Steinberg's rabble peering secretly out thru the eyes of what looks like an adult male. J. is *afraid* of power figures or of forceful characters like Frank Manuel. Part of it is trying to be popular with the underdogs rather than with the overdogs—*feeling* like an underdog, identifying with them.

Some parallel with the "we-they" dichotomy of the prison underworld that Yablonsky describes for the drug addict. Somehow all the bosses, the authorities, the police, the judges, the army officers = "they" (the Establishment, the rulers of the earth). And the prisoners are "we" against "they," the intrinsic enemies.

Also like "labor vs. bosses" (we-they), as if bosses were *born* enemies & couldn't help being anything else, as if this were fixed & eternal, as if the roles were hereditary. Or like the Negro-white split among many Negroes & many whites, who bristle at each other as dogs & cats do.

One of these types—the soft liberal—simply can't stand force, aggression, punishment, violence in the world, & so has to be against soldiers, police, etc. These are the ones who must be permissive, who try to love everybody, who in effect have no standards, & who make weak, inconclusive, indecisive fathers, husbands, teachers, citizens. They try to be popular with everyone, to be loved by all, & so are unable to be in firm opposition on *any* point, & are unwilling to fight for any principle—only *against* the authorities, especially if this is popular & done in a crowd. These were the "liberals" of the '30s who felt guilty before the decisiveness & single-mindedness of the Communists, & fought them only when it was quite late & then feebly & ineffectually. People like Gerry Haigh come to mind, even tho he's not quite right as an example. He claimed once that he had never felt anger!

March 4

Part of this liberal problem & anti-authority is that liberals & "nice people" think of anger as itself bad or evil. One reason they think human nature is bad or evil is simply that people do go into rages & will attack out of anger. Quakers, Unitarians, ministers try not to get angry. Ministers are not supposed to get angry.

So there is a chronic repression & suppression. Plus a lack of preparation for expressing anger or handling it or meeting it in others. This is one job the psychologist can help with, i.e., teach that (righteous) anger is desirable, even sine qua non.

[In Palm Beach, great wealth & great selfishness. What happens to theory of basic-need gratification producing higher personality? Why does wealth make some people more altruistic & others more selfish? (1) Most of these didn't earn it & don't have the self-confidence of the successful man who is not frightened by possible loss of money. If he earned it once, he can earn it again. But these Palm Beachers (DAR, John Birch Society, etc.) secretly know they are incapable of earning. (2) Lots of money doesn't necessarily mean basic-need gratification. Money makes it easier in principle, but not necessarily,

& *also has lots of real disadvantages; e.g., if someone says he loves* you, *is it* you *or your money? Paranoia of the rich. Money is certainly not a sufficient condition, not even a necessary precondition. (3) We should have a strong inheritance tax, out of* love *for our children. To earn them lots of money is to castrate them & cut their real self-esteem (like leaving them crutches instead of teaching them to walk). (4) Money can buy only the lowest basic-need gratifications, background & safety, not higher ones of belongingness, affection, self-respect, SA. Indeed, these higher gratifications may actually be threatened by money. (5) These bastards must feel not only anxiety but also guilt at unearned money. These reactionary political activities are Freudian defenses.]*

March 6

3 A.M.—reading Rilke's *Letters to a Young Poet*. He speaks (p. 34) of what "can so unexpectedly become big & beyond measuring," & it reminded me of the peculiar state I got into over buying the Navajo rugs. It was senseless because I have so many, & it was rash because they were too expensive, & it was all against common sense. (I think we bought about 11 altogether & finally didn't dare to look at any more & to expose ourselves to temptation.) Well, what does it is that if the rug—or any other object—is beautiful enough, I suddenly slip into a realm beyond counting, measuring, costs, etc. It seems then to have nothing to do with price. It then doesn't make any difference what the money price is that is put upon it, because *it* seems transfinite & beyond costs & money, out of the realm of relative value. *Whatever* it costs then seems trivial, or even irrelevant. It was just like that when I first saw the river beyond my house. Suddenly, it didn't matter *what* it cost. The beauty couldn't be measured or counted or priced or even compared with anything. Nor could the rugs then be compared with each other. In Gallup there were three rugs, & we got them all in spite of trying to pick only two. How could one pick 2 out of one's 3 children? This reminds me again of the good way I expressed myself to Mollie & to Storm at Esalen about the massages: "I can't compare one sunset with another. Each one is perfect. Each one is the most beautiful there is. I love each one infinitely. Each one is best." And one could say this of people too. One could say to *various* children or girls or friends that *each* one is the most, the ultimate. Hedy Lamarr *was* the most beautiful woman in the world. So was Greta Garbo. So was Ava Gardner. And so will others be. Each will be *the* most beautiful woman in the world.

April 22

Reading White's *Making of the President, 1964*. Fascinating. But horrible too. And as I read about the Negroes, about morality, etc., I feel that I have part of the answer to all this basic perplexity—I & Walter Weisskopf. [*Bob Hartman? Bert Gross?*] I would think that I (we) should write it down in simple form & then publish it.

First write about the really basic need. It's *not* money, auto, wealth, TV, or boat. It's dignity, belongingness, feeling at home, feeling brotherly & identified, accepted, etc. Money *can* help, but only as a means to *these* basic ends. And they are what every person has a right to. [*Self-esteem = bringing in individualism, freedom to choose, etc., = training in hardships. Training = pride in self. To get stuck on the means & forget the end = idolatry. Also need for structure, firmness, law, order, predictability, mutual expectations, & court. Put this also in terms of the "meaning of life." The only way, apparently, to keep the sense that life is meaningful is to be striving for something. If what is being striven for is the wrong thing, then attaining it can produce breakdown & meaninglessness. If what is being striven for is the right thing, then attaining it should mean happiness (& not disillusionment or disappointment) for some time & then the emergence of higher needs into consciousness. And at the metaneed level, gratifications are endless & can produce happiness without sating, because there are so many different gratifiers, e.g., need for beauty or for truth, etc.*] So I will have to speak about fixation at one gratification level of objects & of safety instead of going on to a higher need. Point out that it's easier to get gratification of these basic needs in Synanon than on Madison Ave. Talk about fraternities, religious groups, or other clan or family or small-town, face-to-face groups. Lack of intimacy in U.S. Multiversity vs. small college. Loss of extended family. Discuss at each of the basic-need levels. Use Walter's stuff on moral economics, on fallacy of G.N.P. & continued economic growth & piling up of objects & things. The life of the B-values (or call it the value life, the spiritual, higher, metalife, transcendent—none of these labels is quite right). Write about the value pathologies at this level & call them "frustrated idealism."

April 26

Still easily stimulated by "motivation & politics," by "adolescents in politics," etc. Perhaps will work it up some. It slowly drifts into the shape of "how to integrate & fuse the B-realm & the D-realm." So many of the youngsters who imitate me are demanding the perfection of the B-realm *immediately*, & it will take them decades to learn about the *slow* revolution, about the necessity of "politics," of getting what you are able to get, & of purposefully maneuvering thru the present realities of power & of possibility & probability. And yet also *I* must learn to understand & accept &, if possible, to *love* the impatience, the idealism, & even the impracticality of the young. Their rush & hurry & unrealistic expectations come essentially out of ignorance, but absolutely *unavoidable* ignorance. They see that shit is shit, & they can't understand why simple enthusiasm, activism, & teamwork shouldn't clean it up at once. This is a kind of simplistic thinking which, in the *child*, is very understandable & endearing. If I were less irritable, I might be able to think of 20-year-olds in the same way. I know I *can* because I don't get mad at Ellen. There I can "understand" it & accept it. Maybe it's because she's also working at PPC [Poor People's Cooperatives], of which I thoroughly approve & for which I'm very proud of her.

[*B + D = Don Quixote + Sancho Panza. The B-realm is the realm of "freedom now," of "perfect & instant justice," the real & witnessed & experienced possibility of loving everybody. And one can see how* easy it is in *principle for everybody to love one another, & it is true that this would solve all our problems. And in this light, how* stupid, blind, insane, vicious & *self- & other-destructive is, e.g., race prejudice, so that one is appalled & aghast & unbelieving in its very existence (in same way that it is still impossible to "believe" that the Nazis really existed & ran the camps, & that the eyes looking at the pictures refused to take them in & are unable to assimilate them). Or that to see people shooting at each other or dropping bombs is so* weird & crazy *that one angrily shouts "Stop all that crazy nonsense this minute, do you hear?" In a word, if we couldn't see the B-realm, there would be no adolescent impatience, no adult indignation, no impulse to improve, to mend, to therap, to teach. Sancho Panza, reduced to concrete (almost), accepts everything as it is to the naked eye. The impatience* proves B-vision.]

May 6

Various thoughts about improving society & then decided to keep it all in revolution file. It could be—*should* be—a big book if I had the strength & time. For instance, speak about the basic-need gratifications & the metaneed gratifications, which are the real "needs" of the people & the proper goals of all political & economic effort, & all other social effort as well. This would also be the place to list all the sociotherapeutic techniques

—T-groups, Synanon, communion groups, intimacy groups, Esalen-type retreats & self-education institutions, Bodhisattva groups. All the self-therapy & self-transformation techniques. All the efforts at helping others to help themselves & be responsible & autonomous (& attack on responsibility-killing & castrating techniques & institutions à la social work). Come to think of it, why don't the social-work associations have any legislative & political & economic programs? Why do *they* not criticize the enfeebling techniques?

Also, changes in the laws to punish more heavily psychopathogenic crimes (that kill trust in others & that create mistrust, suspicion, etc.), like crimes by hitchhikers, or telling the gray lies on TV that make everybody cynical eventually, trusting no one, or feeling *everyone* to be phony. [*To minify, depreciate, lessen, disparage, enfeeble, besmirch, coprophiliac, necrophiliac, the asshole interpretation, the proctological view, denigrating, the mean view, desacralizing, reductiveness, "nothing but," debunking; reducing to a lower level, paranoid, to "dirty-fy," the lower interpretation, diminishing, belittling, debase, to shrink, degrade, befoul, blacken, nigrify.*] (I'm sure the authority-rebellion of the young—"Don't trust anyone over 30"—is partly fed by our advertising mores & the political mores that *expect* any pressure group to be selfish & hypocritical, like the AMA & the druggists who push *anything* that's advertised & sell not what they approve professionally but whatever is advertised heavily. Or the lawyers as a group who are definitely handmaidens of the rich rather than of justice.)

May 15

Thoughts on humanistic "religion" mixing in with other categories: B-psychology, sacralizing, etc. The words "revere," "worship," "adore," should be made humanistically respectable, I was thinking. Certainly, in the love-sex relation that's obvious. I remembered the little "shrine" I set up at Cornell in 1927, with Bertha's picture & a couple of lighted candles before it, & my feelings as I sat before it, which I would now say in retrospect were very clearly "religious." And then I feel like taking the offensive position, on the opposite side, & saying "This must *always* be so if there's any real feeling at all; I would have been abnormal if I *hadn't* felt that way." Same with sexual experience. The person who *doesn't* sacralize it is lacking something in his makeup. Or before new-born baby, or sucking at the breast, or before the erect penis. The woman who felt nothing before this awe-inspiring sight and phenomenon must be regarded as crippled. I think it will soon be possible to write candidly about this, & also to do research on it. Demythologizing has gone too far (desacralizing), & now it's time to resacralize the female, the male, sex, etc., and then to say it all in the context of humanistic religion. Sacrilizing is really *unitive* consciousness; it doesn't mean Protestant-type soberness, humorlessness, antagonism to the body.

Concerning rituals & ceremonies, how about the first menstruation & the first brassiere (as I did with my kids, or *tried* to—they were too embarrassed), 1st ejaculation; kisses could (should?) be less frequent & more sacral. Use example of the way in which too much music around me all the time has finally taken all the kick out of music, of the autonomic kind I used to feel.

Ask question: "Whom do you revere? What? No one? Isn't that too bad—you must be sick." Certainly we revere dead heroes like Lincoln, etc., but why not people before they die? Why not be conscious of the little element of worship, of adoration, of genuflection, of bringing of offerings?

May 16

Reading *Walden* &, at my time of life, completely reinterpreting Thoreau, whom I have always admired. It occurred to me as I read that here is the ultimate Pratychabuddha attacking the Bodhisattva & his way of life. Where are his woman, his children, his intimate friends? I get the picture now of a man unable to love or "do good," masturbating away full-time at Walden. Also, of a man who works out a totally selfish & personal-salvation way of life, forgetting that this is in a way a kind of exploitation of others who are less selfish, like Emerson. He has contempt for the people who manufacture things, but then goes and borrows an axe, buys the nails & the boards for his cabin. His way of life is made possible by other people living in a different way, like Goldstein's soldiers, who could endure, even tho reduced to the concrete, only because other people who were not reduced so could do for them.

That would be OK if he were not so contemptuous. That's like the steak eater despising the butchers. Same for the civil disobedience which is so badly & dangerously used today. I think the activist kids today are proving how dangerous Thoreau's ideas were. Society is a technique for *transcending* individual conscience, which speaks differently to different individuals, a technique for making sure they don't kill each other. This ultimate reliance on the voice of one's own conscience (how about Hitler's individual conscience?) must be exposed again & again as dangerous, unless it is supplemented by validation, by pragmatic consequences, by science. Again, this is the critique of experientialism-solely.

May 21

Going thru Schein's *Organizational Psychology*, & the last chapter on criteria for successful organizations seems to be purely (almost) value-free & technologized. Could make a good example to use to show how *all* social institutions must have Eupsychian goals or purposes or effects, or else they can be used by Nazis or other evil men for evil purposes. Call it amoral social psychology, valueless, or what? Could use as an object lesson in my Utopia class. Here they try to treat the organization as if it were a machine (& therefore neither good nor bad). But if society is in the first place defined as having the function of fostering SA for all, then every part of society has same function or goal. Machines have no goals; social institutions do.

This is also true, I realize, for the various technologized definitions of psychological health in terms of, e.g., effectiveness (without specifying for *what*). I guess something of the sort also applies to the TV & radio demoralizing. The moral or ethical goal seems to be *sine qua non* if the machine model & technologizing (making into a pure amoral machine) are to be overcome.

If we say that wages or pay or rewards, or whatever a perceptive union would try to get, keep on being defined in terms of higher & higher need & metaneed gratification, & that a successful business in a time of affluence & full employment & shortage of skilled top people must use these "higher" wages & metawages to recruit good people in order to stay in business, then this is the same as saying not only basic-need gratifications but also metaneed or B-value gratification. But this means that you can't be value-free or amoral, since he gets *paid* in morals, i.e., truth, beauty, justice, order, law, perfection, etc., etc. Even the pure technologist, whose *only* question is to make a profit, must ultimately have to give moral & value satisfaction & not dare to turn out a fake or harmful product or even an ugly one (at least in principle). Then this itself transcends the polarity between moral & amoral. If one of the wages is the opportunity to do good? Or to rectify injustice? To do things better? To create beauty (including mesomorphic beauty? This is what rewards the

M.D., the good lawyer, the scientist, the novelist or painter. Why not also the manager, the foreman, or even the janitor?

May 25

I thought more about how the liberals & conservatives would be quite shocked at how tough I'd be with the rioters (I'd shoot them if necessary, even to kill if unavoidable—but only, of course, if the society were behind this & could take it in the political sense). I'd jail & punish all the civil disobedients. And for the ones who plume themselves on being arrested, I'd have *real* punishment, anything that they would fear & that would deter them, even if I had to change the laws about cruel & unusual punishment. The point is that punishment must punish in *fact*. I'd bind the society together at its bases for fear of chaos. This is prepotent to "liberties," to rights, to *anything*. The majesty of the law—if it can't be loved, then it must be feared. (Different procedures for lower class who won't be deterred by anything but fear, & for middle-class kids who after all identify with the law, & who can probably be deterred simply by "passing a law" & then backing it up.)

As for unemployed loafers today, in a time of shortages of help, I'd simply be willing to let them starve ultimately. Short of this, nothing will work. As with some, nothing will work ultimately but shooting.

Toughness in population control. Not everyone has the right to have babies or to keep them.

I'd heavily modify the 5th Amendment.

I'd grant the right to suicide, even in hunger strikes, etc., to individuals who prefer to die rather than to work & even doubt that I'd be much influenced by self-immolation as a fact or as a threat.

I'd definitely refuse to shoulder responsibility for normal persons & worry whether or not they might hurt themselves. I'd pay little heed to the maneuver of pseudohelplessness—"poor, helpless me—you'll have to see that I eat"—or the people who refuse to take pills or take care of their insides or drink themselves to death. Beyond a certain & definite warning, I'd let them do what they wanted to do.

I'd make new crimes of people who destroy or muddy the truth or other B-values, e.g., TV, advertising, movies, newspapers, psychopaths who feed on people's best impulses, fake claims, truth-in-interest bill, etc.

Jobs for all could come thru beautifying the country. Through helping & therapying all children & big sisters & brothers. Boy Scouts. Hospital helpers. Foster mothers. Nursery school. Local committees for value protection á la Consumers' Union.]

I think even Goldwater would be scared to go this far. On the other hand, I'd be just as blunt about the necessity for taking care of the 10–20% true incapables in the society, the feeble-minded, insane, etc. The 100% inheritance tax (for real equality for every baby born), the total Medicare, & the best education & psychic therapy for all babies would scare the death out of the conservatives, & they'd call me an extreme radical (correct!). Being authoritarian at the lower need levels of society (most of the "new nations") instead of politically democratic. In view of the events of the last few weeks, I'd now feel it better to turn over Vietnam to China, who would discipline them up to the point where, in a few decades, higher needs would emerge. Of course, the UN would be better, but it's now too weak. But for highly developed & economic democracies, I'd push toward philosophical anarchism.

June 16

I'd been thinking for a long time about the nature of proof, of evidence, of verification. The Cofer & Appley book irritated me to hell, writing off my motivation theory as "not proven." And yet, by ordinary standards, they were quite right. But "ordinary standards" meant for them experimentation, controlled, designed, "normal." *Only* this. But then, why was my motivation theory accepted by everyone, a "classic," reprinted by now 13 or 14 times, known to everyone, used in management, industry, political theory, education, & God knows what else? So far as all nonexperimental psychologists are concerned, *that* is the best we know or can say about human motivation.

Well, for one thing I had discovered at beginning of my Non-Linear summer that it was *silly* to expect to put the theory to the test in a lab or in a controlled experiment, etc. It is a big holistic theory about human beings in the life situation. How could it *possibly* be tested in a test tube? I realized that Andy Kay's factory was a laboratory test. And that's when I really got excited about McGregor & Drucker & all the rest. *They* were *really* putting my theory to the test. And they found it "worked" after "trying it out." And so did Jim Clark, & Porter, & the others. All enlightened business & management is based on this theory now, so *each* factory is another test & another lab.

But how shall I phrase this kind of evidence? That's what it is, & I think that's the word for it—*not* proof, or even verification. For one thing, each factory is a single case. For a normal & conventional design, you'd need hundreds of factories. So the reliability is low, & I certainly *cannot* speak of certainty. Or say "It is a fact" or "It has been proven." What shall I call it? Life-evidence? Which piles up one by one, but in which the person *within* the single-case life-situation can get awfully convinced, & go ahead & *act* on it as if it *were* "true."

That was just the way I weighed Freud against Jung & Adler, not to mention Clark Hall, or Dorcus & Shaffer. Freud felt right. I understood myself better. Puzzles of various sorts were unraveled. He called attention to things I hadn't noticed. He made me feel more perceptive, more understanding, more insightful. It all made sense. I could read my dreams for the first time. In a word, it worked pragmatically. And therefore *I*, testing his *Interpretation of Dreams* against my own personality, could have been considered a single experiment, or case, or whatever.

July 3

Did well yesterday, & so did the audience. Much impressed by their willingness, even eagerness, for metaneed theory [121] & its implications for patriotism, for the real (highest) goals of industry or creativeness or anything else. Talked of *levels* of creativeness & also of levels of motivations to creativeness, up to the B-level, when it becomes impersonal. I waved away the pseudotoughness of *"only* goal is profits" & added all the other goals: low, high, & meta-.

One very impressive thought for future theorizing & research: some products are so fine & delicate that they must have love in their making. Can't be done unless you love what you are doing. As in science, you must be absorbed, fascinated, committed, or else you do a lousy job or, at best, a pedestrian job. The highest creativeness demands, as a prerequisite, love for the problem & the process & therefore the product.

I spoke about my belief that most people in the U. S. are Boy Scout patriots, Bodhisattvas (along with the countervalues & fear of one's greatness & defenses against one's goodness; awe before the B-values, etc.). They all seemed to agree, & with some excitement. Even a few testimonial speeches. Certainly an anticynical group.

Long talk afterward with Bailey about his strong executives. We compared notes, & his data supported all my impressions except one: that they need a female confidante in their loneliness. He agreed on the loneliness & the need to talk freely, but for his men anyone would do who was not a competitor on the same hierarchy—a teacher, a father, an uncle.

I should have added also—of the big shot, the leader, the

success—the loneliness that comes from being rejected, regarded as queer or crazy each time he has a new idea, or whatever causes him to be shut off, maybe for the same reason that the great beauties don't have dates or whatever. (I'm thinking about 2/3 of our grad students or more; they have never taken a course or a seminar with me, & I'm the most successful member of the department, the big shot. But it's my impression that the really good ones *do* choose me. It's the mediocre ones who tend not to, or the very neurotic ones. This in spite of the fact that each single one who worked primarily with me was himself a success, published, did hot dissertations, & then got good jobs & are developing nicely. Do the others *prefer* mediocrity? Are they afraid of me? I don't really know. All I do know is that this is common for successes. I still remember that practically nobody came to Wertheimer's seminars but a few *top* people.)

July 15

Useful thought to work up: thinking about foolish tactics of Negroes & their rioting & burning, splitting among themselves, childish impatience, blaming everyone else & *demanding* manhood instead of developing it themselves, impotence, absence of leadership. Occurred to me that it's as if they had no fathers. [*Their unwillingness to listen to their "leaders" set me off on this. The mobs are leaderless.*] And then I thought of their rejection of the Moynihan report. Their antagonism to law & order, cop hating, special proneness to drug addiction, illegitimacy. Compared them with other immigrant groups who had it worse in some ways: *half* the Jews living were murdered, the Japanese put in concentration camps, the Chinese ghettos, etc. They all worked their way up in the middle-class style by trying, earning, sacrificing for children's education, helping each other. But *they* all had strong family grouping with one or another degree of patriarchy. They therefore learned frustration tolerance, patience, working toward the future, planning, controls on their impulsivity, group solidarity, respect for authority and discipline, for "fathers," teachers, and police, and willingness to take punishment when deserved. They became able to be fathers themselves & to enjoy responsibility. All these capacities the Negroes as a group have less of. They tend to be oral-impulsive, dependent, extrapunitive, nonresponsible, no frustration tolerance, no family or group loyalty, anti-authority. No good male models. Don't know how to be fathers, responsible citizens, etc. They tend to be whiners & to get things by throwing tantrums (to which Mother gives in & Father doesn't). See Fromm on father love & mother love in *Art of Loving* (?).

July 25

Picked up second-hand copy of Mumford's *Conduct of Life* a few weeks ago & last night, just for fun, started browsing thru it. I remembered how very impressed I was when I first read it & the preceding *Condition of Man*. Well, now I have to write him a letter telling him that I must have picked up much of *my* philosophy from him years ago, forgotten about it, & should now acknowledge this debt. The stuff on evil is especially good. It's really a humanistic philosophy-psychology book.

This chapter reminded me more forcefully—or made my "thinking" more conscious—of the way in which I'd write the SA model or the model-ideal person as sage + saint + politician (SSP?) (SaSaPo?). We must be able to get along in the D-realm, or else we become a different kind of monster. As a matter of fact, I guess that's one way of characterizing adolescent-adult differences—the adolescent "idealism" is an insistence on B-realm perfection & an absolute disgust with D-realm politics, tactics, & strategy. Adult acceptance of D-realm inevitabilities, which the kids perceive as *preference* for compromise, as *betrayal* of the B-realm. The fathers sacrifice their lives (à la Harry Golden) in order to take care of their family when they could quite easily run away & be rid of them, & then the kids are disgusted, thinking that the father *likes* to carry coal up 5 flights of stairs, or that he *loves* working 14 hours a day in his grocery store.

The ungrateful child: that's one example of a B-monster, of unconditional idealism. Mumford suggests that this is one reason for suspecting *any* saint or do-gooder. Maybe. I think a deeper analysis would have to take this into account in the countervaluing mistrust of virtue.

One other useful thought I had was on philosophy. *Here* is a philosophy book, & yet Mumford is not a professor of philosophy; nor could any such professor write such a book. Same is true for *Manas*, the best philosophical journal I know. "Professional" philosophy is almost useless, because it has tried to be one department among other departments, one expertise at the same level with any other expertise. Instead, any & every professor should be a philosopher or else not be hired. The whole faculty is or should be *The* Department of Philosophy. Anything else is like having *a* Department of truth, or of Beauty, etc. I remember I suggested to the Brandeis administration maybe 10 years ago (& tried vainly to convince Herbert Marcuse of it) that we should have a *Committee* of Philosophy, with a few professionals to read the great texts & the history, but beyond this to be composed of all those professors in any department who were in *fact* philosophers. No go! Still a good idea.

August 7

Long discussion yesterday with Dick Jones & Harry Rand, neither of whom really understands my point of view. Maybe I broke thru. They quoted George Klein approvingly in *just* the point that I think he got from me at the Washington International meeting several years ago—& quoted it as if I disagreed with it! So I tried to explain that epi-Freudian means that I accept all Freud's clinical discoveries & separate from these the metaphysics & the "image of man" generated by Freud—an image which is profoundly wrong: partly because he never really considered his clinical discoveries as "scientific," but kept on trying to "explain" them with cockeyed abstract theories which are today expendable; partly because he projected his own character into the explanations & theories; and partly because of his 19th-century reductive science.

"Theories" should be what I call "empirical theories," i.e., summarizing, classifications, organizations of the clinical data in their *own* terms (not neurological or chemical). A good example of such an empirical theory is "dream interpretation."

This is approximately what George Klein has been saying. This is what I said at Washington to Klein; i.e., let's stick here to clinical-empirical theory. There Freud is at his best. And I maintained further that this is *more* scientific than the reductiveness he was attempting. The metapsychology, etc., was a suit of clothes that just didn't fit. Also, I made the point that a man can cover himself with any one of an infinity of clothes. (Maybe this is a better example than the "infinity of parallel languages.")

But then all this heated talk led me to crystallize further & to discover new truths as I listened to what I myself was saying. First I made the big point that I didn't like Dick putting me down as a self or ego psychologist. I am a biological psychologist, basing myself on "instinc-toid" theory—& the others don't, not even many of the orthodox analysts. (But I don't think this broke thru to Dick & Harry.)

That is this: that I react to basic-need & instinctoid theory at the clinical & phenomenological level, i.e., of feeling & experiencing them to be raw subjective fact, like a toothache. The need is *felt*. It is a subjective demand, yearning, need. The need to love someone is *not* a construct or an intervening variable. If I instruct correctly as a clinician, I then experience this in the others also as a very profound, basic, irreducible pressure from within human nature. This is like the inner "voice of God," as distinguished from the inner "voice of the devil" or voice of neurosis or sickness, & I think they are *in principle* distinguishable once you've listened to them both. And even today, the person with the strong self, the healthy or self-actualized, has no trouble differentiating the voice of his true, intrinsic self from that of some evil fantasy.

August 11

Sitting waiting while B. antiques, & reading about the horrible Nazis. The contrast was very great with the rosy possibilities I was discussing at Orono. History & current events, what with riots & prejudice & greed, certainly *must* make my lectures sound like rosy dreams & wish-fulfillments, no matter how often I warn that I'm talking about the best ½ of 1% & about what is *possible*.

But then I thought that the Nazis & the Negro haters & the German generals, etc., etc., were most of them not really "sick" in the ordinary psychiatric sense (& I'd call them mostly value-pathologies) &, even more important, that the theories of psychopathogenesis (medical & Freudian) that are used today do not account for the Nazis, etc. And then it dawned on me that I was implying at Orono another approach to psychopathogenesis when I turned the question around from how to account for sickness to how to account for non-self-actualizing. That is, why were people not healthy? Why did they fight the B-values? This is like accounting for stunting and diminution of the *person*; that is, why is he this kind of a less-than-whole person? And then this includes his *Weltanschauung*, his philosophy of life, his basic-characterological attitudes (about self, family, peers, society, nature, & supernatural), his theory of human nature, of the other sex, or who is a brother-human being & who is not, his concepts, definitions, his dichotomizing, his defenses against his greatness, against his growth to SA, against embracing the B-values, against his goodness. Then add his intrinsic guilt over betraying his potentials, his own best self, & not living up to his potentials or of wasting them, or of trying to be someone else rather than himself. Then all the countervalues: the fear of knowing, of goodness, of beauty, of perfection, justice, order & law, simplicity, etc.

And then finally add ignorance, stupidity, false information, & this is simultaneously a theory of pathogenesis (get a better name), a theory of evil.

August 27

Discussion with Harry over bad behavior of J. (son of a psychoanalyst yet!), which is fantastically self-centered. He's just not aware that other people have rights or needs. So he & his co-evils do weird things like psychopaths, not out of deliberate malevolence or sadism, but just out of childish selfishness. Standard pattern for one type of kid. It's as if his parents never affirmed themselves as human beings.

Is this evil? And if so, is it innate? Harry thought yes—that this is just the essential child, which gets trained & covered up & inhibited ordinarily as people grow up, but which remains "there" in some deep sense *under* the controls. I thought no, because it is essentially immaturity, lack of development & growing up. He's still a child.

And then I realized I didn't think of the child as evil. I forgive him his babyhood & childishness. This is an "is" which I don't condemn or evaluate. Since narcissism, selfishness, unawareness of others, is in the cute child, whose nature I accept & enjoy, then *it*, the behavior, is also cute. (Of course, I condemn it in J. On him it does *not* look good.) In a sense, this is the child's intrinsic nature. He can't be any other way. You *must* accept it. There is no alternative. In the grown-up there *is* a choice, & he is less than he could be, & is also less than he *needs* to be to avoid hatred & ultimate downfall. We may be indulgent with the child, but we won't be indulgent with *him*. He is ill equipped to get along with other adults.

OK, is this then instructive? This has to be worked out carefully because no simple statement is possible. (1) The Freudian pessimism (people may behave well, control themselves, & look nice, but underneath, in the id, the dreams, the unconscious, there is the raging animal, totally selfish, etc.) is too unrealistic. First it assumes that what is exposed in the schizophrenic, the child, the delirious, etc., is truly the same as what lies underneath all the time, instead of assuming this to be an operational product of sickness, like pus, which is *not* there in the well organism. (2) We have to remember that the good impulses are also repressed & show up in the dreams, etc., if you are willing to see them (as Freud wasn't). (3) We must work out the exact dynamic, motivational, & reality status of a free association, a fleeting impulse, a dream. Freud assumed the dream, etc., to be a kind of unmasking or debunking. If you *thought* about cannibalism, or had a visual image of it in a dream, or in response to a Rorschach test, then that means you want to do it; you have a cannibalistic impulse which you are controlling. I have never been able to swallow this. In the first place, I think everything & anything; i.e., I entertain all kinds of possibilities (I often have the dream with alternative endings, one after another, trying them out to see how they work). That is, I can *consciously* wonder about cannibalism, speculate on it, think of it as a possibility under certain circumstances; i.e., could I do it if I had to? I just can't give this the same status as a deep yearning, which is not an idle thought but a constant preoccupation. I guess I don't agree that every association, every slip, every thought, is strictly & totally psychically determined. There *are* true accidents. And there are Aristotelian-type associations also. My canoe which I now look at reminds me of the river & of canoeing. But I *don't* want to canoe. The association was not an impulse. The trouble with Freud was that, of the whole welter of associations, reveries, etc., he picked out only those that were scandalous at the time & just didn't notice the others. He definitely selected.

Quite clear then that the 3rd-Force psychology *needs* a theory & description of intrinsic growth, of the intrinsic nature of the organism. Failures in growth must be treated as, let's say, the embryologist treats them, i.e., as pathology, as disturbance of normally expectable processes, like a harelip or the like. The kidney grows thru three separate stages as I remember. If it gets stuck at stage 2, that's pathology. And so J. is biologically stuck, a failure of the intrinsic growth process (I don't know why) rather than being an unmasking of original human nature, a revelation of what we all really & truly are when we take off our controls & habits.

Work it out more.

September 15

Another idea on the hubris problem. Walking onto plane, I recognized a feeling of superiority over others as I walked to the 1st-class entrance, as if I were looking down from a height upon those below. Very hard to describe this feeling: as if I were better stuff, intrinsically superior, condescending, "kind" & "benevolent" (which can certainly express superiority), qualitatively different, etc.

The feeling disappeared as soon as I became conscious of it, replaced by feeling of luck & gratitude that I could afford the roomier seat & the little luxuries that go with it. This seems to be part of an ultimate answer—to replace superiority feeling with luck & gratitude feeling, not only for having more money, but also for having a sound heart or strong muscles or high IQ. This permits the feeling of realistic & actual superiority in capacity or money or whatever, & yet avoids the overgeneralizing which comes so easily & which is *not* true. One can keep the "healthy narcissism," as Harry called it yesterday, which is factual, real, & true, & which should not be defended against, & which is absolutely needed for good work, & yet not get *generally* snotty or grandiose.

Again it comes back to that old lesson I learned long ago in Cuernavaca: the danger is in thinking you *deserved* your good fortune.

I must discuss with Harry also the fact that calm acceptance of one's factual (limited, undeserved) talent makes unnecessary all sorts of external confirmations of this talent: medals, honors, applause, admiration, publicity. Of course, this makes some secondary problems, e.g., for me. The APA presidency is 90 % nuisance & duty, & only here & there a bit of pleasure. (I think ¾ of the pleasure came in the moment when I was told of my *nomination*, which was so unexpected, & just when I was expecting in fantasy to be thrown *out* of APA.) I think most people would enjoy it hugely, instead of feeling trapped & overburdened & tense. Most administrative work bores me, & I don't do it well. I'm just no good with details and routine, & my lousy memory makes it all worse. So I won't even do a good job. And I'll be working with people who *are* good at it & will make me feel slow & inadequate. And at a job I don't like doing. Everybody is happy about it but me. So far all I've gotten out of it is a chronic spastic belly & chronic fatigue. In retrospect, it's quite clear I should have refused the nomination. And if I can ever gracefully resign, I will. Whatever good my election could do for psychology in general, & for bucking up the 3rd-Force people, has already been done. The talks with Harry have made it more & more clear that I love my home & my work, mostly the reading & writing. So there will be less travel definitely, less public affairs, more peace & quiet in my home, less teaching, if I can manage it, less politics, less being the big shot, etc. (I was working so nicely at my metamotivation paper until I went off to APA. Since then haven't been able to touch it; nor will I be able to for some time.) And that's *far* more important than my job & my APA duties & everything else. And nobody else is doing it, & maybe nobody else *can*. How stupid & unfortunate to lay that aside for a goddamned office which is just a nuisance to me. Even the people for whom I accepted the nomination—the Jews, the Brandeis people, the humanistic people—all of these would have been better served if I'd stuck to my writing, in the long run anyway.

Well, what I started to write was that I had long ago decided to *avoid* the public eye & big-shot-hood because of the intrusions upon my proper work, & also to keep my head from getting swollen. Years ago I decided I'd had enough honors & offices, & decided to refuse more in future. This I've done nicely, avoiding presidencies of SPSSI & of AAHP, etc. Also stay away from silly or empty TV or magazine stuff. And also to refuse APA nomination if it should ever come! I guess my weaknesses sought me out in a crucial moment. Maybe I should analyze *them* with Harry.

September 20

Plane home. Talking at Esalen & to Bill Harman last night & the Canadian Broadcasting Corp. is crystallizing what I have to say into condensed form.

We're in transition from one age to another (from one *Zeitgeist* to another, one *Weltanschauung* to another). We're giving up the physical-chemical, objective, *value-free*, impersonal (with the centering outside the human being), mechanomorphic model, along with its accompanying epistemology, ontology, science, facts, knowledge, value system (coming from outside human nature & imposed upon it), religion (same, superhuman); fate & destiny also determined from outside; lower-need technological economics; value-free social work; lower-need accounting, descriptive sociology; purposeless education. Policy-sciences without a policy.

[*Materialistic science (physics, chemistry). Removing emotion as well as purpose, will, need, value. Lifeless, amoral, thing-centered. De-estheticizing of life, of science, & of all social institutions. See MacCurdy on associationism as antipoetry & antimusic.*

Picture of the scientist as sober, grave, unsmiling, unemotional, purely cognitive, rational, cautious, never making mistakes, not really in contact with human beings or with themselves, officially valueless, nonesthetic.

Leads to method-centering, interchangeable scientists, impersonal objectivity & detachment (removal of observer from the observed, with the implication that the observer is a noninterfering camera), positivism, the "expert," playing down of creativeness (& its wildness, silliness, craziness, play, poetic, esthetic), associationism, counting & arithmetic, removing quality from the world (Locke, Berkeley, Hume, Galileo), pure determinism.]

All this has failed. The solutions for human needs and aspirations do not lie within the nature of *things*—the most complete mastery over things, conquest of nature, production of things, economics of things (thing-wealth). There are no solutions outside human nature *for* human nature. The purported extra-human solution solved nothing, & anyway turned out to be only concealed, covert, repressed projections of human impulses, frequently the lowest ones. This is true for the religions, the politics, the economic panaceas, the logic, the mathematics, the sciences (with thing-sciences used as model for personal & interpersonal & social sciences). Even often true of arts (all of them).

[*Big thing is the search for values for the human being. This is what cannot be learned from thing-science or even from infrahuman biology. Even Bronowski's value system of the scientist is a study of a* human.

The basic distinction is between nonlife & life. But even infrahuman life cannot teach us what we want to know, because only humans can be studied as subjects *from within, experientially, as participant-observers. From the spectator study of animals, we cannot learn enough about ourselves, even tho they're better than nonliving things for this purpose. As for physics today, it may be coming to this same conclusion—that what they're studying is largely the nature of human knower à la Eddington.*

". . . no solutions outside human nature for human nature" should read "outside fully developed, higher human nature," because the a priori theoretical systems (Thomism, Marxism, etc.) come from nonpeakers *(nay-sayers, obsessionals, death-wishers, nonpoets in MacCurdy's sense & Coleridge's, people without an experiential base—like Marcuse? or Sartre? or de Beauvior?—or people without instinctoid impulse-voices or inner signals, people with empty & silent insides). That is where & when the highest & most intrinsic human values are perceived by the most highly developed individuals, under the best conditions & in their best moments, perceived within themselves & in the world-at-its-best, seen most perspicuously, & in emotional*

illuminations = good choosers = good taste. (But what can good taste mean to positivistic social science, except sheer indoctrination?)]

The wars, the bomb, exploitation, hatred, greed, the defining of whole peoples *out* of the human brotherhood (treating them as things & as objects), the depression, the Nazis, the fakery of the churches, the inadequacies of laissez-faire economics, of political democracy, of all philosophical "systems," of theory-science (which came to its total & final nakedness in the Nazi camp "experiments" & in atom bomb). All started to come to an end in 1914, when the whole establishment started collapsing.

The great transitional figure between this age & the next was Freud. He was loyal to the objective, thing-science model to the day he died; & yet, with the relentless empirical honesty of the scientist, he kept discovering the depths of human nature, thus destroying the old *Zeitgeist* & laying the foundation for the new *Zeitgeist* of humanism (altho not the whole of it).

[*Psychoanalytic ego psychology is in truth an effort to get out of the "id" blind alley. But it is feeble & not new, being mostly copied from Allport, Murphy, Murray, Bühler, & perhaps from me too. The academic psychologists had been making these criticisms in the '30s & '40s, but have not been credited. I remember arguing with Ernst Kris about my self-actualizing people & their healthy regressions, their* interest *in mystery, their ability to be pleasantly silly, etc. Did this lead him to his "regression in the service of the ego"? Maybe. Also Rapaport all thru the '40s knew everything I was doing & we met regularly. Also he knew the academic literature very well. These loyalists rejected the academic criticisms as well as the criticisms of Fromm, Horney, et al.*]

The new age which is already upon us, in the nonstatistical sense that it is the growing tip of mankind, is essentially the product of the turning inward to the self which has always happened when a culture started questioning itself & when the external systems & panaceas failed. *Inward* to human nature for the answers, because the external answers failed. And I could say also, when the establishment philosophies were not working well, to throw up the whole doubtful business & go back to the beginning of knowledge, & ask what in fact I can believe & trust & count on (Descartes, Kierkegaard, Nietzsche). Also, that we are now learning to go back to inner human experiencing as the beginning of all knowledge, as the beginning epistemology, as the basic bit or quantum of fact or knowledge, the centering point (rather than the objective, camera-eye, external-to-the-thing spectator knowledge of a thing, not from within but from without). We are learning to understand spectator knowledge of things in the light of experiential human knowledge, rather than the other way about. We are learning to understand the white rat through inner knowledge of the human, rather than the other way about. I am confident that we shall also understand physics, chemistry, astronomy, & mathematics in a great leap forward when we start to study them as essentially *human* efforts—that is, as special branches of psychology, rather than the other way about. Furthermore, I am confident that our unhappiness over the stuck-in-a-blind-alley nature of all the psychological & social sciences & their applied professions will disappear when they give up the effort to be mechanomorphic, objective, value-free spectator sciences, amoral & technological, & will embrace their rooting in human nature & frankly regard themselves as epiphenomena spun off by human nature for its own good—that is, when they get defined as being in the service of the fulfillment of human nature. (*Then* we'll get rid of amoral economics, of valueless & directionless social welfare, of technologized & "scientific" nursing & medical education, of psychotherapists who are confident "experts" & "professionals" like carpenters or dentists, or of politics & history & law as the study of who treats whom as a thing, etc.)

The new *Zeitgeist* is value-full (value-directed, value-vectorial), human-need & metaneed centered (or based), moving toward basic-need gratification & metaneed metagratification—that is, toward full-humanness, SA, psychological health, full-functioning human fulfillment, i.e., *toward* human perfection as the limit & as the direction. [*Use in Meta paper.*] Society is then seen as SA-fostering & can be rated as good or bad, healthy or unhealthy, high or low synergy, depending on the degree to which it fosters SA or fails to. By subsumption, then, each & all of the social institutions are definable in the same way & can be given a grade in the same way as good or bad, efficient or inefficient, successful or failing: e.g., education, industry, religion, politics, family, marriage, friendships.

It *revolves* around a new image of man, a new conception or definition, containing both the Freudian-style depths & a higher nature, higher possibilities, which can be actualized under the proper life-history & social milieu & conative history (of gratification permitting emergence of next-higher needs) [*by hierarchical integration*]. Human nature on this side has been sold short. This higher human nature is not in contradiction to human evil depths, but is a superstructure built upon this lower base. History, almost universally, has dichotomized this higher & lower, but it is now clear that they are on the same continuum, in a hierarchical-integration of prepotency & postpotency. The lower or animal nature is the precondition of the higher life & not its antagonist. They are not mutually exclusive. The spiritual life is a higher aspect of the body & is itself animal in nature (instinctoid metaneeds).

This image of man, this human nature, is found to have within its own nature a general structure of intrinsic or final values, which for the (life-loving) human being is intrinsically valid, good in itself, self-validating. [*It is perceived* only *by the life-loving peakers.*] This is a hierarchy of values on the conative & affective side (of basic needs & then of metaneeds), but not on the cognitive or motor or capacity side, where the principle is "It is an intrinsic good to express one's nature openly & in action & in use, to use one's capacities." (The question of controls, discipline, etc., seems to me at this moment mostly a question of Apollo-nizing the gratification & expressions rather than of renunciation or sup-pression.) [*Add the values-from-facts stuff. Also sensory hungers, preferred behaviors, constitutional bent.*] This is not a detailed set of answers to life's problem but a general schema of *what* is good for the fulfilling of the destiny of human nature.

It is also validated in the time dimension (*after* its intrinsic, self-validating, subjective, feeling-good validation), i.e., by science, by pragmatics, because all the consequences of moving toward SA are later found to be good for the individual, for his partners, for society, for nature, & for reality. That is, the gratifications of SA & growth values not only feel good for him, but also are good for his fate & future, & also for everybody else & everything else.

Though these values are intrapsychic & intraspecies values, they also appear so far to be isomorphic with the "values" of (or the nature of, or the descriptive characteristics of) nature, reality, etc.—which is not surprising, since nature selected, rewarded, & shaped human nature to be compatible with its own nature (at least not in defiance of it, or in contradiction to it) = isomorphic evolution. But it is also possible, altho I don't yet know how to express this well, that they fuse & become one—in the mystic fusion, or in the "good death." Which is also not surprising, since human nature is part of nature & is most harmonious with it when it is at its best, i.e., at its most "natural," & when nature is at its "best" (what does *that* mean?). Is this why the fusion & the peak are *like* a good death? Why does it always bring thoughts of death? Why *is* it a death in the sense that one mourns & grieves for it afterward, that it is felt as a death before rebirth? That the same B-knowledge & illuminations come from either peaks or desolations or "final exams"?

October 26

Thought while listening to Chopin & loving it: I've had much pleasure & delight from Chopin, from Schubert, & others whom I love to hear. *But* the *height* of the pleasure, & the degree of peakiness, was less than for Brahms, Bach, Beethoven, which were also awe-inspiring & "higher." The really big or high peak-experiences came from Bach rather than from Chopin, even tho perhaps I love (like, have affection for) Chopin more than Bach (for whom I feel respect, *Ehrfurcht*, etc.). Here may be a usable criterion against which to prove that the *St. Matthew's Passion* is "greater" than the *Forellen Quintet*: how high a peak does it produce? How far up the pleasure-word hierarchy does it go? Up to delight? Bliss? Ecstasy? Cosmic consciousness? Fusion?

November 9

I keep groping toward some kind of crystallization & generalization of this tantalizing feeling that I've been for some years on the edge of,
that truth, facts, insight, honesty, destroy the effects of falseness of
propaganda or advertising, of unwittingly being controlled by conditioning, by stooge effects, by unconsciousness, subliminal conditioning, posthypnotic sugestion (to *some* extent), operant verbal conditioning, false
impressions from experimental deception. [*Add the Asch-type stooge experiment. All you have to know is that they are stooges, & their power disappears immediately.*] Nobody seems to notice that the dehoaxing is expected to remove
all the bad effects & to lose its power altogether. Same for being fooled
by good acting, false front, convincing facade. Insights & facts not only
kill it at once, but negate all its effects even if they've been active for a
long time.

Truth is against the evil of hypocrisy—well, of many kinds,
maybe all kinds (?). Truth is curative & therapeutic if there's enough
strength to take it & use it. Truth is prophylactic & prevents & aborts
illness of all sorts. Truth is psychogogic (ontogogic) & is needed for growth
toward SA.

So many kinds of bad things, sick or evil things, must be afraid of
the truth & of honesty.

November 24

Have been reading Wheelis' *Illusionless Man* & puzzling over its
implications. He sees everything, knows everything, is able to do
everything, & yet it all lacks the element of emotion, of joy, of zest for
life, of exultation in small things. Are depression, zombiehood, etc., definable simply as the loss of the peaky quality in life? I know that I am
feeling low or dry or arid or empty when I can look at the river & see it's
beautiful & yet not *feel* that it's beautiful.Or look at Bertha & peceive intellectually "She is a beautiful woman," & yet get no kick or emotion or zest
out of it, & no impulse to *do* anything about it either. I wonder if I would
want to live on if life were like that all the time? It would hardly be worth
living as a kind of intellectual cognizing automaton. The emotion *must*
be there.

Don't go *too far* in this separation out of B-cognition from the
peak-experience emotion. Certainly the original ecstasy or near-mystical

emotion can die down to a plateau of unitive perception of B-cognition, *but* this must still have the element of happy emotion in it in order for it to validate life. Let's say: the autonomic nervous system must be involved, at least a little. I guess I haven't realized this enough or said it enough. Serene B-cognition *must* be said to have a *little* of the peaky quality in it, or else it has slipped over into depression, death, emptiness, zombiehood! [*Is all this definable as distance from the B-values = a kind of loss of "the instincts"? Tie anhedonic in with evil.*]

Serene B-cognition, or "postpeaky" perception, may lose its high emotional accompaniment as one gets used to the discovery, (is peak-emotion partly a sign of discovery of something new?), *but* it has definitely not lost it completely. It has *not* become purely anhedonic cognition; *that* is a death, a dangerous loss or emptiness. Make a sharp qualitative distinction between the two. At the point at which life & living cease to be enjoyed, at that point death begins. One is not living then. Living ceases for that period. Living must be defined in terms of itself enjoying itself. No enjoying itself = no life. No life enjoying itself = loss of wish to persist & endure in one's own nature. Cannot say that "All things (living) tend to persist in their own nature." When a living thing ceases "persisting in its own nature," i.e., ceases enjoying itself, it results in suicide, death, acceptance of death, the quick dier, the concentration camps. What makes life precious? Joys of living, life loving itself, Thomistic & Spinozistic biological narcissism of the living thing persisting in its own nature. Nonpeaking = death, or, at the very least, the loss of the life-wish. If I call this depression or boredom or anhedonia or nonpeaking or whatever, *then* we can predict drug addiction, alcoholism, not protecting oneself against death, smoking, gambling, desperately seeking for any real emotion, e.g., sadism, masochism, sexual crime, *any* crime, etc.

December 10

Have started back on the metamotivation paper [121] after so many months, & slowly getting back into the mood. Helped along by—of all people—Josiah Royce, *Philosophy of Loyalty.* He raises so many of the basic questions that psychologists don't seem even to be aware of, even tho his answers are inadequate. Anyway, he was groping toward something which we're much clearer about today. (Or maybe *I* am much clearer about?)

One problem I must work up more bluntly—my answers in lectures, etc., have been quite feeble—is the necessary one of differentiating the inner voice of neurosis from the voice of the authentic, real self, of Little Abraham from Dr. Maslow, etc. I must say candidly that this is extremely difficult, because ultimately the differentiation has to be phenomenological. In addition, it can be tested in time by its results, i.e., verified or falsified, & this is *always* the cautious thing to do even if one has already accepted the dictate of the inner voice & acted upon it. Add here to my Chatham point that I can be increasingly confident of the rightness of my impulses because so far they have almost always worked out well, *certainly* in the intellectual realm. On a simple statistical count, I could give myself an index of intellectual judgment & it would be *very* high, certainly higher than my clinical judgment, for instance. The decision can also be tested by logic, reason, systematic criteria. And finally also it must be synergic. But all of these latter criteria come mostly *after* the decision has been made. In the very moment of listening to one's inner voices & deciding on which to act & on which *not* to act, one must know which to trust.

All I can say is that they *feel* different to one who has known both voices, & then it's easy. The biologically sound voices seem to fit, to suit, to sit well, to have a rightness & a suitability & belongingness. The feeling is of recognition: this is *it*. This is for me. *This* is what I've been missing. This is what I was born for. A kind of love at first sight. The pleasant (or ecstatic) surprise of encountering reality, ultimacy, rightness. Like trying on dozens of shoes & then one is just right. Or looking thru dozens & dozens of fabrics for a chair & then one clicks & is just right & suitable, appropriate for the room, the other furniture, etc. Or the athletic youngster who tries out for every team & is good at all of them but who then discovers what he's *best* at, *great* at. Or the youngster who "plays the field" & goes out on many dates but who is suddenly struck by someone across the room & says "This is *it*" in a suddenly serious, sober, awed, quiet, even slightly frightened way. Or one who without warning finds a dance partner who is perfect for him. Or the poet groping for the exactly right word & suddenly *hits* it. It is like sipping at the coffee & finding it too hot & then cooling it down to "just right for you" while your wife heats it up so it's just right for *her*. Or the temperature in your bedroom with the double electric blankets, which can have different temperatures, for husband & for wife. There is always some feeling of *certainty*. Also of recognition, as of something missing hitherto, i.e., recognition that previously life has not been complete & something has been lacking—sense of completion, finality, climax, orgasm.

There is in it something of the sense of a true perception of something real, so that doubt & conflict disappear. As of someone searching quite purposefully for a hammer & then finding it. *Not* a matter of preference or taste, but of the perceiving of something that is real & that is there. As if working out a math equation correctly; it comes out right & you know it's right because you *see* the rightness, as one sees that one line is the same length as the other line. Or in matching colors. (No! Best to stick to the absolute rightness of perceiving the math solution. *That* is the subjective quality when something is just right. Or as in the mystic's illumination, the witnessing & staring at & experiencing reality itself so that nothing can ever convince him otherwise.) [*This discrimination can grow easier & easier with practice & with success & finding experiences that are consciously* used *for the purpose of self-teaching.*]

The false voice phenomenologically lacks this same sense of settling the problem of just-rightness, of certainty, of finality, of suitability. Doubt, uncertainty, conflict, uneasiness remain to an extent (but may be drowned & defended against, e.g., by hypomanic overenthusiasm). There can be intimations of remorse, regret to come tomorrow.

My feeling is also that the poor kids who keep on asking, in effect, "How can I know when I'm in love?" or "How can I know that it's really beautiful or *really* good or true?" They live, like the obsessionals, in a chaos, without any fixed points, no standards, no criteria—like the drug addicts, alcoholics, & other nonpeakers, depressed, bored, *hopeless* ones. [That's *what nonpeaking gives rise to ultimately—hopelessness.* That's *the ultimate (logically & psychodynamically) from which can be derived the boredom, depression, death wish, low evaluation of living & of life, cynicism, valuelessness, anhedonia, confusion, uncertainty, nay-saying.*

December 15

I think one consequence of the hierarchical theory of basic needs is a hierarchical or "levels" way of thinking about much else: politics, economics, religion, etc. It also implies a theory of personality levels. The adult fixated at the safety or love level is a diminished man & must be treated accordingly & *spoken* to accordingly; he can understand experientially only the language for that level. And I think this principle also applies to the law, police, judges, etc. I think it foolish to talk of law enforcement at the B-level for a diminished man, e.g., a psychopath or confirmed subcultural criminal, etc. For my part, I'd fight at whatever level my opponent set. It's ridiculous giving a "low" person the same laws as a "high" person. Supreme Court rulings treat everyone as if he were a Thomas Jefferson. I'd say the diminished person has fewer "rights" than the self-actualizing person. (For instance, all the new protections against invasion of privacy. Does a Mafioso define "privacy" in the same way as Justice Douglas? Does he have the same *right* to it?)

I think this is obvious if we think of insane or feebleminded people: do they not require different treatment than average people? Or how about extremely poor people, for whom food is a desperate necessity? Can I really ask them to be as honest, loyal, truthful, virtuous, as a prosperous man?

December 20

Good way of expressing the attitude of humanistic psychology: to study man as a cause, rather than as caused (as an effect, as determined, etc.). It breaks the determinism/free-will impasse, because this is a testable form of the question "In which ways is the person a determiner; in which ways is he a determinee, a product?"

Better the phrasing: the person is a subject as well as an object, an active agent, a *primum mobile*, a creator, a first cause.

"Man as an end" implies *some* of this, but doesn't communicate as well, has to be extensively explained & discussed. Suggested by Moravia's book of that title. We'll get it.

Use also the quote on p. 1 of *Manas*, Feb. 13, 1957: "Science deals with *caused* behavior, but the reality of human individuality is revealed only in causing behavior," etc.

December 27

Have been struggling for a long time with the basic life-functioning pleasures of just living, breathing, walking, sneezing, kissing, etc. In my files, it's now called "biopleasure" & also "zest" (following A. Myerson). Dissatisfied with both & have a long list of better synonyms, but none quite right. Defining it as the irreducible granting of body-pleasure, of "peakiness," i.e., the smallest discernible amount of ecstasy. So far, the best is "biological functionist." (Function-pleasure? Function-joy? Function-enjoyment?) The thing is, I absolutely need some such concept as a beginning for experiential psychology. Otherwise there is less meaning for peak-experiences, for humanistic psychology, for the difference between yea- & nay-saying. Also, it's a solid base from which to differentiate the real self from the neurotic self, what is authentic from what is not. Also, it makes more sense for me out of depression, drug addiction, sadism & masochism, lower-level "kicks," as with alcohol, danger, pain, new experiences.

I'm calling the absence of function-joy "experiential emptiness," which helps to explain the obsessional (& perhaps therefore the paranoiac?). Also, "experiential function-joy" is a good basis for conceptualizing the worthwhileness of living, the resistance to dying & to suicide. It makes life precious in itself (because it's all full of goodies, little peaks & joys, etc.).

And how about impulse-voice? "Body-pleasures" has the advantage of including sensory, body, & emotion awareness & focusing correctly on the biological, the *real* self, the instinctoid-constitutional, the unmistakably authentic. It's certainly the best place to start if interested in SA techniques à la Chatham paper. Also, it's the simplest & most obvious.

"Body-joy" sounds pretentious & overblown to me. "Body-pleasure" is more modest.

(It occurs to me that calling them "the littlest peaks" marks them off as positive & growth & SA experiences *from* the pain-reductive, tension-reductive, depression-reductive experiences, as well as from the sheer experiential emptiness of Myerson's constitutional anhedonic, born that way, which can lead to desperate measures to *whip up* an experiencing, any old experiencing, à la sadism-masochism. This is good. But see also the hedonism files. This all has to be simplified & condensed.)

Maybe I'll wind up using body-pleasure as the first or lowest in a hierarchy of functionings; for instance, the joy of a good pianist functioning as a pianist, or of an ice skater or lecturer, etc. Or maybe use body-pleasure as less intense than body-joy. "Fully functioning" would seem to be the highest in such a hierarchy, together with peak-emotional experience.

Change SA techniques to self-finding? OK (in course file). Then keep function-pleasure as the general word to indicate body-pleasure, expression-pleasure, sensory-, body-, emotion-, & impulse-awareness. No. Awareness is different from pleasure; includes anxiety-awareness, depression-awareness. Differentiate function-awareness from function-pleasure?

Function-Awareness Subsumes:	*Function-Pleasure Subsumes:*
sensory-awareness	sensory-pleasure
body-awareness	body-pleasure
emotion-awareness	emotion-pleasure
impulse-awareness	impulse-pleasure
tension-awareness	tension-pleasure
anxiety-awareness	
depression-awareness	
emptiness-awareness	
B-value-awareness	B-value-pleasure
	expression-pleasure
	esthetic-pleasure
	mystery-pleasure
	awe-, sacral-pleasure

All the function-pleasures defined *only* as positive growth, not pain reduction.

All of this helps to define SA, identity, self, etc. Recovery or discovery or achievement of real self includes *all* of these. Becoming conscious of them = some measure of control or bringing them about at will. All of it comes under head of "becoming conscious" or "consciously aware" or good reality testing.

Stress the unjaded palate of the self-actualizing person, of the peaker = retention of the most basic, biological, body pleasures & sensory pleasures = a kind of versatility = the ability to enjoy the finest wine *and*

Dago red, the finest cheese *and* local cheddar, great food *and* meat & potatoes, & even bread & cheese.

It is to enjoy the best life has to offer without getting fixated at that level, & *needing* it, & losing the ability to enjoy the simple, the basic, the primitive. Like the dancer-experts who just can't stick with the simple rhythm to repeat it again & again until going into a kind of primary-process state (like my rhumba). They *have* to do tricks & get complicated. For me, this means they're not real dancers.

Also stress that one *must* be able to retain the enjoyment & even the thrill of the axioms, the truisms, the basic sentiments, the schmaltzy & corny music, Victor Herbert, etc. (I tried the Victorian postcards in my class.) This retention of basic simplicity does not interfere with the connoisseur's delight in the finest, the best, the most subtle, the most delicate, the variations & games & exotic, e.g., as in sex. (Good example: the jaded ones lose the ability to enjoy bread & butter, normal sex = a kind of diminution.)

I was reminded of David Levy's finding that the very maternal mothers were more able to love the snotty, whining, sick, ugly baby. *Anybody* can love a smiling, clean, happy, freshly dressed baby. So also for the "bablylover" who couldn't adopt a not-bright child or a Chinese or Negro baby. So also the fake "dog lover" who needs a purebred, certified, diplomaed fancy dog & then crops its ears & tail & insults it with crazy haircuts, i.e., who can't *love* a mutt. So also for the teachers who get interested *only* in genius kids & can't bother with an average kid.

All of this is also the retention for simplicity, realness, & true essence. Like David Levy's taking me to the very fanciest restaurants & then taking me to a delicatessen under the 3rd Ave. El for real pot cheese with real sour cream, which he presented to me with the same delight as he did the wonderful, cooked-from-the-day-before & ordered-in-advance bouillabaisse. And it's true—they were *both* wonderful.

Then add to all this (for the self-actualizing person anyway, but I think also for any strong character, & for the peakers) another variation of this adaptability: the ability to enjoy truly these basic pleasures & also be compassionate, saddened, etc., & effectively helpful against exploitation, cruelty, poverty, etc. It's the dopey kid who *can't* bear to enjoy his meal because there is starvation in India. I feel Simone Weil to have been a dope, stupid, & ultimately cruel to commit suicide unnecessarily by starving herself (because people were starving in France). The little ecstasy of a good beer or cigar or sunset strengthens (rather than weakens) the revolutionary fervor of a Bodhisattva. The good surgeon *must* get a good night's sleep the night before & mustn't feel selfish or guilty about it. Perhaps the mother can't choose which one of her two children to save from death, & might prefer to let them both die or at least not be able to make up her mind. The stern father *must* do the choosing, & not get stuck at the choice point.

1967

Read Freud's introduction to the Wilson book &, as usual, struck dumb with admiration & respect. Awed. And then a good point. This is his realistic & common-sense self. Here he sees what all men see. There's nothing much to argue against here or to reject. But this is different from his system, which is different from his common-sense psychology. When he is *in* the system, then it is as if he put on a particular pair of spectacles which distorted his common-sense view with systematic-theoretical considerations (of what must be so, or *ought* to be so, or "then this follows from that") instead of purely observational & experiential data. Many parallels, e.g., with dogmatic religions, which are agreed to verbally on Sunday & overlooked altogether at other times. Or professors of philosophy. Or, for that matter, the behaviorists. *Any* dogmatics or system-believers. Practically any system can be seen as figure crystallized out—verbally, logically, systematically—from the great ground or apperceptive mass, which has always continued to contradict its verbalized, theorized portion. The solution, since we *must* theorize, is to take the ground, the apperceptive mass, the common-sense, untreated experience, tacit knowledge, as *prior* to and prepotent over the theoretical parts which have been crystallized out of it. *Always* take the former seriously; *never* take the latter seriously (alone). That is, we must always be humorous & light about the theory, must always recognize it as inadequate, which it always is & always must be, even tho it is needed for all sorts of reasons.

Therefore I can criticize Freud's system, his theory, his image of man & of society, etc., at the same time granting that Freud himself contradicted it often in a casual sentence in some unsystematic letter or writing, like this preface. I've told Harry often that, in a certain sense, he is not a Freudian, because in his actual therapeutic work he covertly introduces all the common-sense tacit knowledge that the written system forgets about. Criticism of the written system is *not* a criticism of Freud's common sense, or of him as a human being.

I've been reacting in this way, more & more consciously in recent years, to my *own* system, which I take very seriously in one sense but very tentatively in another sense, e.g., as with Frank or other friends who don't believe it at all, or with students or reviewers who criticize it or are skeptical. I get angry only if they're nasty.

January 31

Bethel.

Visit disappointing so far as data are concerned. Everybody is busy most of the time. Only way to get the contact I want is to become a trainer & be *in* the groups. But is this worth the time? Not sure, & will decide after the Bethel experience. Maybe I could be a container in a presidents' group? I'd certainly go home now if it weren't for B. being in a group & getting a lot out of it. Even the leaders are too busy to talk.

Of course, I've picked up a lot of background, apperceptiveness, tacit knowledge, along with the bits of details & the many additional questions. Will put all these notes & the lecture notes in the aggridant file. One thing I've learned for sure is that this is dangerous stuff & easily misunderstood. Got good critique along these lines from Carl Rogers, the only one, I must say, with sense enough to be badly disturbed.

The facts are there, but they've been swept under the rug. And uncovering them can open a Pandora's box which I couldn't control. One thing is clear: I'd better not chat or lecture casually about this stuff. It had better all be put out in one big lump, in written form, with all the details, explanations, cautions, reasonable conclusions, etc. And this cannot be done in an hour & a quarter. I had thought of this as a presidential-address topic instead of the science stuff, but am more doubtful now. Anyway, I'm just not really sure about anything. No closure yet, only strong institutions, hunches, conclusions that I can't support with data, etc. All I know is that it's terribly important, especially for social policy, politics, etc. For instance, I'm more sure now that "liberal" & "conservative" are both obsolete. Also Republican & Democrat.

Thought: one thing that disturbs me—& also Rogers—is that talking as I did led to self-diagnoses by everyone, not always accurate, I gather, including those I spoke of as schlemiels, which led to clear self-contempt in at least one woman, the trainer in wives' groups. Well, is this good? Bad? Certainly it leads to a stupid black-white dichotomizing into sheep or goats, aggridants or schlemiels. (I'd certainly better stop using *that* word—too contemptuous. Use "poor choosers" or "not-yet-identities"—that's a good one because it implies they can get there yet, which is usually true, if only à la Synanon. *Yes*, definitely. I guess I was showing *my* contempt, which anyway I don't really feel except when they get pretentious or dangerous.) That was one good thing I worked out: that we can be & should be realistic in our diagnoses, but that this definitely does *not* mean contempt or condescension unless for fakes or actors, nonaggridants trying to *look* like aggridants, the non-authentic, or the not-yet-identities. It's easy to accept authentic people, whatever they happen to be, & I guess they are in fact usually accepted, certainly by the other authentics, or the modest, self-accepting psychologist who does well whatever he can do. It's hard to think of male examples, altho plenty of female examples. Most of the less competent or, at least, less successful males are anguished over it & self-punishing & often then countervaluing. Is it possible for this kind of stuff to help teach people to accept themselves, whatever they happen to find themselves to be? (= psychological success!)

I guess one thing that's emerging here—as with creative people—is to move the whole question of success, boss, executive, power man over to the dimension of psychological health, SA, full identity, fully functioning. That is, to think of the tremendous range of *kinds* of authentic persons, & then to define them all as "psychologically successful" or "successful-in-life," etc., & then to ask which of *these* happen to be best for the particular task requirements. And *not* to get taken in by the assumption that we should start from presidents & executives, men who wield great power [= *phenotypes rather than genotypes*].

Let's take this authenticity as *the* great *g* factor here, in this realm as in any other human realm—at least, in those realms that require doing good or desirable jobs or authentic tasks. Then the *s* factors are the requirements of this *particular* job, which means a whole multiplicity of slots, and *not just one* ideal type of executive or boss or aggridant. Then the thing for *all* people to do would be first to self-actualize & to find the real self &, in the process, inevitably, to find out what (& who) one loved & was fitted for & successful at. The succession of successes & failures themselves is a necessary part of this process of finding the identity; i.e., what one is good at & poor at → what one enjoys & what one doesn't → peaks & desolations → what other people love you for & praise you for → what behavior is best for winning all the basic-need gratifications → what *feels* fully functioning & gives *Funktionslust*. This, by the way, places far more importance on vocational guidance & trying-out & on-the-job training & testing & having all sorts of trying-out experiences, for the sake of discovering one's identity or biological self. (I must stress this more in the experiential course.)

In a way, *all* biological selves are equally valuable & respectworthy. *Any* real person is as good as any other real person, just as any real & authentic woman is as good and as admirable, respectworthy, desirable, valuable, etc., as *any* real & authentic man, no matter what their job or destinies are, or social roles, etc. I think I got pushed in this direction this A.M. over breakfast with the women. "What is an aggridant wife?" they asked. Which is a real puzzler. The insecure high-dominance women simply rivaled men. But the secure high-dominance women, à la Ruth Benedict or B.'s mother, are different & quite comfortable being whatever they are. How about the secure *low*-dominance women? I think they too can be authentic &, being authentic & *not* powerful, would then accept themselves as followers without aspiring to be leaders. And yet they could be called "successful"! And so could the man who is secure low-dominance, even tho the culture would give him a bad time.

So maybe I'd better start the lecture hereafter with the question of healthy vs. unhealthy aggridants or bosses, instead of starting as I did with the animal experiments, where health & unhealth are irrelevant. *Or at least alternate the 2 possibilities, since the question of good animality definitely precedes & is *sine qua non* for the question of real identity.*

I guess it looks like this: the necessary first chapter to any future book on vocational guidance *or* the leader (better the various leaders) or the executive or the power person or the 5-star general, or any book on political leadership or the President, etc. (*or* on the good wife or mother), must start with the general *g* factor that underlies any success of any kind in any (worthwhile) realm or task.

Then come the *range* of kinds of persons & the *range* of tasks that there are in life.

And then, only then, would come the question of pathology, of the paranoid leader, or of the functional advantages in specific situations of various kinds of neurosis or immaturity or psychosis—as for the detective it pays to be suspicious, or as for P. S., neurotically identified with the underdog against authority. I might say that, not only do we need all kinds of identities, but also we can use all kinds of mild sickness in highly specific spots—anyway in a highly industrialized & division-of-labor society. And then it's possible even to respect them—if not for themselves, at least for doing a good job where others couldn't (e.g., the patience of aments with autistic children or senile psychoses, etc.). Then might come up the question of LBJ & other "successful" but unlikable people. Do we maybe *need* them? Must we learn to regard affection as irrelevant to certain tasks—and then hope to find people who don't need affection to take the job? And where does B-patriotism or fighting for the B-values come in here? If I were asked to take on a worthwhile job by LBJ, I suppose I'd do it out of B-patriotism whether or not I enjoyed it, & whether or not I got paid off in appreciation, etc. I suspect people like McNamara are willing to be #2 to LBJ for just such reasons.

But even this brings up the fascinating question of the definition of the task-requirements. I thought of myself often as a poor chairman, but now in retrospect I think I was a good chairman (redefining "good chairman"). I had a stereotype of the more obsessional & structured chairman. But this turns out to be trivial by comparison with being a good personnel selector, keeping the family together, having lofty standards & aspirations, etc. By *this* definition I was a wonderful chairman. We still tend in the culture to define *a priori* the role of boss in a somewhat obsessional way. Writing this up would be a great Mitzvah. Thinking of the "chairman type" in a bureaucratic stereotype is ruining the world. They get to be boss too often, in too many slots, & then tighten everything up in a tight-ass way & start persecuting the creators & the originals.

One thing about the wives: they are definitely *not* an impressive group, except for B. & Edith Tannenbaum, but they do seem more aggridant than average. Aggridants tend to marry aggridants, but the correlation seems to be lowish. This puts an additional strain on both wife & husband. No, I must revise that upward as I think of a really average population; these *are* stronger, smarter, more capable than an average group, but still not as impressive as their husbands in any general human way. $r = .5$ or so? And then of course they grow & develop up to their roles, or crack up altogether, or get discarded. (Question: how many divorces here?)

Another thought I came up with this A.M.: rise in status definitely separates out the good women from the inadequate ones, because the latter tend then to get uppity, snooty, mean, & to behave like a *grande dame*, which they are not, while sound women don't change much, & probably get *nicer* in the process, more *noblesse oblige*, kinder, more responsible & thoughtful of others, etc. This is an excellent example for making the point about the real identity. It is *this* that gives stability & continuity & unchangingness *thru* all sorts of environmental changes. They still have the same inner voices, same inner supreme court, same values, etc. But the experientially empty ones will fluctuate wildly with external changes, being dependent largely on cues from the outside rather than from the inside. If they go up, they'll go uppity. Also, since the role is a put-on role & not a natural emanation, it will be stupid, wrong, badly played. That is, the woman—as with South American generals, Josette said—will not behave expressively, but will act out her inadequate idea of what a *grande dame* is in her imagination.

9 P.M. All thru the day I felt better & better about this morning's writing. And at dinner, lecturing to a table full of women about it, it sounded very good & I got quite exhilarated as I told them what I could remember. *Anybody* can be a success—women included. But this is not bland & all-loving. It permits *disapproval* as well. Everyone can become what he is & must then be given transfinite value & respect for this. But this doesn't mean that we have to value gangsters or killers or drunkards or psychopaths in some way. Or phonies, or fakes, or real failures (who try to be what they are not or fail to become what they are). The question came up: how about the successful or self-actualizing gangster or psychopath? In the first place, they are *not* psychological successes. They're diminished & have lost important human capacities & pleasures & rewards. External rewards can't make up for this diminution, because they can't even enjoy their loot, can't really "enjoy" anything in the high sense. Can't love. Never experience real friendship, real trust, identification with others. [*Add this to diminution section of Neurosis paper.*] Certainly get no peaks, only "kicks." Shallow emotions, impoverished consciousness. Die early. Easily bored, can achieve only lower pleasures, which are very limited. No metamotivational pleasure. No ecstasies & contemplation of B-values. Must differentiate financial success, power, status, ownership of things, deference, etc., from psychological success.

And yet, given the wide range of authentics, it is *still* true that some are aggridant, alphas, & factually superior for the particular job requirements. *Everybody* can actualize his IQ, or piano playing, or his high jump. And yet there is only one Einstein or Renoir or Kreisler. For any job requirements there often *is* a best.

February 1

Breakfast discussion with the men very helpful; they asked me to explain why I would now say it differently, as they had heard from their wives. Also set off by discussion of Ardrey & his mistake, which I also made, of extrapolating too directly from lower animals. I would now start with man-as-animal & with his animal-species peculiarities: (1) He is a Persona, which is different, consciously and unconsciously, from his deeper real self, so we can't really know each other well (or even know ourselves well). (2) He is a repressing animal. (3) He has a tremendously wide range of authentic individual differences, far more than any other animal. (4) Aggridance is, in all animals, across the board & general, except in man, where specialization & division of labor & functional leadership obtain most often (except in the case of dictators). (5) We are the most flexible animal species & can adapt to more rules, even to those which are foreign to our real nature; i.e., we can violate & contradict our own nature, & no other animal can (even across the sex lines; but, then, other animals can do that too). (6) We have—maybe—the greatest possibility for cooperation. Anyway, we can either cooperate or compete. Or, better said, we can identify with a love widely—even, in principle, universally. Eupsychia [81] is possible if social & economic conditions are right. Also, respect is possible very widely (this isn't quite right; must work it out more). (7) We are the only animal that isn't necessarily hierarchical. We can—at our most mature moments & under good, sound circumstances—value, admire, respect, & love practically anybody— certainly any authentic person of any type (psychologically successful); also functional leadership; division of labor with equally self-respecting masters of their trade, as plumbers respect carpenters.

But all of these animal qualities are enhanced, purified, & seen at their best in self-actualizing persons, in authentics, identities, the ma- ture! I spoke about psychoanalysis & the depths, & of airing the deep evil & working it thru, & of the change in the quality, e.g., of hostility-self-affirmation, as one becomes more mature in the Freudian sense.

It is *hard*, not easy, to be a human animal (another animal characteristic—add as #8 above). Weak instinctoid. For a cat it is easy to be a cat. But it is hard to become a full member of the human species. The instinctoid animal has to be sought for with special techniques & may or may not be found. Self-doubt. Conflict. Wavering over who one is & adolescent trying-out of various roles & playing nonidentity games. Only the human animal can *act* (there are very few lower-animal instances). Or, rather, #9, the human nonanimal, not-yet-identity, can act & does act all the time, or much of the time, or is not able *not* to act. That's a good way to differentiate the human actors from the few very functional animal instances. The human acts when he doesn't need to & when there is no advantage in it, & even when he tries not to. He can be a willy-nilly actor. Or "nothing but" an actor. Only an actor. Beyond his control. Even beyond his consciousness. Acting in the human is immature-animal rather than mature-human—or at least this uncontrollable acting is. I suppose the self-actualizing people, *some* of them, can deliberately take on other roles, & act other identities if they have to & want to. But would they go in for professional acting? I doubt it. Authenticity is nonacting. So is spontaneity. Authentic expressiveness = SA, creativeness, etc.

"Is this optimistic? Are you hopeful?" I was asked. "Yes, with good conditions & with nature & SA (good animals)." These could be Utopian or Eupsychian conditions, I am convinced. *Certainly* it's true in small groups of self-actualizing people. Firm identities can get along very nicely with each other, permitting & even enjoying the separate & unique identity qualities of other authentics. Use the good self-actualizing marriage as example of a little Eupsychia to illustrate full, self-respecting & other-respecting, nonbossy, nonhierarchical, functional leadership & nice fusing for mutual pleasure & self-transcendence & identification. The more mature, the more self-actualizing, the more a separate firm identity, the more *lovable* individuals become, as well as the more admirable & respectworthy.

[*Partners. Have shared adversities, problems, joys. Sexual gratitude to each other. Each has grown, each therefore grateful. Easy understanding & communication, including nonverbal.*]

[*Respecting each other's roles also. Greater honesty possible. Less "acting." Identification = in many ways they are one person, not two.*]

[*But this too is being a "good animal." That's the way lower-animal marriages are when they occur. At least some are. Anyway, there is nothing in the animal kingdom to parallel our bad marriages.*]

Our "evil" tendencies, matured, become SA, good animality, healthy selfishness, self-affirmation, etc. Good-evil matured & therefore changed in "quality." Good is evil transformed, *not* disappeared or repressed. Every evil quality seems to be the caricature of a good quality, the immature version or precursor of a good quality. We got into this kind of argument—one of them definitely *non*aggridant, not really belonging here, trying to be good, "universally benevolent," & really weak, second-class, I think. He was the only one at the table who couldn't accept my psychoanalytic talk about evil in the depths & its transformation by airing & working thru. He just couldn't accept that we are all behaving well because conditions are good. And that I, & he, would surely become killers under scarcity & jungle nonsynergic conditions. Easiest way to say it is: he is not aware of his evil potentialities (if conditions change), & he would be shocked at himself & at others. When I used the filled-lifeboat example, he just couldn't take it. Nor could he accept the fact of ultimate individual differences & superiorities emerging *more* clearly under Eupsychian conditions. He clung to the IQ as product of good conditions & was very uncomfortable with my insistence that even learning was biologically limited to species possibilities, to uniqueness possibilities, & to physiological limits. None of the executives made a protest. I'd say now that bad conditions are *obscuring* our native individual differences, for which there would be no alibi under Eupsychian conditions, & which would have to be accepted.

I added to basic authenticity to start with, & the job requirements, then sending out call notes which select the correct, useful authenticity for the job, the third element of differential social & economic rewards for different jobs. This is also a determiner.

Also, I'd add just the experience of being successful, rich, powerful, admired as *itself* still another determinant. This helps people *learn* to look & to feel aggridant—like the continually admired & courted girl in the story who finally *became* beautiful, graceful, confident. Also as with B., who is being complimented & admired in her group & is the belle of the ball; she seems to be losing the lurking wives' suspicion that maybe they are accepted only because of husband, & what would happen if he died? So they may feel admired not for themselves but only in role as "wife of," as husband-adjuncts.

February 9

A wild morning, a really big increment in courage & unleashing as I prepared notes for Utopia class 1st meeting this afternoon & decided to frighten out the pikers (for there are too many registered) & wound up half-frightening myself too (that old Jonah complex!). Anyway, suddenly got that old thought: I *must* get this all in print before I die. It will change the world! And then the thought: my God, I *may* die or get killed this A.M. What a pity! So better catch at least a few notes before I go out & risk my life in traffic. First of all, *must* use this for presidential address, with big captive audience. It starts out mildly enough with medical model. Relief from pain & security & safety & seeking for obsessional type, safety-motivated satisfaction of "to be sane," certainty, rigor, exactness, don't take a chance, how not to get fooled, how not to make a mistake, how to be legal, orderly, neat, & tight-ass (& tight-cunt & dry-cunt). And also how to be prepared with a talisman against the horrible & dangerous future emergency. Safety science = a preparing for an unfree future (really preparing *against* it, i.e., to make it *unfree, unopen*). Whatever new turns up, test it! Whatever moves, catalogue it! Whoever new turns up at the village end, first find out "who" he is, who he is related to, where he "belongs," & where he fits in to the orderly plan of the universe, his family, his relatives, his placing. What drawer does he go in in the inventory? How can the new fact be assimilated to the past? How can it be shown thus to be "not really new"? Reminds me of the Bolles motivation text I looked at in which he shackles & handcuffs himself on the very first page or two, i.e., makes an excluding definition, "science is the explanation of behavior," which leaves out 95% of the human data. Testing the null hypotheses, etc., is rabbit-foot science if they are not regarded as mere tools like medicines or computers or hammers & saws in the hands of the *boss,* to do with *as he likes.* All the tools of scientific & statistical method are wonderful *tools!* But to abnegate bosshood, the power of decision, the buck-stops-here executive quality of "*I* am the one who chooses when to use or not use this medicine or this statistic or this experimental design!" This is all fear—fear *against* courage! Free-wheeling, compromising, being ready for anything conceivable that might happen. Use my personnel-administration article on the need for creative people, i.e., flexible, adaptable, "unprepared with rules," *but* quite prepared with courage & self-confidence & not scared to make a mistake now & then, i.e., quite prepared to "experiment" in the oldest sense of "let's try it out & see what happens & then we'll make up our minds." Instead of trying to look certain, calm, sane, unruffled, & lordly, like a bank teller.

March 18

Very important discussion with Dick Jones. I asked him to react candidly to my belief that the Freudian tradition (or extrapolation) was more truly in *my* hands than in Rapoport's, Klein's, etc. (He liked the phrase "Don't be a Freudian—be a Freud." "Freudians" are textbook boys, loyalists, followers, disciples, epigones, Talmudists. Ego psychology, I told him, is an irenic, Talmudic melting into the Freudian infrastructure (throwing away superstructure) with all the academic psychological truisms from Allport, Murray, etc.

Freud was neo-Freudian or humanistic, etc., or Taoistic in this sense: he was the first M.D. to keep his mouth shut, which implies respect for the patient, which also implies his growth tendency, body wisdom, tendency to health, etc. Uncovering, nonintruding, permitting patient his own pace & own style.

Second: he discovered another *kind* of instinct theory, which I am carrying on (no one else I know), & Dick admitted that most analysts neither have a conception of "instinct theory" nor really believe in it. My "subjective biology" impressed him very much. The baton is in *my* hands, while the analysts keep parroting Freud's fumbling theories *about* instincts; they are stuck in his bad answers rather than his good questions.

The real self. "Identity" is an improved version of Freud's first fumbling invention of finding out with the patient what his *insides were like*, what was happening inside of *him*, his inner signals, teaching him to *hear* these inner signals. It is the same as "finding one's real self."

Third: I spoke of my big critique of Freud as being reductionistic with the higher nature of man. This I think comes from Freud's faith in the physical-chemical philosophy of science. But I don't hold this against him; nothing else was possible at that time! Rather, I give him credit for accepting his clinical discoveries, which contradicted this faith in "science." Today we can do better because we know more in 1967 than anyone could in 1890. What I am doing is adding the higher needs & metaneeds to the "id" or to the instincts or to the biological nature of the person. Then they, too, are subject to the Freudian psychodynamics, i.e., to repression, defense, fear, conflict, etc.

In a word, I can purify Freud. But *I* don't think it to be *anti*-Freudian. It is epi-Freudian. And I seem to be the only one around.

This is something like what I've been saying to the rabbis. I carry the traditions of Judaism more than they do, with the ethical, prophetic, messianic & utopian emphasis, which is really all that's good about it. It sounds awfully arrogant & grandiose when I say it, so I usually keep my mouth shut, but that's the way I feel. All the rabbis do is to keep all the crap & the externals; they are really *antispiritual*.

If I ever write up this epi-Freudian version, I *should* finally make a list of the Freudian clinical discoveries that hold true, along with the stuff that has to be *rejected* or rephrased.

Also add the point about Freud being a *clinical*-empirical theorist, i.e., facts first. He tried to theorize to hold together his factual discoveries. (He did it badly.)

1966

April 30

Tie this in with the Esalen weekends. Almost ideal teaching & learning situation. I'd like to tie in also with all this "publish or perish" crap. What *are* the authentic reasons for writing & publishing (not the inauthentic ones)?

Also in interpersonal-relations file, the impulse to share as a basic characteristic of love; e.g., the scene looks twice as beautiful when the discovery is shared with the beloved. (But it has to do also with "secrets" & "privacy" & shutting the world out & creating a private world with secret language, etc.)

Add: parallel McGregor's Theory X & Y management with Theory X & Y education. Change somewhat: what character qualities *must* we assume if graduate education is to work well (also high-school-type education)? How *true* & real are his Theory-Y assumptions for college & grad students?

May 9

Astonished by being nominated to presidency of APA. Apparently I've read the situations incorrectly, feeling out of things, alienated from the APA, rejected & rejecting. Dream fantasies about being thrown *out* of APA. I suppose this is surface sign of a deeper guilt, or self-criticism, etc., about not doing research, about not "keeping up," about being obsolete in statistics, neurology, learning theory, experimental design, & lots more. The ones I admire most are the good theorist-researchers. As I felt the research impulse drain out of me, I guess I must have felt that the right to call myself a psychologist was also draining out of me, & in several kinds of situations I've felt inadequate, not sufficiently trained, etc.

May 16

Talking about this with Harry yesterday, I realized *more* clearly how proud I had been of being a psychologist, how eagerly I had joined APA, how loyal I had been to it. I guess my identity was very much involved. The most important thing about me was that I was a psychologist. And this was very definitely defined as a *scientist*—i.e., a *researcher*. And I think also that this being a scientist & researcher was equivalent to being a man, a male. So giving up research was almost like giving up maleness (not consciously, of course, because rationally that's nonsense).

July 5

Yesterday, at Portners', continuing to speak up freely & got very intense about it, overriding the conversation, lecturing, dominating, breaking in, & in general talking too much & too intensely & too arrogantly. B. says I'm that way often, dominating the conversation. But it *was* a relief to open up & say my say a little more.

Part of the problem showed up clearly in the last week. At Tarrytown House, I simply *had* to take over & lecture them, because they just weren't smart enough, were pissing away the remaining time, so that my whole trip would have been wasted. So I excused myself, said I had to leave soon, & would they mind if I took over & said my say before leaving. At Harvard Business School session Saturday, I got total adulation, testimonials, etc., & was made to feel like the Messiah. It *was* good. And they *were* getting something special. But then, on way home & after talk with Ric, remembered about rejection by grad students. So this up & down business is part of the confusion. High & low. Messiah & reject. Unsettling. Something like the Negro situation that Lloyd Bell told me about long ago: "Better in the South. You know where you're at. *Everyone* rejects you. But in the North, nine will be friends & nice & then unexpectedly the tenth will be nasty." It's very difficult to hit an even balance between arrogance & modesty.

July 8

Elected president of APA. Have to assimilate this, because I had felt outside the APA, rejected & isolated. That's mostly what the intellectual psychoanalysis with Harry was about. I've been feeling more & more out of it, less & less the psychologist APA style, more the maverick. If it hadn't been so unexpected, & so pleasant also to be back in the family again, I'd surely have declined the nomination. Then, as I realized how much hard & unpleasant work it would be & for how long a period of time, I got scared of being elected and sort of half-hoped I wouldn't—voted for Lindsley instead of myself, etc. Now I'm stuck with it, depressed with having to change all my plans in order to become a committee man & a bureaucrat, all the stuff I dislike & besides do badly. Already today I started pulling out of promises and commitments, out of planned researches, etc. Yet the pleasures & advantages are also considerable. Peculiarly, the desiderata that came to mind first were: (1) that a Jew—an Abraham—*should* be elected for the first time in the history of the APA (Jerry Bruner doesn't count as a Jew). (Just looked up history of APA & Joseph Jastrow was president in 1900, so I'm not really the first one. Well, almost.) The other thought that weighed heavily was (2) that Sachar & Brandeis would be pleased. A feather in the cap of the university. And I guess I feel grateful for having been treated so well here. Lots of other advantages too, for AAHP, for adding weight & prestige to my causes, for having a guaranteed hearing for anything I want to say. I suppose more offers, more money, more travel, etc. Trouble is, I don't strongly want any of these, & certainly don't need them. I already feel like a big shot to myself & certainly don't need any additional building up. On the contrary. On this point there's no great meaning to the office. Only half the presidents were really tops; the other half were good organization men or didn't really deserve it. And too many of the *real* big shots were never elected president. I remember how mad I got over the great émigrés, & started a campaign that didn't do any good. Lewin, Wertheimer, Koffka, McDougall, Werner, Goldstein, Fromm—not to mention the other great analysts like D. M. Levy, etc. Skinner and Murray also. I've been nominating them every year. Also Asch.

So it's no tremendous honor.

Bertha & the girls are pleased. I'm not sure why. Bertha thinks I could do a lot of good. Maybe. Ric also. It *is*, of course, good *for the department* & everybody in it.

[*Must start at once thinking of suitable & major presidential address. Maybe it will turn out to be one of the things I was hoping to do anyway. So maybe no plans need be seriously changed.* Except *of course, that I'm stuck with another calendar-date deadline, after I'd sworn not to do* that *again.*

Well: (1) bring motivation theory up to date, with data, evidence, & adding metamotivation; (2) keep enriching the metamotivation paper plus all the methodological comments; (3) additional notes on psychology of science (lots of notes left over, problems unfinished, etc.); (4) "what is theoretical psychology?"; (5) bring the 3rd-Force psychology up to date (I could use the expanded propositions for this; this I could work up on very short notice, so I guess I don't have to push too hard on settling this right away; could let things go as they will & decide a year from now); (6) B-language; (7) critique of self-actualization; (8) redefine "liberal" & "conservative"; (9) evil; (10) truth & honesty; (11) aggridant, strong & weak; (12) synergy.]

July 17

Last night insomnia; read Freud-Abraham letters & got disturbed, as I have always over my relations & conflicts with Freud & the psychoanalysts, & this A.M. talked myself out with B. & it's clearer—& also of intellectual interest. I am repelled by Freud's domination politics, king-of-the-hill tactics, & demands for total loyalty from everyone. He couldn't relate at all to an equal, & was intolerant of differences & debate, etc., as with Jung, who *surely* demanded respect, even at that time. Any other person who had to be independent, autonomous, respected, & self-respecting (let alone anyone *else* who had to be king-of-the-hill, i.e., aggridant) had to choose between "breaking away" or else complete loyalty. (I have experienced this same demand from every "pope" I've ever met: Adler, Fromm, Sullivan, Moreno, Chuck Dederich, Frankl, &, by implication I *think*, a lot of lesser people who accepted me very nicely as a bright young man.) I just can't be & never have been able to be a devoted & loyal follower (as Freud frankly tells Abraham he must be), altho I *could* be & always was a devoted & dedicated *student* & listener with open mouth. So with Adler, who finally asked me after a probing question with implied skepticism, "Are you for me or against me?" And that was the last time I saw Adler. And so, as I read the letter, I get some feeling of repugnance for Abraham the prick sucker. (That's the best way to put the relationship, because Abraham was active, not passive, & he *did* draw knowledge & power from Freud & then use it, like a bright kid with his father, & he did *not* worship or such before any other prick or altar, & he *did* fully accept the humble & subordinate, one-way relationship—he calls Freud "Professor" only, & Freud calls him "friend" or "colleague." Freud says "we" & Abraham says "I," etc.) I think I was able to open my mouth & ears & eyes & take in strength & be deferent & grateful with all of them, but I couldn't give *sole* loyalty to *one*. That's the difference between a good student & a loyal follower. I have never been able to be "loyal" to one person or system or theory which meant an either-or choice, closing myself to all other pricks or fountainheads or sources, renouncing all others.

And on the other side I have rejected all demands to be pope (e.g., for the Horneyans or the humanists, etc.) or to write forewords (in the last week, I refused for Bugental & for Shostrom) or to accept pure disciples (*students*, yes) & prick suckers who pledge total & exclusive devotion, & have always felt slightly repelled by the offer, & have tended to withdraw my prick from these people, get impersonal, detached, aloof—or lecture at them about being independent. I *do* like colleagues, not necessarily smart ones, & I *do* like deferent & open-mouthed students, but *not* loyal, exclusive disciples for whom I then become responsible. (It occurs to me that *this* is the sense in which I am not a "leader," & maybe even the students & younger colleagues feel rejected just because I won't *let* them be prick suckers. But I am a leader in a *higher* & better sense, which allows autonomy for the other, if he can take it. Partial explanation for my puzzles over being rejected by my grad students?)

But the problem with Freud, & with the analysts who should be my natural friends & colleagues, but who aren't, is that I consider him to be the greatest psychologist by far who ever lived, & I feel myself to be epi-Freudian (*not* Freudian) & to be carrying on the best of the tradition, but without being a loyalist. So I've been rejected, condescended to, unused, unquoted, unreviewed by the loyalist Freudians, especially the Talmudic ones like Rapaport. I want to be friends with them, but they reject me. I respect their secrets most; I chose orthodox Freudians as my therapists; I refer patients almost exclusively to Freudians, etc. *But* I respect also Adler, Jung, et al., *anyone* who can teach me something, so the Freudians cast me out. Deutsch kept on misinterpreting in our analysis, assuming always that I wanted to be like him, to replace him, to be an analyst, etc. My respect & enthusiasm & gratitude for Freud & psycho-analysis he could see *only* as a total wish to *be* Freud or a Freudian, rather than as a desire to use it & then build on top of it.

Bertha says *I'm* arrogant & grandiose like Freud. I'd say it's different. The self-confident, stubborn, creative arrogance which is neces-sary for any big job & for real independence & courage is quite different from pope-grandiosity & the demand for subordination.

September 10

Long breakfast conversation with B. over my symptoms & what Harry thought of them (conflict & tension psychosomatic rather than simply physical, small heart, hypoendocrines, etc., as I had thought & still do). Her version of the basic conflict was between being God & wanting to be buddies & friends with all the common people. An astigmatic version of a truth, I thought, & explained. On the one hand, if one is factually superior, as I *am*, in intellect & working creativeness & in actual achieve-ment (a "god" in a certain & real sense), then the job is to accept this instead of fearing or renouncing one's superiority, presumably biological, aristocracy of talent. No "defenses against one's greatness," as with Frank & many others. This is hubris, arrogance, pride, etc., in one sense. It has one meaning subjectively, & can be seen as a problem to be struggled with, even to be feared. Another, from the outside, was the reaction to me in Bill Schutz' group, where it came out *openly*, the God-izing, de-humanizing, love-awe-hostility-uneasiness that they all showed to me; Betty Duff's hurt at my not recognizing her, etc. And I remembered how this feels when I recalled my shock-startle-disbelief at Eliseo Vivas, a professor, i.e., a nonhuman god, pissing at the urinal next to me at the University of Wisconsin in 1928. I had to realize that my image of him had had no kidneys, bladder, or piss. I also had to humanize the great gods who wrote books, & I did this, while certainly admiring, respecting, deferring, imitating the ones I was awed by & hero-worshipped & was filial with. I did *not* have to spit on them or fuck them in some way to save my self-esteem, or challenge them to a gun duel, as Bill Gellerman had to do in my group to me. I just loved & admired them & listened eagerly with open mouth & eyes & ears.

I regard myself as superior—I expect to be listened to rather than lectured at, & I will take *over* the conversation at a point where I can say it better or have more to say. I'll shove them aside, in effect saying "Here, let *me* do it; I can do it better than you." And of course many will get sore (most? all?). *But*, fully realizing this anger, I yet will take over with the ones who should listen. And I really despise those who *won't* learn, e.g., the grad students who won't take my seminars because undergrads are admitted. (In the meeting yesterday where we discussed this, I remembered having attended Wertheimer's Psychology 1 course 3 or 4 times in a row. It was good enough for me & Asch, but not for the mediocre ones.)

So the problem for others often is to de-God me & to rehumanize me. And for me I prefer to be seen as human (even tho very smart, very famous, & very achieving) rather than clothed with *their* problems of transferring upon me irrationalities, magic nonhumanness, etc. I don't *feel* like a god in their sense—*never*, I don't think. In specific situations I am quite conscious of knowing more, of teaching & lecturing, etc., of having authority, but at other times, in other situations I feel incapable, stupid, inept, as for instance at the Board of Directors meeting Aug. 30.

I think this attitude of mine came thru in Bill Schutz' group with the others who were afraid of me, etc. They could get rid of their projections upon me by my behaving in a normal, friendly, & humane manner. I was, in truth, one of the gang only & merely. Except when my knowledge of psychology was of use. But then Solit, the osteopath, was far more confident & capable than I in *his* domain, Bill Schutz in *his*, etc.

The trouble with all of this is that it can be misunderstood as seductiveness, to be popular, ingratiation, to be loved by all, & wanting to be one of the boys, one of the gang. I don't think it is at all. I think it is good, even in a brief encounter, with a stranger, for ten minutes, to be all these, to be friendly, kind, direct, candid, "human," & *not* to stand on one's "dignity" if it is irrelevant to that situation. As I told my group, I might forget their names & not recognize them a year from now, but, in *this* intimate encounter, it could be a real encounter, without defenses or reserve or aloofness (of the kind that I put up around myself in a train or plane where I'd rather not talk with strangers). I guess the Eupsychian solution is to be able to be either aloof if that's best *or* intimate if that's best, & then not to be hurt by the permanent dissolution of the intimacy or encounters.

1967

February 22

Terrible department meeting February 20 with the tight-asses leaguing together to *force* students to take courses that Senders, Simmel, Wodinsky, et al. would require them to. I blocked it & instead recommended splitting the department into two departments—personal & impersonal psychology, or biopsychology & person psychology, or humanistic & social psychology. It's all like a civil war, & I have to fight.

June 2

At Brandeis I just don't exist intellectually except right in class & with my own few grad students. Peculiar.

But now I remember Mike Arons telling me his solution of this. At Sorbonne the internationally famous ones were neglected by the students because they were "there," available, no excitement, taken for granted, old hat. The dynamics here would be very interesting to work out, e.g., countervaluing in order to protect self-esteem, defense against inferiority, against sacralization, against respect & love for the father (keep your cool) & Jonah-type mechanisms. I remember that as boys we talked & fantasied about how we would reject with scorn being courted by, e.g., Greta Garbo, or whoever was *the* female of the time. That would show her that *we* weren't impressed by royalty, that *we* wouldn't genuflect, that *we* weren't stooges & adoring, worshiping peasants. But then the fantasy was that she would persist, even after getting spanked, etc., &, being properly humbled, could then be accepted without loss of manhood. It was all dominance stuff & self-protection against being subordinated & against one's own unconscious *wish* to adore & kneel. I remember the international meeting in Washington where I got first from McClelland, Olds, Sylvan Tomkins, Allport, & Murray the same story—the bigger they got, the more trouble they had with their students. The more they had to teach, the more this was rejected (except by some foreign students, some females, & also an occasional older person).

June 24

End of first Bethel week. Chewing the week over with B. this A.M., & I guess I've learned more about myself than I realized last night when I began getting bored with the whole thing. Also learned more about my attitudes to others & expectations from them. I'm definitely, as they all say, warm, open, casual, easy, etc., but this goes down only to level 2, & that's as far as I want to go, & I don't want them to go any farther. I feel friendly enough & wish them well, & the group works well enough together. But I don't really know anyone there, nor do they really know me. I made a little speech about this last night. It *was* wonderful & amazing that in one week they could drop their defenses so much, make all sorts of changes, even physical ones. It *is* a miracle. And yet, I stressed, it was only 3 inches down. The depths & the mysteries could keep on unraveling for 70 years. These 3-inch-deep defenses I don't think I have, & so I had no progress to make. I had already achieved this thru psychoanalysis, working thru personally over the years, self-analysis, etc. So I told them—& myself—that this degree of mutual trust & good feeling was achieved partly by staying away from everything really *hot*—religion, Vietnam, politics, let alone the deep characterological differences between the warms & the cools, the gullible & the suspicious, the answerable & the malicious. How high a level of respect & trust would be necessary in a group before *such* things could be stated & accepted without destroying the group, let alone anti-Semitism, anti-Negroism, etc.? Then also: I have been a moderating, calming influence, partly because it's clear I dislike conflict, hostility, hurting, & I've been apt to run to the rescue of anyone being hurt. I try to be integrating, synergic, etc., & also to take it easy, be patient & go inch by inch (instead of instant love & instant honesty). But it *is* good to move toward the open expression of hostility & difference—to the point where these can be handled & used well. It's no good avoiding anger & attack & malice altogether, as I did most of my life (until maybe 5 or so years ago). I can certainly manage it better than I could in the past, but I'm still cautious & gingerly & bit-by-bit with it. I told them about my rages, etc., but I doubt they believe it. Partly I've discovered now that, because of my position & status, etc., *my* criticisms can be far more devastating than those from others, because mine are taken as authoritative. So *noblesse oblige*. I can hurt more easily than others can. But also for the same reason I can help more than others can. An act of simple kindness or praise or sociability from me seems to have deep effects on some, especially the rejected ones, the inferior ones. Therefore again, *noblesse oblige*. I'm more clear now that this is *me*, my identity, both seen by myself & seen by others. I simply cannot lay aside my knowledge, my reputation, my achievements, my profession & say "I'm just simple old Abe—one of the boys." It can't be done & it's not true. And partly this explains the level-2 shield that I've very firmly erected under level-1 amiability. I don't *want* people to get thru there—I'm just too busy with my mission, my job, to which I am wholly committed. I don't *want* casual friends, or even deep & intimate friends unless it's tied in with my work somehow. I'd like to be intimate with Harry Murray, etc., but not with the greatest chemist in the world. I haven't got that much time left. And the ones with whom I *would* like to be soulmates are just as busy & committed as I am. So we can be soulmates once a year maybe. So I'm alone, & now it's clearer that I *want* to be alone—from most people. Because I'd rather be doing work than developing new intimacies. The people with whom I want intimacy are too busy or not readily available. I'm lunching with S. today. Nice guy, but I don't *want* to develop it. He's not tall enough or strong enough. Neither are the others I've met here. Warren Bennis is the only strong, big man here and the only one I'd like to get closer with. He feels the same way, & we will—to the extent that busy-ness permits. We're having dinner tonight. (Met Charlie & Edie Seashore & was charmed with them & their beautiful baby. It attracts me to the Higher Education Lab here at Bethel next summer that has been offered to me.)

The ideal group has trust enough to confront the profundity & the unbridgeability of individual differences & to accept their inevitability, & yet to get along, remain a group, no enemies, bitterness, etc., while disagreeing & struggling as in the U. S. Senate in real battles, & *then* going off to lunch together to make fun of each other amicably. I told them about the seminar I ran with Frank Manuel as an example & how I could *value* his disagreement & his thinking me wrong while I think *him* wrong.

June 25

After long A.M. chat with B. over coffee, we agreed that I am really more interested in the depths (& heights) than in the 3-inch-deep defenses being dropped here at NTL. I'm not deeply engaged here. B. pointed out that, when I discuss a psychoanalytic case with Harry, I give full & total attention & am all there. It is true that I'd rather have one case discussion at Stockbridge than 2 weeks here. This dropping of superficial defenses & firming up of the identity, etc., that's going on here is after all old stuff for me. I'm used to it. It's interesting as the human drama always is, & it *is* a good thing to rediscover the truisms. But these have not been for me profound discoveries or illuminations, & so I haven't been really deeply involved or shook up or reactive. It's much better for Bertha, because she's getting a real course in psychology. (Thought: a T-group would make the most perfect elementary course or introductory course in psychology!) She's learning a great deal & profiting a great deal, as she did in Palm Beach. For me it's a professional obligation, a duty, a good thing. I'm glad I came. It's useful & instructive. But I'll be glad to get home, & I wouldn't want to stay for a second session. I'll probably do a co-training session, probably next summer in the Higher Education Lab, but this is definitely a means to the end of contact with aggridants.

So this teaches me the difference between NTL & psychoanalysis (and height psychology).

*   *   *

Joe Bailey congratulated me conventionally on being elected to this office & with the same straight conventional tone asked "And how do you explain it?" [*B. spoke of a "stingy smile."*] And then on to my peak-experience paper [72] being rejected by the *Psychological Review* and the *American Psychologist;* and since then I have never sent a paper into the APA journals (empirical exceptions). I couldn't get a job in most departments of psychology. How come? Something scary going on in APA. I felt out of it, rejected, alienated, & even had thoughts of quitting APA. What does it mean that I was elected? How about the grad-student revolt? How about the tight-asses & the proctopsychologists running graduate instruction & only the obsessionals giving the Ph.Ds? Let me speak for the other characterological half (or ¾) of the psychologists, the more oral rather than anal, the more hysteroid rather than obsessoid, the warm rather than the cool ones, the personal rather than the impersonal, the Theory-Y rather than the Theory-X educators, the Dionysian rather than the Apollonian. (I *won't* say tender-minded, because I consider that I am speaking as a transcender of this distinction. I consider my theorizing *far* more *truly* tough-minded than itty-bitty researches which are well done. The expensive little "nothing," as the women say, or "the mice that have been borne by mountains.") For the ones who are concerned about the dangers to the human species & who feel historical urgency vs. those who play chess or perfect their golf games while the world teeters on the edge of destruction, including science & including psychology; for the ones who seek values, the ethically concerned, the ones who want to help mankind in its troubles (& who feel that, more than any other group, the psychologists are called upon to help) rather than the amoral, the value-free, the "detached" & unfeeling.

July 9

The post-Bethel thoughts keep coming. Just going thru Bugental's book. Most of these friends or acquaintances. And it dawned on me again that I feel closer to so many of the California people than to my friends & acquaintances here. I'd always thought this was the accident of nearness & distance. But now it occurs to me that these are all T-group people, & it makes a difference. They're more direct, honest, candid, undefended, open, feedbacky, etc. And so I actually *do* justly & correctly feel more intimate with them than I do with non-T-group people here. I told Ric last night, & Genia & Harry, et al., at party, that 17 years of friendship with Ric had brought an intimacy that was achieved at Bethel in 2 weeks! And to Genia I said that the only time she had ever been direct with me was 15 years ago when she got mad at me. She smiled & said nothing! It's simply a different kind of interpersonal relationship. When Bob & Edith were here & they asked about my friendship with Harry, I said he was wonderful when he could keep the analyst role. He's always been wonderfully helpful when I *asked* for help. But he's never asked *me* for help. And from him, as with others, practically no feedback at all. I have very little idea about what Harry thinks of me, how he sees me. He rarely says. Genia *never* does. Ric occasionally.

July 19

Save the point, which I've made several times at several places: my courage *still* keeps increasing (almost age 60!), & with increased courage comes a blunter, more honest, more naked version, more true & correct, less hedged, fudged, appeasing, diplomatic, polite, etc. Each time now I've had to revise or bring up-to-date or write a new foreword (as for the Japanese translation of the management book [92]), the foreword is unconsciously more courageous & truer than the book. I'd now call it normative social psychology! Same for the foreword I'm now doing for the library edition of the Being book. Same for successive versions of my courses. I suppose at age 70 I'll look back & see *these* as not naked enough, too timid, etc. I had practically no trouble or tension yesterday with newspaper fuss over Bindrim's naked-group therapy. Compare this with prostration-exhaustion-tension over giving at APA my paper on B-cognition in the peak-experiences, & it took me days to recover. Sheer anxiety over flinging down this gauntlet before the APA. Also nightmares of being shut out of family = expelled from APA, or stoned, etc. But of course this was *courage* too, since I went ahead & climbed over my fears & tensions. Then compare this with my first paper that I was to give before the Wisconsin Academy of Arts & Sciences (on psychoanalysis as a status quo social philosophy). Then I did not have enough courage & simply fled & never showed up.

1967

May 25

A good lead. I've been confused over the question "does high self-esteem and aggridance constitute the healthier, the more self-actualizing, the more fully human?" I think not necessarily. Separate variables are: (1) the level of dominance and self-esteem (in the constitutional sense, e.g., males, for hormonal reasons, seem to be more aggressive than females, more restless, more pushing toward dominance, more angered by exploitation, rape, being dominated, more rivalrous in king-of-the-hill sense); (2) the amount of health, of self-actualization and full humanness (as in my dominance and security studies, where it was clearly possible to be low in dominance *if* one were secure; and the high-dominance subjects who were insecure were clearly unhealthy). SA theory means to be whatever one truly is, even if this is possibly passive, timid, a follower. This falls within jurisdiction of a normal or healthy constitution, as with infants born passive or active. Therefore must separate aggridance-dominance as constitutionally authentic from nonforcefulness as *also* constitutionally authentic. (Maybe aggridance is more mesomorphic then *generally* healthy? Ectomorphs & endomorphs are clearly as healthy or "normal" as mesomorphs. Work this out more. Still puzzling. (3) Still other variables are the XY (cool-warm, blue-green vs. red-orange, anal-oral, etc., in XY file). The *healthy* obsessional (like Walter Toman, where it is not a defense) is just as healthy and respectable as the healthy hysteroid, who is simply more emotional, more personal, etc.

I think statistical thinking, especially factor analysis, would help in tearing out these separable variables. Maybe there are more than 3. I thought of some good experiments to separate the X and the Y. For instance, their color preferences. Do blue-green types maybe actually prefer blue and green over red and orange? Also, as I sit here listening to the harp music, I think: how about preference for harp, flute, etc., over brass and drums? These tastes would correlate with warm-cool variable and also with high & low dominance. Would it also correlate with female and male hormones? Also with mesomorph, ectomorph, endomorph? I doubt very much that there would be *any* correlation with psychological health, or with metamotives or ultimate values in any way.

I wonder how many of the tastes (also expressive movements,

capacities) that I found to correlate with the dominance and self-esteem variables correlated *purely* with it? Maybe I was also picking out healthier ones, since the dominance score did correlate low-positive with the security score.

May 28

All sorts of insights. One big one about SA stuff, brought on, I think, mostly by my deep uneasiness over *Digest* articles. Lagemann started out on metalecture at Academy but has wound up with SA. I realized I'd rather leave it behind me. Just *too* sloppy & too easily criticizable. Going thru my notes brought this unease to consciousness. It's been with me for years. Meant to write & publish a self-actualization critique, but somehow never did. Now I think I know why. I think I had a hidden, unconscious criterion of selection *beyond* health. Why did I get so excited over Arthur E. Morgan just from reading his book—so sure he was a self-actualizing person? It's because he was using the B-language! What I've done was pick B-people! In addition to all the other overt and conscious criteria. People in the B-realm using B-language, the awakened, the illuminated, the "high-plateau" people who normally B-cognize and who have the B-values very firmly & actively in hand—even tho not consciously. Pearl, for instance. Pop Schrank. *All* of them, I guess. When Lagemann asked me about contemporary public figures, I refused. But I *had* looked over lists of people who fitted my stated 3 criteria, & I just couldn't swallow them, e.g., Eisenhower. He *does* fit. So does Truman. [*Mrs. Roosevelt.*] And yet they are clearly *not* B-people. Same for the APA board of directors—*very* capable & sound, etc., *but* no B-cognition. There are plenty of "healthy" people & even self-actualizing people (by 3 criteria) who are far from B-realm and from unitive perception—stuck in D-realm merely.

So I guess I *did* read into my selectees a criterion beyond "health." Maybe I should have kept on calling them "Good Human Beings" (GHB), as I find I did in notes of 1945, or "Wonderful People," instead of shifting over to talking about "psychologically healthy." When did I start that? It's not present in my earlier notes.

There *was* stress on "full use of capacities and actualization of potentials." *Much* better to say actualization of full humanness, as in D-paper [118]. With that paper and with the Meta-paper [121], I guess I needn't think any more of publishing a critique of SA. *But I'd certainly better publish what I saw this* a.m.—*that I'd smuggled in an unconscious additional variable of B-ness, B-values, B-language.*

May 29

The great puzzle for motivation theory: how come war and the "higher needs" take over from lower needs—i.e., patriotism, self-sacrifice, loyalty, etc., take over from food, etc.? Listening to news of Nasser blustering and threatening and thinking how much food & clothes & medicine all his military adventures cost, the mobilization, the international adventures. Good for *him*, or for any leader in a bad situation throughout history; e.g., for the czars in Russia, if there's a division among the people, or if your own government is in danger, then the best thing to do is to divert anger to an enemy, usually external (amity-enmity complex) or internal (Jews in Russia). I think it's quite possible that if Mao gets in real trouble within China, he can pull everybody into a unified nation by attacking some "enemy" or certainly by managing to *get* attacked (à la Pearl Harbor). OK. This is understandable as a way of hanging on to personal power, or even of "patriotically" pulling everybody together into unity, loyalty, hard work. (I wonder if Ben-Gurion may have *deliberately* made enemies out of the Arabs in order—along with other motives—to bind Israel together in patriotism.) But it's still necessary to understand why the masses swallow the bait. One obvious part of the answer: catharsis of anger, revenge, hurt, resentment against lowered self-esteem. [*6/11/67: Is anger here reactive—to threat to basic needs? Or is it in some sense a basic need itself?*] For instance, in Arabs, huge rage must be piled up over past colonial insults, Israel's contempt, & rage over military defeat, which must be "completed" & catharted, rage over poverty, landlords, rich people, politicians, anything & everybody. Ignorant people won't know why they're angry, or may not even realize that they *are* angry. And it's such a relief to cathart, to vent your misery & revenge & rage without inhibition or guilt—even to kill, to fight, to attack. I still remember the excellent article on the analyzed Communists in *Psychiatry* in the early 1940s that showed them to be essentially hostile people who could now be just as nasty & angry as they wished & still feel virtuous. Venting of hatred, *all* the piled-up hatreds from a whole lifetime of past hurts, rejections, insults, wounds; the reservoir gets emptied out, and this feels good.

June 1

I've given up the novels about homosexuals, creeps, and jerks; I've given up the senseless smearing art, the ugly dancing à la Martha

Graham, the upside-down writing world à la Susan Sontag, Sartre, & de Beauvoir & *most* of the others. It's all getting to me more & more. These movies left me depressed, more so after the utterly stupid & vulgar *Impossible on Saturday* we saw last night.

June 11

Very much affected by visit with Murray yesterday & our discussion of the 4 autobiographies (Murray, Murphy, Rogers, & Allport) & the relationship to the B-realm. [*I told him that I'd finally understood from these autobiographies the differences between Allport & Murray. Murray transcended & Allport didn't. Murray understands & has experienced the B-realm, & we could talk casually & comfortably about it. Allport probably never made it—altho very nice, hard working, great scholar, contributor, formally religious, etc.*] I told him of my new discovery of the difference between Eisenhower-Truman SA and the health-beyond-health of the B-person. The B-person may be *more* symptom-loaded and have more value pathology than the symptom-free "healthies." Maybe one is symptom-free *only* by virtue of not knowing or caring about the B-realm, never having experienced the B-realm in the highest peaks (now *that* must be changed also; must separate Eisenhower-Truman-type peaks from those with full cognition of the B-realm).

June 12

Must make a separate job out of the concept of validation and its reconsideration, on the general task of self-validation by experiencing & then the ease of communication of this self-validation to another person who has had the same experiences (as I did with Murray) and the practical impossibility of such communication or proof or validation to someone who has *not* experienced it. One good example is as between peakers, where the validation is via appeal to the other person's experience. You must have experienced it to believe it, and then it is easy. But how to prove the reality of insight into unconscious motivations to someone who has *not* gone through it? How can you prove it? And, as a matter of fact, it has been practically impossible to prove that Freud was right about anything—that is, by external validations. Experiential validation—shall I call it that? —is easy. Use also the example of proving something visual to a blind man. How can you prove to him that red & blue are different? Very difficult.

July 30

Sunday *Times* & talks with E. & decreasing hope that the U. S. will solve Negro problem, education problem, UN problem—*any* problem—until great catastrophes force it. Congress is just impossible. Black riots seem to be the only way of getting reform, although the danger is that they will create authoritarian counter-reaction, away from reform.

It all relates to my presidential address, to my education writing for next year, & even to my humanistic politics-economics, and to the big writeup of Third-Force philosophy & psychology & religion.

The big point is that, if humanistic education, politics, economics, etc., have goal of SA & the B-life, then we must climb the whole hierarchy of prerequisite basic-need gratifications. And this means safety-security, brotherly love, dignity, self-esteem, not to mention the values of justice, truth, etc. Thus, on the Negro's way toward SA, you *must* give him self-esteem. And how is this to be done in a largely racist or apathetic or ignorant U. S.? I had to say to Father Norman O'Connor at the Stockbridge meeting that the riots were better in *one* sense than no riots, i.e., that overcoming fear is better than being cowed. Fighting one's fear is apt to turn out stupidly & with self-defeating costliness, because it is an over-reaction & breaking of the dam, a snapping of controls, adolescent overdoing. Teaching Negroes, Mexicans, Indians, etc., how to achieve manly self-respect includes, then, teaching revolt, hopefully more sensible & efficient (à la Israelis, which is a good parallel after 2000 years of meekness, negotiation, being good, not making trouble, etc.) (Tell joke: Jews being executed by Nazi firing squad. One refuses blindfold. Others whisper "For God's sake, don't make trouble.") If I were Negro, I'd move on every & any front that would help toward higher-need gratifications, including both threat of violence *and* legal reform, job training, education, school improvement, etc. Reformism is not mutually exclusive with violent revolution, in accord with my revolution theory which stresses division of labor.

One cannot become fully human in a blind alley. As soon as hope is cut off for assured rewards & reinforcements for hard work and for *guaranteed* jobs as the reward of training, then the society no longer functions, & one has the right to revolt & be violent—& hopefully wise & directed in the revolt. That is, it ought to be pragmatically successful so long as this is possible. The good general *wins*.

Therefore criticize strongly the hopeless Left, the ones who despair entirely in an unrealistic, adolescent way, à la Marcuse, Paul Goodman, etc., who see no use in any action except destruction & protest. The *Götterdämmerung*, the mass suicide. Relate this to the paranoia, the total mistrust, the loss of realism altogether of someone who is against the Peace Corps, etc., who simply assumes that Johnson & the CIA assassinated Kennedy, who wants to write a book on Provo tactics, i.e., just simply bust up the society; absolutely no improvement is possible; suicide, death, and self-destruction are the only recourses à la Warsaw ghetto revolt (rather than à la Israeli army).

Study the knower first! I *must* stress more the transhumanistic definition of objectivity, detachment, cognition of the Being of the other, the Taoistic let-be, nonintrusive, noninterfering epistemology, which is *most* objective & "true" because it glories in the otherness of the other instead of selfizing the other & assimilating it to one's own selfish, ego-centered, useful-nonuseful, important-unimportant world. It *wants* the other to remain wholly other, as the B-lover wants the beloved *not* to change, *not* to accommodate, *not* to try to please or to be useful, not to modify self in *any* way in order to please, but to be wholly self-ish, since that self is already perfect & *any* change must be a diminution or a worsening. What other relation *can* one have to what is already perfect & is therefore perfectly loveworthy as is. Reminds me of St. John of the Cross & his dark-night-of-the-soul stuff about the Beloved. (God? I'm still not sure that this guy wasn't talking about a human lover—maybe female, maybe male—and that all the pious commentaries didn't come later in order to camouflage. Or perhaps when he saw that his *human* B-love for a human could very well serve as the model for religious, church-type, God-type love of God for man and man for God, he believed them both, or, rather, experienced them both! And which he experienced first really makes no difference. Same for Song of Songs!) Anyway, the beloved is so perfect as to make one aware of one's own shittiness, unworthiness, imperfection (Luther's bag of shit), so that fear, anguish, inferiority, self-derogating, etc., result in a kind of anguish, because how *could* the Perfect Beloved not go away, not disdain, not withdraw his love? But the *miracle* is that he doesn't! In spite of the self-revelation of unworthiness, the forced confession of one's shittiness—how can you be phony & hammy with godlike perfection? One of the first things that happens in B-love is honesty, humility, the confession of unworthiness, the feeling that (1) he has X-ray eyes anyway, and (2) honesty, candor, confession, dropping of defenses and masks are somehow called for. It belongs intrinsically & necessarily to the situation of loving someone perfect—that with great pain & anguish one renounces faking. And then the miracle is that the Beloved keeps on loving! No wonder God is thought of as merciful, all-loving, all-forgiving, gratuitous grace.

A real question for scientific epistemology here. Is the perfection attributed, created, projected? No. This doesn't matter. Take the example of B-love for dogs. If you really love dogs, you love them the way they are! You don't want them clipped or "bred" or certified, or certainly not "beauty-parlored" or taught "cute tricks." Same for women. I really like women. Therefore I like them as they are. I hate dyed hair, nose jobs, girdles—even brassieres, cosmetics, fashions of all kinds. I'd prefer them naked, natural, and untouched.

August 12

Bad night (to sleep at 4 A.M. with Seconal). Turned out to be partly bad dreams, mainly about theory of human evil. Set off by rewriting of page 1 of Being book for revision. It just *cannot* be stated in a paragraph or two—even as an assumption. Just too complicated. How to condense the Socratic notion (supported by the science-fiction book I was reading last night in which IQs went up thru 234 in one girl and to 1200 in the boss) that much "evil" comes out of ignorance & stupidity & low IQ (as in movie we saw yesterday—*The Family Way*). [*Add despair & hopelessness.*] Clearly the world's problems could be quickly solved by intelligence (which would most likely mean greater *virtue* too). Question then is: why do we not as a species really love & admire & trust high-IQ leaders & pick them & support them (which = trust?)? And again, evil is now the basic problem. And in this problem, the area of countervaluing is a basic subproblem. [*How to teach people to love excellence? Alphas? Genius? Aggridants? This too goes with Value seminar.*]

And then my impulse is: for the love of Pete, drop whatever the hell you're doing & write this up. I've got all the notes in the file & enough journal memos to come up with a good definite, humanistic solution (i.e., a realistic & true summary of our knowledge & its ultimate support for the humanistic assumption that evil is mostly reactive rather than instinctoid). But how can I with all the commitments & promises I have? If I could drop the goddam APA! And if I could brush off the Education-3 commitment with, e.g., the Esalen tapes, which contain, for the perceptive ones, most of what I'll be saying a year from now. *Then* I could go into hiding & work up this stuff on evil about the level of development of my Metapaper [121] (I *think*) within a few months. Judging from my dreams, that's what my deepest impulses are to do.

[*Can we cure the Negro riots or not? My assumption is yes, by improving the quality of conditions & therefore of life & therefore of personality. I assume the riots come out of reactive anger (understandable & in a certain sense therefore forgivable). But I must add also: they also come out of despair, hopelessness, death wishes for self & others. At least this we've learned from the riots. But Congress doesn't agree with this & votes mostly for simple suppression = belief that they can never be helped = they are intrinsically inferior-different = an example of ignorance = evil = need for scientific knowledge.*]

To get back to what I started with—evil. I guess I could say that most people think people are evil. My way rather is to think they are stupid. That's more fundamental, because the evil comes *from* ignorance, which comes from stupidity (which comes from not being experimental, empirical, "scientific" enough). My cure for the evil behavior is ultimately more knowledge. (There really *is* no other cure.) [*Science is truth-therapy (better than cognitive-therapy) or reality-therapy. Aligns it then with T-group, psychotherapy, education (responsibility-therapy?).*] Should we go back to churches & priests? Impossible! To authoritarianism? By whom? Jerks who think all human beings are basically stupid & evil—except themselves, who usually in history have been the *most* stupid & evil & lazy & antiknowledge! And self-defeating! Self-destroying à la Hitler, Trujillo, Mao, & all the others. Come to think of it, that's *the* great trouble with authoritarianism—that it gives authority to the scum, to the very *worst*! Science-fiction authoritarianism of last night = boss with IQ of 1200, wisdom, virtue—who would protest against this? How many virtuous tyrants have there been? (Why not? Does power *necessarily* corrupt? How to put this together with Thorndike's *positive* correlation of intelligence & virtue, in kings, etc.? There are contradictions here someplace. For example, why do the bastards win followers?) [*All the B-values correlate positively. Where there is apparent contradiction of this, I suspect it's because of dichotomizing one value away from the others.*]

August 30

Just got a good solution, from *N. Y. Times,* on problem that's been bugging me for a long time. Several items in the paper on *absolute* rights to, e.g., privacy, the Constitution, etc., all making it fine for the Mafia, for criminals, psychopaths, etc., which is *far* more a danger to the U. S. & the world than bombs, Communists, etc. This is like using gentleman's rules with jungle people & is a wonderful technique for suicide, either for a person or for a society. My motivation theory makes it look stupid, as I think of political "levels" (low & high), economic, legal, etc., etc., but somehow I couldn't figure out a rationale or ideology to support my strong *feeling* of profound stupidity of a society shackling itself. Certainly if I were in the jungle, I'd shift over immediately to jungle rules, just as I've actually done with authoritarians, psychopaths, crooks, bastards, etc. I've found it easy to shift over (*downward*) to their rules (if I couldn't do as I preferred, which has always been to break the relationship & never resume it, i.e., have nothing to do with such people).

The answer is clear: there is a hierarchy of *rights*—also different levels of them for different cultures & environments. This is not to say there are no "absolute" rights, but one is entitled to these only in Eupsychia, i.e., under the best conditions only. Otherwise my right to protect my life is clearly prepotent to someone else's right to have a flower garden, or keep his property rights in a warehouse full of food. For me this was & is *the* one big argument for Israel—that even a cornered rat can selfishly fight for his life, for simple survival, & that this outweighs *any* other laws. At this lowest jungle level of sheer survival, I could even make out a case for the rights of the stronger & the more powerful. I.e., if either I or someone else must do, *maybe* I'd try to take away from him his survival food or oxygen or whatever, on the grounds that if I *could*, then that would automatically prove my "superiority" in the jungle in relationship to neutral Darwinian nature, which lets the weaker ones, e.g., without a territory, be more likely to die off. (But maybe it would, at this time anyway, be more diplomatic not to mention this. I remember how angry & disturbed Rogers got at Palm Beach when I talked about aggridants. He couldn't take it. And since then Bob Tannenbaum told me that Rogers was *furious*, more than angry.)

The rights I *have*, e.g., to privacy, are themselves relative to the situation today. I feel we must renegotiate the right to privacy today because of the Mafia, & I'm quite prepared to give up some of my right to privacy, or to buy guns freely, etc. Conditions change, technology changes, & therefore the social rules must change. If *I* were fighting the Mafia, I'd use any rules they use, including assassination or whatever. "Rights" are in a sense just the agreed-upon rules of the game, & I don't see why I have to give the criminal a head start! I dropped out of the ACLU for this reason.

Same thing for duties & responsibilities: they too are in levels, hierarchical. I have more duties to a good person than I do to an evil person, altho there may be some *minimum* rights for *anyone*, e.g., protection from sheer sadism & torture to no purpose (altho if there is some overriding purpose & if the rules of the game have been set by the other, I'd have little hesitation in using *his* rules of killing, or of torturing to get information, or *whatever* he had felt free to do to me).

This is all somehow evolutionary, Darwinian, nature-dictated animal level, which is, after all, our lowest need level, & therefore social-tactics level, e.g., *lex talionis* laws of sheer survival & who chooses to survive when not all can, etc. This is lowest-need-level politics (& economics).

September 19

Plane from Monterey to S. F. Start working thru all the mixed impressions & conflicts & ambivalences from the weekend, & to separate out the superficial from the deep. The place is less lovable definitely; maybe because Mike & Dick Price are gone. The hippie casualness & good humor are certainly there; but the inefficiency & (deep) noncaring for other people (anyway, squares), & the free giving away of things & the hobo element, begging, inefficient work, began to threaten the whole enterprise (Bud Layton, business manager, finds it impossible to be economically efficient because everything leaks out to the beggars). All of this doesn't & hasn't bothered me, especially when I came alone (Bertha reacted with fury to everything). It's like the hippie wedding. I certainly enjoyed watching it & envied them their abandon in their dancing & in their dressing up, *but* it's only like going for a visit to an amusement park or a party or a picnic. And with the baths, the massage, the beauty, everybody smiling & amicable (to me), it can be a happy time for me, a real relaxation & unwinding of the guts. And then obviously they're starting important things there. It's a most important, even revolutionary enterprise. And if it catches on, there may be hundreds of them shortly in the world. It may change all of education.

But it hovers still on the knife edge of self-indulgence, mere experientialism, antiscience, anti-intellectualism, antiwriting. That's what made me mad at the fellow, & their antiresearch, antiwriting, & especially the proctopsychological interpretation by one of them of writing as self-aggrandizement, etc. I felt it also with Bill Schutz, who would be good for Esalen intellectually, but it may be bad for him. Same for the others—Heider, Maupin, Miller, et al.—who may lose fiber if they don't watch out.

Also I spoke very strongly of their being selfish or unselfish, of helping others instead of just experiential auto-eroticism. When someone asked me to come back, I thought: "Yes, if they use Bodhisattvas. No, if they use Pratychabuddhas. I spoke—or rather thundered like an Old Testament prophet—of duty, responsibility, real guilt, selfishness, etc. I suppose deep down they all agree with it & will come around. But it reminds me of the real dangers of hippie-dom, of spiritual masturbation, of the far-out. It's then that I feel most academic, professional, conceptual, organized, Apollonian, scientific.

Peculiarly, I suspect the only one who fully agrees with me is Mike Murphy, who is far-out but still really open, curious, not tied to a system like Skinner, or Rogers as he was telling me, or even like Schutz, Gunther, who would be startled to hear themselves called intolerant, unopen, excluding—& Schutz is the *best* of the group. It's the advancement of knowledge that counts. Not just *any* knowledge, most of which is amoral, but the knowledge that in this moment of impending danger & species-destroying we desperately & urgently need in a hurry. I really don't care much about helping a privileged few to lead happier lives on the edge of catastrophy. This factor of historical urgency as an additional criterion in deciding the question of scientific importance looms bigger with me all the time. It should certainly go into the presidential address, especially since it applies also to clinicians in general, who don't do their share in advancing knowledge, who don't teach us from their experience. If it's not written down (which is the *only* form of teaching that spreads widely enough & covers a quantity of ears + geographical spread to poor countries), then it's selfish & elitist. Maybe talk of collaboration between writer & nonwriter, scientist & nonscientist, as with Harry & me, as a technique?

October 22

This seems to me to be extremely important. I've had to say again & again that the whole 3rd Force psychology of growth & SA is true only for those with a life wish & not for those with a death wish who prefer to die, to commit suicide, or to be killed = the losers. As in the riots yesterday in Washington—for peace no less!—those who put their skulls under the stick, who want to be hurt, executed, crucified. [*Martyrs.*] The generals & "leaders" on both extremes who are looking for defeat for themselves & for their followers—who obviously prefer a kind of *Götterdämmerung*—dont *want* to win or to be effective or to be pragmatic, or to bring about their verbally stated ends; they unconsciously prefer a satisfying defeat. [*I wonder if this could lead to a reinterpretation of Jesus & his crucifixion—which was* sought!]

November 2

A book review claims that the short-story form in its essence, deals with life's victims, the insulted & the injured, the forlorn & alienated (attributed to Frank O'Connor). I think it's crap, & again wonder how so stupid & empirically false a statement can be taken seriously. It's by a Bernard Bergonze, in the *New York Review of Books*, Nov. 9, 1967, which I'm getting on a gift subscription from Ellen. I dislike this magazine very much. It irritates me. It is "stylish," "chic," "smart" in the Greenwich Village style, à la Mary McCarthy, the poison-pen woman—she also writes in this issue. Again I'm reminded how alienated & distant I am from the "intellectual community," or at least the vocal members of it—as I was in the thirties. I'm on a different tack altogether—as I was then. And I think I'm right today & they're wrong—just as in the thirties. I've been speculating: Is it that intellectuals are ectomorphs & the doers mesomorphs? And is this split a constitutional one? Is there something about ectomorphy that nudges one in this fatal direction & gets him to choose the victim, the nay-sayer, the loser? Does he *identify* with the loser, unconsciously feeling himself to *be* a loser? And to admire & follow the dictator, the violent one, the loud-mouth, the paranoid? Why did the intellectuals go for Stalin? And why are they not horrified by dictatorship today, if only it is on the Left side? Why don't they *love* the Bill of Rights?

November 6

Good thought about Presidential address. Call it the *Third Psychology*—& the 4th. Start in: This is a new image of man, a new philosophy of human nature & of all of its works. Then say what it *contradicts*, to heighten the contrast: it is *not* Marxianism—better, it contradicts Marx. It contradicts the Freudian *image of man* (not the detailed discoveries). It contradicts the assumptions of both socialism *and* classical capitalism. It contradicts the basic & foundational assumptions of classical economics & politics. It has very serious questions to ask of political, parliamentary democracy, & discovers shortcomings of democracy, as of many other of the political philosophies which are used today by various countries. It generates a greater sense of specieshood, of the basic similarity of all human beings, & so implies a single world order & world law. Thus it contradicts nationhood & national sovereignty. It generates new approaches to every corner of psychology, & suggests some new corners to poke into. This includes psychotherapy & its professionalism. As a matter of fact, it generates a new conception of the professional-client relationship in *any* type of helping relationship. Professionalism is seen with great suspicion as being often a technologizing (value-free) of *all* the human relationships, many of which much of the time had better be on an I-Thou, older-brother basis. Rather than being an arrogance arising from forming a dominance-subordination relationship between, e.g., the mother & the obstetrician, it should rather be a Taoistic *offering*, being available to the helpee as a consultant, a servant, & *not* as a castrator. *Not* as one who takes people's responsibility for themselves upon his own shoulders. (Injection of an artificial hormone causes glands to stop working.)

This new philosophy offers a religion-surrogate, with much more personal meaning & effectiveness than the established idolatries which pass as established religions. Same for science. Same for work, industry, management. Same for education. (Theory Z goes in here too.) Same for professional philosophy, which has mostly abdicated its general-human responsibilities—it is offered a chance to become an *empirical* discipline at its foundations.

It makes necessary a distinction between yea-saying & nay-saying Existentialism.

It has already generated new pathologies which must eventually force a profound change in the American Psychiatric Association catalogue of illnesses.

Hierarchical-integration instead of atomistic thinking with its splitting, dichotomizing, analyzing, separating, & its tendency to try to be value-free or neutral.

New conceptions of helping.

Add at beginning: I am very aware & am made quite uncomfortable, sometimes get scared, at the fewness of the data. This must be presented as a theory or as a set of hypotheses offered for shooting at & perhaps disconfirming (even tho I consider it all to be empirically based, albeit on too few data). For *me*, it is all a product of data, of testing, of experiencing, of observation, & of many, many quick little exploratory reconnaissances not suitable for publication—& yet good enough to convince me of plausibility & to keep me feeling virtuous about the empirical spirit.

It drags values into science, discovering them, validating & testing them. Rejection of the value-free science model means a change in epistemology & every other branch of philosophy.

New theory of evil, etc. Look thru all the categories in the journals & in the file cabinets.

Even a modified theory of evolution.

November 12

When Mary Bailey asked me so trustingly "What *is* Theory Z?" it stopped me. I just haven't worked it out. One way of describing it, I said, was the transcending of basic needs & to become metamotivated, i.e., to love & to seek primarily the ultimate good things, excellence, perfection, the good job, etc. Another way I thought of was in terms of cosmic consciousness = feeling identified with the cosmos, being an intrinsic & necessary part of it, belonging by right, as in one's own home or one's own family. But this also means to transcend identity, self, etc., & to go beyond into merging & fusing with the world (instead of being a separate ego), homonomy (high), the "high Nirvana." It all recalls the Eastern ways of describing the "Awakened One," who no longer works for, & certainly does not *need*, worldly possessions (& I would add, not to *need* fame or glory or applause or power), where self-esteem is so strong & firm that it no longer needs "supplies," & also strong enough to go on to humility of the self-confident sort, the realistic accepting of one's limits, weaknesses, mortality, vulnerability to pain, to fear, ignorance, etc. Where one can calmly accept all the weaknesses of wormhood & *yet* not really be disturbed by it = functional pride & self-esteem so as to be able to be creative & responsible (to be a strong worm).

Difficulty: if I make the mystical level higher than the Truman-Eisenhower level of self-actualization, then I get all mixed up about "health." Truman & Eisenhower are certainly healthy, but how about many mystics who seem to abandon the whole idea of health—Simone Weil & other "saints," some of them anyway, who seemed to be half-nuts like Weil. Of course not all: Schweitzer, Tillich, et al., are certainly Theory-Z & awakened to the B-realm, & yet they could be called self-actualizing, healthy, fully-human, etc. They were more healthy. But how about Blake? I still don't know if he was also a nut. And then Thoreau? He certainly talked the B-language, *must* have been a peaker. And yet, his turning away from the human species, women and children?

Aunt Pearl is also a problem. She's certainly self-actualizing at the Truman-Eisenhower level. Healthy. Strong. Life-zest. But I know of nothing in her beyond the mundane & secular. Maybe also Mrs. Roosevelt, who specifically said "No!" to my question about having peak or mystical experiences. Compare this with Huxley, for instance. In all of Mrs. Roosevelt's writings & speaking, no *mention* of anything peaky or B-level, no B-language, etc. Even her reasons for being a church-goer were not "religious." She went to set a good example to others. *Noblesse oblige.* To show that one needn't be only selfish, etc. But come to think of it, she didn't have the nonpeaker or antipeaker personality or outlook. Would I have dug out peaks if I had pursued it further? Is it that some people make only secular, mundane, D-realm use of peak-experiences, i.e., no vision of the B-realm or, if so, then not staying there?

November 22

More & more coming to a head—precipitated I think by conversation with Tamara Dembo about the professional-client relationship—is the technologist-value-free-expert-controller. Last few days the struggle over S. S. has resulted in a defeat for me. He's to be kept on by Ric, Simmel, Wodinsky, & Maher vs. me & Jim Klee. It hit me deeply & I dreamed last night of my bafflement, frustration, etc., over this deep characterological conflict between the humanists & the technologists, which finally gets to be a sheer power struggle, a counting of votes, because persuasion is *im*possible. Logic, facts, reason, data, etc., are all to no avail—even with a friend like Ric. I'm sure he likes me & respects me & we can truly be called friends—I certainly feel that way. And yet the difference of opinion (or taste, *Weltanschauung*) is simply irreconcilable.

But as I browsed thru Matson's *Being, Becoming, and Behavior,* which just came, the passage on Rogers fused with the passage on Nietzsche to make me realize that very deep in the technological expert is his *lack* of love & respect for the student, but that this is replaced by total control & power. The young people want relevance, historical urgency, humanistic helping.

November 30

Reading Ritter's *Education.* He insists on absolute self-choice even in schoolchildren à la Summerhill—in spite of absence of data. I feel much more cautious & tentative than he does. Thinking about it, it occurs to me that I would grant wisdom & success of self-regulation for *healthy* kids, life-positive, good choosers, Alphas! But I get cautious with schlemiels, aments, passives, fearfuls, losers, expendables, etc. Maybe even this is an operational way of defining Alpha: give him free choice & see if he thrives or if he destroys himself, as in the chicken & rat poor choosers. This can be done even with infants, I think. Considerable implications for democracy theory—practice, too. (I've made the point often that in the U. S. we already disenfranchise lots of the weak, the senile, psychotic, criminal (*imprisoned* criminals may be the *loser*-criminals; maybe the strong & capable ones don't get caught so often), feebleminded. And many others disenfranchise themselves voluntarily. Maybe it's best *not* to coax *everyone* to vote. Maybe democracy works because so many Zetas don't vote. (Rethink on this basis what goes on in the Communist countries in Europe which are governed by 5% in Communist Party. Could these be the aggridants?)

When I talked with Joe Bailey he implied favoring weighted votes for individuals à la Nevil Shute. At first it seems attractive. But then I always get sobered as I think of the dangers of autocracy, oligarchy, even sage-ocracy. Who would do the weighting of the votes? Chamber of Commerce? Ku Klux Klan? Bishops? And then I get scared by the dangers of all these elitiest notions. Now there's a new danger from the value-free-experts, who are multiplying rapidly.

The ultimate question is how to associate factual superiority, à la the aggridant, with modest, humility, etc., or at least to keep it from becoming hubris, privilege, snottiness. Or becoming mixed up with nonbiological "superiority" as in class & caste connections, e.g., the wife of the aggridant. Should *she* be privileged? His children? These people who come in on the Alpha's coat-tails make much of the social trouble.

How to make these people into the "servants of the people" with *less*, rather than *more*, privileges or luxuries?

I don't dare to publish this stuff yet. Too dangerous socially. Would be used by the wrong people, I suspect, in a misinterpreted way.

Also, might my humanistic education be a prescription for *healthy* kids only, just as the Third-Force psychology *implies* as a prerequisite a love for life? Therefore are freedom, self-choice, democracy, self-regulation all for life-positives primarily? Or *only?*

December 9

On Dec. 6 EKG alarming & put on back at once & brought to intensive-care unit for 3 days. Ischemia. No damage or little damage. Slept for all 3 days & nights. Canceled N. Y. trip & everything else. In effect resigned APA presidency—or made it honorary. Canceled Kairos trip. No thoughts for 3 days. Then got interested in resacralization of nursing. And outlined new article: Is there a profit motive? Will write later.

December 14

Another thought I had: The university world can now, I think, be essentially characterized as value-confused, value-mistrusting, counter-valuing, value-hating. They don't know right from wrong & maybe don't even believe it's *possible,* or that there are any such things. Result of Marxism, Freud, cultural relativism, pseudo-anthropology, the abdication of the philosophers, the physicalism of the psychologists, the value-free sociologists, etc. Also, for the same reason, the taking over of the N. Y. C. "sophisticated" world by homos, poison-penners, "clever" ones, so that review of books, art, poetry, music, are *all* crappy. (Where would Tolstoy be in this crowd? Where would *any* decent person be?)

Maybe this all explains why, of all the youth groups I've met, I like the nursing students best. I think this will mean something for my education writing. Why do I prefer them to the Brandeis kids? Why does the student newspaper get me so mad? Why would I quit if I could? (The only things I've really enjoyed are the "nice kids," HSUNA, LRY, the Upward Bound group, etc.)

December 23

Add to preface not only books already done, with explanation of its place in the total structure, but also books I'd like to write if I had time: (1) education 3 & 4; (2) politics & economics—despite both as based on false & limited psychology, e.g., profit motive, "liberal," "conservative," etc., obsolete. Slow revolution. Moral on higher-need-transcendent economics. *Then* a book on evil, which is really ignorance & schlemiel-hood. A system of human nature & society (stress difference; autonomy of society). Stress biology & specieshood. Announce "Farther Reaches of Human Nature." Announce death-defying journals & book—a style which can be published *any*time. Maybe I should do a posthumous book out of journals prehumously. Stress my eagerness to improve the world & list chain stuff. Tell the youngster I was going to write a youth preface but lost my nerve, but *will* add: (1) there *are* values; (2) beware of the bastards and the mean ones; (3) learn to pick your leaders better. Describe a good one & contrast with the losers who want only a glorious death. Stress my meta-chapter as end of 25 years of work for the peace table. Best to keep on working for the peace table even tho there's a good chance we'll have a catastrophe first. Maybe plan *before* the catastrophe? UN—no veto —bicameral—trusteeships for people incapable of governing themselves to teach them how. The UN should *own* property, seas, poles, places like Cyprus & Jerusalem. Fight national sovereignty, but use it as transitional, e.g., redivide Africa into tribal areas. Must have a UN standing army. Must have population control & stability & *then* can go any place at will. Value cultural pluralism, but *one* language (*any* one) as universal second language, etc. Managerial revolution. The UN *must* have right to go into areas seized by brigands, e.g., Haiti. *Must* be able to run elections, e.g., South Vietnam, & enforce the results. *Must* decentralize, have local government, town meetings for *all*, functions that would be better served so. But then larger & more inclusive units with powers appropriate to *their* size. Must have extended families, 3 generations, maybe like Chinese? Anyway the N. Y .C. family is no good.

December 26

New worries about the journals. What to do with them? The way I feel now, I just don't feel up to writing all the things I feel I ought to, the world needs, my duties. Wouldn't *mind* dying as a result, but I just don't have the stamina to *do* them. So the thought is save it all in little memos in these journals & the right person to come will know what I mean & why it *must* be done. Yesterday I talked with Walter Weisskopf, one of the greatest minds I know, & he evaded the necessity of writing up higher-need & metaneed economics in order to change the world & to destroy the idiotic stuff about profit motives, capitalism, socialism—*all* crap, *all* obsolete, all stale. And nobody but me to contradict it, & I just haven't got the strength. I told Walter his answer, a letter in N. Y. *Review of Books* to some jerk, was too weak. He added to profit motive the power motive. Big deal! *Weak. Cowardly.* How about all the other motives that these managers are working for? How about the hidden ½ of 1% of saintliness even in the toughest ones? He couldn't deny it, but changed the subject, or called me optimistic, etc. Same with Frank Manuel, a great man, whose *Newton* should be a great book, a changing book to change the world & to teach us, each of us, how *we* have been Newtonized, how *we* must cleanse ourselves, how *we* must take up our prophetic responsibilities in a world of idolators; & he too changed the subject & ran away from his great responsibility—like Jonah. Whom can I count on? Henry Geiger? Maybe. He certainly is a wise & perceptive man & he's *not* a coward like the others—but he's got his *mishegass,* his hangups here & there on pacifism, or on Gandhi, or reincarnation. Maybe these won't matter. Maybe I should give him my journals.

I must also be sure to arrange, in case of death, to put together my "Farther Reaches of Human Nature" [144]. I'll list instructions when I get home. Any good editor could do this, I think, but maybe also one of my friends. Bertha is taken care of with insurance & daughters don't need anything. Are they interested? Do they get the message? If only Ric or Paquita got the message or were identified enough with it—they would be absolutely reliable & loyal. Harry is too unpredictable & too orthodox still anyway.

I guess this is one trouble with avoiding disciples & adorees. Nobody to take up the humble, self-abnegating tasks. I must rely rather on good friends who agree with me about my "task" or mission.

Maybe I could dictate from journals all of the stuff on a single heading? I've thought of that.

How about youngsters? Haven't even thought of them. Min Chiang? Art Warmoth? Joel Aronoff? Debby Tanzer?

[4/4/68: Have changed my mind. I wish my wife, Bertha Maslow, to decide what to do with all my journals, who should edit or publish them, who should own them or use them. They are in her charge completely. Abraham H. Maslow. I do this because I feel that her judgment & her loyalty to my wishes in these matters will be the best that I can think of. A. H. M.

I give her permission to censor names of living persons who might be hurt to no purpose, & to use her own judgment entirely. Under no circumstances must any of these journals be destroyed or pages torn out or anything inked out. Such stuff that might hurt can be closed off from publication until death of people involved. Finally, if my journals are used as much as possible & there seems no further use can be made of them at once, then I direct that they be given to the Archives of The History of Psychology, Dr. Popplestone, Director, to be kept with other documents & papers I've already given to him. My belief is that this is a great turning point in history—if we are not killed off altogether—& that any documents will be of interest to the historians.]

December 27

Home after 22 days in hospital. Talked with Fromm (Dr. Hans Fromm) about my nice discovery this A.M. about defense-fear-anger-hate patriotism (that pulls people together) vs. the patriotism of brotherhood & love & identification. Solves the problem that's puzzled mankind so: Why do the *best* qualities in men come out in war—loyalty, unselfishness, brotherhood, etc? Well now I know; the "same" results (not really the same) come from 2 different sources, defense & growth. (Phenomenologically they *must* feel different, even if the behavior is the same.) [*Stress: nationalism-patriotism is being transcended.*]

He spoke at length of war. The Germans, he said, would never go to war. All the youngsters are getting Europeanized; French & German youngsters now transcend their silly nationalism. He was even given a lift, he said, by a concentration camp inmate.

This is the thing to stress instead of all the Vietnam nonsense. Vietnam is no different from other wars, indeed it's *more* virtuous if anything. What *is* different is that the youngsters are transcending nationalism, patriotism, etc. They don't feel the automatic enmity to the "other side." Maybe they don't feel *enough*. The Communists, especially

China, may still be warlike & imperialist & "patriotic" as they were in Korea. But, in any case, this could be *tried*—to be friendly, etc., & only *then* see if China gobbles up countries as Hitler gobbled up Czechoslovakia. *That* was the moment of war. But maybe China wouldn't gobble up anything.

The youngsters of course are getting everything all confused. Pacifism; but we *must* have a police force for One World. Vietnam is immoral, but it's no more immoral than any other war. What they should say is *any* nationalistic war is immoral—& on *both* sides. What they could say is, let there be an election in South Vietnam & if the Communists win it, so be it. That's better than wars. And anyway, all political & economic systems evolve & change. And another confusion: how about Haiti, which is pure evil & banditry? *I* would be in favor of exerting force there, be a policeman, etc. What would the kids say then: should we not fight evil when we can easily? It would be possible to get Duvalier out of Haiti without shedding a single drop of blood. Shall we take nationalism so seriously that we *never* interfere in the "internal affairs" of other countries? Silly! Is the Suez Canal internal? Is Cyprus internal? Was Batista internal?

Anyway, in a full account it would now be possible to offer the youngsters à hope. It's not *all* crap. And these could be listed along with the realistic U. S. critique.

There's so little love in the U. S. family, too. Is this because of the narrowed-down blood family (instead of the extended family à la Auntie Pearl? frustration of belongingness? of the clan? of the oasis in a crappy world?)? I've rarely seen a happy marriage and a happy family. What did this do to the kids?

All the hopes pooped out. Not only the social institutions, but also the ultimate: affluence itself. To yearn for a car or a house and then *still* to be miserable—smack up against the inadequacies of materialism. Materialism is a marvelous philosophy and it works beautifully. It's sparked revolutions & people have willingly died for it. *Until* you get affluence & prosperity & you're just as miserable—even more so.

Shall I add the desacralization of everything, including sex, status, success, victory, etc.?

Does fear of unpopularity take a special place in the U. S.? Among the youngsters?

Also the breakdown of snobbishness, fraternities &, sororities—but *then* realizing that we *need* community. We need fraternities, but of love & inclusion, not snobbish exclusion.

Then add the B-values. We're dying from lack of spirituality. The metapathologies, the value disturbances. We can't stand being poor or crippled or diminished or evil human beings or being cowardly Jonahs. We *must* like ourselves. But this can never be achieved—it must keep on becoming & growing. You have to keep on earning it & deserving it. It's awful to be a bastard; it's awful to be unloved; it's awful to feel cheap, guilty, ashamed, embarrassed.

Add this, too, to the youngsters: why are they so mean, trivial, cruel, nasty to their elders? Doesn't this also make them feel guilty & less human? And it's so awful to feel like a coward, like a rat. And since the nice youngsters keep quiet & let the mean & nasty ones elect themselves loud-mouth leaders, then they must feel ashamed. The Brandeis student paper is almost always mean. Why do kids let the bastards appoint themselves leaders & speech-makers? Spit-on Daddy club.

One real trouble that has to get in here someplace is that tolerance & equal opportunity won't work well enough as between the haves & have-nots, the lower caste & higher caste. You cannot be kind or benevolent: (1) countervalues = you must count on hidden hatred at the injustice of the situation; (2) you'll hate getting, being given, being helped, etc., "from above"; (3) to some extent, fighting to seize & win self-esteem is better than being given it. Conquest = pride. This all makes the helping situation a very delicate one with the dynamics never yet worked out well. Good will from above may not be enough. [*Brotherhood of man. The differences get less & less important. Class, caste, birth, every-thing. Remember the easy integration of the be-in and of the Hippie wedding. Of haves & have-nots.*]

December 31

Manas, 12/13/67, p. 4. "Because it—the self—is supremely valued . . ." This is a good start for a sermon. If I've been lucky—basic needs gratified from birth, identity & self known & accepted, knowledge of introspection, etc.—*then* yes. I can marvel at the self, i.e., my self. I can see how remarkable it is, what a mystery, how beautiful, how endlessly fascinating, etc., & then of course I can realize fully, e.g., I shall *never never* in a million years fully know my self—that's impossible. It is endless, infinite. I can live, see it as sacred, unknowable, all of these things. Then how much less possible is it that anyone else could know it 1/100th as well as I do? If it's a mystery for me; how much more so for anyone else! Also, how much easier for me to totally accept my self, as I accept a bird or a tree, to forgive it anything, to understand why I did that bad thing 30 years ago, to accept simply its suchness, its miraculousness of is-ness & uniqueness & difference from any other self in the world. Its subtleties & nuances are endless. I can stare at it forever as at the surf.

Then—the big step—how possible is it for me to accept *your* self in the same way, as a supreme value, intrinsic, an end, incomparable, like nothing else, something to worship, to be stunned by, to be infinitely & eternally curious & wondering about? Well, why not—in principle anyway? But clearly one thing is quite evident. The 1st step is to totally accept *one's own* self and to sacralize it, & to "know" it in this wondering sense & to value it intrinsically. *Then* I should be able to do the same before *your* self. Then this would be B-love, total acceptance (or the weak word, "tolerant") of individual differences. It would be *love* of individual differences & eternal gratitude that they exist. *This* is chapter 1 in *the* book on individual differences. [*The study of individual differences has as its purpose to learn how to love everyone—or at least to respect, to accept, everyone.*]

And then, of course, if we could do *this*, all men would be brothers and love each other in B-love, & they couldn't possibly hate & kill & hurt in the easy way they do now à la the amity-enmity complex. This could be the basis for inclusive amity rather than *exclusive* amity.

1968

January 7

Thought: The revolution, the humanistic 3rd- & 4th-Force revolution, is essentially an *American* Revolution. As of today, the U. S. is the center of the world of the new 3rd- and 4th-Force psychology (and also Management Theory Y & Z). There is no rival.

But more than this, it is *historically* American also, e.g., Jefferson, Whitman, Bill of Rights, Constitution, democracy, Thoreau, Emerson, Transcendentalism, etc. Fits *very* well in the American stream (altho also in the Jewish, the mystical, the Zen-Tao, etc.).

Again, as in 1800, the U. S. may be the light of the world, morally, spiritually, philosophically, religiously, axiologically, socially, politically. Put this at end of the popular paper (or book), if it ever gets written, on the unnoticed revolution. [*1/26/68: Add Grof to the unnoticed revolution.*]

Includes economics 3 & 4; politics 3 (& 4); post-Marx. Look up U. S. critique file for exaggerations. Also profit-motive file. See the anti-Americans. My "liberal" file. Counter-values. See chapter in Leeper's *Humanizing Education* for exaggerations. Also Fromm, et al.

January 27

Read Grof's book last few days. Big revolution! *Very* important (if verified). Sounds unbelievable, but if it *is* true, then it is a huge validation of the whole 3rd-Force psychology & half of my theories, *plus* a lot more I never would have believed. Will write to him & invite him up. Hit me like the Daytop-Synanon experience when I had to make basic changes in my conception of human nature. I get called "optimist," & these people cure people who are considered to be incurable & make me feel I've been too *pessimistic* about the possibilities for growth & the push toward health in practically anyone. Mustn't write off *anyone!*

January 31

More things coming together. During night reading Esalen's interviews with Wilhelm Reich, whom I've been taking more & more seriously & whom I think I understand better little by little. Grof helped here, altho he himself doesn't know or use Reich enough. I guess my stress on biology, body, instinct, sex, nudism, etc., will strengthen rather than lessen, even tho I seem to be the only APA psychologist who feels this & pushes the body & its joys. Must study Reich more carefully. Same for interview with E.B. Monday as I urged her into "body work" as she starts on her pilgrimage to Esalen. Add my thinking & conflict about Bob Rimmer, Masters & Johnson, & my slow, bit-by-bit dropping of convention & emotions & moving toward an ultimate (Utopian, Eupsychian) acceptance of the body & all its functions à la Reich as *the* basis, the *sine qua non* before all else, before, for instance Freudian psychoanalysis (both Grof & Reich pulled me in this direction), toward full animality & specieshood & disinhibition of the SA & peak-experience kind that Grof winds up with after rebirth.

Just reading my first number of ANKH with its report of Bindrim's nude therapy group (I'll put it in the Utopia file). I feel uneasiness about all of this, & about Bindrim, just as I did (& do) about Masters & Johnson. I wouldn't do these things myself or participate in them—to private? shy? inhibited? defensive? or is this a proper reserve? I certainly enjoy nudism as at Esalen & have no trouble with it. And I certainly think sex is wonderful, even sacred. And I approve in principle of the advancement of knowledge & experimentation with *anything*. Yet the folkways— or a deep reserve & caution or go-slow attitude—are very deep in me.

Anyway, I do think firmly that the question of pace is necessarily involved in breaking the folkways, even stupid ones. So it looks as if nudism is the first step toward ultimate free-animality-humanness. It's the easiest to take. Must encourage it. Only trouble is, I feel uneasy allying myself with nuts, fringe people, borderline characters, e.g. as in this number of ANKH; the tipoff—there are *only* young, shapely, & beautiful bodies. So it's fake, along with the honest Bindrim report.

Yet nakedness is absolutely *right*. So is the attack on antieroticism, the Christian & Jewish foundations. *Must* move in the direction of the Reichian orgasm.

This movement *can* be dignified and Apollonian & *can* avoid pornography & neurosis & ugliness.

February 21

Salk's call set me right off on a job—new, but just ready to be done—humanistic biology (Biology 3). Lousy name. Wish I could think of some word that would reject value-free & imply value-seeking, uncovering, discovering & directional = vectorial (rather than static & descriptive). Organismic? Growth-oriented?

Anyway, my whole psychology is fundamentally biological in a way that nobody else is (maybe Cattell?). Instinctoid in the Freudian-Jungian-Reichian tradition. But also in the Darwinian-evolutionary style (much corrected). Specieshood. Everything I've done could be said to deal with the (obscure) biological destiny & nature of man. Even the synergy [103] & Theory Z [135] & Eupsychian management stuff [92] is all biological in the sense that these accord best with the biological prosperity of the person & of the species (fullest growth, happiness, longevity, freedom from disease & pain & death-wish, avoiding war, murder, killing & hurting each other, sheer survival value & growth-&-prosperity values). I'll put together a memo for Salk but then I want to publish it—full dress I hope. Should be chapter 1 in system of human nature book, if it's ever done.

February 23

Problem of evil in Eupsychia = the problem of evil when all the soluble problems have been solved, when everyone's basic needs are satisfied, no war, lots of wealth & leisure, one world & world law, automation. [*Evil-3. (There is* no *evil-4; in B-realm evil doesn't exist.) (?)*]

Then will come the *real*, tough problems, the insoluble ones. Stress that a happy & serene heaven or Utopia without problems is not possible. There cannot be a perfect world.

There will always be metagrumbles. What cannot be improved? Is anything perfect? Or even if perfect, can it be permanently perfect?

Male & female will always have some trouble. They are too different ever to understand each other fully. Tastes & appetites will always be different. No sexual system will work perfectly—monogamy, polygamy, promiscuity, etc. *Whatever* the system, it's going to hurt someone. Somebody will love & not be loved back. The different physiologies don't mesh exactly.

[*Assume also shared & demonstrated scientific value-system, which also serves "religious" functions. Assume synergic world, one species, brotherhood, love & respect. Help in achieving unique identity via knowledge, testing, guidance, education. Assume free sexuality starting at puberty, more or less lengthy monogamous temporary "'affairs" or engagements. Will slow narrowing down to one most loved person with whom to have children & thereafter relatively monogamous. Or perhaps sex may be divided into nonserious pleasure differentiated sharply from sex as a sacred act with the beloved with subsequent "imprinting," i.e., getting hooked on or addicted to one person, with sex conceivable only with that person.*]

1967

August 31

Underlying sadness over mass stupidity intensified by item in this morning's *Times*. American Sociological Association, 8 to 1 show of hands for unilateral withdrawal from Vietnam, a position so stupid & so heartless that it reminded me vividly of the Stalinists in the 1930s & their awful blunders.

September 30

More & more interested in the healthy, authentic, realistic interpersonal relationships in friendship, love, parent-child, etc. The California trip with all it's quarrels & unhappiness coming out of misperceptions, miscommunications, misattributions, could serve as a model to caution against. Some of the principles are: (1) if someone hurts you, don't assume that *necessarily* he did it on purpose, consciously, with intent & malice afore-thought. Maybe he did & maybe he didn't. Other interpretations are possible. Examples: the dentist or the surgeon doesn't hurt you on purpose. You are not the target! On the other hand, the Freudian point *should* also be kept in mind more often than it is, especially with children, neurotics, etc., that if you are made angry, maybe it *is* on purpose *unconsciously*, even if it doesn't seem so. If your child makes you feel hurt or depressed or angry, maybe that was the idea, the purpose. So this is a matter of recognizing the effect experientially, e.g., hurt, but yet remaining open to the explanation. There is no one-to-one, cause-effect relation between behavior & intent & effect upon you. (Remember David M. Levy's kid who said he'd push back if pushed. "But if it were just an accident?" "Well, I'd push him back accidentally.") (2) Differentiate between the overt behavior & its effects upon you. B., snubbed by Mrs. Sutich & by Mrs. Bronowski—as I myself saw—was angered, felt it to be hostile, & rejected any other possibility & wanted me to be angry for her. I saw the behavior, & I saw B.'s reaction. But my reaction was rather of wonder: "I wonder why they behaved so rudely?" (since I wasn't certain of their motivations). It could have been malice, jealousy, desire to hurt or to dominate or snub, or it could have been awe, shyness, fear (I've seen people fear B.) or illicit love, lesbian attraction, or God knows what. I get this all the time with my students, especially grads, who *often* behave rudely & badly, or at least impolitely, & who often enough make me angry or wounded or sad or to feel rejected. But I try & usually overcome this & stop my counter-hostility because there are so *many* psychodynamic explanations for their behavior, not necessarily dislike. This I've actually been *told* later, e.g., they're afraid of me (which I used to find impossible to believe), or awed, or they assume I'm too busy, or that I couldn't *possibly* want to talk with poor little them, etc., etc.

So it *is* possible to take the behavior at face value, & to dislike the rudeness, impoliteness, snubbing, and to respond to it with a counter-snub, *even* while one recognizes that one doesn't understand his motivations. The bad behavior is itself real & can be reacted to as real—quite apart from motivations. The motivations are just as real but of a different order of reality, a different kind, & are *much* harder to see. As a matter of fact, it's better to assume that we *don't* see them rather than that we *do*. Behavior is a lousy indicator of motives & feelings & intentions. It can be a *defense against* showing or revealing feelings & motives, a way of hiding them. (Example: the Italian movie in which the young Adonis on the beach keeps parading up & down in front of the Italian couple, trails them, etc., until the husband is ready to kill him for trying to seduce the wife, who is responding to all the courting. *But*, the O. Henry ending is: it turns out that the American Apollo is a homo & has been after the *husband*.)

So one mustn't be insultable, thin-skinned, over-sensitive. One mustn't too readily assume that the only conceivable motive for bad behavior is hostility. You just *have* to leave it open in order to be realistic. Last night at Rands', waiting for Jim Byrnes to come, Norma was angry at him for being late, & it turned out he'd driven by, seen people talking (us), went to corner phone & called to see if he was intruding! Who would *ever* think of such an unlikely reason for his lateness (behavior)?

1968

January 18

Polarization between kids & the law: drug agents called "narcos" (contemptuously) in raid on Stony Brook campus, mostly for marijuana. Gets all mixed up because marijuana is not clearly harmful, so it gives kids a good & virtuous cover for rebellion against authority. Reminded me of Madison during Prohibition. I drank Dago red a couple of times & felt very daring & adventurous. I never bought or drank any hard liquor because of the danger of wood alcohol, etc. We *did* swipe pure alcohol from the chemistry labs—I remember Sam Morell bringing some to a party, & then it was mixed with flavorings that weren't dangerous. And we made our own beer, some of us. *Maybe* marijuana has the same (harmless) status as home-made beer? I think LSD is clearly dangerous now, so no conflict there—dangerous, that is, for self-administration.

The point is that, if no value pathology, then narcos, secret agents who caught the income tax bribers, the other secret agents who fight drug addiction, etc., *should*, like policemen, be regarded as not only heroes, but also priests, or spiritual agents protecting the highest B-values of truth, honesty, purity, excellence, etc. I could see myself feeling perfectly virtuous, if I had the nerve, of being a spy against income tax crooks. Same metamotivation as the scientist, i.e., honesty & truth, & down with crooks & liars. Or infiltrating the Mafia. Or as a Negro, infiltrating secretly the snipers & riot-makers & the ones who are preparing for guerrilla warfare. Or being a spy against war-makers, etc.

This would be of the same order as establishing a neighborhood committee to track down & prosecute the crooked garages, TV repairman, etc. This is on the side of the highest virtues. Like Ralph Nader & his war against the auto makers in favor of safety, or Rachel Carson against DDT, or Paul Douglas & his truth-in-lending bill, etc.

But the culture is confused on this stuff, especially the youngsters. They made a hero out of Rachel Carson, & a villain out of the FBI. They use gangster lingo & have we-they attitudes like prisoners against jailers —fink, squealer, spy, etc. This is part of the culture, too, the Mafia gangster ethic against the informer. Even the newspapers & the police themselves show some contempt for the squealer, the one who "sings", the informer. (Put this all under U. S. critique, value pathology, youth.) It brings up again the question of a Eupsychian police academy.

It's all confused because there are so many radio & TV programs in which (virtuous) spies, detectives, "just men," FBI agents, etc., are presented as heroes! In Eupsychia that's the way it would be, just as in Synanon & Daytop where the community is *so* virtuous that anyone will "inform" on a backslider & bring him up on charges. Use this as example of *ultimate* Agapean love, or team spirit. Now I remember the woman at Synanon, soothing me down after my apologetic speech about values, etc., by telling me "Remember that's what we're all here for—to *pick up* the square values". Same for the Seventh Step & convicts. Just the toughest ones, who have hit the bottom, *most* appreciate Emerson, middle-class & bourgeois values, square values, values that our indulged & gratified college kids get so contemptuous about. Also use example of Garrett girl brought up in Synanon on the edge of informing against her lying roommate at Radcliffe—to the *horror* of my Utopia class, especially the two "activists." Garrett said finally she didn't, but only bawled out her roommate personally because she decided that the deans would not understand her motives (true!)

January 20

Item in *Times* (filed under U. S. critique): students from *best* (psychologically) families, "liberal, affluent, & permissive," may be expected to "demand" most, to be rebels, activists (Roger Heyns interview). Fits in with my motivation theory, i.e., gratification of basic needs → metaneeds. It satisfies for a time, but then emerge still higher needs (& values). See notes in motivation-data file. Also grumble-theory file. They're really the same thing. See gratification file, too. Satisfaction leads to higher dissatisfactions. Put this in preface to new Being book? Good idea! Say "I had thought to have a separate preface for the young & then decided not to because it seemed too pompous & condescending, & I'm not that close to them anymore to be *that* sure of myself. However I feel quite confident in making this minimal statement at least: Much of the dissatisfaction & disturbance & rebellion of youth I think of as anger against corrupt values, hypocrisy, phoniness, etc., which is *simultaneously* the same as saying they yearn for values, for something to believe in, to love & respect, to sacrifice themselves for, to devote themselves to. As all the conventional "value Establishments," the churches, the schools, the politicians, etc., turned out to talk one way & act another, e.g., as with Negroes; as all of these seemed to be phony to youngsters, they entered the interregnum period of valuelessness, and also of youthful ineptitude & lack of pragmatic experience in achieving the beautiful values they espouse. So they often are self-defeating and occasionally just plain stupid, for instance, in picking their leaders so badly (violence, defiant, authority-rebellious, psychopaths, paranoids, spit-on-Daddy, bold & driving, phallic).

Or to say it most simply & succinctly: many youngsters, students especially, espouse the highest & most intrinsic values & reject the destroyers & vulgarizers of these values; but they are not wise enough & experienced enough (& not tolerant & democratic enough to be compassionate about individual differences) to try to persuade & educate, e.g., the racists, but must fight them instead, or lose all hope because a racist doesn't become a saint in 24 hours. In a word, youngsters are not sages (how *could* they be?). The true sage (Tzaddik) is not only wise & saintly but also pragmatic & practical in the sense of being a "winner" & not a "loser." That is, he wants to achieve in actuality & has good reality-testing about strategy & tactics, so that in fact he is more *likely* to bring about the actualization of these values.

Youngsters are more apt (1) to be impatient; (2) to be perfectionist, & to demand all or none; (3) to be mercurial & cyclic, i.e., too early disillusioned, defeated, lose hope & withdraw; and (4) to have too great an appetite for excitement & enthusiasm & too little for patient, long-time, slugging hard work. They're willing to die for their beliefs, but not willing to do the mimeographing, committee work, long-term planning & administering, etc. They're not able to wait (one of the results of the permissive & gratifying, child-centered family). I remember a student in my class, disgusted & defeated. "The faculty pay no attention at all to the wishes of the students. It's a fake. No use trying." And he turned his back on the whole thing. I was surprised because the faculty & administration & student committee had just in fact achieved almost everything the students had wanted. It turned out that this was all *nothing* to him, & it was all a fake, because the faculty had rejected his demand that the students alone select, hire, & fire all the professors.

Also the students have a tendency to procto-interpretations—they see with only one eye & are blind with the other. They see our society as *merely* & only hypocritical, materialistic, unspiritual, phony. They see the U. S. as *only* a nightmare & are blind to the fact that there is also a U. S. dream & that this is one of the best societies ever achieved in the whole history of mankind & certainly *the* best *ruling* society that has ever been. Proctopsychology says all men have evil in them (true). But it is also true that all men have good in them, too. Same for the U. S. (Like seeing neurosis & psychosis as signs *only* of sickness & hopelessness, instead of *also* as signs of growth & possibilities of growth, as in Duquesne paper. Or use example of Negro riots. This is *higher* than not daring to riot for fear of lynching. Compare also the Negro achievements with what *I* expected in 1920, 1930, 1940 = a series of unbelievable miracles.

February 24

Norman Mailer in *Harper's* has set me off on the "liberal" that I've been struggling to understand. I think I've got it, & may change the name!

I think the key is around the question of ambivalence to authority vs. postambivalence. The *real* liberal is strong, enduring, fighting (but with good humor, non-neurotically) & is himself a people-lover & a nice man, e.g., (Upton Sinclair & Norman Thomas, the heroes of my youth, old Bob Lafollette maybe, George Norris, maybe Adlai Stevenson, FDR, *maybe* Sen. Eugene McCarthy(?), some of the Senate liberals (but I don't really know enough about these people), Pop Shrank, Jane Addams, Mrs. Roosevelt, Ruth Benedict. The true liberals are postambivalent, in the sense that they are no longer ambivalent about strength, winning, authority, responsibility, fatherhood, leadership, achievement, decisions —in a word good cops, good ship captains, good generals & bosses, good administrators of justice, good superiors.

The more usual "liberal" (put it in quotes because it's phony & not real) is ambivalent to power, authority, responsibility, etc. [*Neurotic, immature.*] He must be perpetually out-of-power because of his unconscious *fear* of being *in* power, a father, a decider, unpopular, saying "No," punishing, giving orders. Rightly so, because he'd do a lousy job of it, what with his guilt, conflict, & confusion. He can't take on the stern father role, he does well only with the son role. Lots of psychoanalytic stuff available on the adult who secretly feels uneasy among the men & suddenly feels like a boy among them, & then unconsciously has to worry about being unmasked & exposed.

If he is to be regarded as immature unconsciously, easily regressing to adolescence or childhood unconsciously, then, of course, like a child or youth he will *identify* with the weak, the young, the losers, cripples, the small, forlorn, powerless, the prey! And then simultaneously he *must* logically (though unconsciously) be *against* or hate or fear the opposite number. The father, boss, strong man, the predator, winner, aggridant, elite, the cop, the judge, the ship captain, the general, or even the strong mother (or, extremely, any female, because he can change them all into mothers, i.e., strong ones).

But then this goes along with the whole business of identification with the aggressor, the prey who loves & admires his predator, the mouse who loves the cat. On the one hand this involves the whole covert unconscious homosexual—the tendency to present to the dominant one, the dreams & fantasies that go with offering yourself up to the strong one who deserves to be the fucker & penetrator & mounter (it is suitable, fitting & proper, just & right, apposite, appropriate). Like my monkeys, the Gaze determines instantaneously who presents & who mounts. This secret sexual life of the ambivalent "liberal" might go over into overt behavior? Good research project. Will they tend to marry dominant women? To then play the son role? All researchable questions.

No wonder then that he must be a loser & "throw the game" if he's on the edge of winning. He feels afraid of, uncapable of taking responsibility, deciding, punishing, hurting, refusing, being unpopular, losing the love of any of the other "kids." He will falter & feel guilty when about to win, or when elected boss or captain. And if it's thrust on him, he'll try to keep the *love* of all the subordinates & so crap it up (if he's not strong enough to learn, to change, & to *become* a boss).

March 7

It was important for me then to understand the anti-Semitism which hurt so badly during the first half of my life & which was simply a puzzle to me. I could never understand it. It was occasional, unpredictable, & its motivations were mysterious. Certainly I'd have *stayed* depressed if there weren't also "angels" around at every juncture, few in number but enough to keep hope alive. (I'm sure one deep reason for the whole study of self-actualization was to turn to studying these small percentages of good & kind people, i.e., not *everybody* was a bastard, only *most* people.

Well the correct parallel is racism & hatred in general. We still don't know enough about it. So the violent Negroes are making everybody pay for the hatred toward them & their fathers. (I amended my bulletin board notice, "Time Wounds All Heels," to add "or their children or grandchildren.") So now *we* had to pay for the South of the last century.

Then too, I was sad & depressed especially after the Spanish Civil War defeat, watching evil triumph, & the Nazis & Fascists & Japanese militarists all sweeping everything before them. The same appeasement & failure of nerve now as then, the same unwillingness to believe that authoritarianism is evil, the same loss of faith in democratic politics, the same refusal to count our blessing, to love the Bill of Rights, etc. Also the same lack of brotherly love, as when the League of Nations failed, the same insistence that patriotism & nationalism must have self-interest as its *only* motive. (Even when the U. S. is unselfish, it's justified as self-interest.)

That was when I decided to change the whole tenor of my work toward psychology for the peace table. I've got the outlines now after 25 years of work—but now it needs to be used, to get around, to soak into politics, economics, philosophy, etc. From one point of view this is happening with great rapidity, but when I'm sad it seems to be creeping along so slowly that catastrophes may come first.

I must add, if I ever write this up in a personal way, that I consider also that this work was determined (unconsciously) by the Jewish passion for ethics, utopianism, Messianism, the prophetic thundering. My whole value-laden philosophy of science could be called Jewish—at least by my personal definition. I certainly wasn't aware of it *then*. And maybe all of *these* trends are responses coping with anti-Semitism, trying to (1) understand it & (2) cure it by making universal brotherhood, etc.

The funny thing to add here is what I've realized recently for myself—& clearly relevant to theory & research in these areas—that I don't really expect very much from people in general; i.e., I'm not perfectionistic—I accept evil, stupidity, ignorance, laziness. But then I'm *very* appreciative of the angels, the good ones, the ones you can count on when they do appear. It's easy to get misinterpreted in this area. If I study the good ones, then this gets called "optimistic," altho statistically it's rather on the pessimistic side. To look for the Olympic medal winners doesn't mean you consider everyone to be a winner—altho for newborn infants, anyone *could* be a winner.

May 5

A point that helped me to understand the youngsters: as they cut themselves off from the elders—don't trust anyone over 30, etc., anti-authority = anti-father, etc.—what they are in effect implying is that you get stupider as you get older, more venal (sell-out), or defeated or hopeless (cop-out). But this implies the same thing for *themselves*; they must unconsciously see themselves as deteriorating, growing stupider, more cowardly, etc., as they get older, i.e., they must see growing up as going downhill. *Must* be unconscious conflict.

I asked a youngster: Do you expect to learn anything during the next year? The next 10 years? Will you be wiser or stupider 5 years from now? At age 31, do you expect to be "untrustworthy?"

Who should teach whom? Youngsters teach the elders, or vice versa? It got me in a conflict about my education theory. I've been in *continuous* conflict for a long time over this, over Esalen-type, orgiastic, Dionysian-type education. Bettelheim's Freudian-type lecture really made me think of this again, i.e., of authority, & of trust in authority-teachers-elders vs. impulse-ridden, Nirvana *now!*, grab the gratification immediately. I tied his lecture in with the principle of limited good, i.e., his slum kids grab *now* for a good realistic reason—scarcity. His education theory is that the reality principle must win out over the pleasure principle—delay, postponement, which in turn means trust in parents & teachers.

The adolescents & college students clamor to be listened to, as they were as children. Contra-patriarchal. And for youngsters and children something of the sort is required as in the psychoanalytic therapist = client-centered. But they must be seen as *for the sake* of developing ultimately the reality principle, the ability to listen & to learn from the elders. At *this* point, i.e., at *my* point, what does freedom consist of in my classes? Why should I waste my time in listening to adolescents fumbling toward insights which I already have. It's certainly good for *them* if they haven't found identity yet, as it was in my Utopia seminar a year ago. I became a consultant & shut up, so they didn't "learn" content about Utopias. What they *did* learn & got enthusiastic about was T-group style intimacy.

October 3

Have been trying hard to answer all the autobiographical questions I get about the SA work, how it started, the B-psychology, etc. The SA work started in 1935, trying to understand Ruth Benedict & Max Wertheimer, & I remember voluminous notes on them, lecturing to Brooklyn College classes about it, but never submitting it for publication for years. Finally Werner Wolff got hold of it—how I don't remember—& published it in his new journal (which soon folded). And of course this stuff kept on generating things in my head, slowly I guess, & maybe also I was too scared to let loose until much later. Then while I was in California, somewhere between 1947 & 1949, I got the big flash on the electric train from Peoria to Kansas City (or was it St. Louis?) & wrote it all out. It was called "Higher Ceilings for Psychology" & all the real points were there—of deriving a psychology from healthy people rather than sick ones. I put the whole thing in my *Motivation & Personality* book [57], toward the end. Why I dropped this title I don't remember.

October 4

Much of the background of sadness & worry of the last year or two or more—with the whole thing personified & brought into my own home—has been the self-destructiveness & unrealistic foolishness of the liberals & radicals who, with their good & desirable ideals, the B-values stated in so many words, yet help to bring about the very opposite of what they wish by attacking the basis of *everything*: government, stability, peaceful change, lawfulness, orderliness. [*Theoretical & research problem: How do you bring about the opposite of what you wish?*] Everything that is good, that is "high," justice, brotherhood, truth, beauty, rests on safety & security, on *respectful* opposition to unjust laws or rules or folkways, on *respect* for the system, the Establishment, the police, the law, the judges, the parents, the teachers. [*11/11/68: The first thing the destroyers (the militants who feel that you have to destroy the whole society & that out of its ashes will emerge the perfect society) do after they have won their bloody revolution, & in fact have all power, is, before everything else, establish law, stability, order.*] *If they* are attacked, *everything* is thereby attacked, because the alternative is no government—chaos, disorder, lawbreaking, riot, looting, vandalism, cop-hating, government-hating. And then, of course, there must be inevitably a regression to the safety-need level for many, many people, especially all the obsessionals, the anxious, the frightened, the authoritarians, even the normal conservatives, the *average* citizen who sees all the disturbance, the heckling of speakers, the taking over of buildings, all the tactics of the activists & militants, as nihilism & also as just plain unfairness, injustice, hatred, violence, willfulness—& then get tough finally. *First* come safety, security, structure—& only on this basis can we seek for higher needs & higher values.

One part of the sadness is the willful refusal to learn from history, as well as the refusal to learn from the psychology of motivation. (That's *my* job. I must make this more explicit. These same kids who are electing Nixon & maybe even Wallace *say* that they are basing themselves on humanistic psychology. I must remind them of the *hierarchy* of basic needs & the prepotency of the safety needs.) Every time the idealistic demands for justice, etc. have gone violent throughout history, every time they've been based on hatred, e.g., LBJ & Nixon dartboards, injustice, e.g., drowning out a speaker, & chaos threatens, *then* almost surely comes the swing back to stricter authority, to authoritativeness, & finally to authoritarianism in the hands of one or a few individuals, a dictator, or a military regime. In a word, a reaction, a regression. [*"Backlash" often means regression to the safety-security-law-order level.*]

This, even in the name of ideals & B-values. There are definite limitations on what can be done, & the pace at which it can be done. Hence my theory of the slow revolution, which is *really* democratic, because it assumes that you must *convince*, coax, seduce, teach those who disagree with your ideals or with the highest values. You can't really *force* them to do anything at all except with a big or huge majority, which means "How do you get a majority on your side?" By frightening people? By calling the police pigs? (Now the police seem more & more to be going to the right, toward Wallace. How else can they fight back against contempt, hatred, lack of appreciation & gratitude?) By being unfair, discourteous, impolite? By contempt, hostility, violence, injustice? Or by compassion, Agapean love for the opposition, B-respect for the frightened ones, the ones with the jungle world-view, the authoritarians, the reactionaries, the greedy & selfish ones. This can go along easily with the firmest & most determined & most unrelenting continuing fight against them. As a matter of fact, that's the only way in most situations, anyway in the U. S. (Be sure to make explicit the necessity for violence when the law has broken down, as in the South of 10 years ago, or as with the Mafia, or as in Haiti, or Batista's Cuba—altho even here, B-politics & B-revolutionaries must expect the possibility of going to the other extreme & getting a Left dictator instead of a Right dictator, so that even a revolutionary war against Batista or Duvalier or Wallace or Sen. Eastland must be compassionate while being absolutely fearless & strong & unrelenting. (As in fact we were with the Germans after Hitler even tho for political rather than compassionate & magnanimous reasons.) If we could truly understand these awful people, our arm against them would be strengthened, *not* weakened. We would be *more* effective, not less effective. The B-person, in a godlike way, could even execute them compassionately & for their own good, in a kind of euthanasia, as we might with a hopeless & therefore unhappy & anguished case I heard of with neck severed, a vegetable. Many of the dictators, especially the paranoid ones, Hitler, Stalin, Joe McCarthy, Mussolini, must be understood as unhappy, deeply miserable, anguished. Assassinating them would be like putting them out of their misery, without in any way losing our ultimate respect for the sacredness & uniqueness for every baby born into the world, & our feeling of great sadness at the unlucky way in which they went so wrong that they had to be killed off like senile psychotics or thalidomide babies or terminal cancers. The pious Christian or Jew should *pray* for him while killing him.

Then deal separately with the sociopaths & psychopaths like the Southern senators who were absolutely convinced of their righteousness & therefore had no guilt or misery; like the professional criminal who is really a member of another culture with a different set of folkways & values, which we *professors* could certainly criticize theoretically as antisynergic, etc., but which wouldn't much help the present *actual* situation of the Mafia or Al Capone or a pimp. Here understanding at the B-level could also be compassionate & magnanimous while being also tough, unyielding, necessary, realistic by Synanon-like treatment, the therapeutic chance & by imprisonment or exile rather than killing, & by continuing to research other forms of recovering the little seed of healthy humanness & helping it to start growing again. How to reverse regression? How to *de*culturate the unguilty criminal? How to rehumanize the professionally proud gunman or gangster?

October 20

Led me to think of 2 kinds of education, 2 goals for education, & therefore 2 kinds of students: (1) those essentially looking for personal growth, for personal therapy, for self, for identity. Still rebelling. Still working for Esalen-type freedom. This is what I think could be called general education, which certainly has as a basic part of it this personal development from immaturity to maturity, this throwing off of dependence, passivity (seen as domination), adolescent, pre-adult growing up.

This is in contrast with (2) the ones who know finally what they want & where they are going, who have found their career, their fate, & who are eager for it. They *know* they want to be doctors, teachers, psychologists, etc., & now want good *training* & are now impatient with what they would consider to be "crapping around." They want meat-packed, content- & skill-centered training (like Everett Hughes' medical students who are very impatient with anything that doesn't help toward being a doctor). Thus they are interested more in how skillful & knowledgeable the teacher is, how authoritative he is, his reputation, his contributions, & less in how nice a guy he is, how much they like him, how amusing or entertaining or lovable or admirable he is, *less* in their inter-personal relations. In a certain sense, I could almost say that they are more interested in the extrinsic learnings (which however they've made their own if they regard the professor as introjected & therefore part of the self). If they have firm identities, they can *use* the IBM machine, the technologist, & don't worry about being "mastered by the machine."

A confusion is the possibility that this second group is made up of two groups: the first of oblates, but the other of conventional "good boys & girls" who like to do what they are told. (But, as we know now, in grad school anyway, they may start out being merely dutiful & then, via immersion in the work, fall in love with it à la functional autonomy—as I did when I was hired by Harry Harlow to do a million boring delayed reactions with monkeys.)

Partly these two styles, personal growth vs. professional training, parallel my differentiating general education (undergrad & lower) from grad school & professional schools. Different roles of education.

December 10

Bill Laughlin called up last night & in effect offered me either 3 or 5 years of the freedom (less 10-15%) I had asked for—*still* leaving it somewhat vague, so that details have to be discussed with his people when I come to Esalen. For instance, I don't know if this means moving to California, selling home, resigning job. Can I do a year of tryout? Or is it truly what I want? A blessing thru & thru? And yet, instead of getting happy & high, I got confused, depressed, tense, as if I were fearful. So had some drinks & spent the whole P.M. chewing it over with B.—& it kept me up most of the night too. Why this paradoxical reaction? Various thoughts—I'm a teacher, a professor, a Brandeis University man. This would be like a divorce—or like a change of profession at age 61! Also moving, giving up home I love, area & neighborhood I like very much & even love, especially my river view. And yet the last week of cold has been giving me angina, keeping me indoors (yesterday for the first time since heart attack a year ago, *no* exercise—too afraid of the cold & wind & too embarrassed to wear helmet or mask to warm the air, etc.). Definitely pushed me toward a warm climate, like around Stanford, which is also very beautiful & elegant. Better for my health by far & Bertha's too. Not that I couldn't *manage* here, e.g., indoor exercise, get used to wearing helmet publicly, air conditioning in summer, etc. But each time now it's a matter of sheer will power to *force* myself to walk.

Felt sadness over ending of a career which I used to love. Teaching is less & less fun year by year recently. My respect & affection for students is also less. Theirs for me is less & less, I think. My scorn for faculty & intellectuals generally grew greater & greater year by year, especially this last year of politics. Also felt something of the depression mentality, i.e., value, job security, pensions, etc., until I realized this was nonsense now. I could have any one of a hundred academic jobs if ever I want one. Or better—since I *don't* want one—I could make a living by royalties, lectures, seminars, *guest*-teaching, etc.

December 21

I think Jeannie has helped me answer the question I've been puzzling over for 30 years: Why do we love children so much? Analyzing my total B-love & giving over to the tiny baby, part of it = experience of perfection, i.e., she looks perfect & miraculous in her tiny perfection (it's more a miracle than with a grownup). Experiencing perfection subjectively (peak-experience), with permission to express it all out—post-ambivalent, perfect completion (like a perfect, total, complete orgasm), uninhibited expression (leaving nothing over), not 99% but 100% Dionysian, orgiastic, finish, no conflict, no defenses, no controls, no brakes, no monitoring, no editing, no self-observing = loss of self is partly perfect expression all-out, postambivalent, 100% enjoyed & 0% unenjoyed or worried about, loss of inhibition. (Add this to kinds of transcendence.) This is the only kind of expression that is *all* satisfaction, i.e., expression without any inhibitions whatsoever, without need for vigilance, alertness, caution, worry, concern (more than in romantic-sexual love, I think).

There's a kind of Dionysian (is Phrygian more totally orgiastic than Dionysian?) wildness & happy insanity & delirium that a baby can call out & which feels peaky. I've seen mothers go nuts over their babies in public—like an epileptic or psychotic seizure to the point of screaming.

Why do littleness & tininess make the perfection seem more perfect? Also: does the *helplessness* of the baby (or of a child's pet or doll or toy) make it better because it can't fight back, or resist, or because its "wishes" need not be taken into account? I.e., we can be totally selfish without taking thought or being careful not to offend or to be rejected, as with someone else's child, whom you may *not* pick up & kiss wildly & hug totally. Could it also be that the seeming absence of sexuality & eroticism (or so the culture says) permits one to behave in a sexual way, like a lover or a sweetheart—as one is *not* permitted to behave even *with* a sweetheart? I.e., one can be an all-out lover without running the risk of anyone's or the culture's disapproval. Maybe more completion-of-act is possible than even in most sexual acts? This is "purer," without "selfish" return (altho of course, at the B-level, it is totally selfish, total metahedonism, total happiness, pleasure, self-indulgence, giving oneself pleasure, seizing pleasure without any guilt whatsoever)! The crazy non-Reichian culture doesn't permit a man to love a woman all-out because of the suspicions of "Is this a line to cover up the personal, sexual pleasure?" "Is the love a coverup or camouflage for selfish sexual pleasures?" Just as a rich woman or man just can't avoid the suspicion that he is being "loved" for his money.

There's another example here to support my belief that all peak-experiences come from experiences of perfection & are completion-feelings, the 100% experience, the 100% response to a 100% stimulus. Talk also of 100% gratification (by contrast with anything less).

1969

January 22

Feeling better all the time about going & staying. I forgot (!) that I had promised Bill Laughlin to move to his area if I got 4-5 years of fellowship. So that's settled. Altho it disturbed B., who still feels tense & insecure about the whole thing even tho it's *her* dream come true also.

We both felt much better when it occurred to us we could have *two* houses in Calif., one in town & a hideaway that we've both always longed for & could never afford. Means selling *this* house & giving up my blessed river, New England, Brandeis, etc., after we make sure all is OK out there, & that everything is really as good as it looks.

Thought: in 4 years I'm 65 & will have Social Security, retirement money, royalties, &, if I want it, income from lecturing weekends or even teaching—that is, if Laughlin doesn't renew after 4 years.

Thought: will have no schedules, so can drive south in leisurely way, visit relatives, Geiger, friends, Kays & loaf along the way. Also can loaf when we get back here. Still not sure about London meetings in August. That would be fun, but traveling is so stressful. If B. wants it, then OK. Otherwise probably not.

Nice call from Laughlin, just to say how pleased he was.

February 10

Everything continues to look good, better & better, after initial panic & depression over high prices of houses & apartments & disappointment that San Francisco seems not practical to live in. My ties to back home get less & less very rapidly. Even reconciled to giving up river view, New England, etc. Living in furnished apartment (Del Medico Arms in Mountain View) is quite OK to my pleased surprise & would be acceptable to me forever (altho not to Bertha). Very quiet, convenient, less responsibility, shopping & walking very easy & interesting, dozens of different kinds of restaurants, easy drive to office, etc. My work is going *very* well & did from beginning. Every time I realize I'm free of classes & schedules & duties I get nice surges of happiness.

But *must* have 2 bedrooms. Developed in last week constant postnasal secretions that wake me up, make snoring worse, & made throat raw & scratchy. From climate here? Weather delightfully warm by comparison with Boston now.

B. has been hunting for house daily almost since we got here February 1. Fatiguing. No luck yet. But seem to be plenty of apartments available for rent until we find a house. So at least we don't have to worry. Everybody at Saga continues to be obliging & very helpful, including wives.

March 3

Reading Aronoff's marvelous chapter on motivation—definitely an improvement on my work—& he takes this as a basic proposition in my work: "First he argues that every human being has an intrinsic inner nature, with needs, capacities, talents, temperaments, & inclinations. The human being as not an empty organism to be filled by Society." This corrects the "liberal," Rousseauistic, environmentalistic, nonevil, non-sickness model of the human being, in which all you have to do to make him perfect is train him right, give him a perfect environment, trust him to be *only* & entirely intrinsically good (a contradiction of the empty organism), thus denying that he might behave badly even in a good society, even with good parents, etc. Make it explicit! My theory of evil accepts the data: people *can* behave badly sometimes even when loved, gratified, in a good environment, etc., as the present revolt by *best*-treated youth testifies; i.e., they want everybody *else* to be well treated too, & (stupidly) acting this out = metapathology (general) or Frankl's "lack of meaning," etc. Better say lack of B-values. No! Better say demand of immediate, perfect, & universal incarnation of all B-values.

This is starting to get all confused. Just the way I am these days about 3rd-Force psychology, Esalen, et al.—conflicted.

He goes on: "If this inner core is denied, sickness will result. With the discovery of these internal forces," he argues, "it is possible to build an absolute code of values. In other words, what is in us is healthy, & we should structure the world to provide a means of gratifying it" (human nature's essence). Well, this means real right & wrong, good & bad, healthy & sick. And *this* is what the wobbly liberals can't swallow. They're still with cultural & ethical relativism—except the puzzle that they'll forgive anybody else anything, refusing to say "That is evil!" while at the same time forgiving *themselves* nothing, or anyway forgiving their brothers nothing. So they *do* mind "Red-baiting" but don't mind "American-baiting." Add: therapy for evil.

March 24

Monterey. Up in A.M. & struck by view of bay. Very happy, grateful, privileged, etc. Talked it out with B. & a little clearer in my mind about all these things plus "deserving," humility-pride, conservative politics (of pro-capitalist bookstore in motel).

(1) I do *not* "deserve" my genes, my father's courage, the Jewish heritage that sent me to school books and libraries as a matter of course, the history of U. S. & Jefferson, Lincoln, et al. How can *I* take credit for American affluence & democracy & social mobility that allowed me to rise to just where I want to be, *should* be (for the sake of others & of work that I can do which not only pleases me but helps society), etc.? So I should count my blessings, be consciously appreciative & grateful, have humility & not be proud in the hubris sense. Furthermore it is OK to enjoy my good luck, my blessings, my "picnic on the road," my casualness about time, money, etc., but since they're a gratuitous grace in part, & since I don't altogether "deserve" them, & since my duty to my talents, fate, destiny, oblation, my calling, remains in force *behind* the loafing & casualness, I should never get to *need* or demand absolutely, as my right, these luxuries. They must remain expendable, & I should be free of needing them. I should be able to give them up with good humor, not get bitter, angry, depressed, discouraged, disheartened, etc. They must remain enjoyable non-necessities, especially to the extent that they help my mission (which they *do*).

(2) *But* also, in a different sense, I *do* deserve all the good things I am getting, & may permit myself to feel pride of a certain kind—because I made the fullest use of my fortuitous, undeserved "good luck," of my genes, of my opportunities, of my culture, etc. I took good care of what was given to me; I made *myself* into a good psychologist. I worked hard, disciplined myself, did things I didn't feel like doing, & sought out the best teachers in the world, etc. This kind of pride (& contempt for those who waste their talents) goes along perfectly well with the humility & nonpride of nondeserving, & is perfectly realistic; i.e., I *am* in real fact the best man for certain jobs. No *false*, unrealistic humility here, no masochism, no guilt. I don't even have to feel guilty about my nondeserved good luck. Just mustn't get nasty or snotty or smug or feel that I fully *deserve* my good luck. I must be willing here to recognize B-justice & injustice. (Who said "God has given me the Papacy; now let me enjoy it!"? One of the Borgias I think.) OK to enjoy it, but keep in mind the equivalent of "There, but for the grace of God, go I."

Make up suitable words for the 2 kinds of pride & the 2 kinds of humility. Point out that this is the only way to avoid repeating the historical mistake of identifying success or privilege with feeling that one deserved all one could selfishly get, along with contempt for the unlucky, the handicapped, the *socially* unjustly treated. Political conservatism often assumes an absolutely perfect correlation between what one deserves what one gets, & what one has—no matter how gotten. The equivalent liberal mistake is to assume that *no* one deserves at all what he gets & that it's *all* society's fault, with *none* of it being the individual's fault. My twofold attitude makes a good integration I think. Certainly far more realistic & pragmatic than either doctrinaire, liberal or conservative. Bring in here also the difference between social injustice & biological injustice. Conservatives stress the latter & forget the former. Liberals stress the former & forget the latter.

Can say it in another way—liken it to a lottery, a gamble, or a sweepstake. It all *begins* with a toss of the dice, but if the dice make you eligible to stay in the competition, while excluding many others without even giving them a chance, then it's still up to you about making the most of your opportunity, or of wasting it.

Or, if you have been chosen, if you are *one* of the elect, that's when the work *begins*–the practicing, rehearsing, planning, striving, training, the finger exercises.

April 10

Kairos weekend, much of it, on humanistic politics (politics 3). (Humanistic radicalism? Slow revolution? Humanistic revolution, of which humanistic politics is one aspect?) Get the tapes & transcribe them. Also Esalen tapes, last A.M. on politics. My impression—& Bertha's—was of a very sympathetic & interested hearing. Stress absolute values of truth & therefore the Bronowski-scientific means to truth, to open communications, & therefore to evil or wrongness of SDS breaking up of debate & classrooms, etc. Specieshood as an absolute desideratum. Democracy same. The rules of the scientific community = personal autonomy ultimately, each man an emperor, absence of leaders, hierarchies, or popes, absolute openness & no secrets, no patents (?). Polanyi's scientific values.

Also, as an absolute value, no self-obliteration, one world & lots of other consequences. Work out very carefully that *usually* it means personal sovereignty, choice, & one man/one vote, but that this has exceptions which ought to be faced: Whom do we order about? Incarcerate? Deprive of vote, of liberty, etc.? I spoke of the UN as a trustee for underdeveloped countries that need authority from above, not yet ready to make wise personal choice. UN trusteeship = older-brotherly attitude, not a selfish colonial one.

Another message from Jeannie after a wonderful visit; she represents good humor, cheerfulness, gaiety = another of the B-values. She needs no excuse to smile or laugh. It just equals good functioning.

Then it dawned on me, as I wondered about imprinting & getting hooked & addicted on a baby: it's a matter of perceiving the *uniqueness*, & this takes some time & contact. One must learn & perceive the idiosyncrasy, the individuality, the difference from anyone else in the world. Imprinting on a baby takes a little time. And I think it's deeper for female's than for male's because Ann & Bertha actually fed & cleaned & clothed the baby, while I just spectatored & enjoyed. It's the difference between enjoying a house you *buy* & enjoying a home you build yourself.

Also I notice of the baby, there is no prejudice, no morality, no conscience = no self-punishment, guilt, shame, or embarrassment. There is id, there is ego (will, self-choice, decided tastes & distastes), but there is no Freudian superego.

April 15

On same subject of evil, add, after reading Sidney Hook's article on student violence (evil file): the faculties are so weak & have no fight in them because they lack a theory of right & wrong, of evil & so don't know what to do in the face of viciousness. This nontheory of evil, it occurred to me, is one peculiar version of the "value-free" disease (which is the same as ethical relativism, of Rousseauistic optimism, of amorality, i.e., nothing is wrong enough or bad enough to fight against). I was thinking of Voltaire—was it Pangloss?—whose life philosophy collapsed with the Lisbon earthquake & of whom it was said "What kind of idiotic philosophy is it that has no place for earthquakes?" What kind of educational philosophy is it that is unprepared for ill will, for bastards, for mean & vicious kids? It's a philosophy in which nothing is bad or sick or wrong or evil.

April 16

Big insight over breakfast conversation. B. was talking about her cleanliness as a reaction *against* childhood filth & evil. And suddenly it dawned on me that it had been the same thing for me & my mother (father too). What I had reacted against & totally hated & rejected was not only her physical appearance, but also her values & world view, her stinginess, her total selfishness, her lack of love for anyone else in the world, even her own husband & children, her narcissism, her Negro prejudice, her exploitation of anyone, her assumption that anyone was wrong who disagreed with her, her lack of concern for her grandchildren, her lack of friends, her sloppiness & dirtiness, her lack of family feeling for her own parents & siblings, her primitive animal-like care for herself & her body alone, etc., etc. I've always wondered where my Utopianism, ethical stress, humanism, stress on kindness, love, friendship, & all the rest came from. I knew certainly of the direct consequences of having no mother-love. But the whole thrust of my life-philosophy & all my research & theorizing also has its roots in a hatred for & revulsion against everything she stood for—which I hated so early that I was never tempted to seek *her* love or to want it or expect it.

All so simple, so obvious—& to discover it at the age of 61! And after all the psychoanalysis & self-analysis! And after all the talk about Bertha being the opposite in many respects of the world view of her foster-parents! Insight never ceases.

May 24

Bertha had a very good idea which I seized on because of my depression & puzzlement over all the campus insanity, which seems to have no bottom of meanness & revenge on the side of the (2% of) student "leaders" (backed up or tolerated by perhaps 50% of the students & fought against by practically none) & the weakness & helplessness (in the face of evil & violence) of the administration & faculties (here at least there is a fighting back—the Committee for Rational Alternatives which I joined has about 80 members on the Brandeis faculty out of about 300). My psychological knowledge did not prepare me for all of this (except for grumble theory & hierarchy of motives theory—& even that wasn't enough to explain the viciousness & nihilism & destructiveness of e.g., SDS). All of this makes Freud & Jung with their evil id look better. And how much of this is plain & simple Oedipal stuff unresolved? (But add to this my Mexican paper [75]. The weakness of parents whose traditional course of values has been destroyed without a new humanistic source to take its place yet—so that in effect we have weak parents, & especially weak fathers, which leads to phallic, gang-type, baboon-type adolescence & contempt & rage against the fathers for *being* weak. This *must* be added to the total picture. *Why* is my Mexican paper so neglected? Must include it in next book.)

Anyway Bertha's thought helps: It is that the kids are reaching for higher grumbles & metagrumbles *without* yet having basic-need satisfaction & while still having classical identity neuroses. Metagrumbles while bypassing the basic-need gratifications—or at least the good *results* of the basic-need gratifications. This can explain in one blow the depressing & confusing combination in the 2% leadership of (neurotic) meanness, hostility, destructiveness, irrationality, acting out but *all* in the name of the B-values: truth, justice, love, brotherhood, peace, autonomy, self-government, self-actualization! The yearning is there (consciously) at the same time that the violence & hatred are there (unconscious sources), especially the wild & total hatred & rejection of the elders & authorities, law, order, security, etc.

But to make the picture complete, I must be more pluralistic & add in the contructivist portion of the student's (I don't know how many) who *are* basic need gratified, & who are *not* neurotic, & who *are* prematurely self-actualizing, especially some of the girls. Then try to figure out why they back up the sick nuts or at least tolerate them & refuse to oppose them. Is this the age-group and peer-group solidarity (à la Kibbutz) against the elders no matter what? Because they have been brought up in peer age-groups rather than in 3rd-generation family groups, à la Mexico?

By the way, this is not really a campus or education problem except that the campuses have been so stupidly managed & education has been so idiotic that *they* are now most vulnerable, & most pitiable & weak when confronted with the fundamental issue that they have been avoiding for so long. Education is the most traditional—& conventional of all our social institutions. Even the Catholic Church is moving faster.

I'd say now that the rebel leaders in my seminar last semester, all of whom were classically neurotic (but syntonically), were also evil in effect & in some cases in character. Met R. a few weeks back, &, of all things, he too asked for a letter of recommendation! Which I refused to his utter surprise & which he argued against!

May 25

Set off & depressed by a blunt article (finally!) by Arnold Beichman. Letter from Columbia in *Encounter*, May 1969 (filed under youth). The goal-less destroying has to be explained pluralistically, i.e., various groups with various motives, dynamics, & explanations. Finally it is clear that the destructivist students & youth (it turns out they're almost entirely college students of which a disproportionate number are Jewish) have no goal or purpose except the exhilarating process itself of destroying in a we-group. [*This is the pathologizing & neuroticizing à la Horney of the Jewish tradition of ethical-"religious"-spiritual-Utopian-prophetic-radical critique of society as only Outsiders can—messianic.*] It is *not a Putsch*, as Beichman calls it. When Columbia is destroyed, these kids (& their profs) will walk away from the ruins. They *don't* want power or control. They have no program nor purpose, no past & no future. No history (& to hell with it), at least not *conscious* history, & no plans. [*Politics 3 includes Freudian past.*] No wonder they often like Che Guevara. He was the same, exhilarated with the *process* of revolution, fighting, killing, & bored with building a good society. Gave it up to go kill some more. Will the SDS types be as stupid & self-destructive as he was? If I am right & they are "acting out" all sorts of Oedipal conflicts, neuroses, & metapathologies & just plain rage, revenge, & contempt against the weak fathers, then *of course* this will be & must be stupid, self-defeating, & self-killing. For instance, what will they do when they are faced with a firm & wise authority (*not* reactionary & overkill, *not* frightened) like Brendan Maher & Saul Cohen? My guess is that many of them would *like* it & respond with a sigh of relief. Not all however. The death-wishers would get themselves killed or failed.

[*All this is relevant to humanistic politics = must be in good faith, consciously & unconsciously. Must have goals & plans both for good person & good society. Must rest on compassion & respect & brotherhood for, e.g., cops. No we-they dichotomy.*]

The constructivist kids, the nice ones, the Peace Corps types, are different; they *do* have goals, plans, hopes, purposes, & therefore *can* be satisfied, & *can* work with authority, & *will* be glad to get power & will use it well. What's mysterious in them is their loyalty to or at least nonopposition to the SDS, whose pretensions, issues, & slogans are obviously in *bad faith*, quite fake & phony. In a word, they also choose lousy leaders, or let themselves be captured by any leaders who push themselves forward. They have not yet developed leaders themselves, who would be tough, firm, unyielding, & ready to fight back, physically if necessary, & who would be ready to take the offensive against the SDS & the black militant counterphobic destroyers.

Even some of the hippies have been "radicalized" [*pseudo-radicalized, destructivized*], "politicized" (no word for "angry-cized," "violent-ized," etc., e.g., the local "free university"). In a word, seized, captured. A few years ago, one could count on them to be nonviolent, nondangerous. Now many have become thieves, cop-haters, compulsive law-breakers & even violent mobs. Will Esalen be captured in the same way? AAHP? (I see signs of it in the current newsletter.) Watch this to see how it goes. [*How much of all this = counter-values?*]

But the big point that I started out to write is about the failure of will, responsibility, "elderhood," & parenthood in the faculties & administrators (very well documented in Beichman). Occurred to me, as I contrasted them with the firm & strong & healthy ones, who, like the self-actualizers, are quite definite about the difference between right & wrong, good & evil, that this failure of will & decisiveness is *another* product of the lack of a theory of evil! And is therefore a *theory of will & responsibility.* How can you will something or decide something unless you have a principle of differentiating desirable from undesirable, what you want from what you don't want? [*Beichman talks of "paralysis of will."*] The stubborn or "strong-willed person" is one with good impulse-voices (like Jeannie, who knows exactly what she wants & doesn't want & lets you know unmistakably & can't be changed), with good inner signals. Will have to include these principles of good & bad among the impulse-voices, the signals, the triggers to like or dislike, to enjoy or reject, to be pleased or to get angry. The weak liberal—& now I must add the weak intellectual, professor, student—is weak-willed & therefore weak to disapprove or fight back or to take the offensive.

Think thru: what does all this have to do with value-free science & ethical & cultural relativity, which claims that there are no absolutes, that nothing is definitely right or wrong, good or bad? But see also how destructive radicals, e.g., in SPSSI & among sociologists, also reject value-free social science but practically throw away science in the process. *All* absolutes gone, not only from tradition, from churches, from education, but also from science, leaving us valueless in the metapathology sense—value-free in a different sense.

The Beichman article brings up to clearer consciousness my suspicion that I'll have to work up an "isomorphism of fighting tactics" or something like that. It started with the Mafia. Slowly its success has made clear the inadequacies in 1969 of the Constitution, Bill of Rights, system of law, 5th Amendment, presumption of innocence, etc. The Mafia is something like a smart lamprey eel or tapeworm that takes off its 10% of blood without killing (unlike SDS, which wants to kill). The Libertarians have finally gone nuts altogether, preferring the Mafia, street crime, the breakdown of law *rather* than cut in on the possibly innocent by even 1%. It seems to me to follow from the hierarchy of motivation theory that living at the different need-levels means *living* at those levels—taking on the rules necessary to survive in, e.g., the jungle, the slum, the world of drug addicts, the jail full of criminals. For myself, I'd just naturally do in Rome whatever was necessary to survive in Rome & not piously stick to my back-home rules. If the Mafia used assassination, I'd certainly try to assassinate *them*. I'd use *any* tactics that would serve to keep me alive & maybe win out.

Now the question comes up again about SDS & other deliberate destroyers. The ordinary academic assumptions of reason, good will, rule of truth & logic, politeness, etc., have been renounced by SDS. This makes it a different game, or rather war, so rules must change. I'm willing to fight by the usual rules, but if those rules are broken why should I continue unrealistically to stick to them & thereby handicap myself in the war? Whatever tactics were used against me, I'd feel free to use back.

One new set of laws we need today are against a Fifth Column within, the Communist Party of the 1930s, the Mafia, the SDS, i.e., any *group*, qua group, which is in a conspiracy against the society & which does *not* accept its basic rules. *Any* member of the Communist Party, the Mafia, SDS, etc., must be taken as an enemy simply by virtue of his announced membership or loyalty in the group. Any crime of the group is *ipso facto* his crime & I'd consider him punishable for it without further proof of his individual responsibility. But we have no such laws, at least not adequate ones.

What shall I call this? Levels of law? Isomorphic levels of law?

Hatred is dangerous. So is violence. So are meanness, nastiness, cruelty. Beware of anyone showing these, especially "leaders." Brotherhood includes generations. Beware of full-time "revengers."

Must be constructionist. Violence as *last* recourse & only when law & orderly change processes are broken down or totally blocked, & even then must be "shrewd," i.e., have a good chance of winning, since sheer survival comes first. Recognize that avowedly good goals & slogans may cover up all sorts of Freudian stuff. Must *choose* good leaders, not yield to self-chosen "leaders" who are apt to be bad, falsely decisive, etc. All this pushes brotherhood up to a most basic & beginning position, from which both ends & means can be deduced. Leads to compassion rather than hate, including rather than excluding, splitting, polarizing, we-they, amity-enmity. Look thru biology 3 paper. Stress that big problems require good persons (which SDS & Afros clearly are *not*) plus good society (which SDS & many "libertarians" & anarchists don't want—have they too accepted Freud's & Hobbes' belief that society, *any* society, must be bad, evil, freedom-destroying & repressing?). So politics 3 must early on make these points: (1) that society & politics are unavoidable, and (2) that they can be either good or bad, humanistically speaking; i.e., living in society can make good persons *more* likely than, e.g., living alone, à la Thoreau, or in a small community.

June 15

"Psychoanalysis was never meant to be a philosophy of life but rather an impartial tool designed to enlighten the patient. . .so that he can make wiser, more fruitful choices." The word "impartial" here can mean "loving the truth" or "having faith that the truth will be for the best." It does not imply "not-caring" or "I don't give a damn." I can *love* & respect the truth which is going to be uncovered, even tho I don't know what it will be. "Impartial" means I want it to be the undistorted, uncontaminated, untwisted, really correct truth. So "impartial" means I'm not going to interfere or twist or stack the decks or tip the table or in any other way make it nontruth or less-than-the-perfect-truth. The truth is best; therefore, wanting the best, I want the truth. If I am a member of a group, & we are all tested to see who is the fastest runner or the best at arithmetic or chess, then I, identified with the group, wanting for the group the very best leader, no matter who that turns out to be, whether me or someone else, will get indignant at someone who craps up the test so that it does *not* pick the best leader but picks me, who will *be less* than the best & who will therefore handicap the group. For the best results (a fusion word, normative), it is best that the testing be noninterfered with, perfectly accurate, impartial. That is, for the good of the group which I love, I want the test to be as impartial as possible, because *that* will bring the best result for the group which I love.

Therefore, as I claimed in the H paper [95] (I think it was), psychoanalysis *is* a philosophy of life, at least in part, because it has faith in the healing power of the truth—*whatever* it may be, however painful it may be.

July 30

The insight—which I had partially at *that* time, too, when I realized that the responsibility of being the pope-sage was just too great for me, too much was expected of me, the adoration just too frightening &

demanding—was this: Any big shot or top man, in no matter how small an area, gets to learn *first* that all the other big shots are extremely or moderately imperfect, &, pretty soon after, that he himself is too (if he hasn't known it already—or if, as in my case, he carries the load of the shy, timid, low-self-esteem boyhood). And this produces *real* trouble too. The big shot *knows* he doesn't amount to *nearly* as much as the worshippers & admirers & would-be followers think, (Flash: no *wonder* I've refused popehood, presidencies, writing forewords, pontifical positions, being the Stork-God for the frogs, etc.) They, not knowing big shots, can & do keep their innocent illusions & perfectionism, producing in him real conflict feelings of phoniness, not knowing how to break the news to them of his imperfections without looking mock-modest ("In humility, I'm tops!"), shaking with fear before their worshiping expectations of great revelations & home runs, which he privately knows are over-inflated. Yet how can he hurt them? I still remember the Esalen lecture in the San Francisco Unitarian Church (& the year before in Grace Cathedral), my last big lecture when I got so sick, exhausted, tense, terrified, apprehensive, wound-up (as if for the Olympics, or Carnegie Hall, etc.) from my terrible responsibility of living up to their expectations. Really their *demands*, & now I remember my awful feelings ·& slinking out after my *failure* to hypnotize someone for the Dale Carnegie group way back in the '30s, which traumatized me. But why must I hit a home run? Why can't I take the occasional failure calmly? Why do I *always* need to knock them dead? My *own* perfectionistic demands upon myself! They expected me to be the pope, the sage, the great teacher. All those innocent, wide, admiring, eagerly expecting eyes. Tickets so expensive. People fighting to get in & couldn't. Lecture piped to crowds outside. Poems written to me afterwards. People weeping on my shoulders. Love expressed. The fee so big. Supposing I were given a fee of $5000 for a lecture. It would be *worse* because I'd have to deliver more, give them their money's worth. $10,000—even worse. The father *knows* he can't live up to the perfect ideal, godlike attributions of omniscience, omnipotence, X-ray eyes, of his young children. How to humanize himself in their eyes? Realistically? Almost impossible to do. They *have* to project upon him too much that isn't so out of their *own* needs. This is after all a sign of the (immature) human urge toward growth, improving, perfecting, of the hunger for excellence & for the B-values.

It's all an extension of my psychoanalysis, but which fell short. This tension is *not* just the fear of retaliation, of dominance-struggle, of the phallic fears of finding that the "big prick" is just a fake, of rivaling the father & therefore being afraid of retaliation & castration & being put down. This is all true, but at a lower level of discourse. It's all true, legitimate, & justified. *Nobody* is that good. It's a false expectation & demand. The demand from the *other* is unreal. It's not just Oedipal, with the big mama & the little boy & his overgreat ambitions. It's also like the pornographic stories in which the female expects him to be superhuman, to screw 10 times & to produce in her 100 orgasms, etc. It's only part ambition-fantasy; it's also fear of inevitable inadequacy because the demands of the other are just too great, too unreal. You *must* feel like a phony, a fake, because that's what you know *they* expect & what *they* will say when you must disappoint their godlike expectation. But this seeks out every last bit of unworthiness in you, both neurotic, historical, & now *real*, real, real! You *know* you are not perfect. Thought: I bet this could be detoxified a little bit at least by Bill Dyer's trick of saying, "Let me share my dilemma with you," & then speaking the truth about one's fears & conflicts before starting the lecture. Use the story of Carnegie Hall, & the Menuhin debut. "It's not hot for us pianists!" This would be the true & real & not phony humility, & would say "*You* may have these unreal & unfulfillable expectations of me, but I don't have them for myself even tho I *do* respect myself &, by my presence here & acceptance of the fee, *do* feel what I have to say is worthwhile, even if once in a while I *do* fall flat. So let's us not expect too much or we'll all get uptight about it, me especially."

November 3

To summarize new impressions of Jeannie: The advent of walking has made a difference. So also her grunting & cooing—clear efforts to communicate as well as to announce. They've made her less passive & dependent, & I see the first real signs of willfulness & therefore of conflict of wills, frustration, anger, crying, & the like. She can no longer get automatically everything she wants. The period of full need gratification is over. She wants many more things & activities than she did because of her new activity. For the first time, we had to worry about her endangering herself, & it's so hard to deny, to frustrate, to take things *away* from her. And so tragedy begins—& maybe the first introduction to evil & suffering & anger, at least from her point of view. I saw for the first time an "evil" impulse, sibling rivalry, taking Ellen's hands *away* from Bertha & then herself possessing B. exclusively. She did this twice, & Ellen was very definite about claiming a look of anger & maybe hatred directed against her. This was the only emission of "evil" possibilities from Jeannie. Everything else was her awareness that there is evil & tragedy in the *world*, frustrations, etc. Saw her with a little 2-year-old boy who placidly accepted her babyish curiosity—she poked her exploring finger in his eye. But sooner or later, even *before* a sibling rival which I'd thought would be the first tragedy & evil, she'll conflict with another child over who possesses a toy, who hits whom, etc.

Also she's more a nuisance & a problem to Ann & Jerry. They're still perfectly patient & accepting, but how long can *that* go on? Soon they too will disappoint or frustrate her or punish her. She's too insistent already on having her way, on "talking" perpetually, so we already talked about the necessity of "teaching" her to stay away from dangerous places, glasses that might shatter, etc. Also her *demands*, are becoming very imperious—to be picked up or fed, or be "read to" from her books, etc. So the adults are beginning to express *their* wills too.

Also she's starting to use forks & spoons & insists on using them even tho she's hardly able to. So, very messy, something new, & first mild complaints from Ann, or at least sighs of impatience, half amused but half serious too.

So the whole relationship changes. She's no longer a little flower, something to love wholeheartedly & intensely = to adore. It's not a total addiction without question, wholly admiring, drinking it all in. Now it's an interrelationship between persons. For instance, she was hooked on B. as usual, but for 3-4 days fended me off altogether, very definitely. I couldn't kiss her or pick her up or put her on my lap. She was absolutely definite & strong willed about it until past middle of visit. She rejected me in effect—& I could feel a little jealousy of Bertha, slightly saddened, etc., even insulted & offended. And it took real will power & respect for her tastes & wishes not to just pick her up willy-nilly to embrace her or feed her. (Loving-respecting-Taoism.) Nonintrusion isn't altogether easy. So she is now able to deal out hurts. For the first time her wishes force me to restrain *my* wishes. She's very "active," imperious, willful, decisive, definite (as always) about what she wants or likes or doesn't want. I can't play with her as I could with a puppy or a doll or a cute *thing* without will.

But also she's more actively affectionate, or at least is able to be, & toward end of visit was with me too, or when I was alone with her & there were no preferred rivals around.

She was for me less sheer pleasure & happiness than during the last visit here—more someone I had to take account of, a sovereign entity, to defer to, to inhibit myself with, someone who *limited* my enjoyment because of her tastes & preferences. I can't just use her anymore as one can with the nonwalking, nontalking infant with whom one can play as one wishes. So *I* felt frustrated for a time. She has rights which I cannot trespass.

This doesn't express it very well. But there is some difference between the infant & the "person." Ann now sighs & says she doesn't have a real baby anymore & yearns for another one. Bertha loves her just as much but gets tired more easily, so there's some ambivalence about leaving to go home; on the one hand she misses the baby terribly, to the point of tears at the end of the visit, but on the other hand she can use the peace & quiet & rest.

A test of the whole thing: Crockett wanted me to go to Cleveland with him for OD workshop & I jumped at it but had date in Santa Cruz I couldn't change. The eagerness to visit Jeannie was there in full bloom even so soon after leaving, even at the real cost of fatiguing & unpleasant travel & work, & money, too, because B. would surely come too. That was the emotional reaction, even tho my head tells me about being rejected again, maybe or probably, etc., etc.

As for "evil," it looks as if it can't be seen for the first year of life in a healthy, happy, well-loved baby, but starts coming in soon thereafter.

There's a loss of babyhood—a real loss to mourn—but on the other hand new tricks to laugh at and new ties with a new "person." For instance, it's marvelous to watch her respond with rhythm & "dancing" to a record with strong rhythms. Her grinning & laughing is just as delightful as it was, but there's less of it. No more the "silly idiotic grin" of babyhood—as we were reminded when we saw another baby do it.

December 6

More & more on my mind & in my notes is the importance of feedback, of pragmatic knowledge of actual results, of what is the case. It's been crystallizing into a very basic, even crucial, axiom of the whole 3rd-Force psychology and 3rd-Force sociology—the basic element in truth & honesty therapy, NTL, Synanon, basic encounter groups, existentialism, psychoanalysis, etc. There is not only self-exposure (openness), but also somebody around who is strong enough to feed back both good news & bad news. It's part of the Eupsychian credo—to be the stern father as well as the Rogerian-humanistic-type motherly father. And I think this "soft" impression could come out of my writings, too, no matter what correction I make. (Add this to *Motivation and Personality* preface? *Farther Reaches* preface? Yes.) But it's partly real & true, too, that I have been often the motherly father (as Walter Toman said), enthusiastic, hopeful, encouraging, accepting, nongrading. I haven't said often enough: You have failed. You are *not* capable at this task. You *don't* know enough. For the first time I did this with my last education seminar at Brandeis, à la Synanon, when I called them a bunch of shits, etc., & rejected all their crap instead of keeping my mouth shut as I always had for fear of hurting. Must *not* be afraid to hurt for good purposes, as doctors & dentists do. It felt awfully good when I spilled my guts & told them what I thought of them—& *still* do. I do *not* want to waste my time on them & have been rejecting their overtures. The stern father must give honest feedback, often unpleasant & painful truths, à la surgeon & dentist, for sake of ultimate health.

Add: my growing suspicion & distaste for the intelligentsia, I finally figured out, is certainly *partly* due to the fact that they don't get realistic, immediate feedback. They can continue for a lifetime passing out crap & how can they know it? No feedback, no failure, no punishment, no profit-&-loss statement. The businessman & the athlete are best examples of excellent & impersonal feedback, by contrast. Therefore more "realistic," more capable of dealing effectively with real world, firmer, sharper, truer self-image, i.e., they know what they can & cannot do & where they stand relative to others, as in tennis or chess tournament.

Advantage of T-group over psychoanalyst, getting feedback from a dozen people, all unanimous, is difficult to deny or contradict. With a single analyst, you can disagree with him. Group consensus is more "real" than individual judgment. Is the same true for a psychoanalytic *group*? After all the point of analytic experience is to be as tough *as possible*, i.e., to proceed at the fastest pace an individual can *manage*. To go faster or be tougher might drive the patient away. There's a contradiction here someplace. Maybe it's the qualitative difference, à la Asch, of group judgment over even the toughest individual judgment. Maybe analyst X could go much faster than he now realizes in a group analysis. Maybe the classical individual analysis is so long because it *is* individual rather than group. I think of "group atmosphere" as still a different variable, e.g., Theory Y, Utopian, Eupsychian atmosphere is much more powerful than the accepting atmosphere of a psychoanalyst's office. OD atmosphere is much more a "world," a whole culture, than an individual psychoanalysis could be. Maybe in a synergic "world" realistic feedback is much easier to take in a nonparanoid way. The whole thing of "belongingness need" may come in here, all the LeBon-type psychology of crowd & mob, the contagion of group emotions & judgments, release from guilt, shame, etc. Qualitative change in personality itself by being part of a group, crowd, mob—if everybody's looting, that turns you into a looter or lyncher, or killer soldier. But not *only* regression & down-leveling, but also up-leveling, rise to nobility, self-sacrifice, etc., can also happen in crowd with buddies. Contagion from *either* high or low group, or atmosphere, or person. Also, leader's feedback is more "real" than from a weakling, more convincing & compelling & acceptable.

Granted that reality-feedback is the best of all, & that feedback from humans approaches this as an asymptote, & is more or less good but never as good as feedback from reality—the research phrasing would be about any feedback, how closely it approached 100% reality-feedback.

How much of this comes from the fact that: the real is not afraid to hurt, & most humans *are?* Also: people are actually less hurtable by the real than by human feedback, because one can't attribute motives to the real; i.e., to reality one can feel "I am not the target," but from people hurting me it is a possibility that I *am* the target. The less paranoid I feel, the less threatened, weak, frightened, sensitive, anxious, self-derogating, the less suspicious I'll feel & the more accepting of the feedback as truth, honesty, real. But then I wind up with a *real* difference between people & stones. With the former it's sensible to feel suspicious sometimes; it's correct to attribute motives to some. With stones it is *never* sensible or correct. This *normal* paranoia I'm speaking of is a necessary, logical, realistic possibility in any interpersonal relationship, but not in relations with reality or nature.

Perhaps then add the dimension: the more "real" the feedback person (in Rogers' sense, in the self-actualization sense) the more it would work just the same way as reality-feedback. The self-actualizing person is less afraid to hurt therapeutically (or any other way), & also is seen as less *wanting* to hurt; i.e., there will be less attribution of hostile motive to him.

December 26

Reading Brian Moore's *I Am Mary Dunne* & it brought to a head in first few pages a big sadness, which broke thru. All the procto people, the ones with shit-colored glasses (I must use this label—it's the best one—even if it offends some people), the dyspeptics, the despair & malice people, the hopeless ones, the copsophiliacs, the coprophiliacs, the Sartres', the sourpusses. All the books I've been reading, including this one, are about pimps, neurotics, homos, rich stinkers & schlemiels. And I sit here listening to Bach, looking out at the bright-red plant Bill Laughlin sent over, & my beautiful trees, & think of Jeannie & remember what a nice day I had yesterday visiting, a whole day full of decent & good people (especially the spunky old ladies). The world is full of beauty & so many precious things to see & people to know & books to read (Spinoza, Epictetus, Marcus Aurelius in the last few days), & so much to think about. I was all involved with Darwin & Kant & Freud & Jung & Schweitzer & Aldous Huxley & all the mystics & John Gardner & Gunnar Myrdal—& then all these shits start dumping their crap on me, *my* intellectuals & *my* liberals. In a world full of beauty & inspiration & miracles & progress & defeat for evil, why do these people have to smear shit all over the place?

1970

January 25

Baby sick off & on for several days but today really came to life & is an absolute delight, an intrinsic good, self-validating, sheer end-pleasure. As Ann & I talked about this & drew consequences for her writing, we realized that much of the women's liberation stuff, female discontent, *must* come from lack of this ultimate & finalistic B-love for the baby. Because if one regards the baby as sheer joy, an absolute & unqualified blessing, gratuitous grace, just plain, undeserved good luck, how could one conceivably talk, e.g., of self-sacrifice, of being trapped, of being discontent, of anger and resentment against the man who makes it possible, etc., etc.? Clearly they must be lacking in maternal feeling. Ann regards herself as just plain lucky, blessed, & misses the baby an hour after she's put to sleep. We all do & were tempted to wake up the baby so we could play with her. (I remember that we actually did this when Ann was an infant, woke her up for a little snuggle & play, & she went right back to sleep again.) Same for Bertha who gets the sheerest, most final delight from the baby. For me too, it was like recovering peak-experiences all over again in my old age. Like falling in love profoundly. And I suppose it must be much stronger for Bertha & Ann, because I have no impulse to diaper the baby, can go back to my work after playing with Jeannie for a while. Their joy must be more intense because they seem never to tire of her, or to get bored, etc. I've never seen Ann impatient for a second, nor irritated, nor anything negative. That is total acceptance of the baby & her total nature, no conflict or ambivalence or *anything* negative or qualified. This really is "unconditional positive regard."

I've seen nothing at all yet of any impulse that could conceivably be classified as "evil" or anything like it. Less than at Columbus. But she can dish out pain & hurt. As usual she rejected me for first few days or at least totally preferred Bertha. And as usual I had to be patient & build up a whole campaign of slowly making contact & being accepted. I complained about this to various people & discovered it was not uncommon. Never heard of it before. Anyway babies can hurt by their preferences & favoritism & therefore rejection.

February 12

Visit was a delight. Jeannie more fun than ever because of her new talking & communications & games. No sibling rivalry seen because no siblings, but she *can* dish out hurt by preferring & nonpreferring. It's painful to me to be rejected for a long time. Of course no intention to hurt—especially since I *am* acceptable when B. is not around. So we all planned to let me pick her up when she wakes up. I light the fire for her. One or 2 other things that she turns to me for. And finally after 3-4 days I'm accepted. "Evil" must include dishing out pain whether or not intentionally.

I summarized for someone: Why do we love babies? Because they exemplify every good quality we love & admire in human beings at their best (list them), except for knowledge. And because they lack all the qualities we dislike & hate in human beings (also make list).

1968

March 8

Good idea for preface to Being book revision [128] awakened me at 6 A.M. & I *had* to write it down. What's missing from the book is the problem of evil, & these were about the only revisions I made in the text. Thought was: say this & explain briefly the transcendent point of view on the subject, i.e., of reconciliation with evil from point of view of psychology 3 & psychology 4. Good way to say it occurred to me. If neurosis can be seen "from below" or "from above"—i.e., from below, as just sickness & symptom or from above, as a stupid striving toward health & humanness, of which, however, one is also afraid (ambivalence toward humanness)—so also can evil be seen in the same way, from below or from above. Seeing from above is easy enough for an intelligent man to do for, e.g., tigers, ants, etc. I can learn to see the tiger as not "evil," but just natural & tigerish, & I can be detached, disinterested, objective—or, better, I can be godlike or Olympian, & from a high (& safe) perch on top of Mt. Olympus I can watch a tiger bring down a gazelle & be reconciled to it as necessary, part of the order of nature, etc. (*Much* more difficult if it's me & not the gazelle, but still possible in theory.) I can watch a war between red ants & black ants & be neutral.

April 29

Memo on empirical approach to the psychology of evil (in journal, in evil, & in yea-nay files). Very pleased. All sorts of ideas came up in conversation with Hilda, with cabdriver, with B., with Peter Hollis in Buffalo.

Also ties in with direct approach to friendship investigation: ask directly each of the former friends where it's gone sour & ask why. Example today: John & Claudia Andrews left Brandeis without visiting, calling, or writing us. I was a little shocked & felt less friendly. Today passed their house, asked to come up but needed rest because of fatigue & declined. Only later realized that, if I'd felt more close & warm, I could easily have rested *there*. Also a little constrained about asking if B. could stay & get delivered to Bennises'. Later Andrews came to visit us in Bennises' apartment. Would candor & direct confrontation work this out?

Also I should remember I'm here in Buffalo because of affection for Warren Bennis, all other reasons secondary, & have refused hundreds of other invites. And I feel quite at home here. Relaxed, shoes off, helped myself to a drink, to Warren's books, etc. Also B. came because of feeling for Clurie which came out of T-group-type confrontation & candor, so that B. feels affectionate, maternal, & also welcome.

Add to evil file: much evil comes out of good men, good will, etc., doing their expert, specialized jobs very well but atomistically, discretely. For instance, the mimeo bureau or the highway commission or the dam builders may each & all be devoted, angelic, patriotic, unselfish, hard & efficient workers, & yet let loose upon us a flood of mimeos or roads or dams. Put it all under the head of holism (a society has to be held together organismically) & administration techniques (which is also holistic). Here the villain is the atomistic conception of the expert, where he does his thing without reference or tie-in with anyone else & is thus dehumanizing his job, technologizing it, losing human values. Being a good nurse (or doctor) defined holistically is just less essential "figure" against more essential "ground," i.e., general-humanness. *First,* one must be a good general-human, & only then is it possible to be a really good nurse.

I think if the problem starts here with the figure-ground, organismic relation between a man & his job, *then* holistic organization of the social machinery, which will integrate with each other the mimeo, the road builder, the dam builder, the nurse, the doctor, etc., then becomes possible.

Use my old example of the Battle of the Bulge (in homeostasis file), in which all of the specialists suddenly gave up their specialties & became general-soldiers, which was *the* basic & general function of *all* of them. Use body example too: the stomach is *not* merely for digesting food, or the eye for seeing, or the kidney for collecting urine; *all organs* have the same end-function—to live, to keep the organism alive & healthy & growing toward SA & beyond. So an eye ultimately has the same function as a kidney. They just get *holistically* specialized (rather than atomistically or discretely specialized).

In evil file, see my notes on review of Mumford book, where sins of cities, technology, etc., are called evilly *motivated!* Not so. "These are the environments we *choose*, the forms we tolerate, the ghastly anonymity we seek." Not so! Nobody *chooses* smog. They just don't know how to make large-scale social arrangements for *not* making it. Good example: it turns out *I* am & was a polluter because I have a cesspool & it drains into the river. I'd *prefer* to have the sewer extended to my house, but how do I *do* it alone? I tried once, & went to City Hall, but it takes a combined campaign by as many as 50 families, all willing to spend about $1000 each, who will then as a unit confront City Hall & *its* budget, & the major, etc., etc. So I gave up—rather than give up being a psychologist—& I continue to be a river-polluter. This evil consequence comes out of good motives, well-meaning people, etc., but is due to the difficulties of society, of huge numbers of people living together with old social arrangements which worked fine when the population was 1/10 what it is now, & everyone could dump his waste into the river & it was OK. Or burn his trash & *that* did no harm.

See also revolution file, Daniel Bell's marvelous review of Michael Harrington's book on the difference between good ideas & good, pragmatic, effective programs which get the ideas done. In my Utopia class, I demanded, along with good ideas & goals, some specification of how to get it done in practice. Pure truth, pure justice, pure love—all fine but *how?*.

June 3

Solution: fear is not a motivator; it's an antimotivator. It *prevents* reaching out, needing, desiring, wanting, yearning, expecting, hoping (& therefore it prevents action & growth). One *could* say with Rogers & Goldstein that there is only one big motivator—SA—*if* one could then add that there is at least this one countermotivator or countergrower (actually also sloth, inertia, fixation for various reasons, etc., are also counter-growth forces, i.e., antimotivators). This all requires defining motivation *only* in positive terms of need & yearning. Easily enough done in the system book.

Anyway it *is* easy then to simplify all of Freud into the discovery that fear & anxiety are the main root of psychopathology. And this fits in OK with the definition of psychopathology as fear or evasion of growth. Add fixation à la *My Secret Life*, in which sex was so powerful & so rewarding that he didn't seek anything else in life. Same for the feeling of endomorphs? Or the athletics of mesomorphs? Or the music & art & thinking of ectomorphs? Or the perpetual pregnancy of highly maternal women? See Fenichel again on fixation from *both* overgratification (or, better, say over-reward, as when the tit tastes *so* good the baby doesn't want to let it go) & undergratification (if you starved all thru childhood, food & eating can become self-rewarding, functionally autonomous, valuable *per se* as an evil).

Then all of this can be relevant to the theory of evil, too. Fear as a cause of evil. Fixation as a cause of evil. Fear as a cause of regression which causes evil, etc. (But be sure to add the other stoppers of growth, especially inertia, sloth, laziness, etc.)

June 5

News of Kennedy shooting. My reaction to these things has been sadness & depression, then anger about the gun laws, then a determination to get to work, to *my* job of understanding individual & social illness, violence, malice, & stupidity. The attacker is probably a single sick man, so the real question is: What kind of a society is it that permits him to have a gun? What kind of a society permits & protects violence as if it were a sacred right? How can the National Rifle Association be *so* dedicated, so rich, so devoted, & so numerous as to block the U. S. & the Congress from making violence less possible? Why is there still no good book on violence at all its levels & facets & *all* its determinants? Here is a clear example, like all the other killings & shootings, to analyze out the difference between the intrapsychic & the societal determinants & their inter-relations. Norma just asked: "How can a human being be so malevolent or so malicious"? Even the wife of a psychiatrist must think as if he were personally responsible & sane. And of course *most* people will think in this "psychological" way, & not think of "societal arrangements." I guess I'm thinking professionally; after the first stroke of sadness & unhappiness & something of the same feeling I had at the news of his brother's assassination: "My God, the world is falling apart." Then almost immediately came anger over the gun laws (*not* anger at the shooters). That is, anger over the stupid societal arrangements that permitted this to happen.

Then I think of my immediate getting to work. This is *my* responsibility & only people like me can do something about it, to get the ultimate facts & understanding that we need here—let's say, by contrast with the cardiologist I'm to see this afternoon. Reminds me of the movie with Warren at Buffalo & the question again & again of "arrogance," & the same with Mann, & at the Transcendence Conference where I came thru as "arrogant & authoritarian" to at least one person. And my answer has been "yes," in terms of responsibilities & in terms of the good I think I can do & of the secrets I have & can teach, & the anger & impatience with those who won't hear me or won't listen or, as I learned yesterday with Mann, with those who won't help me & support me. No wonder it sounds like Moses & the Tablets, because in a way it *is* like that. I *do* feel I'm on the right path & that I *do* have the lessons to teach & that very few other people do—just that special group who *should* be supported by the UN & who should not waste their time as Murray has. Rogers is now entirely free. Bennis is getting a good training. So is Argyris. But Dabrowski should be freed. And so should I. And so should Weisskopf & Geiger. Sutich should be entirely subsidized. Well, I can be arrogant for *them* & they can be arrogant for me, as, let's say, Mike Murphy is.

But on the other side of the coin, right along with the feeling of arrogance, responsibility, special vocation or call, goes the profound feeling of not knowing enough, of general ignorance & feebleness & helplessness about *doing* anything yet, because we just don't know enough & are far from it. Maybe the anger I feel is this feeling of impatience to get on with the job that so urgently & obviously needs to be done & my contempt & anger at the people who keep filling the *Psychological Abstracts* with such a large percentage of off-the-mark stuff that I was reading this A.M. (along with some terribly important *bits* of information). Maybe it's also *just* that deep feeling of "My God, the world is falling apart" that pushes me so hard & makes me feel such urgency & impatience & anger. I recall Koestler's fantasy (or dream) of lying in a ditch beside the road being beaten by attackers & screaming for help to the passers-by, who pay absolutely no attention. Well, I'm screaming like that, I guess. Maybe Bertha was right about the preface, which she said was "screaming-like." I *did* tone it down very considerably, but my *Farther Reaches* paper [126] apparently sounded "screaming" to the Transcendence Conference people, including Polanyi (but *not* to Murphy & Bellah, who, I guess, share my sense of urgency & also my sense that here the answers are, in *this* direction).

July 5

Bethel experiences add up to one final medicine: honesty, candor. Same for Freud & all the other department psychologists. Saw Bill Schutz on TV a few nights ago & he's gone even further in one couples' group at Esalen in having them reveal the hidden secrets to each other, even tho it often led to violence, etc., & certainly made the interviewer uneasy (me too). Bill is, however, convinced it works & is worth the pain. Thinking about this on walk today, & sorry that I can't go to Esalen for the schizophrenia conference; it occurs to me that they are making the case for candor even more unanswerable. The fear always has been that the truth might ultimately be *so* traumatic as to produce insanity. But now what they're saying—Grof, Laing, Dabrowski, Silverman, & Mowrer too—is that it is worth even *this* risk, that the psychotic insights can be retained (& *not* forgotten as always has been thought) & under proper guidance, à la LSD, can be a great growth experience (like Harry Rand's patient of 10 or so years ago who went crazy when it dawned on him what a bastard he was, but who came out of it a good man). If you take the fear of insanity away, the ultimate fear, then what possible reason is there for *not* being honest?

July 8

I've been speaking & thinking & writing more & more about specieshood, experiencing oneself as a member of the human-animal species. Occurs to me to put this together with the search for identity, for self, etc., as self-discovery, both of them, but at different levels. Discovering one's basic needs & metaneeds, which everybody has, is discovering one's specieshood. But the individual variations on the theme, the *differences* from the others, this is identity. (In a *sense?* After all, they're *both* identity; they're both subjective.) I guess discovering one's total real self includes both the personal subjective discovery of what is shared by other people & what is *not* shared by other people—but in the moment of experiential discovery, one is not aware of such differences, of whether this experience has happened to others or has not happened to others. *Experiencing* being a Mozart can be no more startling than experiencing being a boy or a girl, or experiencing sex. It makes little difference that billions of others have experienced it before. Discovering *this* is extra-experiential, just like discovering that not everybody composes music in his head easily. It's that latter extra-experiential comparison of one's own-made life with others that makes this differentiation possible between our shared & similar experiences & our unique & idiosyncratic experiences that other people *don't* have. I don't really know what it feels like *not* to be a psychologist, *not* to have ideas & observations & theories playing around inside my head most of the time. It seems perfectly natural & easy. It has been difficult to learn that other people have other things in their heads & don't get fascinated with what fascinates me. Perhaps that's part of that bad experience I had at Bethel, when I was billed as a celebrity. I don't *feel* like a celebrity. There is no such feeling or experience. That's something *other* people tell you. Why does it irritate me? Well, they don't let me feel natural & normal (anyway, they try to prevent me, but I don't let them), but make me feel as if they were seeing only my persona & not me—& the persona is what they have created. They are, in a certain sense, then, seeing themselves, not me. If somebody calls me a "name professor," it irritates me & gets me mad. It's like the rich man who dislikes his wealth to be the only topic of conversation, or dislikes to be seen as "the wealthy man" rather than as just a person.

Or put it this way: If I'd been on a desert island for life, I think I'd have written everything I've written (in principle) even tho I knew no one would ever see it, or if I knew (better example) that nobody else in the world was interested. No, that's not a good example.

Say it so: Authenticity covers *both* being an authentic human animal *and* being authentically an idiosyncratic human animal, different from other human animals.

July 29

All the confusions & contradictions about the data supporting my motivation theory are leading me in the direction of wondering if I need the additional variable of degree of aggridance in the whole structure, i.e., that aggridants have more of the higher needs & metaneeds. More growth-tendency & growth-needs, more tendency to self-actualize. More peak-experiences. More insights & illuminations. Reading new biography of Eleanor Roosevelt brings up the question of how much possibility there is of *inherited* aggridance (genetic), because she came thru to SA in spite of awful conditions throughout early life. She disclaimed peak-experiences á la Ruth Benedict, Fritz Heider, & others who were transformed in middle years by an illumination. So also for the "coping studies" with badly treated children who yet did well.

In the industrial work, it often looks as if the blue-collar workers are *content* to stay at the lower need levels. Certainly this can be learned & cultural, but might it also be in part genetic? Perception of one's own inferiority? Scaling down of one's aspiration levels? A form of biological *noblesse oblige* like the "inferiors" who are killing themselves with drugs, etc.? (But does the Synanon experience contradict this? Not sure, since it's possible that only aggridants come to Synanon & stick it out, à la volunteer error. But they *call* themselves weak, oral, addictive, like the AA people who say "I am an alcoholic" in the same way B. says "I am a diabetic"— "but I am managing to overcome or avoid this bodily weakness." As so many of the Synanon grads frankly say, they *have* to stay in Synanon & might slip without its support.)

August 11

1. Kids "need" training & lessons that they don't desire. It's "good for them," especially for the future, to learn to brush teeth, not to eat too many sweets, to learn arithmetic, courtesy, etc., or else they'll get clobbered outside the family & later on in a future they can't imagine or understand. [*Not everything that is needed is desired, & vice versa: not everything desired is needed.*] In these respects, it's best to call them "stupid" as Synanon does. Good example: necessity for Negro parents in South in 1900 to teach their kids how to accommodate to white domination to avoid death. Same with Jews in Europe.

2. Kids have needs which they unconsciously desire from parents: discipline, law & order, limits, a parental superego to blame for their own

fears, e.g., girls pressed for sex cannot now say "My parents forbid me" & so get into sex that they don't want. He "desires" to be punched when he has sinned, i.e., justice. He "wants" a united front of parents & elders. He does *not* want a weak father (altho seems not to mind a weak, indulging mother).

3. He functions better, is happier, less bored, has more fun in life, if he has hope, desire, something he has *not* got that he can look forward to getting, i.e., a future, hope, anticipation, something to work for, to dream about, to plan for, to be eager for. Levenson speaks of the "boredom of opulence," which is to be *given* everything at once, to have too much. All this removes "something to strive for, to work for," goals not yet attained & therefore to be drooled over. Striving for something eagerly wanted organizes the personality & galvanizes it into pleasant activity.

4. Factually shaky self-esteem = unearned applause & confidence, not based on pride of *actual* achievement, victory, skill = no self-confidence, no sense of capability = parents are fools in his eyes for believing in his capacities even when he doesn't have any. [*See Levenson, p. 130: "A bad report card means that the teacher is wrong,"etc.*] Doesn't know what he is actually *able* to do.

5. Kids, testing limits of parents' reaction & finding no limits, are like kids for whom there is no fixed, stable reality. In a world in which they could influence the sun, the moon, & the winds, they'd be scared to death. E.g., if a kid is separated from his parents in a shipwreck, earthquake, or gets lost, etc., why does he go into panic? What has removal of parents removed? Protection. Strength. Security. Safety. Knowledge. The ones who know. The experts. But supposing they stop supplying strength, protection, safety, knowledge of what's right & wrong, what can be done & what not. Then what difference will their absence or death make? *No* difference! So the child with a weak father, indecisive, controlled by the child, is reacting like someone whose father is not functionally *there*. No wonder he gets mad at him, contemptuous, disrespectful à la Mexican paper [75].

6. Kid has no chance to "earn."

7. He is deprived of hardship, toughness, endurance. See Outward Bound Program.

8. He is permitted to "use" his parents.

9. He learns to control by temper tantrums, by withdrawal of love, by not eating, etc.; i.e., he learns that these "punish" the parents.

10. All of this is non-Taoistic. It does *for* the kid instead of letting *him* do it. It is a taking over of the kid's responsibility for himself, enfeebling him, a kind of castration, a subtle overprotection, lack of respect for his own autonomy. He must exercise his own muscles.

11. Use the old Margaret Mead idea that there *is* no healthy adult concept, only that which the culture wants. To some extent true. Kid in

this sense "needs" (it's good for him) to learn to talk English or Swahili or whatever the group talks.

Read back from troublesome adolescents & what's wrong with them. This gives some retrospective clue to what they "needed" to learn as children, e.g., patience, ability to work, long-term planning, U. S. culture, respect for parents, elders, authority, law, ability to enjoy, ability to strive, ability to love, ability to relate to older people, frustration-tolerance, boredom-tolerance, control of impulsivity & acting out.

August 25

Possible beginning for presidential address: "I will choose, as a strategy of presentation, to begin with a vast oversimplification & then later fill in the details, struggle with the complexities, etc.

Let me call behavioristic psychology the first psychology, Freudian psychology the 2nd, and humanistic psychology the 3rd. And then what I think of as a real possibility, what I am fascinated with, is the psychology of transcendence & of ends, the transhuman or transpersonal (really *should* be "transcendent") psychology = the 4th psychology.

Sleepless night. Midnight, but the thoughts keep blazing. On behaviorism, say it's done a lot. It was the beautiful program of Watson that brought me into psychology. But its fatal flaw is that it's good for the lab & in the lab, but you put it on & take it off like a lab coat. It's useless at home with your kids & wife & friends. It does not generate an image of man, of philosophy of life, a conception of human nature. It's not a guide to living, to values, to choices. It's a way of collecting facts upon facts about behavior, what you can see & touch & hear thru the senses.

But behavior in the *human being* is sometimes a defense, a way of concealing motives & thoughts, as language can be a way of hiding your thoughts & preventing communication.

If you try to treat your children at home in the same way you treat your animals in the lab, your wife will scratch your eyes out. My wife ferociously warned me against experimenting on her babies (I was working with monkeys at the time).

Behaviorism is nonvectorial (scalar). No directions, no ends, no principles of choice or of guidance. It is concerned only with means (instrumental) & not ends (axiological), so it has in itself no hints about good & evil, right or wrong. It's purely technological, & is *just* as available to the evil man, the dictator, as to the good man or the people helpers. Value free, value neutral. No help in finding out *what* is good or *how* to lead a good life. No morality. (Same for psychoanalysis, which also *tries* to be value free, an impossible task.) It takes for granted the intrinsic rewards or reinforcements, as if they already existed & did not merit examination; but if they *were* examined, they'd turn out to be approximately the same as my value theory, i.e., the "nature" of the species.

Add also about verbal operant conditioning that it often disappears when the truth is known. Same with all stooge experiments (à la Asch), the Baker-Metzner experiment, posthypnotic suggestion, advertising propaganda, censorship, subliminal stimulation, repression, lying. These all rest upon truth concealment, where the Third- and Fourth-Force psychologies rest on truth valuing & embracing, & think the truth is not dangerous but healing. Jeffersonian, Synanon, psychoanalysis (?), T-groups, democracy = the truth-concealing or mistrusting society. (These are better words than "free world" or "totalitarian" or "authoritarian.")

August 29

4:30 A.M. Humphrey nominated. Very sad, couldn't sleep. The whole process of the convention saddened me & disturbed my sleep. Have tried to learn from it, as I watched the "liberals" cut each other to pieces & probably split the Democratic Party, beat Humphrey, & elect Nixon. (1) The demand for absolutes, the seeking for perfection. The extremists insisting on this or breaking up things. The spoilers. (2) I suspect McCarthy of pathology of the schizzy sort, so I couldn't understand the tremendous loyalty to him of so many. Same for Robert Kennedy. *Not* so for McGovern, who seems like a very good & decent Theory-Y man like Humphrey. Why did so many juveniles therefore not follow him, but follow 2 very doubtful characters instead? Humphrey also seems a Theory-Y, nontranscender self-actualizer like McGovern & many of the other good politicians. McCarthy is the most Theory-Z man I think, but neurotic. (3) Something like this, plus more for the demonstrators who *hate* Humphrey, will spoil or break up (or try) the convention, the Democratic Party, the 2-party system, & may elect Nixon. Their attacks on the police in authority, their seeking to harass the police into making martyrs of them, & then the extremist delegates going along with them instead of with the police, the siding with the criminals, the chaos-makers. The rioters called the demonstrations "free speech." The complete conformity at the Left extreme about law & order, which they seem to hate as much as the Right extremists seem to *need desperately.* (4) Then the attack on friends rather than foes trying to destroy the Democrats, not the Republicans. Same for the Negroes, many of whom at the 10% extreme first shoot down their friends & their leaders & allies. (5) The weird goings-on with the peaceniks who don't seem to *see* the faults of the Communists, or don't seem to *think* anything of their sins, while attacking so bitterly a liberal who's spent his whole life on reform, as if he were a villain.

Lesson for evil stuff: the dangers of seeking perfect human beings, especially among human beings. The danger of seeking absolutes & perfection in the D-realm, i.e., in society, which *must* be D-realm. Same for 2-party politics. Absolutes mean multi-party system, as in France, which doesn't work. Two parties mean broad coalitions & alliances of all sorts of people, with the parties overlapping by 50% to 75% & with the centers of the parties not *too* far apart, so that they compete for the middle 50% of the voters. The perfectionists & absolutists will reject Humphrey because he must compromise & form a broad coalition. So many of them really don't care for a majority, like the Goldwaterites, absolutists who prefer to lose rather than form coalitions & alliances, to give in & compromise. [*Quarrel with Ann over politics.*]

August 31

Reading Glasser, *Reality Therapy.* He too goes in for setting up his own church & the "narcissism of small differences." He stresses the word "responsibility"—quite legitimately—but instead of showing it as a neglected facet, or as one needing more underlining, he deliberately misunderstands Freud & all the others, in order to stress how *different* he is.

But *I* can put it all under the head of parallel languages, different ways of saying the same thing, with each language having its own advantages & disadvantages for various purposes.

All the therapists are saying that step 1 is acceptance, an act of truth-awareness, taking it upon your own shoulders & admitting that you are sick, etc. [*All of this involves "going to the bottom of the barrel," having nothing left, complete breaking of pride, of will, of self, humility, request for help, admitting weakness. Must start off with the truth, & away from the big lie of pride & trying to* look *better than you* = *phoniness. This admission of illness is itself a healthy step. The double view here: to say "I am sick" is to start toward health.*] Can use this list to make the point of basic similarity & surface, but there are real differences of language or interpretation.

For the conventional man, step 1 is the acceptance of: "I am not adjusted to the society. I am different." For Freud it is the acceptance of: "I am sick. I have been regressive. I have been unaware." For Glasser: "I am irresponsible." For Synanon: "I am stupid." For T-groups: "I am defensive, not real." For Reich: "I am armored, rigid." For Adler: first "I am compensating" and later "I lack *Gemeinschaftsgefühl*." For the Church: "I am a sinner & a wrongdoer, with real guilt, needing forgiveness." For

Gestalt therapy: "I am not here-now experiencing." For Esalen: "I am not fully conscious, aware, free." For Moreno: "I am not spontaneous." For Rogers: "I am not open, congruent, actualizing. I hate myself, feel unworthy. I am not loveworthy. I lack courage. I am fear-motivated. I lack values & commitment. I am less than fully human. I am less than fully functioning. I am not growing. I can't feel."

October 13

Add comments on testing as itself a destroyer of the mood, as in being turned on by love, peaks, LSD, or as in my Synanon trial testimony where I agreed with Dederich that testing the Synanon residents to see if they were *really* clean was equivalent to mistrusting them & controlling-from-above, the very opposite of the Synanon procedure.

Reading *Psychological Bulletin*, August 1968, Campbell & Dunnette on effectiveness of T-group experiences. *One* thing it shows, along with their conclusions, is the inadequacy or clumsiness of classical scientific methods to test subtle changes—or, at any rate, the great difficulty with using them. See their attack on $N = 1$, i.e., the single-case method, & criticize it. On the one hand, every case *is* unique & noncomparable, just as Mozart is (imagine saying "For my experimental group I want 40 Mozarts & for my control group 40 Debussies!"); so, to be understood, there is no alternative to studying it *as* a case, idiographically. On the other hand, uniquenesses can be added, or at least particular aspects of them can, just as sunsets or beautiful women can be added, subtracted, etc.

This has *some* connection or parallel with the experimental concept (the blood-filled concept rather than the helium-filled concept) in which the abstraction is made up of experiences (which must be unique).

Connect also with my old paper on experimentalizing the clinical method [37], in which, post hoc, unique cases can be used statistically. This is again the equivalent of saying "give your all to the case, as a good therapist does. Forget about everything else while you're doing this." But *afterwards*, after you have awakened from the trance, the absorption, the fascination, in which you are simply receiving, you can recollect & *then* compare & arithmetize.

Don't test or arithmetize or be detached or compare or take notes, etc., in the middle of a high. I'm *still* suspicious about the Masters & Johnson data on observed sex. How could you have a peak-experience that way? And how can you assume that nonpeak sex is the same as peak sex? The observer intrudes & perhaps changes the very *nature* of what is observed.

Bull-in-the-china-shop science.

Why did my self-actualizing subjects refuse to be tested? When does the tester (or the test) look ridiculous? Funny? Childish? When does it seem out of palce? Are some things too private, too sacred, for this kind of intrusion? Are some things—enthusiasm, gaiety, light-heartedness, laughter—not available for testing because the testing halts them at once?

But notice that none of these objections apply to the I-Thou "interview," to rhapsodic interviewing or conversation or the joint exploring of something *jointly* felt or experienced, or at least sympathetically received. (Will I show my baby pictures to a baby hater?)

Add: remember that the *point* of objectivity is that it is supposed to get more accurate data, less contaminated by the wishes or fears or expectations of the researcher. But Taoistic objectivity & interviewing get better data, more truthful. Therefore it is *more* objective than laissez-faire, spectator objectivity for *some* data at least, especially intrapersonal & interpersonal data.

Also use the example of the little Negro boy being tested by the white psychologist. Interruption for office party for a Negro woman whom the psychologist kissed. Boy's IQ immediately went up.

Effect of pollster-interviewers. Discuss.

Use example of my psychoanalysis. It was *so* successful, so meaningful, so crucially important to me, & changed me so much that I don't care about *100* experiments that fail to prove psychoanalysis has any effects. I just *assume* that the experiments are poorly done or are inadequate to the purpose. If I *saw* the goldmine in the desert with my own eyes, I'd pay no attention to those who disproved its possibility (altho I could understand, accept, & be sympathetic & not angry or insulted by their skepticism).

How would you test for the effectiveness of love experiences? Or even of good mothering? Or of good education?

Or how would one make scientific use of Bertha's great insight this last June in Bethel, which I saw as extremely & profoundly changing & effective? In fact, I'd say it made a different person of her for the month or two following, until the counter-effect & disappointment with her group's not sticking together, not keeping promises, not making contact, etc.

Debby Tanzer, with her childbirth interviews, got so many peaks, value-experiences, etc., that in retrospect I'd think this proved her to be a good interviewer-person, i.e., a good person. A bad person, or one not understanding, sympathetic, or identifying, or committed or enthusiastic, could not have gotten those data. That is, not getting data may turn out to be a judgment on the defects of the personality of the researcher or perhaps on the methods of the researcher. *Not* getting data may mean very little.

In the same number of *Psychological Bulletin* there is a summary of researches on managerial motivation, doing partly what I've been urging myself to do for a year (see file on data for *my* motivation theory), i.e., testing of my motivation theory in industry à la Porter, et al. Totally unimaginative. Sticking entirely to classical model of research à la physics lab. All the subtleties missed, also all the humanness, in their eagerness to look "scientific." I should really write "What Is Research?" & talk about the first exploratory stages, the delicate probings of the humble, *ignorant* man who is starting out to try to know. At that stage, all these fancy experimental designs, with fake vigor & phony exactness, all based on inadequate data & tests & dopy questionnaires, are absolutely premature. Like trying to use the highest power of the microscope to start with (instead of to end with). *This* is when the Taoistic, I-Thou, joint discussion & probing is the *only* right thing. Or the really good, novelist-style case history (like Hannah Green's *I Never Promised You a Rose Garden)*, or even the really careful & open autobiography. Maybe that's the way I should write it, for, e.g., the Warren Bennis case-study section of the *Journal of Applied Behavioral Sciences.*

November 9

Someone talks of the ultimate (value) "questions of truthfulness, justice, & compassion." For one thing, reminded me of my incompleted file on truth (& add "truthfulness") sitting there all the years since La Jolla (June 1961–January 1962). If I'd had another month or two I'd have finished it. Lost the impetus when I left & got involved in teaching. When I came back in summer 1962, got all absorbed in management theory at Non-Linear Systems. I should consider this a priority job.

But how to treat compassion & Agapean love as B-values? I don't think they are ultimate values in the sense that B-values are. So far I've treated love & emotion as attitudes *toward* the B-values, like awe or mystery. The B-values *command* love & awe, gratitude, etc., in the beholder. *He* loves; *they* are lovable & loveworthy; *not* the same thing. Truth, excellence, etc., are cognitions of the nature of reality; i.e., they are out there as well as within the beholder. Awe is *only* within the beholder & should not be projected out there as part of extra-human reality.

But can also see Agapean love & compassion as *consequences* of contemplation of B-values. Also it stresses the holistic view, the view from above, the Olympian, godlike perception of the world in its oneness + holistic comprehensiveness, i.e., of the complexity of the oneness of its internal holistic structuring & dynamics & vectorial directions in time.

This is because compassion = understanding, forgiveness, acceptance, reconciliation (as with pain, death, evil behavior)—as I asked John Holt's class to make the point about compassion for Hitler, et al.: "How would *you* like to be

Hitler? How would *you* like to be a son of a bitch & at the same level *know* willy-nilly that you are one?" Also I stressed with them that this kind of compassion or understanding does not necessarily mean forgiving or a weaker arm; it usually means *greater* firmness in acting, with *less* conflict rather than more.

If one can see from above, holistically, maturely → "I *am* my brother's keeper" → sense of oneness of mankind, specieshood. I am responsible for Hitler & Stalin in the same sense that I am for my brother Paul or my sister Sylvia.

All of this goes also under the heading of maturity, this suggested to me, *both* chronological and also personal, characterological maturing. [*Also social maturity, moral-ethical maturity, cognitive, motivational, axiological, etc.*] Discuss the overlap between these 2 kinds of maturing. Could they be put on a single continuum? I.e., is personological immaturity the same as getting stuck or fixated at one of the stages in chronological maturing? Like IQ, where it *is* possible to talk about mental age independently of chronological age? Could one speak of levels of "personality age" in the same way? [*Make test?*]

Stress the need of holistic view. Reconciliation with evil, compassion for sick & sinner, tolerance for & patience with immaturity, etc., are impossible *unless* one takes the holistic view—that the world is one (does *not* mean that the world is homogeneous).

This brings to mind my limitations on truth-telling, which I've been thinking about—or, better, the paving, the style, the strategy & tactics of truth-telling & of candor. For example, for the immature, who couldn't understand isomorphically any mature truth; for the inexperienced, who won't fully understand until they experience for themselves; for the paranoid, where the *only* thing I can see to present is unrelenting honesty & truth, even when it hurts, i.e., to avoid suspicion; for the schizzy, where a hard truth can throw them over the edge of sanity; for the haters, who think they love everyone; for the Peaceniks, who are obviously hostile & violent, e.g., the girl in my class who is all of these & whom I could kill with my authority. I would refuse to cut her with my truth-scalpel unless I had time & willingness to heal up the wound.

Add also the Freudian defenses: repression, denial, reaction-formation, rationalization, etc. [*Also T-groups. Also Rogers.*] Fold in: psychoanalytic techniques, the strategy & tactics of truth-telling *and* receiving, getting *acceptance* of the truth & only thus getting it to have its healing effects. Also the training & the selection of the psychoanalyst bring up the question of *who* is the best truth-teller. What are the analyst's resistances to seeing the truth, being able to dish it out effectively, to have compassion for the blind & fearful patient (Agapean love), to be fascinated with each patient accepted so as to get love-knowledge, receptivity, & Taoistic objectivity, being able to wait & not be impatient?

Also the use of psychotic insight into the unconscious à la Laing. [3/24/ 69: Savage Sleep, *Millen Brand re John Rosen.*] Jourard, self-exposure. Mowrer, confession. Theory-Y communication up & down. Feedback à la T-group, à la Rogers, à la tape & video recordings, à la seeing yourself thru the eyes of your child with "play therapy." Being able to listen. Little mouths & big mouths &

open ears & closed ears. Confession with forgiveness, contrition, penalties which relieve guilt & bring completion (putting perseveration to an end).

Then ask: *why* does truth heal? But is this the same as asking: why does beauty heal? (Or any other B-value?) Is this the same as Socrates & Plato talking about contemplation of the B-values as the ultimate happiness, the highest activity of man, etc.? But then you can ask the same question again: why does it have these good effects? Instinct? Species-specific characteristics? And then go on to consider the *machinery* which mediates these effects: the nervous system, endocrines, biochemistry, genes, etc. = a partial explanation at one level. If you ask: *"why* this machinery?" then the only answer is evolutionary-historical.

November 10

Last night at Cohens', long discussion with Abe Zaleznik of Harvard Business School. He's more or less rejected T-group, Theory Y, McGregor ("trying to make a heaven on earth"). Against Esalen, against Schutz (altho has never been there & doesn't want to go). Straight Freudian interpretations = "to mother the world." Schutz is really depressed & defends against it with hypomanic & exaggerated reaction-formations, e.g., "joy." *To me:* "What is a big man like you wasting your time for with those kids?" All a good, straight Freudian reaction with all its strengths & weaknesses. He's realistic about his limits of usefulness in analyzing one (upper-class) person by one. He can't do much for the society (but with the implication that no one can). He says "I am modest about doing well the little that I can do." When I said I could integrate with Freud all sorts of other people & theories & data, he was skeptical & asked "Why do you do this? It will kill you." He questioned my high aspirations—partly, I sensed, because it couldn't be done & partly because, if it *could* be done, it's such a heavy task it would strain & hurt me.

If he had a choice between going to Esalen or to, e.g., Rome, which would he pick? "Rome, of course," which means he doesn't *want* to learn or experience the Esalen kind of thing, even after I spoke of the benefits, of what massage & body awareness did for my back.

When I agreed with many of his criticisms & of Bertha's, & Saul's, who is sort of amused by the whole thing, as with children playing, then they asked me why I went anyway. I said "Because it is the wave of the future, because these experiments have to be done, because one-by-one psychoanalysis is socially useless (except as experiments to teach writers like *me* about the basic, intensive study of human nature in individuals, i.e., of raw material, so that the ethical-social-humanistic-Utopian-Messianic-scientific people like me can use the raw material to build upon). *All* movements were once just as 2nd-class & doubtful as the Esalen

& Eupsychian movements are now considered. *Their* experiments are just as important as the Freudian experiences were as raw materials for the people like me—that is, as first-stage science which I could make use of in my theorizing & scientific planning & hypothesis-for-testing production. I spoke also of the great yearning for religion surrogates, saying that the Esalen people *paid* for these seminars & traveled long distances, that their experiences were often truly happy, that their defenses & rigidities & body armor truly dropped before my eyes (altho I admitted I *knew* little about how lasting these effects were, altho I felt they are lasting, just as I feel psychoanalytic effects are lasting altho nobody's been able to *prove* it well).

Z. said: "Remember, not only are they children at Esalen, but they're in a permanent state of childhood."

D. said: "Esalen people are unable to commit themselves to a woman" (they also tend to choose very young girls to sleep with).

I said that Esalen-type education is good for the Puritan, rigid, inhibited types who are unable to feel, express, or enjoy, or to be I-thou, to be good, deep friends, to love. Good for the overintellectual & over-restrained à la British. Teaches them to be more Dionysian, to be less acculturated. How to be childlike again, playful again, wondering again, really looking & listening & experiencing again. Joy once in a while. Peak-experiences *encouraged* rather than feared. (Critique: They're *just* playing. How about work & discipline? How about study? Service? In addition to personal identity? Such people seek it only for themselves & for their own selfish good.) Z.'s critique: each one sets up his own stove, his own kiosk. He made fun of their "discovery" of sex & nakedness. I said for many Americans, it *has* to be rediscovered à la Reich—body armor & rediscovery of the body & of pleasure. He said also: they're mothers & not fathers, & at the same time *hostile* to mothers, age, elders, authority, fathers.

November 26

Finished Fromm's new book, *Revolution of Hope*. Disappointing, even tho one must agree with the general thrust. His work has gone steadily downhill. Reaffirms for me again the desirability of the empirical, scientific attitude & of scientific experience & training. For him it's all black & white, exaggerated extremes, polarized; he can't think in terms of degree. He comes to definite & final conclusions (rather than tentative ones) without the slightest hint of the data or experiences upon which he bases these certainties. His opinions are presented as if they were facts, & they're generally so sweeping, so all-or-none, that they are not testable.

No hint of percentages; he seems to come to a picture of a type of man & then talks about Man, without regard to the exceptions. He doesn't build upon other people's work as scientists do. So he rediscovers things that have already become well known, & in a necessarily amateurish way therefore. So there is no progress, no collaboration, no building up of a joint structure of knowledge. He doesn't seem to read, so he's totally ignorant about, e.g., Theory-Y management theory.

[*12/12/68: Add to preface of education book my shame & embarrassment about my colleagues, about tenure, about retaining all guild privileges, about their resistance to any innovation even when data supported it, i.e., anti-intellectual, anti-empirical. Statement: Why I Left the Academic World!*]

December 6

B. had good insight into the problem of post-T-group disillusionment—namely, that we really did *not* want to get closer & stay close forever, because most of the group were not really simpatico or good as long-time friends. As she & I discussed whether or not to form a continuing group here at home, & both found ourselves hesitant & reluctant, it broke thru simultaneously. We'd been repressing the realization that the intimacy *did* feel good while it lasted, but we didn't *want* to be close with people we couldn't deeply care for. Then how to explain the hurt & the let-down feelings when others didn't respond? Conflict? Repression? I feel better about the whole thing now, when I know what to expect & *want* what I expect, i.e., to have a happy time for 2 weeks & then say goodbye & go back to my privacy. But to confront this consciously & bring it out on the table for honest discussion. I remember now that I brought this up 1½ years ago at Bethel when I pointed out that they didn't really know me—only 3 inches deep. And also that the intimacy & communion that we achieved were based on careful avoidance of *deep* issues that we'd seriously disagree on. I asked if we could discuss Vietnam & they all agreed we couldn't.

But this is also one aspect of the Esalen critique I've been so involved in this semester. I must sober them down in their exhilaration over what is like the shipboard romance. It won't last & they'd better accept it—& *enjoy* the transient intimacy as Bennis suggested.

Somebody also brought this up at the Orizon evening in D. C. when she questioned the wisdom of another group's plan to continue with follow-ups of the T-group. I think one good way to view the whole thing is thru the eyes of the psychoanalyst. Do this systematically before going out to Esalen. Start talking about repression, defenses, the difficulties of self-knowledge & self-analysis. The Esalen techniques only *com-*

plement the depth techniques & succeed upon them, being really success-ful only with the already analyzed person, i.e., the person who knows himself in depth. The end goal of psychoanalysis is identity. Same goal for Esalen techniques. (Who am I?) But which work better? If only we had good evaluation methods, good ways of assessing improvement!

December 12

Add to my NTL etiquette notes of last summer: if I ask you "Do you want wine with dinner or not?" then this is not merely polite but B-polite; i.e., it assumes I really want to know. If you do, I really want to get it for you, because (1) I don't want to waste money (give up being a "sport," a show-off, a big-spender type—all phony); (2) nor do I want to force it on you, so that you, out of D-politeness & hostility-fear-defense, will have to drink wine that you don't want or mustn't have; (3) nor do I want "politely" to have to drink it myself so as to put you at ease & so that you won't have to feel guilty about drinking wine all by yourself & then apologizing, so that I'll have to apologize & reassure; & so (4) we can avoid *everybody* doing what they don't want to do, with money & wine being wasted & with bruises left over, real hostility & irritation, etc. Use the Japanese code of politeness-as-avoiding-insult-&-hostility-mechanism as the contrast with the etiquette, politeness, manners of authenticity.

So I can say out of authentic etiquette, "Does anybody want some wine?" And the ones who really want it will say "yes," assuming my question is authentic, & those who don't want it will say "no." Or I could say "Are you a wine drinker (or wine lover)? If so, I'll order some wine. Otherwise I won't because Bertha & I don't want any." Or even: "Shall I order a half or a whole bottle? How much wine does each of us want?"

Authentic etiquette permits authentic, *real* questions, which mean exactly & only what they say & have no subterranean implications. And they permit authentic answers. But either this means lots of training in "healthy selfishness & honesty," which even neurotics could pick up to some extent, or else it requires fairly healthy people to be *able* to ask authentic questions & give authentic answers (rather than the questions "Shall we go now?" = "Let's go now!" *or* "Would you like some lunch?" = "I want you to have your lunch now").

Authentic etiquette is the same for *all* cultures. You don't have to know the local code of unspoken meanings & implications, e.g., "Isn't that a beautiful painting you have" = I *must* give you the painting (= I don't dare to admire anything). Or, as in so many cultures, giving a gift "means" that you have to return a gift or even double the gift à la Chuckchee.

But this cross-cultural, species-wide etiquette actually exists *already* among authentic individuals of any culture. And, as with the Blackfoot, all that is necessary to avoid any offense or blundering is to say, as I did: "I don't know your customs. If I offend, it is ignorance. Please forgive me & tell me what I've done wrong." And then this worked. When I did something wrong, like stepping over the chief's outstretched legs, they told me, or their reacting was of *good-natured* amusement at my mistakes, as I might be with a foreigner's funny misuse of the language.

I think I *could* break our cultural rigidity about halitosis & sweat odors, but *only* with (1) long-time friends who (2) also are quite strong people. Use G.'s sweat smell as an example. I *didn't* tell him, altho I hinted e.g., "Wouldn't you like a shower?" But he's strong enough so that I *could* tell him if I get to know him more closely. Similarly with bad mouth odor, have said this only with my own family, not anyone else. (I *could* say it with, e.g., Mike Murphy, if he had a bad smell, but he never has.)

Our society has no built-in ways of rejecting, without insult, an invitation to a party or visit unless with a polite lie about headaches or whatever. I can't say to many people (I've been doing this more & more recently with students, colleagues, close friends, but still get caught with unwelcome invitations or visitors without being able to say, simply, "Let's postpone this") "I'm working well" *or* "It will tire me out" or even "I just don't feel sociable right now." No! Come to think of it, I *have* been saying this more & more easily, but only since my heart attack. This gives me a marvelous alibi & also courage to be selfish, forthright, etc. Also, as I was saying to Murray last night [*he's in love—at age 75 or so!*] at the Bob White party, my heart attack permitted my superego to die, & therefore allowed my intrinsic conscience to reign. That I am less & less a good citizen, dutiful, thoughtful of others, responsible, "nice," & more & more permitting myself the healthy selfishness, which is synergic for the world. But just *now* came a call from Hilda about a former student worried about her college-age son, coming in today when I wanted to be alone in office. I had told her over the phone I would see her only in office hours. But I thought, as long as I had to be at the office at 4:15, I could see her at 4 without trouble. Compassion? Do a good deed with very little cost? Lack of strength? I feel it to be the former & maybe old habit of being neurotically unable to say no. Why else do I want to go off next year in the winter, or even for the rest of my life if I could, to a totally isolated & concealed place where even my friends couldn't get to me, but I could get to them? It's partly to save myself from my own tendencies to be compassionate, helpful at little cost, amiable, etc. Plus what's left over of superego as well as intrinsic conscience, as well as just plain "normal" etiquette, as with Mary Hall's coming, whom I would rather not see—too many visitors recently—but I just can't say so because I'm "her boy" to the extent that I take her $1000 a year as consultant *plus* enjoying the backseat driving I do with *Psychology Today*.

Or we have no way to terminate a visitor's staying too late, or one who just shows up unexpectedly at the door, or who *asks* "Can you put me up overnight?" Tho, since my heart attack, I can say "Yes, for an hour, but then I'll have to excuse myself & rest." But that's also often under the head of a good alibi, i.e., a gentle white lie that the culture permits, & serves instead of bluntness.

(Example: the *forcing* of too much food on the guest, where the hostess *has* to, & the guest feels he *has* to eat at least some of the food even tho unwanted.)

Contrast with this T-group etiquette (which is transitional to truly authentic etiquette). Also Esalen etiquette (the same). The first time I was impressed with this was the Air Force group at Maxwell A.F.B. in Alabama in 1954. The strong men, self-respecting & therefore without need for defenses or phony games of masculinity, king-of-the-hill, etc., startled me with the easy way they could speak their mind bluntly, & yet without offense since the others were known to be strong, able to take it, *preferring* it. Then, second, with Drury's novel about Senators, & my follow-up; that's the way *they* behave too, each like autonomous persons who assume that the others are also strong & autonomous, so that real profound disagreements, bluntly stated, are possible, & then they go off & have lunch together, or you hear they are good friends. Also: the thinking I've done over the phoniness, & therefore harmfulness, of the "I don't want to hurt you" type of doctor-patient relationship, which is *supposed* to spare pain but produces *more* pain, I think, & paranoia besides.

This all involves the excesses & artificialities of "trying" to be authentic or spontaneous, which is a transitional state between, e.g., being a crook & being, gracefully & easily, an honest man. [*See "trying" file.*] The "trying to be" state is gawky, awkward, artificial, a little phony because it is willed rather than truly spontaneous, like an Arthur Murray dance. And yet we must learn to respect it or at least tolerate it—as with Negroes today *"trying* to be men" but doing it immaturely. In a certain sense we may be said, *all* of us, to be in this *"trying* to be" state, & only rarely in the Being state. Tie this in with the will-volition paradox of *"trying* to be" nontrying, e.g., trying to be spontaneous, natural, simple, to relax, to be Taoistic. "Trying" is *not* the opposite of Taoistic; it is a step along the path to that end of being able to not try & yet do right. The opposites are apathy, hopelessness (*that* form of nontrying), & trying & striving for the wrong ends (which will not bring happiness, serenity, fully humanness).

1969

January 7

Better use the distinction I've made between hard-nosed & soft-nosed, tender- & tough-minded, X & Y scientists. I've been thinking of it as essentially characterological & taste & attitude differences between those psychologists who came in from physics & engineering, etc., & those who came in from art, literature, philosophy, the humanities, or as helpers. This is testable, e.g., with Strong's aptitude tests. When I took it I was rated high in psychology, art, & music. And I'd rather be a truck driver than be in math, physics, or chemistry, etc. But our experimental psychologists, Morant, Held, Neisser, Stecher, etc., all came in from physics, engineering, & the like. This comes back to the "personal & the impersonal scientists."

I think this can be used as part of the psychology 3 differentiation from behaviorism—& maybe even from Freud, who after all did hope to reduce psychology to quantity, physics, & chemistry. See McClelland's *Roots of Consciousness*, first chapter, comparing Freud with Hull.

Also use the distinction between interfering & controlling science (experimentation) & noninterfering, observing science, e.g., microscope, telescope. The hard-nosed, interfering, controlling, experimenting, impersonal vs. the soft-nosed (loving the object too much to dissect or kill it or change or destroy it or to do it violence), personal, curious for the sake of understanding & helping & enjoying & contemplating (rather than mastering, conquering, reducing) = really interpersonal I-Thou relation with object of study (in contrast with I-It).

I guess, too, the interest in the individual case is humanistic & personal vs. statistical, average, "law," which disregard the exceptions = impersonal, mathematical (rather than the sacred & unique individual). McClelland speaks also of Hull's loyalty to the "system" rather than to the individual, inexplicable, exceptional facts = also impersonal.

January 27

Thought on plane: a very useful paper or lecture would be on the stupidities of youth, their unwisdom, lack of experiences of all kinds, their usual freedom from all responsibilities & duties, e.g., earning money, supporting themselves, let alone supporting someone else; their innocence about death; their me-me-ness, impatience, perfectionism & absolutism; dichotomizing & either-or tendency with inability to think in terms of degree & of shades of gray; their tendency to consider all problems soluble, & quickly too, with belief that if they are *not* being solved, there is a villain someplace with malice & ill will; their tendency to project blame outward; their innocence about money & where it comes from; their innocent assumption that avowedly good ends justify *any* means, so that they think too well of themselves because of their ends, but also get taken in by *any* jerk so long as he talks good values. [*Juvenocracy. See "younguns" paper.*] They haven't learned to differentiate people whom you can count on from those who are unreliable. They need companionship, belongingness, affection, applause; but *too* much leads to poor judgment of people, so that they are too easily taken in by decisives, by bigmouths, by defiant, daring, violent ones (they admire daring & violence too much & caution not enough). The "cause" must be exciting, gay, fun with togetherness. They go too easily for amity from enmity rather than from including. They hate to practice, e.g., the piano. They are unable to be alone, unpopular, ostracized, unloved, laughed at. *Very* hard to resist the crowd. (Would Asch's experiment work in the same way with older people? Self-actualizing people?) Many of them are still struggling out of dependency, i.e., Oedipal, authority hangups, *unable* to be friends with elders. Pulled around too much by sheer sexual drive. Need other people too badly. Underlying feelings of inferiority lead to neurosis. Generally have not yet developed compassion, Agapean love, unrequited love, unrequited respect (too often *quid pro quo*—I'll love you if you love me; I'll praise you if you praise me). Generally far too much misunderstanding of elders, their pleasures & pains, their goals, etc. (Quote Ellen, age 10, on how awful our party was. Why? Because it was so quiet! She thought they weren't having any fun.) In my class, note also the weirdly neurotic transferences; e.g., I was Mark's father, I was Pat's mother, I was Trudy's father, etc. Generally they've never experienced B-love. They are at the metagrumble level without awareness of all the pregratified needs this rests on; they don't count their blessings & so are stupidly underestimating the worth of these gratified values (you could solve the whole youth rebellion by having a depression, or by cutting off their allowances). List all the experiences they have not yet had: marriage, parenthood, career, executive responsibility, e.g., captain of the ship, ordering people around, firing people, being postambivalent, being grandparents, having friends & family die, the dead parents & the work of mourning, confronting real evil in the world, becoming fully conscious of their own evil, being a success at a job, contributing to the world, feeling the world is better off because they have lived in it, having people totally dependent on them. Confronting real hatred & emnity, real enemies. Stupidity about economic necessities in a complex society. (Use the plastics example in *The Graduate* & other "youngun" movies. Compare with the fool in Christ legends, the superior wisdom of the ignorant, the innocent, the pious. Say about the plastics & also the lawyer, the dentist, the real-estate man who told me that his work wasn't worthwhile. I said *any* work which is necessary & needed is worthwhile & can be sacralized, & that includes garbage collecting, running a bus or a truck, etc.) Rethink Thoreau & his snottiness about the lives of quiet desperation which now I don't believe. It must often have been simply snotty projection; he thought they were desperate because they didn't have Thoreau's tastes. He couldn't see that running a farm could be a profoundly sacralized life. I guess he too was a big kid. Emerson was the great person, not Thoreau, even tho Thoreau was the better writer.

Good way of saying this is autobiographical. What lessons have *I* learned since youth? Am I wiser now than then? How exactly?

Also use Harry Golden's examples of the unsung heroes who sweat their lives away for the sake of their families.

February 1

On plane to San Francisco. When Ann & Ellen were born, they made the psychology of the time look trivial & totally inadequate. Certainly weaned me from behaviorism anyway. Now Jeannie is also uprooting psychology for me. As yesterday, on the edge of depression & tears before leaving for several months, to what can I attribute this except to pure love, just deeply instinctive feeling? The delight is pure, unending, esthetic, perpetually surprising & (esthetically) shocking. And intrinsically rewarding, without extinction of any kind that I can see. [*3/26/69: Add: Jeannie looks gentle, nonhostile; no malice, no hatred, or even anger for more than a moment.*] And what could it have to do with extrinsic rewards or reinforcements? With my self-esteem? With aim-inhibited sexuality? With pride? Or with *any* other secondary thing, or explanation of any kind, or excuse or means-to-any-end? She just looks intrinsically beautiful, fascinating, lovable, & charming. I enjoy endlessly looking at her, kissing her, hugging, holding—& get a terrible & ultimate happiness when she suddenly smiles at me in her baby way, or opens her mouth silently wide in a laugh without sound, & when she looks merry. It all seems to appeal to some fundamental architectural structure in me, in Bertha, in Ann, & in Jerry. We are all triggered in a kind of reflex which *feels* as profound & biological as anything could be. It's the *same* feeling & syndrome as being in love & therefore makes romantic love look awfully different. The sex *must* be regarded as *not* of the essence, but as some sort of gratuitous grace, an extra which is not *sine qua non* but is simply a perfect completion, a climactic ending which is not really attained with a baby, but is *almost* attained. Hugging the baby tight is terribly satisfying & has some of the climactic quality, & yet one can't let go altogether; one can't *crush* the baby. One must restrain oneself in a way not necessary in sex where the total Dionysian letting go without care or restraint is possible. One feels the impulse to hug the baby harder than is permissible—the gentleness *is* necessary, after all. You can't go completely wild physically, even tho you *can* with words, emotions, gestures, etc.

Anyway you love the baby—or anyone or *anything* else—because it's lovable, loveworthy, *calls* for love, demand-character, & then the words come up: first it's beautiful, & then it's perfect (& excellent) & couldn't be improved or bettered. And then there is the perpetual sense of good luck, of gratuitous grace, of not really *deserving* it, of not really having *earned* it—the pure gift. I thought of the thousand terrible things that could have happened to an embryo, to the bad luck & bad accidents at births, to the tragedies & sicknesses & other blows, as if any baby had to run a gauntlet of a thousand blows, so that one gets the sense of miracle & disbelief & incredulousness at the very moment of staring at what actually & improbably exists—a perfectly beautiful, healthy, charming, & lovable little thing, with the whole sense of miracle intensified by the very fact that perfection, if tiny, is somehow even more perfect.

February 19

Walking in San Francisco today, passing lots of hippies & rebels. Thought: when talking with Mike, realized that I was a bridge between the 2 worlds, of radicals & conservatives, & lived in both of them & could get along with both of them. [2/21/69: *One aspect of "conservatism" is the belief that human beings are fundamentally evil, stupid, greedy, sick, & nasty, & that therefore they needed strong repressive & suppressive controls. Well, my reading of available data indicates that there definitely is evil & stupidity, etc.,*

*a great deal in some & at least a little in most or all men. And this does need
controls, rules, etiquette, laws, codes, folkways, & habits to hold it all under
control. But just as real is the good, the wise, the beautiful, the generous; & this
needs (or can well use) freedom, spontaneity, the absence of control. This is an
example of the way in which the emerging knowledge of human nature makes
obsolete both classical conservatism & classical progressivism (liberalism),
which assumes that everything will go well & people will behave well if they
are treated kindly, i.e., that good social conditions & good people will make evil
& sickness disappear. This is definitely true for some people & just as definitely
not true for all people—how many we don't know. Some people have so much
evil, malice, selfishness, lack of identification & compassion, etc., that it is fair
to call them simply "evil people." But there are few such people in my (selected)
world. I meet in my world more fine people than evil people.]* Remembered
talk with Bill Crockett. Can I get Mike Murphy & Jim Fadiman & Bill
Schutz, et al., together with the Saga people? I like both groups, feel I
understand both, & I think both like me—altho I wonder how they'll feel
when I write my political credo, which in some ways is far more
"conservative" than the conservatives & far more "radical" than the
radicals. *[2/27/69: Radical? I'd try any & every experiment, including both
"radical" & "conservative" ones, to see how they work out & who is right. I'd
turn over a few schools & colleges to Negroes to run entirely, even specifically
militant Blacks, like Cleaver or the Black Panthers, etc. Make a Malcolm X
University to see what happens. Colleges run entirely by students, with faculty
& administration as employees. An Ayn Rand college. A Communist-run
college. A Reagan-run & administered college. But, of course, many extant
colleges are already experiments of this kind, e.g., Bob Jones U. But how about
evaluation & validation? Harrad College? Funded by the state or U. S.? Why
not? We could learn a lot from seeing which is more viable, which not, & then
also pre- & post-testing in all conceivable dimensions. Why not several
Summerhills? I guess this is mostly a radical suggestion because so many extant
schools are already run by conservatives, authoritarians, religion nuts, etc.]* On
the one hand, I would be far more firm with the lawbreakers & far more
tough with, e.g., the campus disrupters. I'd arrest & prosecute them
all—not just disperse them, & certainly not bargain with them, etc.
Anybody attacking the police, or insulting them, I would regard very
seriously as striking at the roots of the whole society & of civilization in
general, so I'd take it *very* seriously. In the APA I voted against removing
the next convention from Chicago. I supported Hayakawa to Mike's
surprise. Etc., etc. But on the other hand I'd be *far* more radical in helping
the Negroes, no matter what it cost. And I would change radically the
whole of higher education, in a sense, then, destroying it. I'd have real
equality of opportunity for *all* children starting at & before birth, medi-
cally, psychologically, educationally. Including a very high inheritance &
gift tax so that no baby could be rich, so they'd start even, which would

encourage everybody to take care of *all* babies, not only one's own. I'd leave the harmless hippies alone & make absolutely no fuss about such folkways as don't matter, e.g., length of hair or style of dress. Stress this folkway point, since it has nothing to do with intrinsic values. But stress also the *pacing* of change & the tie-in with compassion for the conventional people who are pained & threatened by breaking the folkways, regarding them as ultimate & real & eternal laws. Etc., etc.

Must keep on trying this coming clean with Crockett, Murphy, & all the rest, to see how possible it is to have authentic dialogue even in the face of irreconcilable individual differences & disagreements.

You can *never abolish* poverty, because it's relative, the only way would be absolute & universal equality of income, & even this is impossible. That is, the *equality* is, as can be seen with kids, whom parents try to treat equally. They'll be sure to find *some* inequality to quarrel over.

If you gave to every individual $2000 a month, which would make *everybody* rich by current standards, then what would this solve & what new problems would it create? Certainly absolute poverty, i.e., of lower biological needs, would be wiped out thus. Would it reconstitute the Negro family? Maybe.

Could you get rid of racial tensions by making it official policy to reward interracial marriages, adoptions, business partnerships?

I'd *punish* criminals—instead of assuming that punishment is *per se* punitive or barbarous or that it wouldn't teach. I'm sure that it *would* teach or at least control hoodlumism & a fair amount of crime. On the other hand, I'd make prisons therapeutic & educational & growth institutions à la Synanon. As for student criminals & delinquents, I'd expel them automatically for a year or so & throw them out permanently for the 2nd offense unless & until they grew up or got therapy or changed.

Question: what word to use instead of "change agent" for the society-improver? Change is not a fusion word because it has no direction; it is amoral.

No tax exemptions of *any* kind.

Much higher taxes to cover cost of all these programs & also to reduce the number of wealthy people (bad for most of them).

Welfare programs to be paid by federal government.

Police upgraded by sabbaticals for education which would mean higher pay & higher standards. Much more on-the-job training. [*Educationalize all of life. Sacralize all of life. Everyone is a policeman.*]

Tremendous expansion of vocational counseling of the ultimate sort & Job Corps training & retraining → self-actualization.

Stronger antitrust legislation & limits on size of any corporation.

Healthier, nonfreezing union laws & compulsory arbitration, resulting in general adaptation to change while keeping the unions strong. Mustn't kill them. Limitations of right to strike when it hurts society. Some principles of determining just pay in relation to the skill needed, the length of training needed, etc., rather than just power of blackmail.

Much strengthening of the means of fighting the Mafia, to include tougher laws & less rights for known criminals. They should be under permanent probation.

We could be benevolent as hell (liberal) if only we were firm rather than wobbly before lawbreakers, destroyers, U. S. self-hatred, haters, neurotics & psychotics, enemies of democracy & of society (conservatism).

Collect in one place all this politicist-program stuff. Look up Fromm's socialism stuff, ADA programs, Harrington's radical program. Put it all together, but include the duties & the responsibilities.

Change adversary law → humanistic law to transcendent law (law 3 & 4). Same for economics. Same for *all* social institutions. From Theory X to Y to Z. [*Put all this kind of stuff under revolution & politics 3 (humanistic politics) & politics 4 (transcendent politics).*]

February 21

One Esalen experiment has been a failure (in terms of what was expected, i.e., the hypothesis). The staff, mostly young people, & many in the hippie or near hippie style, treated in the Esalen way & presumably having the massages & nudism & easy sex & the therapy & seminars & the Utopian atmosphere, have turned out as a group to be contemptuous of the squares, *not* friendly, compassionate, loving or brotherly or even helping, therapeutic, Bodhisattvic—just snotty, arrogant, neglectful too often & for all I know really hostile or cruel or sadistic (*this* I don't know). That is, they've formed an amity-enmity culture, good with each other but not with "outsiders." Bertha caught another pathology, too, that has not been overcome: the whole culture is a youth culture essentially, or at least youth-centered, youth-worshiping, acting like youth. The resident elders are hardly grown up or mature, at least the ones I know, except Mike Murphy & Dick Price. (But again, caution—there are lots of them I don't know, & I mustn't judge them.)

Don't know whether I wrote this down or not, but it's an important example. The community of science & scientists is in a very strict sense a Utopian community, truly anarchistic, no leader or bosses, no orders, no domination, no killing, no violence, no lying. Honesty & truthfulness are the rule, generosity of a synergic sort (publishing = giving away but it also means getting praise & rewards), strong code of ethics, oblation in the service of truth = one of the highest values, etc. The social rules & social system are theoretically perfect—& yet, are all scientists noble & virtuous? Or even wise? Obviously not. I think they *are* better than the average in some ways, but not outstandingly so, & not in all ways.

So obviously, good social rules are not in themselves enough to make men virtuous, altho they *do* help & may be necessary though not sufficient. Tie this in with psychotherapy, which often helps people to become more virtuous *without* changing the social environment. What kind of combination of good society & good therapy & growth efforts would be best for helping people to become good, wise, beautiful, affectionate, good humored?

February 27

How to say this? I'll just ramble from the place I started this A.M., looking at Jeannie's most recent picture, which I just can't get enough of, & to which there is no extinction or negative adaptation yet, none at all. All thru the night when I woke up, for days past, all day today, I keep staring at it with fascination & with true esthetic shock, unbelieving, each time with the fullest enjoyment, as if I just couldn't get tired of it. So I wrote a note on love: "Jeannie's picture produces the same level of delight time after time." And then I remembered that I did the same thing with Ann's baby pictures when I was away on the Blackfoot reservation. I missed her awfully, so kept looking at the picture & reacting as if to something or someone totally loved. Yet when I was *with* Ann actually, I didn't bother looking at her picture. I certainly enjoyed her, & later Ellen, totally, & loved them completely & without ambivalence of the slightest degree. Well, that's not a good example because I reacted to my own children with the perpetual, never-changing, always fresh, total love, fascination, esthetic shock, esthetic surprise. (Each time I saw them, I'd get startled by how lovable & beautiful & miraculous they were & how much I loved them, as if my memory in between looks were absolutely unable to keep up with the reality—which lasted until adolescence, when it *did* become ambivalent & mixed with anger, depression, etc.)

[*If it's* not *forgotten, as in love, call it "perpetual stimulus power"? That should be a good test of love, i.e., perpetual trigger power. The maintenance of the novelty reaction (always new) & resistance to boredom.*]

Anyway, what I was starting out to say was that one can overlook his love, his blessings, etc., because the person is always there, so that for most people they don't realize how happy they were until the baby dies or disappears. They don't seem to be able to enjoy their blessings until they are snatched away, & then retrospectively. They don't appreciate what they've got while they've got it—only when they no longer have it. (Not true for me. I just keep on actively appreciating my blessings & being grateful for them, so I'm not a good example, not average anyway.)

Should I call it "gratification-produced change of values"? Or "postgratification change of values"? This has some relation, somehow, to Colin Wilson's St. Neot's margin, but I'm not quite sure how.

Anyway, one obvious remedy for this idiocy is to be able to "count your blessings," which means insight & remembering & appreciating. But how many people can do this? What kind of exercises? Can it be taught? If only people could use the simple exercise of imagining death, either one's own or the other's. If you can really imagine it, that alone does the trick. Then I can look at the person in an appreciative, grateful way. If I think of Jeannie's dying, my blood runs cold. Or of Bertha, or the time I thought Ellen had been killed, etc. It's easy enough to do. Why, then, don't people do it, even when I call their attention to it? Maybe most people can't imagine death—maybe it has to actually happen. Only then can they realize how much they loved, or how lucky they were, or how wonderful the husband was, etc.

This is part of the sadness of life—that loved people have to die before they are fully appreciated. In a certain sense,·then, many such people are happy only retrospectively; i.e., it's a postmortem diagnosis. See exercises. [*Postgratification devaluation? Gratification-produced devaluation & retriggering?*]

The constant presence makes you overlook the preciousness of what you've got. You fully appreciate what you no longer have.

You have to consciously cultivate appreciation & gratitude.

March 4

Impressed with the connection between the behaviorists' "behavior therapy" & the Synanon "behavior therapy." "Changing behavior is the easiest thing, so we believe that if we can change that first— regardless of the underlying cause or problem—deeper changes will [might] follow." (*Especially* if the character structure is compatible with the behavior, as in my "behavior therapy" of 30 years ago, when I tried it with high- & low-dominance characters whose behavior was different from their underlying personalities. I got them to behave like their underlying personalities, & it took *very* easily.)

Tie it in with role therapy. Bring up the whole question of behaving congruently, naturally, spontaneously, i.e., in accordance with true personality—in itself good therapy, growth, self-acceptance, ease, lack of strain & artificiality, etc.—like not lying or faking, like not keeping secrets, like not playing a role, etc. I have no doubt that anyone can learn to behave like what he is *not*, i.e., like a spy or a swindler. But show that this must be costly, a strain, effortful & fatiguing, destructive of deeper self-esteem. ("I am really a fake! If they knew what I was *really* like underneath, they would hate, despise, reject, ridicule me.")

Ultimately the recommendation is: let yourself behave as you really are & feel. Let it show. Don't keep yourself a secret. Be honest. Be congruent, integrated, one. If necessary, let yourself be despised, laughed at, rather than telling a permanent lie.

Yesterday a talk with Bill Crockett, with whom I am trying dyad-group therapy or T-group, trying to be honest, both of us, candid about opinions, politics, anything, so that we can know each other truly = authentic interpersonal relationship. He said "I much prefer being hurt for the moment rather than being kept in the dark" (which I think leads to "normal paranoia"). I told him I thought he was strong enough for this, hurtable (as we all are) but not crushable, & preferring the truth to phoniness. But I also told him I felt this couldn't be for me a universal policy because so many people are *not* strong enough, & fear the consequence of truth too much, or are not ready for it yet, or must take it bit by bit in small doses as the psychoanalyst dishes it out, i.e., *offers* it so that you, the patient, can swallow it or not as you decide. I *do* think it's a viable policy for almost everybody *if* you are willing to spend the time, recognizing that it entails responsibility for therapy, for healing up the wound, for enduring the hostility & enmity, etc. And most often I'm *not* willing to take on such responsibilities, so I *do* say polite & courteous things, believe in normal social etiquette, which allows me to keep my cool distance without either hurting or helping until I decide whether I want to take on the responsibilities of closeness & candor *or* decide that this person is strong enough to "take it" easily—like psychoanalyzed people who can talk much more freely & revealingly & honestly than others can.

I thought my doing this with Bill was a great compliment to him, & he took it that way. We agreed to keep on working in this direction, especially since we will work together in OD—& I think also in my Eupsychian politics & ethics.

Reminds me of Bethel, 1967, when I pointed out to the group that they knew me only 3 inches deep, & that our degree of intimacy did *not* permit talking about really hot topics, e.g., Vietnam, LBJ, etc. (with which they agreed), & nobody even tried to bring up these topics. Question: can Bill & I come to real disagreement & yet remain friends, colleagues, & truly respect the individual differences that lie behind disagreement? To be 2 Senators together, 2 sovereign powers, 2 autonomous people who yet respect autonomy of the other & even *like* it?

March 12

Savage Sleep brings up again the whole question of Freud & my relations to him, to his writings, & to his followers. Talked about this at length in the Havemann interview yesterday & said it well, I think, in all its complexity. But this book brings up depths of psychosis, as in the waking dream à la John Rosen, depths of orality & anality & infantility which for me are just hearsay. I never experienced that deep. So should I trust Brand or Rosen or Lewin, etc.? Rosen's results have not been proven yet, & I hear skepticism from good people. Must have long talk with Harry Rand about this. But even then it's hearsay & needs verification.

[5/14/69: *Did I ever write down the point of Toman & others that psychoanalysis is essentially frustration therapy rather than gratification therapy? (Millen Brand would add "understanding & communication" therapy i.e., understanding of the id & communication with it, plus the fear-allaying infantile, oral gratifications.) The refusal to gratify arouses anxiety, irrationality, depression, etc., in the analysand, all of which are the material which is then available for analysis, & also to help the patient become aware of how sick he is & where & how. It permits the sickness to come to the surface of consciousness where it is more easily seen. Need-gratification would cover up the irrationalities & infantilities in the expectation that the gratification would cure them. Both are right, of course, at various times & places, & any wise therapist would have both rationales in his armamentarium.*]

And then, even if it's all true, is it really an exposure of *my* depths? Or the depths of ordinary or healthy people? That just doesn't seem holistic enough. If my skin were flayed off me, wouldn't the exposed surface be different from what it is now, intact? Dare one judge from such acute & profound illness, where we don't even know the causal factors? (Curing with words or with love or milk does *not* prove anything about causes, no more than curing a headache with aspirin proves that the headache was caused by lack of aspirin. I'm convinced there are genetic, chemical, physiological causes in schizophrenia as well as psychic ones; i.e., it's more than a simple deficiency disease—the predisposition must be there.) Are we infantile or psychotic or oral & some additional state overlaying? Is the id of the psychotic the same as the id of the healthy? Maybe even the archetypes are different? What does Grof's work say about all this? Even there, the same question comes up: if we regress under LSD, is what we regress to, & now show openly, the same as what was there all the time hidden & waiting in unchanged form? In what sense does my Babinski reflex now exist in me? Can it be said to "exist" now at all?

Then another big criticism: I said to Havemann that I thought the psychoanalytic method & system of pathology is the best we have for dealing with our illnesses, or depths, or whatever is infantile in us, or neurotic. *But* it generates a false or partial image of man & of society & of life in general. The good & noble & healthy & beautiful in human nature are *not* just marks of phoniness behind which hides the truer reality of psychosis, etc. Am I more "real" than Brand's patients? Yes, in the sense of being more fully human, of having fewer losses & diminutions & more capacities & unleashings.

Even I would deny the parallel or identity of the infantile patients & Jeannie, if only because they live in terror & depression & hopelessness & she lives in joy & zest & without fear or hate or envy or self-rejection or self-punishment. They are damaged & sick & she is not, & perhaps they *try* to get back to being like her as an acting-out (which is not the same as doing or being), as I have fantasies about being young & healthy & playing tennis, etc. It's something I'm longing for—not something I am.

[2/15/69: *Baby-love thought: all (most? some?) of the qualities that are lovable in Jeannie are also seen in well-adjusted, well treated ament adults. Then I thought: why aren't they loved for these qualities? And then: well, maybe they are for all I know (= good investigation). And then: if they're not, why shouldn't they be? In principle, they should be lovable (= again, a good investigation). Maybe they're easier to love than normal adults. Maybe it's easier for the feebleminded to retain the lovable childlikeness. I think this body of theory would make people less ashamed to love them. Is this a critique of our culture? Because if we don't as people love them, & if they should be loved & are lovable, then something is wrong with our preconceptions (= critique of U. S.).*]

A thought: Freud has made more discoveries than any other psychologist who ever lived—but also many mistakes (even tho I can see what he was *trying* to say with his mistakes, & in each case he was trying to say something important, something that now *has* to be said even tho in a better way).

March 16

Bill of Rights book: more thoughts on levels of politics (I like that scheme more & more; it's a very powerful aid to thinking, I've been finding). Principle & perfection cannot be the only guides to action at any of the three levels, not even the B-level. Questions of selection, choice, division of labor, strategy & tactics, & individual differences must also be used as guides. That is, fully granting agreement on B-values & B-politics, good men can yet do different things. Essentially it comes down to the fact that no single person can do everything. He has to choose & limit himself. I pick my several favorite charities & causes & limit my money & activities

& libido to those, while granting (& *hoping*) that individual differences will make other people choose not my favorite causes but others. If there are a thousand injustices, you can't fight them all. I throw into the waste basket most of the begging letters for all sorts of good causes & stick to about 10 or 12. Grounds of choice? Absolutely personal & selfish, i.e., those that just happen to engage *my* tastes, personality or professional interests. I'll help fight injustice in APA but not in dental association, for instance. This is on the same principle that I have more responsibility for my family than I have for strangers, all else being equal. Or for Jews rather than Buddhists, everything being equal. For example, say *everybody* is starving. I have some extra food, but I can't feed everybody—only ten people. Whom to choose? I'd choose actual human beings I knew (Pedro Lopez = Mexico), closer to me, identified with me, etc. Americans rather than Afghans. My neighbors rather than my daughter's neighbors. Cases where my emotions & therefore my responsibilities are more directly involved, where I can *see* it with my own eyes. There is an economics & politics of compassion, of responsibility, of love; a strategy & tactics of truth, beauty, virtue, excellence, etc. = B-politics. Even in the B-realm & in Eupsychia you can't do everything; you must choose, must select & reject. And it's most efficient not to feel guilty about what you *cannot* do (choose not to do), or about choosing selfishly in accordance with your own commitments & character (demands being equal), since guilt will make you a poorer, weaker, less healthy helper, & also since you must assume division of labor in the Eupsychian community; i.e., others with different tastes & different superiorities will take care of those other causes that you neglect. This, by the way, is one of the ways I choose for money giving. If it's already well taken care of & lots of people are interested, e.g., Red Cross, then I won't bother, but will choose causes that are neglected & that have few backers; e.g., I've been fervent about AAHP & *Journal of Humanistic Psychology*. But now it's on its feet, lots of patriots, so I can turn rather to the new *Journal of Transpersonal Psychology. Manas*, which I've helped, is *not* widely helped & therefore needs my help far more than does cancer research or heart research.

Therefore I must reject what doesn't engage me, or I can't libidinize, however virtuous it may be. And this can look cold-hearted, selfish, rejecting, or neglectful of the B-values. So there *is* a B-politics & B-economics in the strictest sense of how to choose among scarce goods.

Therefore I must make up my own mind about what is urgent, & permit others to make up theirs, & not get mad at them if they choose not my causes but some preferred others. (If they choose *no* causes, *then* I can get mad or contemptuous.) Therefore any ultimate Bill of Rights must take account of this in various ways, e.g., *not* demand universal, positive, active support. Even the hard sell for virtue or philanthropy is suspect. But consider the pressure of the Jewish community to insist on rich men donating more than poor men. It works in general & is fair in general, but it winds up forcing Mr. Cohen, an atheist, to help pay the rabbi or to donate to a Mikva, etc. Or take the wars within the Sierra Club, Audubon societies, SPCA, et al. All ultimately virtuous, & yet can get nutty & can divide on equally virtuous solutions, on which good men can differ violently.

What started me off here was John Altgeld correctly pardoning the Haymarket victims & thereby killing off his political future. Real question: good case could be made for protecting his political future & letting the men hang. *He* couldn't do it, & he is universally respected for sticking by principle. And yet, he might have been President or, as governor, saved many *more* lives with his power. Tough decision. But B-politics would have to accept *either* solution. The no-compromise-with-principle in effect helps to make sure that all power-holders have no principles whatsoever. But then the force of the good example, à la Schweitzer?

I must dissent also from Brant & the pure libertarians & strict constitutionalists about, e.g., the 5th Amendment. The writers of the constitution could not foresee the Mafia; the Jeffersonian assumption doesn't take enough account of evil & pathology & anti-any-society, or of U. S. self-hatred, or of the number of Quislings or secret fifth-columnists clearly planning to destroy a virtuous society in favor of a tyranny, people who openly plot & league to take away my life, liberty, property, etc. There was no *organized* crime in Madison's day. No one has a right to ask that the U. S. castrate itself. But changing the Constitution can be done legally, democratically, & constitutionally. It should not be frozen into a new sacred Bible or Talmud. To the extent that it protects the Mafia, a cancer within its own body, to that extent the Constitution is a danger to the U. S. & to democracy. I think it quite possible to be libertarian & yet adapt to new social situations, which were unforeseeable. The test is, I suppose, ultimately the self-actualization of each & every individual. All of this is recognized in the Constitution by accepting different rules in time of war. Well, it *is* war with the Mafia, & it was with the Communists in the thirties (even tho not today, & I wouldn't bother them on the grounds that they are not a danger; if they became a danger, then I *would* regard them as at war with the U. S.). Another example is the fear of going out into the streets at night. Liberty has been restricted thereby, & the viability of the U. S. threatened, & the appeal of Fascist authoritarian reaction increased. Therefore, I'd regard it as a war of a new kind, & fight it in new ways, e.g., *not* permit bail to the known professional criminal. The more crimes he commits, the fewer rights he should have, because I deserve my rights—civil, legal, etc.,—more than he does whenever there is an irreconcilable conflict between his freedom & rights & mine. In Eupsychia I think there is no question whatsoever that he would be regarded as sick & given no more rights than a psychotic or ament. He'd be turned over to therapists &, if cure was not possible, confined for life (with all the liberties which would not endanger normal people & normal society). Same for psychopaths whom the law just can't handle now. The precedent is with the insane, the feebleminded, & soon with drunks & drug addicts.

April 30

Talking with Chris Argyris about his newspaper study & the cynicism of reporters. He says they believe strongly in a bad human nature. "You can't change human nature. Don't trust anyone." Rivalry. One-upping rather than collaboration. I thought them, I said, to be sort of peeping Toms, removed, nonengaged, on the fence—as a defense against intimate involvement & engagement = not expecting much from people. Also, permission to mock from the fence.

But then somehow we got to talking about the failure of the liberals, & my diagnosis of them as lacking a theory of evil, so they can't get really indignant at a wrong (unless it's fashionable to, & the whole pack does) because they don't really know right from wrong. A peculiar mixture of Rousseauistic Utopianism (like McGregor, Rogers, et al.), masochism, guilt, self-blame, even self-hatred.

And somehow they reminded me of each other. One has no theory of good (which means no theory of evil). The other group has no theory of evil (& therefore not much theory of good). So what they have in common is a lack of a way to differentiate good from evil. The weak liberal has no real place in his psychology for bastards, mean people, psychopaths, paranoids. The reporter has no place for anyone *else*. He can't believe that there are good people. The full person can encompass *both* good & bad people. Better add this as a characteristic of self-actualizing people &, of course, as a desirable norm to strive for. This relates also to my impression that the self-actualizing people let their anger loose more totally, with less inhibition, guilt, conflict.

May 2

When I talked to the graduate-student group on Tuesday, I realize now that I changed the order of priority of bases of psychology 3. I told them that I thought *the* basic axiom of psychology 3 is that man has a higher nature which is *instinctoid*. And that if this were not true, then the whole structure of humanistic psychology would fall. And that this would be the source of conflict within psychology 3 psychologists, because most of them cannot accept any version of instinct or instinctoid theory— Fromm, Rogers, Allport, most of them I guess. And so I disagree strongly with them on this basic point.

May 14

Problem: leaders are generally superior to those whom they lead in IQ, talent, courage, health, vigor, being agent & not pawn, liking for responsibility, metamotivation (?). If followers loved & respected the superior leader, then his say-so would be enough. But today authority is suspected, not loved. But in *either* case, show how trusting the say-so of authority is not good for the strength of the follower (it castrates him gently). And in other cases it's clearly best for him to be the organizer of autonomous opinions, of autonomous people, keeping communications open, & believing in democracy even tho he is in fact superior.

But how to reconcile this with my advice to me, to Sutich, Mike Murphy, Andy Kay, Laughlin, et al.? You're the boss. Insist on that. Don't consult too much or take too many votes. In each of these cases, the leader is quite superior to the others. When to hang on to power, when to give it up? Again the business of self-trust, of arrogance, is involved. If I'm sure of myself, then I'll push to have my way.

Clearly the democratic way (Theory Y) is generally better. And yet I make exceptions, but haven't worked out a rationale for those exceptions. How to use the aggridant in a democratic setting?

May 16

Walking thoughts: I'm *definitely* settled on writing up the difference between SA-seeking education (humanistic education) & calling-vocation-destiny-work education (after one's identity & calling & value commitment have been *found* well via education 3 or any other way). In the latter, stress apprenticeship, listening, deference, modesty, humility, looking for supervision, memorizing, repeating, endless practice, skill rehearsal, being shown how to do it, eagerness to learn & impatience now with all the identity "crap," à la Hughes medical students. The teacher's function is entirely different. Show how. No longer student-centering.

Content-centered, skill- & methodology-centered. Can't learn content in a T-group. Psychology is a poor model to use for content education, even tho it's a *good* model to use for humanistic education, because the content & the self overlap. For content education, chemistry or plumbing is a better example. But watch out for overlap & *against* overdichotomizing education 3 from content education. There *is* room for T-groups, etc., in medical school. So talk about humanistic identity-seeking education & then humanistic vocation or content-seeking education. *Each* stage can be humanistic.

Another thought: thinking so eagerly about seeing Jeannie tomorrow night, like a drug addict or alcoholic. I certainly loved my own babies totally. Why the addiction phenomenon? Answer (partial): supposing I had been able to see my own children only every 2 months! I would have developed the same addiction phenomenon then too. *Any* normal mother or father would. I *did*, as a matter of fact, when I was on the Blackfoot reservation & didn't see Ann for 3 months. Same craziness with pictures, dreams, yearning, impatience to get home, etc.

May 17

Jeannie even more a delight: still whole-hearted, preambivalent, preconflict, *total* & 100% attention, curiosity, enjoyment; her smile & laugh is *total* (unlike any adult's, where there are always *some* brakes on it), so that occasionally it goes over into an orgiastic frenzy or wildness (could this be called Dionysian ecstasy?). Also body things are 100%, hunger, sleep, complete definiteness about her impulse-voices & appetites (what she likes & dislikes, wants or doesn't want, is absolutely unmistakable). Negatively stated, I never see her bored, jaded, blasé. She seems to be totally interested in whatever she's interested in, altho she is easily enough distracted by something else that's fascinating, & then her total attention & interest are given to *that*. First signs of fear = startle & crying to sudden loud noises. She's now a smily child, smiling much of the time = eupeptic? [*She smiles a lot for no reason. Unneeded, unmotivated smiling. Do adults ever do that? No external reason needed for smiling. It can be pure delight in just being = zest, biopleasure, joy.*]

[*6/3/69: No deception in baby. Plenty in adult. When & why does it start? What are its benign (as well as sick) functions? How is it taught? Reinforced?*]

More struggle for good labels & phrasing for getting stuck within one's own psychic world & not being able to appreciate another person's inner world, or, worse, being "psyche-centric à la ethnocentric" & judging everyone *else* & their ways by one's own psyche = if it's different from my tastes or values, then it's wrong, stupid, bad, sick. [*Imprisonment in one's psyche?*] This lack cuts off the possibility of sympathy, compassion, toler-ance, charity. If you simply & wholly disapprove of an alcoholic ("Why can't he control himself?" "He *shouldn't* do something so unhealthy." "He's perversely doing it to irritate me.") without also getting some sense of his anguish, self-disapproval, guilt, self-punishment, etc., i.e., being able to "feel" oneself into *his* psyche, then you get—what shall I call it?—something like moralistic, intolerant, but not quite. It's a sort of blindness, a kind of imprisonment in one's own mind. I've thought of making up some new words from Greek & Latin roots—maybe after one last session with the thesaurus for "imprisonment, locked up, not being able to see or feel, blindness." The word "ethnocentric" is perfect to label the equivalent cultural phenomenon, but "psyche-centrism" just doesn't do the job well (egocentrism & self-centering already have other mean-ings).

Also it cuts off the possibility of accepting or liking individual differences = no   democracy.   Projection → paranoia.   Reading   Tom Wolfe's *The Electric Kool-Aid Acid Test* about Ken Kesey's Merry Pranksters, the ultimate in drug culture, impulsivity, rejection of controls, stress on Dionysian feelings, orgiastic, wild. Very clear that the Esalen, hippie, & LSD cultures must think of this as one extreme possibility. I get a smell finally of sadism & masochism, of schizophrenic "freedom" (total loss of controls & of integration), & finally of insanity & death. Also I was reminded how mysticism can & has so easily gone over into magic (astrol-ogy, Tarot cards, I-Ching are among the developments I've seen).

May 20

A. & J. bring to mind my prison-cell, existential model of interper-sonal relations. I could start & say that the SA model of interpersonal relations is correct. We *do* get our happiness & our growth toward SA from & with other people. But I've learned by now that this is *so* easily misun-derstood in an ideal & perfectionistic direction, as if this were a reasonable expectation (rather than a rare one) that all should go well & smoothly, & that growth toward SA is an *average* probability, so that if it doesn't occur in a marriage or a friendship, they're shocked & surprised. They expect more than they have a right to expect from what I know of human nature. As I was saying, people can live together only if love (or compassion) transcends justice, if one accepts & tolerates, & swallows shit. It's a *great* achievement to get along well, *not* an easy one. This is because people simply are not that good & pure & perfect. (Here is another example of the necessity for psychology 3 of a theory of evil to round out the theory of good.) One must not expect too much of them, because if one *does*, then disappointment most of the time is almost guaranteed. One must be *sur-*

prised & *pleased* by strength, virtue, loyalty, kindness, love, etc., in another person. These all exist & certainly are potentials in many (most? all?), but I've stressed that SA is *rare*, not common. Same for great peaks & great insights! All you can reasonably expect or hope for from another person is that he struggles (for a whole lifetime) *toward* these good goals rather than away from them. And even the *best* people, the 1% of self-actualizers, are shitty part of the time. There is no permanent heaven or happiness or serenity or contentment—& certainly not in interpersonal relations. This is an unreasonable expectation (in the sense of unscientific) from what we know of permanent grumbles & the need to want (need, lack) something. Also from what we know of the wide range of individual differences within the not-sick range, let alone the various sicknesses.

So I think if I were to lecture on interpersonal relations, or marriage or friendship or parent-child relations, I'd stress at the very beginning tolerance, acceptance, & giving up the hope for justice & fairness & *quid pro quo*. I'd talk at length about individual differences, changeable & unchangeable, & our tendency to get irritated, offended, & threatened by these differences from ourselves. Then I'd stress compassion as a necessity (love is too difficult to expect); e.g., "How would *you* like to be George Wallace? Or Stalin? Or Hitler?" Also tricks: "How would you feel abut him if you discovered he was dying of an incurable disease? Well, he *is*! Everyone is!" Or "Suppose he were blinded. Could you then be compassionate & forgiving? Well, he *is* blind. *Everyone* is!"

And then I think, as a strategy, I would finally start with the cellmates-in-prison model. Supposing you were locked up for life with another person whom you disliked or perhaps even hated, & from whom you expected little or nothing. What would you do to make the situation less difficult, more bearable? Remember there's no exit. This starts from the most *unpleasant* situation as a centering point rather than from the most ideally happy & pleasant situation as model ("and they lived happily ever after"). Then whatever positive turned up would be a plus, a pleasant surprise instead of something so taken for granted as not to be noticed consciously. (In the perfection model, only imperfections are noticed consciously.)

Maybe it would then be useful to balance off the whole picture more realistically & refute Sartre's "Hell is with other people." This can be true, *but* (1) a worse hell is to be without people altogether, & (2) also heaven is with other people.

Stress grumbles: permanent happiness or even contentment seems not to exist or to be possible. We *must* expect discontent sometimes (& also content & happiness sometimes). But (1) it's better to have higher discontents rather than lower, & with metagrumbles even the discontent is "divine" & can be "enjoyed"; also, (2) it's better to be discontent about *something* than about emptiness & *lack* of goals, needs, troubles = better to lack & need something worth seeking for than to be apathetic or totally sated, blasé, & bored = better to be with an irritating person than without any person.

Another good way to stress the injustice & unfairness of compassion & love is to point to its giving without receiving. One must give compassion without the demand to get it back, *quid pro quo*. Parent & child make the best example here of giving without return in kind. Who looks for justice in such a relationship?

But then comes the miracle often enough, even if not always, that the freely given compassion breaks the vicious circle, breaks the polarizing into mutual antagonisms, & melts the person down enough to melt his defenses & counterattacks & "cure" the whole mess. "Perhaps only a world clean-stripped of meanness & injustice, & peopled with saints named Smith & Jones, would have enabled George Orwell to live in a state of inner peace" (who *never* had any inner peace).

Plus, make the point that needs making: it is not sensible to judge as *more* real & true the awful attacks that come out in anger. If anything, these are *less* true & real, in contradiction to Freud. They are designed primarily to hurt, to attack, to fight back. And they almost always involve an attack upon the weakest spot, that which will hurt most. The aim is to hurt—not to tell the truth, even tho in such moments concealed truths may emerge. That is, though these concealed truths may hurt, the considered, thought-out, measured, mulled-over statement is far more apt to be true & correct. Angry emotions are *not* more true than are considered, thoughtful, weighed conclusions.

Thought: call it magnanimous. I remember hoping that the Israelis could be magnanimous after the 6-day war. Here was their chance to be generous, big-souled, justice-transcending, compassionate. They weren't, & they're still in trouble. So with individuals in interpersonal relations. The word "love," even "Agapean love," doesn't get across as well as compassion, *caritas*, magnanimity.

June 28

More affected than I realized by Vasconcelos last night, about trust in man. Talking about the conservatives & reactionaries in the Assembly, his experience is that the ones he knows are sincere & decent but just don't *know*. But when they *do* know, then they change & improve. So he too said: "Don't give up trying. You have to have faith in them, & their good will, in the power of truth & communication, & in their ability to change in the direction of this truth." And then his validating report: "In my experience, even with myself, it works." Which in effect means "I have tested the 3rd-Force psychology in my life, & it works; it is valid & correct."

Which is also an answer to the dilemma: there's so much evil in the world, but so few evil men! Must the *evil* come from malice, the will to evil & to sin, the *love* of evil or the desire to be a devil or a Satan, or the desire to be hated or loathed? No, it must come from sources other than these, sources not on their face evil or in themselves evil. The voice of the divine within is counterposed *not* by the voice of the devil within but by the voice of the timid, the basic-need-deprived, the ignorant, the superstitious—in a word, by the voice of the schlemiel within, *not* the voice of evil within. When they lash back & revenge them, in resentment, in disappointment, it is in principle *so* easy to melt them down into decency, à la Sorokin's experiment for instance, or by therapist-like understanding—in a word, by returning good for evil, or better, refusing to return evil for evil, refusing to get into the *folie à deux*, by *not* being shaken by the momentary aggression (understand it as hurt & revenge for hurt = please *don't* hurt me; please love me, respect me, take care of me & my needs). Toss in here, as a necessity for this theory of evil to work well, that we must *not* take seriously, as deep or more real truth, the wild overstatements said in moments of anger, of desire to hurt, etc. The regret & remorse over our "slips of the tongue" in anger & desire to hurt show that they are not really *true* statements; i.e., they are lies & seem to be lies as soon as we add in reflectiveness, editorial criticism, second thought, rationality. [". . . *the recklessness of a writer for whom second thoughts do not exist." Why edit? Rewrite? Improve one version after another?*]

We've gotten too uncritically accepting of Freud's assertion of the profound significance of these expressions. But they are of just one part of us, *not* the whole of us, *not* the voice of the real self but rather the voice of the child within us, something which disappears so easily with catharsis & which is not "really meant," for which one expects to be forgiven. What we do while catharting is not the realest us. How shall we phrase this better, so that we learn *not* to take this as final proof that our "deepest" selves are evil? Maybe this way: It's the child in us, & we certainly do *not* take it as a final, eternal revelation of the truest, permanent wish of the child when he says "I hate you" or "I wish the baby would go away, or disappear, or had never come" or when he *acts* & tries to hurt his new sibling. As adults, we understand this to be childish, immature, ignorant, & something he'll mature out of, "outgrow" when he "understands," gets wiser, more sophisticated, more knowledgeable. Also, in marital counseling, you learn & they must also learn not to take "seriously" the lashing out in anger, the words spoken *in order to* hurt. They must be interpreted as *just that*, the fleeting impulse which is in itself real & must be acknowledged—as anger, hurt, desire to hurt back, self-defense—but which is less real, partially real, than this same impulsivity of childishness *plus* criticizing it, looking it over, thinking about it after the hot anger has died down, integrating it into the larger structure of wisdom about it, to see it not close up, to see not *only* it, but to see it in all its network of relationships, its frame of reference, as figure against ground, not only to express it & cathart it but also to understand it, to go beyond limitation to the here-now by including the future & the past & B-cognizing it all. To take it alone seriously& to make *per se* is like being scotomatic, to be reduced to the concrete (to be reduced to the here-now,to be reduced to the emotional). It *is* being reduced, if one takes this partial reaction as if it were the whole, & as if one were unable later to be holistic about it & place it in its larger context.

July 26

Good A.M. Good job. Writing critique of self-actualization in revised *Motivation and Personality* preface [142] is a good idea & will be quite a document, also serving as a marvelous catharsis & fighting-back for me. Partly out of dreams (?), partly out of the movie last night (*Popi*), which was so touching I had a hard time keeping my tears quiet, partly out of all the irritating reading I've been doing (the intellectuals, liberals, students, Negroes, professors have turned out to be 90% schlemiels). The whole revision of *Motivation and Personality* has done this for me. Makes me feel good to say my say, fight back, declare myself, have an influence which is so badly needed, complete the act, feel effective & influential, etc.

But it also dawned on me, as I was fighting back against instant love, instant community, etc. (read *Modern Utopia* yesterday—almost entirely crap), that *I* should write on how to build a community—& with whom & whom *not*. Then, as I discussed it with M., it dawned on me that not only am I theoretically & academically qualified to do this, but also *I've been thru* community experience: 10 years or so of great success at Ocean Ave. [Brooklyn], failure in Madison with the Communists in the old rotting house that we rented together, & then both failure & success at the shining new Adams St. [Madison, Wisconsin] house.

Succeeded with decent, solid, reliable people, none of whom *needed* community, but who came together out of economic necessity. B. brings up good point: the one who actively *seeks* community probably *needs* it in the deficiency-need sense, & therefore is probably too neurotic to be able to function in a community. She points out that all the individuals who did well liked privacy too (Rod Menzies, Paul Settlage, Pop Schrank) & were responsible, active agents—solid, reliable, & trustworthy. The ones who crapped up the living together (L. G., radical & totally selfish & narcissistic, & his stooge & pawn, C. M., & J. Z.) talked big words like brotherhood, freedom, etc., but were personally selfish, unreliable, liars, loafers, poor workers with anything that didn't turn them on, unable to do anything that bored them, exploitative (especially of Bertha & probably all women).

Rule for good community: keep out most radicals! I'd certainly keep out the contemporary equivalent—hippies, revolutionaries of all kinds, dropouts, certain kinds of neurotics, narcissists, immatures, Dionysians who just can't stand to be bored, who can't work at the chores, etc.

Differentiate, as Horney does, the neurotic need for love from healthy pleasure in love. In the same way, the neurotic need for community & togetherness is totally different from healthy pleasure in community, friends, etc., which goes together very nicely with their simultaneous need for privacy.

Our experience, where economic need forced the community, puts greater stress on the common task or need-focusing of togetherness.

Also: the good requirements, it occurred to me, would mostly be called middle-class values, bourgeois values, etc. Critique needed here.

Reminder: most of the failures I've been reading about—of the hundreds & thousands that the hippies & the resisters & coffee houses like Ellen's have tried & failed—involve the usual story of 2 or 3 workers, with the rest becoming parasites & progressively lazier, shifting responsibility to the workers who are expected to do everything, & with the workers finally giving up in disgust & pain & disillusionment at the discrepancy between (1) the words, pretensions, & enthusiastic beginnings, & (2) the failure & betrayal in the long, hard work, chore-doing, being there when needed, slogging along thru the long haul. They do well with excitement & enthusiasm, but get too easily bored. Old apothegm: they're willing to die for the revolution, but they won't peel potatoes for it.

August 19

I've thought often about Jeannie's state of innocence, cleanliness, purity, lack of evil or malice, her easy state, her preambivalence, her frenzies of happy, crazy burrowing into Ann or Bertha in a kind of kiss with her little mouth wide open—it looks like a kind of orgasm, a wildness that's ecstatic, beyond joy, *too* much, as if she'd gone happily crazy & delirious for a moment. But soon she will know tragedy & therefore evil, & will herself emit evil, tease & finally torment her mother, show hostility, anger, revenge, etc. I think the *big* moment of tragedy & evil, if no accidental tragedy has come first, is the birth of a sibling = sibling rivalry. But this is felt erroneously & stupidly as evil by the baby, because in fact the new infant is not a rival in a win-lose game. Mother can love them both. "Knowledge" (of tragedy, of loss, of betrayal, of abandonment by the mother, & of usurpation & dethroning & expulsion by the infant) brings evil into the world for the infant, & ambivalence begins. Until such a moment or one like it (perhaps the mother is confined to a hospital with tuberculosis, & this is seen by the "stupid" child as permanent abandonment), the baby is *preambivalent. [Good word.]* If it's lucky, it may come thru to moments of postambivalence in the forties & perhaps a plateau of postambivalence in the sixties or seventies.

Stress, however, that though knowledge & experience bring evil, it is a very low level of knowledge, really a misinterpretation, that we, at a higher level of knowledge, can see as erroneous & call stupid. And then my thought came: perhaps knowledge brings evil & tragedy into the world *because* it is poor, low-level, erroneous, stupid knowledge. Here the whole concept of levels & of B-language again becomes very important.

September 3

We've noticed that Ann is a perfect mother in all ways, including that we've never seen *any* sign of irritation or anger with the baby. Total acceptance, unconditional love, infinite patience. She demands nothing in return, accepting the baby totally just as she is & delighting in her just the way she is. Perfect B-love.

So my walking thought tonight was: (1) if we could only be like that with adults! If Ann could be *that* loving, patient, accepting, need-gratifying, undemanding with her husband or her sister (she's getting to be that way with us, with Bertha & me), then that would solve all the world's problems. (2) There's isomorphism involved.

Because of the baby's purity, innocence, & total lack of evil (& she's totally lacking in fear too), we are totally disarmed, & drop our coping & defense mechanisms, & don't bother looking for justice, logic, or *quid pro quo*. Yesterday Jeannie peed on all 3 of us in one day, & we all thought it was cute. We forgive her everything & blame her or disapprove *nothing*. So we become totally expressive, spontaneous, unconcealed. That is, she brings out the best in us (because the worst of us is not needed). Paralleling her lack of evil, we lose our evil. Because she exemplifies B-values, we become closer to them also, & therefore exemplify them more. (In relation to Jeannie, Ann becomes a perfect human being.)

So we can love babies because they bring out the best in us, transform & improve us. And this feels good, being loving, unselfish, accepting, open, undefensive, need-gratifying, benevolent, expressive. They therap & grow us, & transform us into good people, into saints (as great people, sages, saints, & lovable people do, as Aldous Huxley did— they permit us to be lofty, noble, pure, good, excellent), & so we love them for it. As we will love anyone or anything that makes us love ourselves better, deservedly (since we behave so well, we *deserve* to like ourselves more).

Then I can also love the baby for this ennobling effect she has on Ann, &, to a lesser extent, on many other people, strangers who smile at me & speak cheerfully whenever I'm carrying the baby. She seems to be a therapeutic force, just as *we* would be if we could have all her virtues & if nobody had to fear us (her tininess also makes her less fear-inspiring).

September 8

I haven't paid enough attention to the need to admire as well as to be admired, (parallel to love as well as to be loved). To want to be loved &

admired & protected is certainly a deficiency-need. But how about the desire to protect & to be responsible for, to love, to admire? Is *it* a deficiency-need? I don't know. Even if yes, it's in a different meaning. It's all giving rather than receiving. Surplus. Overflow. Generosity. Probably also has instinctoid determinants. Overflows from health. Kids this A.M. playing with Jeannie, nice kids, & all 3 generous, eager to take care of Jeannie (instead of to hurt her or ignore her as with "not-nice" kids, vengeful, hostile ones, suspicious ones, jungle types, etc.).

We could certainly study the "need" (?) to admire, to look up to, revere, worship, e.g., a good leader, father, boss, elder, hero, older boy in gang. We certainly hate to work for a boss we can't admire. And not being able to admire your father is ruinous. Same with teachers. Same with guru-guide-tzaddik-model.

But the whole thing is shot thru with B-justice; i.e., the admired one must *deserve* it. Can't do it by fiat, by sheer will power, & we won't take "the best of the poor alternatives available." We'd then rather admire no one than someone unworthy. This therefore is in the metarealm of B-values. Justice, excellence, virtue, beauty—all *demand* admiration, & we then admire willingly or unwillingly. Virtue, truth, justice, law, order, etc., then all press us to admire what deserves admiring; i.e., we *should* admire, we *ought* to. It's fitting & proper, suitable, makes a good Gestalt. It's then an ontological act, in accordance with & in cooperation with the true nature of the world. It affirms the B-fact-values-essence nature of reality, of the world, of Being. It affirms the truth instead of fighting against it. It accepts reality & *embraces* it.

September 20

Yablonsky's *Hippie Trip* very good & useful. An extensive page-by-page review or commentary would be the equivalent of my whole Esalen-critique file, not to mention U. S. critique, Eupsychian ethic, metamotivation, Utopia, evil, & a lot more. [*Education. Youth.*] This is Utopia by fiat, by resolution, by enthusiastic moments—& it works for some, but very few, & then only the good ones (the strong, the healthy, the zestful, the seekers & questers, the good workers—in short, the ones who have already been seeking & working & thinking, & *then* can make a big conversion in what looks like a single moment).

But mostly it fails, & mostly thru ignorance of the facts of human nature & of social arrangements. It fails because of all sorts of *a priori* convictions (illusions) with which they come already equipped, all sorts of "shoulds" & "oughts," all sorts of already-defined axioms—which happen to be wrong. They misdefine & misunderstand freedom, love, SA, anarchism—but most of all they misunderstand evil. They think they can abolish it by *resolution*, & are therefore absolutely helpless when confronted by violence, laziness, selfishness, craziness, impulsivity, or (when they find it in themselves) when faced with responsibility, hard work, boring work, delay, persistence, temptation, self-sacrifice. Then their weaknesses appear (lack of knowledge about themselves, false expectations of themselves & others, the "Nirvana now!" impatience, the childish illusions about societal arrangements, etc.). It is the immature acting *as if* they were mature. Self-actualizing people, or even "decent" people, *could* do all the things they want to do; they *could* have successful communes; they *could* have leaderless anarchism; they *can* allow other people to do their own thing; they *can* live by impulses, spontaneously (& trust them to work out well); they *can* be open, compassionate, sharing, generous, brotherly, affectionate, responsible, etc. Just as we all were at 1232 Ocean Ave., & as we were in Madison with Rod Menzies, Paul Settlage, Walter Grether, & as we were *not* with the Madison radicals, with L.G., J.Z., Polly (who was later very good to live with at Ocean Ave.), C.M. (not bad in himself, but awful because of being a stooge for L.G.)—in a word, with either healthy or responsible or mature or just plain good middle-class-virtue people, nonevil people.

[*9/27/69: You do your thing & I do my thing & nobody interferes = a denial of any evil (one "thing" is as good as any other "thing"), & the hippies don't interfere even when evil men are attacking them or their friends, according to Yablonsky.*]

But all this living together is impossible with childish, selfish, immature, irresponsible, not-sensitive-to-others people, let alone neurotic or malicious, contemptuous people.

So the hippies & the SDS types, & the "Movement" people, & lots of others like them with good stated goals & values, want to achieve these ends simply by jumping right *into* them, without the prior growing up via experiences of all kinds, without "middle-class" maturity virtues that are necessary for living together even in *twos*, as in a marriage, without discipline. All the philosophers & psychologists of spontaneity, self-trust, openness, doing your own thing, etc.—Huxley, Leary, Rogers, Fromm, etc.—every single one of them (1) is older & (2) has mastered a discipline & therefore (3) *deserves* to feel competent & self-trusting & doesn't need a guide or an elder anymore. Parallel: they're already good pianists because of a lifetime of assiduous work, boring practice & finger exercises, actual competence & achievement—& therefore they can *afford* to say to themselves (& foolishly to others): "Be spontaneous. Be open. Be loving. Transcend the dominance hierarchy—glory, money, power, competition, mistrust, rivalry, etc." They can manage it because of their previous history of hard work & success.

And also these very same achievements, disciplines, experiences, & "wisdom" make it more possible for them to be good prison cellmates, to get along with other people, to function well in a commune. (Paradox: it's the person who's experienced enough to value his privacy & who doesn't *need* the perpetual puppy-snuggling with others who is best able to make it in a commune.)

"Wisdom" & experience certainly consist partly & *necessarily* in having worked up via experience a theory of good & evil in human nature, of what to expect & what not to expect & from whom to expect it & from whom not; i.e., a theory of individual differences is also necessary for choosing which people to trust & which people to mistrust—not to have illusions about human nature. *Which* illusions? They have no idea how *hard* it is to be affectionate, responsible, loving, brotherly, open, compassionate, relaxed, good natured enough to take shit without seeking for immediate justice, frustration-tolerant, loyal, persistent, hard working, reliable, thinking-of-others, etc. Use the example of how difficult it is for *two* people, *with* sex thrown in, to get along well together! How much more difficult, without sex, for larger groups of people, for 3 billion people, for prison cellmates, with immature children & their irritations to take care of.

Partly they're also suffering from the peak-experience interpretation of life (added to the instantaneous SA interpretation of life). Human nature is at its best in the turn-on of enthusiasm, of mob excitement & happiness, when anything seems possible (well, it *is* possible for the moment), in the exhilarated, ecstatic moment, in having fun, when everything is going well & you're having a good time, as at a very happy & gay & pleasantly silly party where you can be impulsive & do crazy things & it all works out so well & "God *does* provide," & there is in fact no evil (because everybody else is at his best too).

OK, that's part of the theory of good & evil. You have to *earn* the self-actualized way of life. (Why does everybody overlook that all my subjects were older people? That they were so infrequent? That they were already "successful" in life? That they may have been the best of the crop to *start* with, the unusually good material? That they each & all had a beloved job? That they each & all were unconfused about right & wrong?)

And, second, peak-experiences are *not* a way of life, & you really can't build a style of life upon them exclusively. And it seems not to work when you try to get them regularly via LSD or weekend workshops at Esalen. It looks as if it's better to wait for them to happen (while you keep working to be a better person who *deserves* to have them; i.e., it's better when they're earned). Good parallel: better not to keep on stimulating sexuality artificially via pornography, erotica, or unusual kinds of situations & stimulations. Best to be "natural" & to be content with meat & potatoes & bread & butter & not get to need the exotic & esoteric & unusual—which leads to impotence anyway.

But all of this interpretation of commune failure & Utopia failure, in terms of lacking a theory of evil, is also a critique of Esalen, of psychology 3, of big-bang revolutions, of shortcuts, of sudden insights, illuminations, & revelations as not only necessary but also "sufficient" (insights open the door to working thru & to self-imposed discipline). Also, for Marcuse's & Brown's nonrepressive society, you need highly evolved human beings or else "good, middle-class, responsible ones" who keep their neuroses to themselves; i.e., it's possible to be a good commune member even tho "privately & nonsocially" neurotic.

In the William James APA symposium I read last night, someone was perfectly correct in pointing out (it was Nevitt Sanford, I think) that grad students in psychology jumped to my kind of psychology in their search for a philosophy of life, forgetting the discipline of Freud which we older people had assimilated & now took for granted as a *foundation* for the higher life. [*Use in* Motivation & Personality *preface.*] *Say* this! Use the Sanford quote.

To go back to the evil stuff: use the hippie illusions as examples of what *should* be included under the evil rubric but rarely are, i.e., how *difficult* it is, how *hard* it is, to be brotherly, etc. The hippies & commune-ists get disillusioned because they don't fully realize the shortcomings of human nature over the long haul, when the problems start coming, when the baby has colic or is teething, when the mate is not screwing because she has hives or dysentery & looks awful & behaves like a shrew or a witch, or when boredom sets in, or when inertia has to be overcome, or when there's repetitive dull work to do, e.g., dishwashing. Then the hip-pie (the perfectionist, the full-time peak-seeker, the one who expects life to be lived always at its peak) gets disappointed, depressed, disillusioned, bitter. (Say it: How not to be disappointed? How not to be disillusioned? How to get rid of illusions? *Which* are the illusory expectations?)

Also point out the kids' misinterpretations of their elders' values & pleasures. They keep talking of the plastic society, of the dull family life, of the lack of excitement, gaiety, & happiness in their parents. Use exam-ple of Ellen, age 10 or so, commiserating with us because of the dull party we had to endure (to our surprise, because it was for us a wonderful party). When we asked her where she'd ever gotten such a cock-eyed notion, she said "Well, it was so quiet!" So kids don't know how wonder-ful it can be to earn money for one's family, how one could love children so much that it's a delight to sacrifice for them, e.g., my teaching summer school at Brooklyn for $200 a summer so that we could get the kids to the beach at Coney Island or up to Connecticut at Derby. Or that it's a great pleasure just to sit around & do nothing & just chat with one's wife casually about trivia, & look back at it as a peak-experience. The kids don't understand their elders' pleasures, judging them always by adolescent, phallic, motorcycle, rock-music, frenetic standards, & can't understand that they may be living a good life & having a wonderful time, even if they do prefer quiet to noise & activity, privacy to a gang, & middle-class virtues to hysterical & Dionysian ones. The kids are apt to think they've "sold out" because they're wiser & more experienced & expect less of life & of society & of human nature than adolescents do, with their "idealism," which is partly ignorance & inexperience & perfectionism & a big-bang interpretation—because elders prefer the quiet voice to the scream, gentleness to roughness, "getting along" with the cellmates rather than insisting on absolute justice & equity.

I'm including the class-transcending values in the meta-epilogue chapter of *Farther Reaches of Human Nature* [144]. Maybe I should also have youth-transcending, middle-aged values too? *Yes*. Especially include the stuff above, i.e., what I'd call experience, wisdom, a theory of human & social evil. Accommodating to evil & living with it are exactly what the perfectionistic, "idealistic" kids are apt to scorn, to despise, to think of as a betrayal, as "selling out" or "copping out" or cowardice (which they can truly understand only when they themselves have become middle-aged). Shall I include all of this in the evil chapter? I think it belongs there because the kids (mistakenly) see it as evil in fact. And I'm including lots of other stuff that's mistakenly defined as evil, i.e., the semantics of evil—much evil disappears from the rubric. A wiser, more experienced Olympian would *not* regard middle-aged acceptance of human limitations as evil. That's it! The kids refuse to accept human limitations, e.g., laziness, slovenliness, revenge, resentment; i.e., they refuse to accept *any* evil in human nature as intrinsically & unavoidably & eternally necessary. If I say they lack a theory of evil, that's what I mean. They expect perfect wives, partners, colleagues, teachers, friends—even perfect *selves*. They are B-monsters. And of course, insofar as this produces evil—e.g., the generation gap, nastiness to elders, the spit-on-daddy club—to that extent it's another example of evil boiling down to ignorance, inexperience, immaturity, just not knowing enough at a high enough level, Socratic evil-thru-ignorance. Because the hippies go in for a doctrinaire rather than a realistic nonviolence, they *create* violence & attract it & give it food to feed on, as in Yablonsky's book—lots of examples there. To turn into a lamb is to call out the wolf in some people. To lay down one's arms absolutely is to attract & create aggression & sadism (like the masochistic girl in the press who was *murdered* because she didn't resist the aggression but almost asked for it, anyway accepted it). Same for encouraging the violent wine-drinkers, the Hell's Angels, the Methadone-freaks, the psychotics, the psychopaths. I wonder how many people I'd pain or kill if I were absolutely exempted from any penalties. Or if I had absolute power. Or if I *knew* there would be no resistance.

This too goes under the evil rubric, that is, unrealistic nonviolence of the hippie sort. Just as the SDS types elected Nixon & the unilateral "Peace! Peace! Peace!" types are war-bringers (if the U. S. disarmed totally at once, or left Vietnam at once, it would bring *more* & *bigger* wars, not fewer wars).

All of the above also serves as a critique of McGregor & Theory-Y management. You *cannot* establish a Theory-Y organization by announcing its advent as of next Thursday, when everyone will, starting at 9 A.M., be trusting, open, friendly, loving, intimate, relaxed, & generous. Point out that here, too, it's a hard & long & skilled job & won't always succeed, &, even if it does on the whole, there will still be recalcitrant individuals who will have to be fired.

Looks as if this evil stuff is growing into a book rather than a chapter. If I were teaching, I'd offer a course of lectures on it. It's just ready to put together. If I do any voluntary teaching around here, that would be good to work up, record, & transcribe. I guess also this stuff about reaching for the ideal prematurely goes nicely as an example in my 3-level political theory. There are dangers in "idealism," & it can bring evil results. The impatient, "Nirvana-now," B-monster perfectionists are endangering all the good goals. The Eupsychian ethic, the good world, has to be built up solidly, floor by floor, & on good solid foundations, *testing* everything as you go upward. There's a place for caution, reserve, not going too fast, testing the ice before you go another step, i.e., doing it in the scientific, technological, engineering way (Apollonian) rather than by spurts of enthusiasm, faith, greediness, & sloppiness. Test everything & go step by step. Fits right into my theory of the slow (unnoticed) revolution.

September 27

Reading "University 1970: The 5th Estate," an article by Judson Jerome in *Change* (procto file), in which almost everything is procto-interpreted, i.e., explained exclusively by attributing *lower* needs rather than higher. A kind of cynicism, wise-guy attitude which irritates me always—a sort of diminishing of human nature, a refusal to believe in "higher nature," or else it is a deliberate pose to look "not-fooled," sophisticated, knowing what's going on behind the scenes, & what ordinary people are not in on. To know the secrets, to know what other people are being fooled by. To know what lesser people don't know is to be smarter, cleverer, "hip," to be savvy, to feel superior, to be in on things.

Of course, it's a safety device, like a gambler afraid to bet & take a chance. It's also the fear of being open, of being trusting, of "believing" & having faith, of taking a chance (this is a form of *not* taking a chance). It's the stance that we attempt to "cure" with T-groups, therapy, psychology 3, Synanon, the Eupsychian network, Organizational Development (OD), Rogerianism & Esalen openness, candor, etc. That is, it's a sickness; it is incorrect, false, untrue, blind, cognitively untrue & axiologically untrue. Like all fear-inspired defenses, it is a form of blindness or, anyway, interpretive blindness.

Work it out more. Why are they afraid or mistrustful or disbelieving of higher motives? Why do they think the *appearance* of higher motivations, or the claim to them is a fake, a put-on, a hypocrisy? Because they *a priori* believe it doesn't really exist (B-values). When they see what *looks* like unselfishness or altruism, of course they can't believe *it*; they feel it's phony necessarily, & unreal, & go looking for the *real* motives that are concealed behind the facade. Of course they despise the "do-gooders," Boy Scouts, bleeding hearts, Christers, Pollyannas, etc., etc. (They don't even have a *good* word to describe metamotivations; it doesn't really exist except as a phony facade.) That is, they despise the ones who are sincere, i.e., taken in by their own propaganda, who really *believe* that they're being unselfish or compassionate & who don't "realize" that they're sim- ply being taken in by themselves & don't know their own "real" motives, which are deep, dark, & dirty necessarily & only. For the ones who do this put-on & faking & are *not* consciously sincere, (i.e., the *conscious* fakes, the psychopaths, etc.), they have a kind of affection, a sort of "respect for their honesty." They prefer conscious crooks whom, after all, they can under- stand as sharing their theories of human nature, & who are "realistically" taking advantage of the repressed bleeding hearts, "screwing them"— which, after all, in an adversary, would mean that the crooks doing the screwing are the victors, more honest, more knowing, more hep, more realistic, not fooled. So the two people who are hep & who are not being fooled certainly can understand each other, & can wink & grin knowingly at each other.

But explain also the *hatred*, the malignity, the out-&-out sadism of the procto-knower, the cynic, against the do-gooder. Why doesn't he just laugh at him or sneer at him? Why must he go to such lengths, to such trouble, be so persistent in destroying him? For fear of being converted unless he can expose him as a fake, or at least as a failure? (That way of life doesn't work, & therefore I'm correct in my view.) If the good guy is *really* saintly, then the wise guy is wrong, profoundly wrong, & has all along been a fool rather than sophisticated & knowledgeable. If he's been wrong & a fool & a jerk, he is & has been ludicrous, laughed at, not superior but inferior—exactly what he's most afraid of, exactly what his whole way of life is designed to avoid. He must *not* be laughed at or look ridiculous. That's *why* he mistrusts & is wary & won't drop his wise-guy defenses. (Good example: Ratso in *Midnight Cowboy*.) He's afraid to be taken advan- tage of, fooled, manipulated, controlled, looked down upon, put down. It has to do with dominance-subordination. Somehow he feels that his savvy, knowing what's really going on behind the scenes, gives him superiority, in about the same way that the peeping Tom feels superior to the one who doesn't know he's being peeped at. Secret knowledge makes him feel superior to the naive & unknowing one, the one who is fooled, taken in, innocent & ignorant, doesn't know what's going on.

Why is this also a form of humor? The very standard amusement, superior amusement, with the standard farce theme of the husband who's being fooled & cuckolded, the man who walks innocently thru the whorehouse thinking it's a girls' academy, etc. If you can get someone to believe what isn't so, the put-on, the line, then not only can you feel superior & stronger, but also you can laugh at him. This is certainly in- volved with the dominance-level & with the dichotomizing, adversary, zero-sum-game iew of social life. A full description of the levels theory should certainly include this. This is all kid stuff, at an immature level, in the D-realm. The B-language would transcend the whole thing. I guess this is the negative side of the B-language & communication & instant knowing-each-other at the B-level. All a guy has to do for me to place him at the D-level is to say "Publish or perish." Then I *know* he's a cripple.

September 29

Slowly crystallizing into consciousness: to cosmocize & univer-
salize my critique of Esalen into an examination of benefits & booby-trap
exaggerations, not only of Esalen & its whole chain, but also of the hippie
culture, psychology 3, Synanon, NTL—in fact the whole Eupsychian network. Much of it is a *misuse* of my thinking. But the misuses are all old
philosophies & issues: romanticism, pro & con; anti-intellectual, antiscientific dangers. Is instant Nirvana possible (insight vs. working thru)?
Do illuminations come in a moment, or do you have to work at it for a
lifetime? I.e., is it a search for wisdom? Is it painful & difficult? Can you
reach love & brotherhood via elitism, contempt, & condescension, excluding people rather than including them, without compassion for all? Theory
of evil, etc., etc.
      Esalen is only a single test-tube case which I happen to have
handy. Mustn't take it (individually) too seriously. Must take all the individuals there, & problems, mistakes, & solutions, as *instances of the general.*
      Also the question of validation: What kind of human beings does
it create? What kind of interpersonal relations? What kind of societies?
      Do peak-experiences (+ mystic + plateau + untrue) come from
glimpses into the B-realm? From glimpses of B-values? That is, from perfection, duty, B-truth, B-love, B-completion & perfection & excellence,
etc.? Once I thought it might be generalized as "triggered off by anything
done very well or perfectly." Maybe this is better phrasing because it is
more general & inclusive.

November 6

Reading Rasa Gustaitis' *Turning On* (Macmillan, 1969), on the Esalen world, & very much irritated by it. Summarizes the whole crappy side
of the "turning-on" world. She falls for Perls, Schutz, Rolf, the hippies &
gypsies *only*, while she rejects the squares, the intellectuals, & can't listen
to a famous existentialist lecture (May ?). Struck me that everything &
everybody she admired added up to the way of life of psychopaths—
living only in the here-now, not thinking also of past & future & of the
world in which the here-now is placed, of being impulsive & admiring
any impulse or whim or word & the *acting* on it, of a kind of contempt of
the straight & squares, putting them on & panhandling from them, of
having shifting, fluctuating, transient, inconsistent interpersonal relationships, sexual or nonsexual, of being unpredictable, unreliable, without

loyalties (stealing from each other), "expression-is-all" & totally without controls, even of human turds, of dirt, of sores, garbage, etc., of implied irresponsibility to their children (all these attitudes = lousy child care = lousy wife care). Work is bad (*this* part of the Protestant ethic they've picked up—only they act on it). The Dionysian & orgiastic are for them somehow better than Apollonian planning, delay, control, measure—à la LSD. A peculiar kind of narcissism, something like the psychopath's self-absorption & not caring about anybody else except for here-now usefulness. Seeking for parties, the party & picnic ethic, & can be really fun at parties with their carefree, unworried hedonism, having-fun-only hedonism = doing *nothing* unless the impulse hits you, or if it's not your bag or your scene = a wild self-destructiveness as in the Morningstar Ranch story, where a very little effort could have saved the whole thing. [*This can also be considered a form of personal immaturity. Work it out. Many of these kids* talk *SA, but their whole life is* anti-*SA*.] She's also picked up from the "gypsies" their antagonism & contempt—as with hereditary enemies—of all authority, rules, laws, etc. The shiftless life. The hobo life (restless—they come & go on impulse) = a short life as with psychopaths. Read Cleckley again to make the parallels = living entirely by the pleasure principle, rejecting radically the reality principle of Freud.

No identification with other people. She felt that the motorcycle gang might rape her & her "friends" wouldn't lift a hand to protect her. No solidarity, even *within* the amity-enmity group. No loyalty.

My vague impression is that this is much more a male wish-fulfillment than female. The male fantasy is of unlimited screwing without responsibility of any kind to woman or child, a modern version of the older "stag" fantasy—fool 'em, fuck 'em, forget 'em. Women & children get the short end of things here, as I remember discussing with X, who yearned for continuity, a home, & a child instead of getting screwed by some transient male every once in a while, which she didn't even enjoy.

Of course all of this makes community impossible. This type has to be screened out of communes or fired out.

Also part of the syndrome is the attack upon *any* rules, *just* because they are rules & therefore constraints upon total liberty; this includes, also, any & all the folkways, traditions, customs, mores of any society. Of course, this gets silly because the folkways just don't mean anything special & are just not worth the bother of revolting against, especially since other folkways necessarily take their place anyway; e.g., their slang becomes conventional language, their clothes finally become conventional, their music, dancing, places to go, things to do, style. [*Also rejects planning, future* = *much reliance on chance, the aleatory life as in much contemporary "art"* = *a going over into magic, astrology, cabalism, etc., etc. Can be seen either as one (distorted) version of Taoism or as helplessness, fatalism, the ultimate of being a pawn.*]

But anyway the point should be made that revolt against constraints *must* bring up the question: once the shackles are broken, *then* what? What to *do* with freedom? It's not a life-career, breaking one's shackles again & again. It's the whole question of life-goals, life-purposes; it brings in planning, the future, ties to other people, to society, the place of "helping," etc. The hippie here-now, hedonistic path is *one* opposite of the Bodhisattva path—it is one example of personal salvation seeking, the Pratychabuddha path.

The best way to handle conventional rules is to be *aware* of their rootlessness, as an ethnologist is, & *never* to take them seriously, to be light & good humored about them as about traffic rules, to let them set lightly upon our shoulders, easily & casually dropped off when *too* inconvenient or growth-frustrating. It's the difference between being *able* to be naked without fun & without pleasure when that's the functional thing to do & being a doctrinaire "nudist" who makes a big cause out of it & expects too much from it. This implies *not* pushing it too hard, offending your neighbors, feeling "oppressed" when you have to keep your pants on in such & such a place. It's just not that important. Same for hairstyle or clothes. Those who are *bound* to any particular style, even the currently rebellious convention or style, are enslaved.

[*It is also revolt against "the forbidden," against any structuring (e.g., the "system," the "Establishment"), against stable & continuous enduring. "All is flux." That statement also needs modifying to include enduring.*]

Same with the Esalen techniques: they're all good or useful for certain people at certain times, but do *not* constitute a way of life. They are all outgrown, & all lead to the ultimate life questions; i.e., they are only steps along a path, means to an end. Many of them are only reparative & should not be necessary for adults, who should have been finished with them in childhood.

It occurs to me also that in her book there's much attraction to the exotic (the "mystic guest from Hawaii"), to the strange, the unusual, the "romantic," etc. She's missed the point of Zen: to sacralize the *ordinary*. The faraway places, the novelties, the use of drugs, the magical, the mysterious—all can distract from the task of learning to see the miraculous in the face before you, in the flowers in your own yard. That's one reason I mistrust so much of her book & of the "far-out," "turned-on," stoned, extremist hunting for ecstasy out there rather than right here. That too is akin to the psychopath's easy boredom & need for novelty & excessive triggers & stimulations. It all leads to selfishness, magic, sadism, death.

The latter part of her book makes me compassionate rather than disgusted. A poor, mixed-up, confused woman.

November 16

Good insight on *evil*—maybe a breakthrough. The enjoyer & the nonenjoyer-perfectionist can debate with each other in a circular way—

which I think shows "good & evil" to be attributions & projections, & maybe in a certain sense beside the point. The perfectionist must of course be disappointed with anything or anybody, & then he often attributes evil. The discovered flaw proves it's evil. Then the nonperfectionist says: "No, you're expecting too much. You're responding in terms of your own inability to enjoy, your sourness, etc. If you expected or demanded less & accepted reality, then you could enjoy it more." The perfectionist (unable to enjoy whatever causes the other to enjoy) then can respond: "Yes, that's just what I mean, & you're agreeing with me. Men are always disappointing, flawed, liars, weak, greedy—you can't count on them, on anybody. You're crazy for calling them good." Clearly 2 people of different kinds talking about their different subjective reactions & in effect one is saying "I cannot enjoy" & the other is saying "I *can* enjoy reality just as it is."

What is added by speaking about "out there" being either good or evil? It's OK & real to say "People hurt me & disappoint me" & just as real for another one to say "People *don't* disappoint me & I like them & enjoy them." It's like the PTC argument when one finds it tasteless & the other finds it bitter. Is it "really" bitter or tasteless? Better talk only—at this moment anyway—of the various subjective experiences rather than about the attributions & projections & generalizations & labels.

Nobody can argue against finding out *why* there are individual differences & where they come from, & maybe whether they can be changed by therapy, etc. Is the perfectionist a nonenjoyer? Biochemically or neurologically lacking something? A nonpeaker? Maybe dyspeptic or depressed or with some other temporary illness? Maybe the peaker is hypomanic or sees reality falsely because of rose-colored glasses? What?

And, second, nobody will argue against enhancing pleasure & happiness & enjoyment & decreasing pain, if possible.

And, thirdly, just as we accept the nature of trees or rocks or infants or puppies without even *thinking* of whether they're good or evil, maybe it's better also to try the same attitude toward people & anything else now labeled good or evil; i.e., just accept reality Taoistically & realistically-scientifically, know the nature of reality as accurately as possible, & then pick for yourself which portions of reality you want for yourself. E.g., do you prefer to be with paranoids or with healthies? That is, don't bother saying "He is more evil than that one," but rather "From him you will get more pleasure & less pain than from that one" *or* "The statistics are that you can trust garage men so much & as much." At the very least, this approach will lessen surprise, shock, disappointment, disillusionment. Use the Bossom experiment as an example to show how this can be researched & that one could then say that secure people see more realistically & correctly than insecure people. This is very tricky in one way. It involves giving up the neurotic oughts & shoulds—"He is not the way he ought to be" or "People *ought* to be more courageous"—in favor of knowing just what people are in fact & then adapting to *that*. The trouble is that part of their realistic nature is what they *could* be, what their hidden potentials are. So must differentiate carefully the *a priori* "oughts" from the scientific "coulds." One imposes a norm which is unrealistic; the other uncovers the norm which is intrinsic to human nature itself = "What are people like?" rather than "What should people be like?" or "What do I expect or demand that people ought to be like?"

Also, this approach lays much greater stress on description of individual differences & acceptance of them (until the time you can differentiate the neurotic-incorrect from the true-correct-healthy).

If you tell the perfectionist "Enjoy yourself as much as you can," he won't fight back as he will if you tell him "People are enjoyable—or good."

Shall I call this the transpersonal attitude toward good & evil? Certainly that's my attitude to everything that is not human *and* adult. Maybe it can be carried over to people, too, as well as to cats or trees. And stress: this attitude does *not* give up finding out who is right & who is wrong objectively—altho it accepts also the ultimate reality of a self-report or feedback; e.g., "She looks ugly to me," "The whole world looks gray to me today," or "I have a bellyache," or "I had a peak-experience over X" (over someone I later discovered to be a thief, so I couldn't get peaks from him anymore).

November 26

B. suggested, in regard to the female-male meeting last night, that I could be misunderstood on the statement that every baby, & potentially every person, should be regarded as capable of SA & of creativeness. A better phrasing came out of the discussion. I should stress that it has nothing to do with "talents." *Any* job, almost, can be "creativized" (sacralized?) because it can be done with excellence, perfection, elegantly, efficiently, parsimoniously, unitively (etc., for all B-values). That is, it can be done with dignity, trying to improve it, do it better & better, so you can take pride in it, so you can lose yourself in it, so you can pour yourself into it totally with self-forgetfulness, "give it everything you've got," forget time & place, do it for its own sake as one does a painting or something beloved.

I remember one such discussion long ago where I maintained that even driving a bus could or could not be done in this style, creatively or noncreatively, which means actualizing the self, here-now, & making the growth choice (over inertia, hopelessness, etc.). I think of the carpenter who did our deck & certainly acted like an emperor, totally self-respecting & doing a *fine* job. Psychologically, the immersion in the process & the results for self-respect, self-acceptance, & competence-pride were all the same as Beethoven composing—subjectively, anyway.

November 28

Discussion of Organizational Development (OD) philosophy with Lew yesterday. He makes a good critic. Also long discussion of X, a jungle type, "low person" rather than "high." Tried to describe levels of evolvement of personality, but it was difficult. Must work it out better, try to write it down with lots of detail. Said: all the words you use to describe him are not either-or; e.g., is he loyal or disloyal, trustworthy or not, plotting or not? They all have layers of meaning rather than being either clear or unclear on a single positivistic plane, like Flatland. If you started with the basic assumption of "First comes #1," i.e., of trusting no one really, of feeling the need for defense of oneself, that everybody else is out only for himself, then the simple hierarchy of values by which to judge persons becomes not good or bad, but strong or weak, hammer or anvil, wolf or lamb, & only on the basis of achieved wealth-power-status, with the assumption that this comes about only by ruthlessness, selfishness, toughness, Hobbesian "realism" & Machiavellian "methods, strategy, & tactics," the sole principle of interpersonal relations, mutual exploitativeness at best &, at worst, who gets screwed—you or me? The whole thing is antisynergic, zero-sum-game, adversary, win-lose *Weltanschauung* of limited good; i.e., my advantage must necessarily be your disadvantage. Therefore, if you have good luck, I *must* have lost something & therefore feel chagrined, envious, put down, defeated, & therefore angry & ambivalent to the winner (since I also admire "'strength" of the jungle sort = safety-danger level strength), or loyalty-shifting, temporary, Machiavellian alliances for mutual advantage against someone else with no implications of anything enduring beyond this transaction (à la France, which has good relations with the U. S. whenever she *needs* the U. S. &, when the need has passed, can lapse into normal impotent envy). Is this person loyal to Lew? Probably yes, at this moment, *if* Lew is undoubtedly the unchallenged boss (it's best to get along with the king of the jungle), but he would have to be on the winning side, & with whoever might become the next king of the jungle, à la Lindbergh or Petain with the Nazis = "best to be on winning side." Then of course he could be expected to weigh & calculate & not be loyal to Lew, but to engage in intrigue with the probable overthrower of Lew, i.e., the next king. And *certainly* to be counted on, if the king has actually been dethroned, is the pleasure of revenge for his past humiliations, brown-nosing, ass-kissing, appeasing, ass-presenting—by kicking the fallen elephant in the ribs, spitting on him, contempt, asserting open dominance over the formerly feared one. It's apt to be *cruel* dominance, as with my monkeys, after the overlord was dethroned, who would pick him to death unless stopped. See parallels paper [78] for good examples. Also authoritarian paper [33].

A letter: "You don't remember me, but I was a student in your class 20 years ago. A word from you will open the door at Brandeis for my son, who is applying there." To seek for privilege, to use pull, to trade on acquaintanceship = view of the world of magic & luck, of people who can be appealed to arbitrarily to let loose a lightning stroke by whim, for no reason, regardless of deserts! Like elbowing into line ahead of other people. To pull rank or to appeal to rank for special arbitrary privilege. "She just happened to catch the eye of a producer at the lucky moment & he made her a star" = don't work for goals, don't earn, don't deserve = there is no justice, just luck—virtue is not rewarded in this world, nor is vice punished, & maybe even the opposite is true.

But this letter exemplifies the profound stupidity & self-defeating quality of jungle people, who are not aware that they are actually *damaging* their own cause, bringing about the opposite of what they intend. She has no idea that this letter might offend or anger me & thus might work *against* her goal. Low people don't understand Y & Z people, [135], while Y & Z people *can* understand X people; e.g., Lew, who's a decent man, a Y, can easily outsmart the X person who is blind to Y & Z.

Bill Crockett last night describing the State Department world, politicians' world, newspaper world as essentially jungle worlds, so he quit & finds the business world at Saga far better, & spends his time trying to change jungle world into family world. My academic world, I told him, has been changing from the pure world of Depression days (profs took vows of poverty & humility & devotion to truth out of sheer love of truth). But affluence changed the academic world more & more toward a jungle world—even the world of science, altho it is still possible to remain pure & clean if you really want to, at very little external cost. I was able to do it & even got rewarded for renouncing extrinsic rewards.

Has my point of view about the world & about society & human nature been too much shaped by my specially good world? Supposing I'd stayed in Maslow Cooperage—would my psychology now be different? I don't think so. I'm in the middle of Roman history now & that's about as nasty as you can find, & that all can be integrated into psychology 3, as also can poverty, underdeveloped nations, India's misery, war, etc. I pick the *best*, the tallest, the Olympic team. That's how good people *can* get. That's what's possible for *any* baby born into the world—but *not* guaranteed, or, in many places, not even probable.

And yet it's still a fair question: why not a Zoroastrian equal struggle between good & evil, defense & growth, jungle & synergy? There *is* evidence, more really, of fear as prepotent; also of regression & defense. In this sense, fear is stronger (prepotent) than growth. If I say growth does win out *under good conditions,* how circular is this? Is a rosebush, grown healthy & tall under "good conditions," *more* a rosebush than a stunted one? There's circularity here too. Perhaps I should say rather: "If you prefer a tall rosebush to a stunted one, then there are the conditions necessary." Similar for the jungle world vs. the brotherly world: if you prefer the latter to the former (which everybody does who has tasted both), then how do you go about getting it? [*Which world is closer to the "natural bent"? Answer has to be hierarchical. Both are "natural" & sensible, under low & higher conditions.*] Same for jungle man vs. B-man, or X vs. Y; if you can get people to taste both, they prefer Theory Y to Theory X. Given really free choice, this is what they choose = wisdom of the body. After all, this is true after therapy, after Synanon, after T-groups, after peak-experiences, etc. Like saying human beings choose happiness over pain, misery, & anguish, freedom over inhibition, courage over fear. Only real trouble is getting them to taste *both* if they're stuck in neurosis, or in the jungle, etc. See review of Fromm's *Revolution of Hope* in *Contemporary Psychology* of a few months ago. Take it seriously as a critique & try to deal with it.

Jungle World	Brotherly World
Rivalry, competition.	Collaboration, team work.
What's good for me? No responsibility to others (or else it doesn't pay, is not rewarded).	Duty, responsibility. Response to requirements of the situation. Principles. Impersonal law responsibility to others pays off, gets rewarded.
First principle = loyalty to self.	Principled. Moral values.
So little identified with others, so noncaring, so self-encapsulated, that opinions of others just don't matter (e.g., slum lord, psychopath).	Intrinsic rewards (B-values) & compassionate & forgiving understanding of others' bad behavior. Transcend opinion of others. Love & compassion & pity transcending justice, fairness, & "rights." To pity the person who has to shit on your head = higher than love.
Personal chauvinism, single-self, restricted self.	Species chauvinism; enlarged, including self. Ecology, transhumanism, fusion with the world.
Lies OK for low "personal" advantage, for putting down, for dominance struggle, for remaining inscrutable, mysterious, impenetrable, poker-faced.	Candor, honesty.

Jungle World	*Brotherly World*
People *either* weak or strong.	
Flat-meaningfulness. A or not-A. Either-or. Dissective. Dichotomous.	Layered meanings. Levels of meaning.
Virtue is not rewarded & vice is not punished. It's either luck, magic, accident, or perhaps just the other way about.	Virtue is its own reward & vice is its own punishment. And anyway, in good world, virtue is rewarded & vice punished.
Generally can't understand Y & X people & their ways = blindness = all sorts of stupid mistakes in trying to manipulate Y or Z.	If healthy, the Y or Z man *can* also understand the X man & so has a great advantage in a duel (*if* willing to be isomorphic about weapons & tactics, i.e., to give the other the choice of weapons & then to use the same weapons).
The ultimate of power, status, wealth, & therefore freedom to obey any whim or impulse = Marquis de Sade or the Roman emperors.	Ultimate goal & ultimate pleasure = to be sage-seer-saint-doer. B-power. B-freedom (freedom to love B-values).
Social Darwinism. "Survival of the fittest" = whoever survives & wins. Individual struggle for survival.	Kropotkin: survival of the cooperative group.
Anybody can be bought. Everybody has his price (= money, power, status). Bribery is a realistic tool.	Metahedonism. Metapay. *Not* anybody can be bought with money-power-status, but anybody *can* be bought with B-values, etc.
Proctopsychological view of life. Shit-colored glasses or denial view of life with rose-colored glasses.	Realistic view of life.
Nonpeakers, lower joys only. Blind to B-realm, B-values, metapay. Ecstasy, bliss, joy not possible. No unitive perceptions. Totally secular, profane life.	May be nonpeakers but much more likely to be or become peakers. (See Theory-Z paper.)
It costs too much to be virtuous, honest, generous, etc. One gets punished for it. Evil eye.	Virtue pays, is rewarded & reinforced. Costs little.
Elitism goes with privileges & more rights. To the strong (who are therefore superior) belong all the spoils, all the power, deference from others. (This is justice at jungle level, shared by both predator & his prey; i.e., *both* think the strong deserves by right to be the predator, & the weak ought to be the prey.)	Superiority = responsibilities, duties, *noblesse oblige*, metapay, renunciation of many (low) privileges. Predator privileges are not sought or enjoyed, & are even repugnant. Same for "prey privileges"; they are equally renounced.

Jungle World	*Brotherly World*
Using prostitutes, buying people, using court jester, humiliating people, naked expressions of power over others, of subordinating others, of "mounting" others. Using or being used.	Transcending domination & subordination of baboon type. Transcendence of using & being used. No *need* for power over other people.
Dominated by money, power, status, one's own or others'. *Needed* for self-esteem.	Wise use of money, power, status as means to good ends. Not "needed." Not basis of self-esteem.
Dominatizing of sex & sexual organs. Symbolic acting out. Sex as a channel for domination & subordination.	Sex is sex, not dominance. Penis, vagina *not* aggressive, dangerous, frightening. Sex is mutual, not transitive. Sex positioning not dominating.
No *real* anger at evil, since it's accepted. Real guilt? No real shame over evil. No impersonal enmity against evil unless it hits personally, but even then with secret admiration. Identification with the carnivore, the tiger.	Moral indignation. Full anger. High, principled, suprapersonal hatred & enmity against evil.
Basically paranoid position. Suspicious. Attribution of low motives of hostility. Down-leveling of motives.	First trusting, give him a chance, & only after the fact judging, realistic judgment of motives, both good & bad. Truth despises paranoia.
Contempt for other's honesty, altruism, affection, forgiveness, justice, etc., as weakness, as unrealistic stupidity, as not strong.	Admiration, affection for honesty, etc. Taken as signs of strength, maturity, trust in self, lack of fear.
The blindness, coarctation, & unrealism of fear & suspicion. Abstracting into either dangerous or usable, into weak & strong.	Full perceiving. Openness to the world, to reality. Less abstracting into dangerous & not dangerous.
Loss of human capacities. Domination of humanness. Neurosis. Inability to drop defenses, drop body armor. Never turn your back to anyone = can't relax, play. Always wary, alert, vigilant. Psychosomatic diseases.	More fully human. More healthy. Less illnesses of stress, tension, loneliness, lovelessness, mistrust.
No impulse to help except in put-down way, condescending, good-natured contempt, e.g., big tipper, showoff, buying flattery to feel big.	Bodhisattva helper. Pleasure in helping, parental pleasures; pleasure in growth & SA of others.
Puzzled, suspicious, disbelieving, confused.	Pleasure in contemplation of B-values in people, in world.

Jungle World	Brotherly World
Jungle economics = you have a right to everything you can get & no obligation to others. "It's mine" = absolute statement.	Moral, brotherly, humanitarian economics. Others' needs are to some extent my needs also.
Jungle politics = struggle for power, status, wealth *by* the strong & powerful & wealthy (excluding the weak, the prey, or else using them, fooling them, exploiting them, etc.). Politics of alliances against.	Family or brotherhood or species-hood. Politics of unselfishness. Politics is the B-politics. Every individual, however weak, incapable, or low, has some sacredness, irreducible dignity, rights, etc. "I am my brother's keeper, especially the sick brother." Politics of duties & responsibilities *as well as* privileges, jungle power, personal rights, selfishness. Politics of justice, love, compassion, & forgiveness. Holistic politics of one world & one species = transcending of atomistic, separative, excluding, or amity-enmity growth politics. Ideal politics.
Safety-level world view. World is full of dangers. Protection against dangers is first & prepotent life task. Reduction to concrete à la Goldstein. Blind-man model, spy model.	Higher-need world view. World is *not* essentially dangerous, or its dangers are easily taken care of.
Reservoir of revenge, conscious or unconscious, as very important hidden motivation.	Nonvengeful. Compassion, affection, friendliness, reactive aggression & anger.
Theory-X laziness avoids responsibility, doesn't care to do a good job; stupid, incapable; prefers idleness; must be motivated by reward & punishment; unambitious; strong need for security; must be watched, controlled, supervised.	Theory Y prefers enlarged & enriched job; prefers responsibility; prefers to work & to do a good job; self-direction & self-control. Good communication. Motivated by higher needs & SA & metamotives.
Samson complex necessary as defense against being weakened. Jonah complex necessary as defense against envy, jealousy, assassination, evil eye.	Samson complex not necessary; can permit oneself to love, to be softened, to be tender, to take off armor & to be not tough, to be vulnerable without fear. Jonah complex not necessary. (If it occurs, it's neurotic.) One can dare to actualize all talents to the full without danger, & perhaps even they will bring rewards of love & respect instead of pain & punishment.
Disadvantages of antisynergy.	Synergy. Pleasures of teamwork, of belonging, of being rewarded for being at one's best.

December 12

At Center, visiting Barker & chatting also with a woman philosopher who asked about the 3rd Force psychology & then countered: "But feeling good, as in peak-experiences, can be just an inner emotional state having no reality reference, can't it?" What impressed her & Barker were the *experiments* (of Debby Tanzer) where not only peaks but *also* better interpersonal relations between husband & wife enhanced the masculinity of the husband, etc., i.e., objective effects of the subjective experiences. So also for the brain-wave work with alpha waves (objective) correlating with (subjective) serene states. Grof's work. LSD stuff & other "altered states of consciousness" research data.

I think this helps with the relativity problem as between world X & world Y. Why choose one rather than the other, especially when it's conceded that an X world sometimes calls for an X person? I.e., it's "better" at some times & for some people.

Stress more the sacredness of the ordinary, the miracle of the usual. Important as aspect of plateau-experience, the easy state. Also, in letter I wrote to someone rejecting astrology, magic, the voyages to India, the straining after unusual states, the romanticizing of homosexuality & schizophrenia, etc., I thought these to be possible defenses *against* & flights *from* self-confrontation right here at home. The hunting for the exotic & the esoteric hides the problem in the kitchen, in the back yard. Same criticism against perpetual hunt for novelty. (All this is in Esalen critique too.) It's too much stress also on the Dionysian, the "turning on," the big bang rather than the plugging along & working through. Or screaming rather than the quiet voices.

Plateau-experiences include quiet, nonorgiastic sense of miracle, quiet sacralizing, quiet wonder, gratitude, awe, incredulity, fascination = the quiet peak-experiences, more cognitive than emotional. As a matter of fact, it's *always* cognitive, & sometimes the peak is not.

1970

January 18

Also democracy (real & compassionate) *needs* a large proportion of active agents (rather than pawns) & produces them as well. With too many pawns it would break down into authoritarianism, i.e., the strong *using* the weak rather than *taking care* of them. But the latter can also be a *kind* of authoritarianism. In a democracy the strong also take care of the weak, but the latter should be, ideally, only the irreducible proportion of the population composed of aments, children, the aged, crippled, etc. (10—20%). It's partly a numerical matter of degree. How many could-be strongs are *made* weak by the society, as with Negroes, et al.?

And then also, must think thru the different kinds of political choices possible to the strong, like Sherm & his VPs. There was no question about the different & real increments of capacity from the FSDs [Food Service Directors] to the RODs [Regional Operational Directors] to the VPs to Sherm. Probably a bigger proportion of Republicans to Democrats at each higher level, & of conservatives to liberals, & of Goldwater-Darwinian conservatives & liberal-conservatives.

The *pure* Darwinism would insist on both (1) real equality of opportunity, a competence-elite, & against being "born to the purple" & to privilege, hereditary classes, or castes, & therefore in favor of heavy inheritance taxes; and (2) simultaneously giving great privileges & rights to the gold-medal winners in the (real) competition, & being tough on the losers, perhaps taking care of them & perhaps not, &, if taking care of them, then not treating them with the *same* respect as one does winners = a real class & caste structure, but based absolutely on real competence = giving rather little power to the less competent & strong. Keeping power in the hands of the strong. (À la Ayn Rand? Better read her stuff.) [*Aggridants are all active agents, but not all agents are aggridants? They both need better definition. Theoretically anyone can become an agent.*] Very few candid conservatives, saying publicly what they really think. Maybe I should write out, frankly, the whole range of theoretical political possibilities. It's all muddled now because of the secret thoughts, not written for the public.

This Darwinian conservatism can yet be perfectly democratic in the sense of perfectly equal opportunity for every infant throughout life & perfectly fair & real judging of the Olympic games, of the tests, of competencies—as in the world of athletics, where *real*, actual differences incompetence emerge in perfect justice, & are perfectly-justly rewarded without reference to *any* variable other than competence.

At the other end of the gamut of democracies is the B-level democracy, à la Eupsychia, where every individual is sacralized & irreducible, with multivalued (& ultimately transfinite & idiosyncratic) scales of value & of competence (rather than a single ladder of competence). "One man, one vote," equal political power of the voting-power sort, moving on finally toward the goal of brotherhood, family or team spirit = less & less use for political power, & more & more movement toward philosophical anarchism, with B-justice toward self & toward all others equally = functional power of the Blackfoot Indians in which a man was the leader by general agreement in just that *one* activity in which real competence is superior. But since there are *so* many areas of competence (so many scales of value, perhaps even an infinite number), self-esteem is possible for all, based on actual competence & achievement in *some* area of life. One can even sacralize oneself just for being a male or female as in the B-analysis appendix of the religion book [102] = basic, healthy, real self-esteem for anyone & everyone.)

Against this background, real generalized aggridance is still *also* a possibility (or reality?) as figure against ground. [*Summarize evidence for Terman-type general aggridance.*] That is, it's true but less important & not exclusively important. Also it is separable from self-satisfaction, smugness, & the feeling of having "deserved" it since: (1) It is in fact *not* deserved, & came only because of biological injustice. (2) Everybody is sacralized anyway. (3) If one doesn't deserve it, & it's luck & gratuitous grace, or "gratuitous responsibility that wasn't asked for or sought," then there is *noblesse-oblige* sense of duty & responsibility, of fatherly love & compassion for the less aggridant. (4) One is already metapaid, as others are not. (5) Lower pay is less important. (6) Simplicity à la Thoreau becomes more & more important. (7) Any society needs to *protect* aggridants against envy, the evil eye, & assassination, & to foster the feeling that they be loved & admired. Therefore they must get *less* pay, *less* power over others, *less* privileges than others & be *more* B-humble, more the servant of the people rather than the master. But they also must be more godlike, *both* stern & merciful, *both* maternally & paternally loving, both lovingly kind *and* just.

Thus Darwinian aggridance is compatible with democracy & doesn't necessarily mean fascism or pecking order or noncaring for the weak, or anything like that.

Also, if we were less afraid, wary, cautious about the aggridant, we would give him *more B-power,* not less; less interference & shackling; more decentralized freedom to do his thing, to manage, to do what he's good at, unleashed (= more metapay).

The Theory-Y boss is *non*controlling; the Theory-Z boss or manager or leader is even less so. Spell out. And yet this is all compatible with sternness, *real* justice, including firing (as in Steinmetz book), where just firing makes the man *better* off rather than worse off for various reasons, not to mention the upholding of justice, order, excellence in the world &

in the eyes of others, along with all the other B-values. Steinmetz is *partly* correct in his scorn for the weakness & "mother-hen" softness of the manager who's afraid to hurt, to fire, to criticize, etc. Theory Y or Z, I think, gives *better* bases for guiltless & compassionate stern-justice. Must also spell this out in OD, T-groups, etc. "No ecstasy without agony," à la Blanchard, *Psychology Today*, December '69; in same issue see article on the feminizing of boys by female teachers—this can be generalized.

January 21

Suggested by reading Amitzioni paper making a case that there *might* be basic needs & they *might* be testable (!). Those sociologists are really weird. Beautiful examples of scientistic stupidity—they're difficult to test; therefore they don't exist. Therefore the opposite is true—that everything must be & is learned, & is culturally relative! It's as if I were living in a totally different world of beliefs, assumptions, axioms. Same for the economists & the politics people—all assuming at the beginning a totally crappy theory of psychology! They're really antiscientific, antiempirical—they're really *a priori*, like some dogmatic religious groups & doctrinaires.

Also Donaldson reprint paper on growth-stopping & psychosomatic-illness effects of chronically suppressed anger. Also longevity-cutting. The point is that it's biologically & phsysiologically bad to be for a long time in a state of rage. But that's the state of emotion (& stress, vigilance, alertness, jumpiness, fatigue) in the jungle world, Theory-X world, neurotic world. Anybody reading his paper would *avoid* that state if he could.

It all goes back to the ultimate questions: What is the good (desirable) person? What is the good (desirable) society? And who says so? And on what grounds? And can you prove it? What are the goals of therapy, of education, politics, economics, family life, parents, philosophers, sociologists, etc.? But these are still moot & certainly argued over & disagreed with. At least as I present them, they purport to be plausible extrapolations from empirical & clinical work of all kinds. But these in turn are claimed to beg the question. And even the empirical work (e.g., NTL or OD or Esalen or Synanon) is all of it an unproved, premature (scientifically) leap of faith in the whole humanistic psychology. Also maybe even ethnocentric—would the Japanese or Hindus or Russians have evolved or "discovered" such a system?

So another methodological question occurs to me. Phrase it so: what are the ways of discounting or eliminating my personal beliefs or hopes from the whole system, in favor of checking by *other* people's judgments, or by the free choices, or by objective, quantifiable, public, manipulatable criteria & tests à la Kamiya? In the beginning of my work, e.g., with SA, this was impossible. It *was* wholly subjective, circular, a leap of faith. Now it's different; there are non-me data available to check the whole system at various points, e.g., Personal Orientation Inventory, motivation-data work, the effects of therapy, replications by others, its fruitfulness & usefulness for other people in *their* work, etc.

Bill Laughlin started the whole OD thing at Saga not for profits or the like, he says, but just because "that's the way people ought to live." How about Bill Crockett? Why is he devoting his life to OD work? I must ask him. American, religious, "liberal," man-of-good-will reasons? There are *some* data to support his belief, but mostly it's still a matter of faith, belief, taste, etc., namely, that "It's better for people to be honest & trusting with each other." But what does "better" mean here in objective, researchable terms? Or what does "ought" mean in Laughlin's statement? Or in the ones who started NTL work at Bethel? Sometimes it's easy philosophically, as for Chuck Dederich, who had a simple & unquestioned criterion: to cure drug addicts. Or even for Argyris when he asks how to increase interpersonal competence. I'm in the middle of Likert's new book, & I think that's the most impressive "scientifically" so far. I wish I could hire some Marxian critics, some tight-ass logicians & analytical philosopher's, some obsessional methodologists, some real skeptics like Frank Manuel, to go over all this system & all the data & try to tear it apart.

The mere fact that the higher levels & states exist doesn't prove that they are better. Nor even in itself does the fact that people yearn for them, strive for them, value them. Maybe not even the fact of free choice. That just proves the fact of preference, which is still different from "better or worse." (Must add up all the appetite data & all the wisdom of the body stuff & all my self-choice stuff & then show the generally good & desirable consequences, & *justify* the word "wisdom," which implies a norm, a criterion of value, of better & worse.) In the propositions book, I guess the beginning had better remain as is, essentially descriptive. But later in the book, all these philosophical, value & method & logic problems have to be wrestled with. The "higher" states of being need some kind of external validation. [*Beyond "feeling good" or "feeling bad." But isn't this also avoiding pain, which is universally accepted as valid?*] Add this to the meta-chapter? Maybe I've already done some of this in the Theory-Z paper [135], which will also be a chapter in the *Farther Reaches* book [144].

The other way about too: if I can prove that SA is an objectively desirable or better state, then this proves that intrinsic values (better & worse) can be found *in* human nature.

The jungle person—I pity him. Am I justified? Can I prove it? Maybe he'd pity me. Who's right? Same with music: I like Beethoven & he likes junk. How to prove it? Is one "better" than the other in objective ways?

January 31

I haven't dared even to myself to accept some of the thinking-thru of taking our own evolution upon our own shoulders. But I find myself secretly entertaining all sorts of "cold-blooded" possibilities, & now it's precipitated by the full acceptance that we must evolve ourselves, as we take over from nature & natural selection, & be just as neutral & unfeeling & nonanthropocentric as nature is. I think back to that day in Washington Square with the Manuels when I saw the drug users as performing a kind of biologically unselfish act, a sort of *noblesse oblige* for the good of the species & voluntarily killing themselves "for the good of the gene pool." And the private political thoughts I have (& millions of others must have secretly) about "It's better *not* to give foreign aid to any country that won't start birth control." Or the lurking thought that wars & famines are after all doing nature's work, that the world would be better off if half the people alive died. Or my reluctance to abolish capital punishment for those who would hurt the gene pool, or even those who would culturally hurt their children. Sooner or later, after the catastrophes force us to pace the overpopulation, we'll stop with all the crap about more food, or better strains of rice (which just *produce* more people). How can we give up on humanitarianism? But how can we *not* permit voluntary (or maybe involuntary) euthanasia & suicide? One day we'll have to talk about the exposure or killing of monster-babies, or even of healthy *surplus* babies. How about selective breeding? Who dares mention it? What shall we do with the frustrated maternal impulse? Perhaps a *real* reason for multiple families is so that 6 or 8 people could share the one precious baby! How could I do without Jeannie? What would my life have been without Ann & Ellen? But come to think of it, they *were* shared, & that was OK & even desirable for everyone.

How about facing the problem of cutting down India's population whether they agree or not, e.g., by medicating the water supply? How about paying for sterilization?

This all ties in with the aggridant question, which I don't yet dare bring up publicly except with aggridants. If aggridance really is a *general* superiority (all desirable traits correlate positively), what then? If these are genetically better & worse, what to do about it? Anything? The genetic forces are so weak that it might be better to do nothing at all until social injustice (inequal opportunity) is abolished. But *then* it will certainly have to come up. Meanwhile I can keep my thought to myself & do battlefield surgery, i.e., what energy I do have goes to the strong ones rather than to the weak (genetically). I do run a kind of natural selection with people, paying lots of attention to the promising ones & brushing off the losers, the incapables.

I think this is all OK & is *not* subject to the dangers of the circular reasoning of social Darwinism because (1) *everybody* is sacralized & can be seen unitively, & (2) we just can't yet define "fittest" or aggridant. *I* may personally rely on my judgment, but I don't care for other people to rely on *their* judgments, which would almost surely be screwed up with "family," class, caste, race, poverty, etc.

February 5

2 A.M. Not what people are, or have been, but what they *can* be—that is the psychology-3 question. Under a hierarchy of good conditions (defined in terms of the hierarchy of basic-need gratification, which in turn can be conditioned upon a hierarchy of good external conditions that make *possible* security, friendship, trust, generosity, etc.), there eventuates a hierarchy of better & better human beings.

Make the parallel with plants or dogs or horses or Negroes (compare 1970 with 1870). The history of what actually happened is not a very good criterion. It may be simply the record of how early human potentials can be destroyed.

Only under the very best conditions can one know how superior & tall & healthy a person can get. Same for *any* living thing. We know how awful people can be, & we know something about *how* they can be made awful (psychopathogenesis).

And yet we must build into this theory the ultimate limitations of the individual. My discussions yesterday of Carl Rogers, Ev Shostrom, Dick Katz, Viktor Frankl, Köhler, Asch, Gardner, Murphy—all at the top & yet all limited. Same for my list of most influential thinkers for *Life* magazine & for the Laughlin Fellowship—the top are far from perfect. (See Network-people file.) My recommendation had to be like what I worked out for the proposed Brandeis Institute of Advanced Studies—let each one be king of his own hill. So many prima donnas are unable to work *with* each other amicably & Taoistically. This king-of-the-hill stuff then raises a real question for OD: how possible is it for the top ones to get along together? How about under a boss? Ultimately, "good conditions" may have to be defined as being a boss & not *having* a boss. Well, how possible is that? All or most of the self-actualizing people were their own bosses. But there *can* be Taoistic bosses. I think I was a Taoistic chairman. But what did that cost me? I was certainly eager to be rid of the job.

I think the administrative proposals I made at Brandeis could work here too—any 2 men could give the M.A., any 3 men could give the Ph.D., & with no other criteria except their own personal taste or judgment. No veto power from anyone else. This is compatible with no departmental rules, no across-the-board requirements for all students. The thesis could be open to *anyone's* criticism, but the final decision would still be in the hands of the 3 signers. Then could use any number of autonomous kings of the hill, each with his own church. Let them run their own show, & still not require anybody to agree with anybody else. Then Rogers wouldn't have to agree with Frankl, etc.

February 25

Continue thinking as I drive thru Pleasanton area via Foothill Rd. We find it even *more* beautiful than we remembered it (& then it actually was during the Depression days & Okie days). Breath-taking. Exhilarating. New-born lambs playing, cute as hell. And then we pass the site of the old Hearst Ranch where that poor anguished woman committed suicide—in the *midst* of all that beauty! How is it possible? And in Berkeley we were reminded of poor Else Frenkel-Brunswik. *So* bright! So pleasant! Seeming to have so much fun. And then suicide! How does it possibly fit with my perception of the world as so beautiful & so precious & so full of Jeannies? Just the thought of Jeannie alone is enough to validate life & the world & everything social.

Again the only answer I could figure out was sort of Zoroastrian but with biochemical trimmings. It just couldn't be any other way. The suicide *must* be sick in some specific way that makes impossible zest, good impulse-voices, feedback from the good processes of life; e.g., it must vitiate the joy of plain eating, or fascination, or else there must be some definite evil & pain & depression producer. That is, the positives can be taken away & leave a zero, a kind of deChirico flat plain, a sort of depression, a nothing, an absence of pluses. And then, too, there may be definite minuses, like actual pain, remorse, guilt, self-loathing. The first I remember after that goddamn operation on my teeth & gums 6 months ago or so. I got *so* much anesthesia that for a whole day afterward I felt agitated in the way that Jack seems to be normally. I could enjoy nothing. Nothing attracted. Nothing was worthwhile. I couldn't read or sleep or eat or listen to music or chat or *anything*. All I could do was pace back & forth. What a life!

But then I remember the absolute negative misery of the postsurgical gall-bladder days, 3-4-5 of them, actual pain, nausea, tube in my throat, etc. All I could do was be stoic! But for how long could I stand that! Supposing I knew there were to be 5 years of it? OK. But supposing it could *never* be any different? Then I think I'd certainly want to die. In the just-zero life, at least I could help others & be useful. So no suicide. And pain & misery for a fixed period of time can be borne & endured against the ultimate relief, & then normal living, which is *so* precious that I could endure *years* of misery if I knew normal life would come at the end of it. But the suicide must be zero, plus miserable, plus no prospect of anything else at all ever. Only in that way can suicide make any sense.

So maybe, I thought, we must think of 2 *kinds* of people in this sense too, those who can enjoy & those who just can't. So maybe I'd better not judge the whole of mankind by Nevitt Sanford & Felsovanyi & others who love their work, or by Jeannie, for whom there is nothing *but* zest & fascination & fun. How can protesters be so resentful of life & of society, no matter how much injustice or exploitation there is in it? Even in the concentration camps, moments of beauty came with a butterfly.

Maybe I'd better be realistic about my reports in at least the sense that I admit they are the reports of a happy man (this was *such* a happy trip!) who loves his work & finds *enough* wonderful people & enough joys & beauties & hopes to want to protect the whole of life. That would be like reporting on the knower & the kind of spectacles he has on his nose. I wonder what would happen to my whole psychology & philosophy if *I* were in a concentration camp or were doomed to die soon. I don't think my report of the world would change much. I think I could recognize that I was seeing only the asshole of life. Why should I forget the rest of it that I wasn't seeing? As a matter of fact, I *am* doomed to die—maybe soon——what with the possibility of heart surgery. Or without collateral circulation, a heart attack would very likely kill me. So what does this have to do with my report on human nature? Might not one person, even with very bad luck, recognize the beauty of life for others than himself? Yes, I think so.

But this must all be included in the evil theory.

March 7

Last night, female party & discussion convinced me more than ever of instinctoid differences between female and male (à la Benedek, H. Deutsch, primate babies, human infants, etc.), *but* with a wide range of individual differences, especially in maternal feelings, *and* with a very heavy overlay of culturally relative, learned expectations. So that the whole theory *has* to be tied in with psychoanalysis as an uncovering technique, not only for discovering one's own inner, constitutional identity (one's "original nature"), but also as a scientific technique for getting the data. The usual scientific techniques, studying the surface, the habits, the defenses, etc., are not very useful, & may be useless altogether unless supplemented by "uncovering techniques." I found the best example to use last night to be the Benedek & Rubinstein book.

March 13

A.M. Awakened by angry thoughts. Grumbles theory with post-gratification forgetting helps us to understand the peculiar phenomenon of children of affluence, of indulgence, & of safety & security, the ones upon whom love was terribly centered—of just these getting aimlessly violent. The safety needs are of no importance to them because they have never been called into question. They are not afraid of chaos, fear, insecurity, because these were never experienced. They were just taken for granted. [*What's missing here is compassion, e.g., for elders, for the lower-middle class, for the uneducated. Supposing these kids could think of their enemies not with elitist contempt, but as if they were all relatives in trouble? Brothers behaving badly. "Neighborhood concept."*] I took hot water for granted until I went to Wisconsin at age 20 & learned that it didn't just flow out of a tap; it cost money & had to be paid for. This was a surprise, I remember. Well, why should it not have been? It came free without question, without effort, in the same way that air did. It just occurred to me—as I was going to write "air & water"—that *water* doesn't come free either, but we *can* take it for granted—we needn't notice it. If it stopped flowing, it would become precious, & my attitude forever after toward it would be different; i.e., it *might* be taken away.

So with the kids who've had it *given* to them without effort or work, as a right somehow, something not even rising into consciousness. *That's* one big difference between them & their parents.

And so they can play with violence & revolution, attack law & order & peace, call all authority into question without realizing that they're touching off in their elders (who still have a profound *need* for safety, security, peace, order, lawfulness) profound anxiety & counterantagonism, & the feeling that their roots being chopped at & the ground is shaking under them. This feeling is so widespread that no politician has a *chance* if he wobbles on law & order. And it's *still* possible, if an astute Napoleon or Huey Long came along who promised law & order, that political democracy might die. Only their stupidity has saved us from Joe McCarthy, General MacArthur, George Wallace, et al.

The kids can in principle be handled very easily. Firmness & justice would do it à la Hayakawa, but that's been missing in the intellectual community. So that's a basic question too. Why? I think I could by now put together a pretty good explanation for the weakness of the intellectuals before violence, decisiveness, determination. Lots & lots of notes & materials. But I doubt I'll ever do that.

I keep on fiighting off good ideas as if they were seducers & sticking only to what's most basic for essential, basic theory, & in the longer run. Mustn't deviate from my plans except where I can do something easily & quickly. Best thing I've done this year—besides all the thinking, notes, memoranda, & journal writing—was to revise *Motivation & Personality* [142]. *Very* satisfying feeling. Very pleased with it & myself. Best use of the time. Now, except for quick & small pieces, next best thing to do is to get on with *Farther Reaches* book [144] & keep on resisting temptations & seductions.

March 22

Exclaiming to B. about pluralistic democracy. In the B-psychology there is the *extreme* of individual differences, i.e., idiosyncrasy, the sacralizing of the single person, a kind of transfinite pluralism of transfinite individuals. (This is stronger & more extreme than the "cultural pluralism" of ethnic groups, sexes, generations, castes, & classes, since these are all *groups* rather than idiosyncratic individuals.)

This implies an infinity of "ways of life" or "styles of life" from among which to choose in accordance with one's own bent—destiny interacting with an SA-fostering culture & *its* opportunities. It includes the philosophy of each person "doing his own thing" with as much let-be & noninterference (Taoistic) as possible = permission for eccentricity, for "characters," for (French) "type." All of which, of course, implies the whole apparatus of finding one's own personal identity, of therapy as uncovering, of vocational guidance of the meta-type, of values-counseling, etc. But must make sure to avoid the exclusive stress on identity, on SA, on privacy, etc., because there are also weak, incapable, dependent, helpless people who would be merely frightened by autonomy; also feed in here sociability, groupiness, the ones whose personal bent is toward being in groups & teams rather than alone. Or as with the choices set before females, which ought also to be pluralistic, it ought to be OK *either* to achieve outside the home or *not* to. To be maternal, esthetic, interpersonal, family-centered, as, e. g., B. is, or Edith Tannenbaum. To do the home & family & extensions of family among friends (as last night having the Leavitts over for dinner) all as works of art, of elegance, taste, & enjoying & enriching the friendships = supplying a modern, "portable roots," nonforced, nonconventional *choice* of one's "extended family & community & friends" = *not* like the extended Italian family, which is compulsory & gives safety, security, roots, ties, *but* at the cost of personal growth & at the cost of *so* much time required that achievement becomes difficult &, for the female, impossible.

All this leads in to the discussion of the kinds of cultures & subcultures & small groups & communities & communes, which are all then defined in terms of their usefulness in fostering basic-need gratifications, SA, & transcendence of self. But clearly, if we take individual differences (better call them "idiosyncratic differences" = better stress on single person rather than groups) *really* seriously, then society must be very pluralistic, a smorgasbord of *many* kinds of life from which to choose in accordance with one's own bent & taste, & finally in accordance with the joint tastes of one's family, one's love-identifications = the Taoistic society, to stress the let-be, the nonintrusive, the noncontrolling. This can range all the way from the hermit, all alone in his cave, to the herd of cattle, the group of puppies, the gangs of children.

Since society is then seen primarily as a *satisfier* of personal needs,

& is judged primarily by how successful it is in *this* job of personal fulfillment for all, *then* we can go on from there to deal with the inevitable losses of freedom & autonomy that we have to pay to society in return for the far greater blessings it gives us. How to maximize personal SA while minimizing social costs? What *psychological* taxes do we—must we—pay to others & to society in general, to the earth, to nature, the cosmos? (E. g., for ecological reasons, we should now restrict having babies, which would be for many a tremendous personal loss.) What *must* it cost to love a wife, a child, a parent, a friend? What responsibilities, controls, loyalties, unselfishnesses, sacrifices do I commit myself to when I make a friend or have a child? Point out the "rules" by which the society or the group or the commune or the family agrees to function together which don't cost *anything*, or almost nothing, e. g., traffic rules, chess rules, noise rules, privacy rules, rules at meals, etc. These have little or nothing to do with the freedom of the person—or *shouldn't* anyhow. One must be very suspicious about the mental health of any person, even a youngster, who makes a big issue of such working rules. For one thing, if he doesn't like the rules of a group, he can secede from it—or should be expelled to go seek some other, more compatible group. For another thing, such turmoil is often either neurotic or else dominating, or at least tries to dominate others, which of course violates the basic social philosophy of personal autonomy & freedom. Even for children, such freedom of choice of rules is more possible than our nuclear-family-society allows, e. g., Kibbutz style, Blackfoot style, extended-family style, in which a child is free to go to his aunt or the neighbor when angry with his parents.

The question is then one of strategy & tactics of politics, of how to combine autonomy *with* the blessings of community & society & *with* the personal responsibilities of love, loyalty, commitment, & "B-sacrifice" (which one *enjoys,* & with which he is fulfilling himself, à la Harry Golden, *thru* his children, friends, leaders, etc.). If the goals of the society or group are clear, then these problems are only means-problems, at the politics-1 level of homeostatics.

Reminds me that I've been insisting on calling myself "revolutionary" & denying the term to the destroyers, the clowns, the haters, & the death-wishers. Use the phrase "constructive revolutionary," contrasting with "destructive"? Or build constructivism into the definition of the humanistic revolutionary? Or talk of the effective revolutionary vs. the ineffective revolutionary? *Or:* of the feedback people vs. the *a priori* people? The feedback revolutionary (empirical, scientific-3, pragmatic) vs. the doctrinaire revolutionary (*a priori* dogma, unchangeable principles, closedness to new data)?

All of this leads to some redefinitions of "crime." Most crimes are now obvious, but there will also be new crimes against humanism, autonomy, against the basic needs, e. g., destroying of basic trust, of shaking one's faith in authority by breeding paranoid suspicion-secrecy-down-leveling, of being antilife in general, of dominating, of being non-Taoistic, controlling, manipulating, dishonest. Even, perhaps, of being immature, neurotic, antirational. Certainly the question of violence will come up. When is it criminal & when not? Supposing you make people feel unsafe or insecure. What rights do elders have *against* youngsters—as well as the other way around? Useful example: since, as I believe, female-male differences are instinctoid, what rights do females & males have *against* each other when their natures conflict (which they must often)?

  If all this is the Taoistic, pluralistic, idiosyncratic, humanness-fulfilling democracy, *then* come the questions about the tactics of dealing with those who are incapable of living up to such a society, e.g., XYY people, feebleminded, schizophrenics, etc. Should they be disenfranchised? What would be done with them *within* a loving family? Perhaps that gives most of the answers. Add in the major implications of *loving* authority, of love for the elders so that they are trusted, their advice followed, even their *orders* followed, since B-love is not called into question, any more than when I trust my doctor or nurse & "obey" them. As a matter of fact, there ought to be a chapter on obedience. *When* is it needed? How often? Also the self-control & Apollonian controls that come out of our good feelings for others: affection, trust, respect, loyalty. How shall we relate to an eccentric, senile elder, to a schizoid relative, to a dying father who was a bastard all his life?

March 25

  Nice arrogant joke I thought about last night. "I've never understood economics, so I created one that I could understand." But it's also serious; maybe what I couldn't understand was the assumption of lack of brotherhood, the assumption that one necessarily used superiority for domination & exploitation. Maybe I was a socialist for these reasons. I gave it up because our Flatbush Ave. co-op lost money even with all our volunteer labor. But I think, in retrospect, we just had a lousy & inefficient manager, even with his good will. So I've come to appreciate the good entrepreneurs, managers, & businessmen, & efficiency & competence (rather than just good will & nice *a priori* doctrines). But my version of socialism + free choice + competition + etc. is acceptable. Then also, at that time, Stalin & the Communist Party taught me that socialism could be tyrannous & that it *had* to go with political democracy. But that means free choice & equality of opportunity, & *that* means inevitably an elite of the Jeffersonian sort. So you *still have* to face the problems of how the elite relates to the nonelite—& then you *have* to talk about brotherly love, etc. So both socialism & democracy & efficiency all merge finally into Agapean, realistic, pragmatic, specieswide free choice, equality of opportunity, Agapean love, Taoistic let-be, Bodhisattva helping, metamotivated, competitive (for the sake of free choice, of feedback, of empiricism, of discovering which is most efficient & capable, etc.). Also have to add the unitive B- & D-realm difference & its consequences for, e.g., self-esteem & esteem for others, etc. Should all of *this* go into the meta-epilogue too? I could wind up with a brief statement of all the axioms that will form the politics-3 book, i.e., all my basic propositions.

March 26

I don't remember where I wrote the stuff on tears before the surf at Big Sur & Carmel as partly due to intimations of mortality (death file?), but now I think that's only part of it (tho a *real* part of it). I've been writing in my back yard in the sun, facing the bougainvillea vines, & with birds on it & twittering all over the place, & it's snowing in the Midwest, & everything has been going so beautifully (reading Ann's letter to *Psychology Today* helped too), & it all adds up to the edge of tears. But it's from the piling-up of sheer beauty & the good luck of it all. They're really esthetic tears too. And then I'm reminded of tears after sex. What would that be called? Sheer ecstasy & joy? Or rather *aftermath* of? Relief from? Letting go of all the one-pointedness, & the building up of a total, integrated oneness of the whole organism? It's certainly been *called* death & rebirth, "the little death." But I think we have to add to that the fact that sheer beauty is too great to be borne. It's just "too much." More than we can assimilate or comprehend. It goes beyond our powers & is more than we can manage & control. Maybe the tears are the happy giving-up of control? Of will? A sign of happy helplessness? Maybe, also, the element of disbelief & of miracle (it's just too much; it couldn't be so; it can't be real!). Maybe it's a piling-up upon a piling-up upon a piling-up—just now across the face of all this unbelievable beauty a butterfly flies by! Just as at Esalen once, when everything was already too much as I walked up from the massage & the baths, looking at the sea, just then a hummingbird flits in front of my nose—& broke the camel's back! That was too much! So to the edge of tears. Maybe that's a signal that the organism has had more happiness & beauty & miracle than it can calmly & integratedly accept, & then this is ecstatic disorganization?

I suppose there's also something isomorphic about the whole thing. I've certainly been feeling happy & lucky & graced. And it's certainly true, as last night driving home when I realized, *yes*, I'd had such a good evening, but then everything instructs me & fascinates me & cheers me. But is this really altogether so? I wonder if all the beautiful surroundings & freedom, etc., are not very helpful in building me up to this pitch? Maybe even *sine qua non?* Could I manage it in the slums? In an apartment with cockroaches? If I had a lousy job or a lousy boss? No, I think the beautiful environment lifts *me* to the B-level. Anyway partly. Or at least, a more beautiful world *helps* my innate tendency to enjoy. I think I *could* enjoy life in a slum apartment, roaches and all, but maybe less frequently & less intensely. But question: why do I *select* this beautiful environment, & why do others *select* the roaches & the garbage cans of the East Village? Some choose what is *not* voluntary poverty & simplicity à la Thoreau, as I've said. Thoreau would never have dreamed of living there. Never! Choosing *dirt* & the underbelly of poverty, almost in a masochistic way. It's like choosing friends (it *is* a choice). If you choose jerky friends, then why? Why not choose really good friends? Why did I have such good teachers in N. Y. C.? I sought them out! They were my choice. It was not an accident. In a very real sense, I deserve credit for my wonderful teachers in N. Y. C. (at the University of Wisconsin less so; I had to take whatever I could get, whoever was there).

Why did I bust out bawling uncontrollably when I was telling someone about how wonderful Jeannie is, & Ann is, & Jerry, & how she sent him flowers for helping at the birth? In this same sense it was just *too* much, too right, & too miraculous. And it got to me also that somehow I had helped to bring it all about, thru the peak-experiences stuff, & Debby Tanzer's thesis, which probably convinced Ann & Jerry about natural childbirth, which helped to give me that lovable baby, etc., etc. The mystery & wonder & miracle & sheer good luck & fortuitiveness of it all, along with the paradoxical mystery that somehow I had *helped* to bring it all about! & so on!

Is this all one explanation for the easier tears of older people? But there are many other possible explanations too—weaker autonomic nervous system; weaker controls & defenses; self-pity because of approaching death; imminent death producing tension between observing the eternal & realizing one's temporariness, so that everything becomes doubly precious; increasing freedom from cultural disapproval of weeping (a dying man can certainly tell the conventions to fuck themselves), etc.

March 28

Bright idea yesterday: if our mortality produces in us appreciation, gratitude, unitive perception, feeling of good luck, B-cognitions, plateau-experiences, etc., then it struck me, as some kids went by gaily, they don't feel mortal. Subjectively, kids are immortal. But this can help to explain the generation gap. We say of the kids, & I remember about myself, that they are really selfish about their parents & elders, ungrateful, not fully aware of their parents as ends, only as means & as suppliers; they don't count their blessings & aren't even aware of them often. Whatever is *now* is taken for granted as not being in question, as being *always* there, immortal as is without past or future. It just *is*. Doesn't really have a history. (Do we appreciate time, becoming-being-dying sequences, because we are aware of death?) This gives nonmortal ones a certain smugness. They will *always* be able to run & climb & jump & stay up all night. They will never be sick or get rheumatism or have operations. Those are peculiar weaknesses of "those others," who then become a nuisance. So that kids are not "sympathetic" to the mothers with migraines. Or as I was not to my father's foot. I *behaved* well, but I didn't really *feel* anything; I couldn't identify with him in his pain. Does this also help explain youngsters' impatience & demand for perfection? I. e., they are not compassionate about elderly weaknesses & shortcomings, can't identify with them, so no "pity." They don't have empathy & can't intuit the inner feelings that they have not themselves ever experienced. Does that have to do with nonmortality, or is it just the general product of the lack of these experiences?

The ones who have made their peace with mortality give up competition. (I *still* wonder that maybe what I've called SA has reconciliation with mortality as a *sine qua non*.) Maybe also their pity & compassion for themselves as dying creatures make them able to pity others? Maybe it is also that frustration & deprivation themselves, by producing subjective consciousness of blessings that have been taken away (deprivation *creates* awareness?), thereby enlarge, enrich, & expand the consciousness of others & of the world. Therefore, to the extent that death is a depriver, it *produces* the enlarged awareness of many things otherwise not perceived, as well as helping to produce sympathy, compassion, pity, identification with others, empathy, intuition & understanding of others. [*Death-exercises for the enrichment, expansion, & heightening of awareness? Relate to LSD, postsurgical illuminations, peaks.*] Also, since my awareness on the beach of the contrast between *its* permanence & my mortality produced such an intense feeling of the preciousness & beauty of what I was looking at, maybe death helps to create the feeling of sacralization = unitive consciousness, plateaus, peaks (both sunny ones & clouded ones), of archetypical, symbolic, eternal, transcendent experiences. Kids can't do this; they are still positivists perceiving only what their (external?) senses can bring them. Does death-awareness *produce* the transcendent, transpersonal, transhuman?

There's another step in here someplace. Why is basic-need gratification such a catastrophe for many? As if *only* striving for something needed was living. As if they didn't know what to do with themselves once the basic needs are gratified & the D-striving stops. Why don't they *automatically* rise to seeking the B-values? Why is it so hard to be wealthy & to have surplus in this realm? It must be partly the *habit* of defining life, pleasure, & happiness in the only terms we've known, i.e., scarcity. Just as it was a small tragedy for me, a grief & a loss, to give up looking for bargains in second-hand bookstores & to just order full-price whatever I needed or wanted. Now I've gotten used to that & enjoy being able to order at once whatever I want. But that "working through" took years. (Is that why the Rockefellers & Fords, etc., use their wealth so well? Because they don't have the habits of scarcity? We were wondering what we could learn from them about bringing up kids well.)

Thought: how does this all relate to B-love? From the above, this should have something to do with mortality-feeling, witnessing the eternal. Well, kids certainly do this less well than later on in their lives. D-love is certainly partly gratitude, appreciating, feeling of (undeserved) good luck, & all the rest above. Think this through including the B-exercises, unitive exercises, sacralizing exercises, etc. They probably would automatically help toward B-love.

March 31

The whole question of the aggridant, strong-weak, & a lot of other things has to do with the politics-3 book in the sense that weakness has negative survival value, while strength or aggridance has positive survival value; i.e., they are the "fittest" in both biological & social ways. [Add to politics-3 book: the scientific community as our nearest approach to a Eupsychia. See Eupsychia file & various science files.] I saw a TV program on an Odyssey House in N. Y. C. for juvenile drug addicts, with an M. D. complaining of no money from the city. Could this be due partly to unconscious "battlefield surgery"? Let them die because there are biological advantages in it? Better that the limited money should be used for the healthier, the "fittest," rather than to save the death-wishers from their own "suicidal impulses"?

I remember 3 or 4 years ago, with the Manuels in Washington Square Park, the insight emerging as we walked among all the hippie kids & their drug "culture" that this was after all a culling-out of the "unfit," just as a hard, impersonal nature does for older, weaker, crippled prey who are the ones the predators live on, or like the least-dominant rats who succumb first to famine while the Alphas survive exactly the same hardship. (Instead of this "survival of the fittest" vocabulary, which is circular & begs the question of defining "fittest," use simply the question: "Under conditions that threaten survival, who is most likely to survive & who is least likely?" This is a scientific, researchable phrasing, putting stress on biological essence rather than on cultural epiphenomena.) I remember becoming conscious for the first time of feeling, like a judge, "Well, that will improve the gene pool." Perhaps there are advantages in letting them die from their own folly. Perhaps even this could be seen coming out of the depths of their unconscious, as a form of noblesse oblige, like saying: "I am made of poor stuff. It's better for mankind if I die. Therefore, I will sacrifice myself for the good of mankind. Better I should die than that worthier ones should." A form of movie-like heroism, like the man on the life raft who lets himself drown so that the others can more likely live. Or like the Eskimo grandmother in times of famine, who exposes herself to death so the children can have more food, etc. A form of voluntary self-euthanasia, as I might for instance kill myself if I knew I were going into a long senile psychosis which would impoverish my whole family to no good end. I recognized, also consciously, this same general attitude toward suicides: "Well, maybe they knew best. Maybe it's better for them & for everybody else too." *Along* with this, the simultaneous, rational recognition contradicting this, that suicidal impulse is often just a passing mood of perfectly fit people who should be prevented from acting on this transient impulse & who can then be wonderful people, even self-actualizing like Lincoln, Wm. James, Ruth Benedict & others who transcended depression. It was the same rational recognition I had even for drug & alcohol addicts; I learned from Synanon that, if they can be saved, they can turn out fine. If I ever say this in public, I'd have to stress that, if I were in charge, I'd permit any overt or covert form of voluntary self-euthanasia *only* with agreement of a·Board of Others; i.e., the death-wisher's own unconscious judgment is *not* a good prediction of his later worth to society, or even a good diagnosis of whether he is now or will be weak or strong in the biological sense. Especially for youngsters, who might possibly be damaging the gene pool in *fact*, would I not leave it to their own immature & ignorant judgment, but would demand agreement from a Board of Human Geneticists, & even then might permit only self-sterilization rather than suicide. Suicide is OK when the social costs of one's staying alive to *others* are just too great. When would *I*, being brotherly, fraternal, Agapean, etc., decide that *I* should commit suicide? Or *should* have in the past? It's funny that, tho I was a depressed youngster, really unhappy, alienated, or at least feeling alone & unloved & unwanted, & later in life going thru a period of *conscious* depression, I have never in my whole life experienced a suicidal impulse(?). What does this mean? Even if I *had* had such an impulse, I *should* have been prevented from carrying it out, since I've turned out well. (But what with proneness to coronary attacks & diabetes in the family line, maybe I would have been forbidden to have children in a Eupsychia with zero population growth?)

The whole predator-prey model which Bob Ardrey is writing about certainly has truths in it which are being repressed & suppressed, & yet the model just *cannot* be carried over from animals to men. That's the point: perhaps because of our refusal to face all this consciously, & because of repression leading to defenses, we are unconsciously using the predator-prey, strong-weak, alpha-zeta model in a neurotic, irrational way, when we should *not* be using it altogether.

Maybe that's a good reason for going ahead publicly with my aggridant theory, which I've been keeping secret because it can be used as a rationale for social Darwinism, i.e., survival not of the biologically fittest, but rather of the socially privileged.

Anyway it *is* also relevant to question & contradict the statement of the M.D. "treating" young drug addicts, that this is a "disease" rather than a crime, with her assumption that it was *entirely* the fault of society, like typhoid, & could be totally prevented & completely cured &, in effect, had nothing to do with genetics. Maybe yes & maybe no. My own guess is that it *is* a "disease" (or, better, a necessary symptom) of nonaggridance, i.e., of biological weakness. Same for alcoholism, which also may be a sign of across-the-board (across-the-chromosomes?) genetic weakness, i.e., poorer biological stuff. Anyway this shouldn't be ruled out, or swept under the rug, or suppressed.

If there is anything to my suspicion that aggridance may be a general, biological, holistic, across-the-chromosomes superiority (as in Dove's experiment), i.e., that all biological desiderata & superiorities are *positively* correlated, as in Terman's study, then we'd better accept the fact that some "diseases" are *not* diseases as contagions are, i.e., not a passing accident which, like getting killed by lightning strokes, has practically nothing to do with genetic "fitness." These *are* "diseases" of general biological weakness. Social policy is another story; maybe in some instances we *should* permit newborn monsters or Mongoloids, or gene-pool worseners to be killed—as in fact many of them are unofficially by parents & physicians. (That's a good point to stress: there certainly is euthanasia, if only in the sense of working less hard to keep alive the terminal cases, the senile, the dilapidated schizophrenics, etc. You can permit someone you love to die out of love, or, even, if he begs enough, help him along. Bertha & I have made such a pact, & I'm sure this must be very common. But because this is illegal & must be kept secret, it may be very inefficient & sometimes a mistake. Here, too, publicity & confrontation would be better. *Cultures* also repress, deny, have reaction-formations, etc.)

All of this will be *doubly* true when we have to go to zero growth or even cut back the population. We'll *have* to have some choice criteria. It would be stupid to choose by flipping coins, i.e., by chance. I guess this has to be a problem to face right now if we anticipate a Eupsychian one-world, because it's absolutely certain that we'll then have to choose who will live & who die, who will be a parent & who not.

It's strange, but that will amount to bringing back, voluntarily & consciously, the equivalent of nature's animal model of predator & prey, of survival of the fittest in the animal sense. Strength, health, SA, maturity, personal evolvement will then have—in *addition* to their growth values & experiential values (better conscious life, more fun, etc.)—sheer survival value, sheer viability. Which in turn adds up to a really strong approach to my effort to demonstrate the external as well as internal & intrinsic validation of "higher states" of personal growth. (See file on levels-validation.)

Also, if this first were true,—that drug addiction is ultimately the *noblesse oblige* of voluntarily resigning one's commission—or to the extent that it *is* true, then our proper attitude toward it is more Taoistic, letting-it-be, noninterfering, permitting people to decide for themselves. I think this is what is unconsciously & semiconsciously going on anyway. (If they want to kill themselves, let them. Maybe it's all for the best.) Certainly there *is* a political attitude, easily seen & rarely openly stated by, e.g., the Goldwater types & the social Darwinists. In the politics-3 book this *has* to be faced. To what extent are they right? Maybe we'd better add to the notion of the sacredness of every individual the sacredness of the species, i.e., of the gene pool, & then, for political purposes, integrate the two concepts rather than half-unconsciously letting either of these principles become absolutes.

If politics 3 is a politics of specieshood, i.e., of Agapean love or at least of brotherly responsibility, then it is certain that we must talk of suicide for the sake of others, & of euthanasia too. Of self-sacrifice.

Come to think of it: involved in this whole mess of associations was also my thinking about the Negroes yesterday in a discussion with Mrs. Harvey of the Wright Institute, all confused à la liberal about the Black Panthers, etc. What finally convinced her was the survival argument; i.e., these may be death-wishers or death-acceptors, voluntary suicides, but it's worse that they are also lousy generals. Not only will *they* die, but they will drag along with them thousands of others. They threaten not only their own survival, but also that of the group they're trying to lead over the edge of the cliff into civil war, which could be only a slaughter if it ever really got going. The Jews (& also the Negroes up until recently) survived, in contrast to the Indians, who didn't, by *not* using force when they couldn't do it usefully, by *not* fighting back, until the moment came when they could fight back effectively, i.e., shrewd fighting back. Even then it could be pointed out, with the Israelis who fought back so well, that they get arrogant rather than magnanimous (as they *were* with the Germans) & are now placing the whole country in real jeopardy & threatening their very survival. Successful violence, even when absolutely necessary, breeds its own dangers & outsmarts itself.

[3/31/70: *Bet. It's better for Israel to make real peace with the Palestinians by paying them off & even restoring their land to them when & where this can be done & then buying it back if necessary. Also by announcing an offered peace-settlement package deal which gives back occupied territories, most of it to the Arabs, little strategic pieces to the UN, or offers equivalent land someplace else instead, or offers to pay for it. My bet is: sooner or later they'll do all of these, either voluntarily or involuntarily.*]

April 7

Useful for crystallizing my ideas about the essential harmfulness of the repudiation forever of power, control, etc., is an article about the *New York Review of Books:* "A Close Look," by Eugene Goodheart in *Dissent,* March 1970 (in garage file & marginal notes). He overlooks the meanness & nastiness of the magazine (itself one of the weaknesses of "weak liberalism"), & also he overlooks the general sickness of the anti-U.S. stance (like the statement I saw in a liberal journal recently, summarizing the horrors of war "from Hiroshima to My Lai" & overlooking "from Pearl Harbor to Hue"). But he does raise useful questions about the fashionableness of the New Left in the *N. Y. Review of Books* & their tolerance toward the fascism of the radicals of the New Left. (The most searching statement I've ever seen of the Marxian dilemmas on means & ends, of ideology as class-produced only, of the rejection of objectivity & of scholarship, of seeing the whole political, judicial, social apparatus as merely an exploiting-class tool, etc., is still Polanyi's "Notes on the Hungarian Revolution." Use it.)

Main theoretical question is: is it *possible,* or desirable, to remain permanently out of power, & to renounce power, because one considers it intrinsically evil & therefore is repelled by it as by a disease that one wouldn't want? Is the role of the critic (solely, merely, permanently, totally) a good or useful thing to have in the society? Same for the permanent revolutionary? Years ago I would have accepted the usefulness of the permanent opposition, of the permanent critic like Voltaire. But now I don't think I could, at least where it's possible to get power to take control & leadership. Such a critic forever renounces participation & experience, along with its feedback, its learning, & therefore its increasing pragmatic effectiveness & realism & success-in-the-world. (Like the priest who is also a marriage counselor.) Use the example from Synanon: only experiencers can understand fully, can help, can cure. Tie this in also with my conception of the B-monster, the evil perfectionist, who can *neither* be satisfied ever with what is, *nor* do anything to make it better. This derives directly from psychology 3 as experiential. Experiential knowledge must be different from & less than spectator knowledge (& in this case I'd add "critic knowledge," opposition knowledge, knowledge by enmity). Refusing the experience of power, of responsibility, means forever remaining adolescent & immature. Not really competent, not *able* to take control or responsibility = not *able* to construct or achieve. It stops growth toward SA, maturity, humanness, which after all include competence (no solid self-esteem without competence & effectiveness).

April 18

Can use sex machines as a very blunt confrontation of the love-sex principle. It's clear that a vaginal-sized vibrator is physically better than any human penis could ever be. Also clear that it's easily possible to manufacture to anyone's prescription, for personal tastes, a female sex doll which could physically be "better" than any conceivable human female, e.g., vibration, pulsation, squeezing & relaxing, "milking," with temperature variations & anything else desired. Like Philip Wylie's *The Disappearance*.

Now the question is: who would prefer the mechanical contraptions, machines, & dolls, & who would prefer a person? Clear operational differences between merely sex & sex-love, or maybe better call it person-love.

April 19

Got into big uproar at conference over preface to my religion book [102]. Critical of astrology, Tarot, numerology, & I-Ching as having no evidence. Jim Fadiman objected, saying there *is* evidence. Also Grof, Katz, Weil, & others. Farthest-out group in the country. Finally agreed to speak only of "fads & cults" without specifying, even tho I feel their "evidence" didn't amount to much. Half because I didn't want to offend my friends & half because I wanted to hurry on to talk of the plateau-experience. Now I think I should have stuck to my guns, even tho it doesn't matter very much. No, it *does* matter. I still hate to lose friends. Next time the matter comes up, I'll say my say—only I'll do it more carefully, & take whatever time is necessary. *These* people may want to leave the door open, & accept doubtful evidence, but meanwhile the world gets flooded with crap. I guess now it is my duty to make a serious statement next chance I get, talking to the intelligent persons, instead of a casual *en passant* reference.

I agree that it's best not to close doors & to deny the possibility of anything, & to keep all possibilities open, to "entertain" them in one's mind. That's freedom of research & openness to consider *any* possibility, instead of being *a priori* about it. And yet, if the "evidence" is so thin & doubtful, & even better explained in other ways, I should say that too.

April 21

More learning from Jeannie, who's cuter than ever & no signs of evil this time. Nobody to be rivalrous with? Much more accepting of me this time. Still very "reasonable," i.e., good frustration tolerance & quick ending of crying when, e.g., taken out of bathtub against her will. No sulkiness, no whining, almost no anger. *Always* cheerful & frequently totally merry, except upon waking up, which takes her awhile to achieve. Even then she's not whiny, only dazed & sleepy.

The thing I saw this time that I would add to the B-values is the total openness & innocence with which she turned & stared at me while on my lap. *Total* trust. Totally unleashed & unguarded. Absolutely nothing withheld. This totality, also of expression, of happiness or anger, or of looking, suddenly gave me the sense of ultimate "completion," finality, completeness, & total giving over, of 100 percentness. The B-value of completion needs more working out, but this is certainly part of it. She is totally unleashed; there is no shackling, no hindrance, no set, no brakes or inhibitions. She is totally her real self. No dissociation into a persona, into shoulds or oughts or ought-nots, into a sick self & healthy self. She is all of a piece, one peice. She is just *one* thing, not split into different kinds of pieces (which is B-oneness, B-simplicity). But the B-completion & finality also = B- perfection & excellence. It occurs to me also that B-humor is also involved in all this perfection & completeness & oneness. Is she "cute," amusing, delightful, laughable, smile-making (B-humor) because she also exemplifies all these other B-values? Our highest response to great beauty, truth, etc., is to laugh with delight. Better call it by some special name to differentiate it from lesser laughters: B-laughter? It's a kind of ultimate delight-exultation-exaltation-disbelief-etc. Look up Nietzsche on this.

But she herself is also merry much of the time (should be a "higher" word for this). So she both is a stimulus to B-humor & also responds with it, with pure easy-state amusement ranging on up to delight & laughter.

So again I wind up with Jeannie being the pure B-values, exemplifying them all. No wonder she is lovable. And also no wonder she produces peaks & plateaus, both serene ones & teary ones (the ones which contrast your own temporality & mortality with the eternalness of what you are looking at). But this too can be generalized in another way; i.e., the B-values *are* eternal, sacred, mysterious, awesome. Maybe when we respond with peaks of any kind or plateaus of any kind, it's always (?) a response to the eternalness, perfection, beauty, i.e., B-values, of whatever sets us off?

But why do I respond so much more strongly to Jeannie, & as I did also with my own babies, than to *any* other babies, however lovable?

There seems to be also an element of "getting hooked" or imprinted or addicted. What does that mean? It's certainly not "one's own blood," etc., because adopted babies get just as B-loved as one's own. It's just repetition, familiarization, habituation, getting used to, etc. (This is the extremest example of "preference thru familiarization"! Why didn't I think of that when I wrote up the experiment?)

Just noticed another "reminder of the eternal." Jeannie has discovered for *herself* what every baby independently discovers as a game —the fun of walking in her mother's shoes. It's like watching instincts—& getting awed. But this is only one example among many. Not only is it cute to watch the infant & baby rediscover instincts & universal games (peak-a-boo, getting tossed in the air by Daddy), but also this is all eternal, evolutionary, biological, & one thinks of the species within the baby. I guess this must be part of the sense of the miraculous we get from babies—just as we stand goggle-eyed before chicks breaking out of the egg, or before *any* instinct. The ethological literature, & also, I remember now, my course in embryology, produced this sense of the eternal, like watching the surf. But the baby is far more purely instinctoid & far less acculturated than the adult. So that in the baby we see the essence far more than we do in the adult, where we see mostly accidentals & localisms & habits & folkways. It's as if the baby were more *real*, more truly human in the biological sense anyway, or at least more undisguisedly human. I think Horney's real-self idea fits here.

April 26

Columbus, Ohio. In the various talks I made about evil, some good phrasings came up. In the first place, it's become more & more clear to me that my theory of evil is needed to combat the perfectionism & impatience & unrealism, mostly of the young, but also of the "inexperienced" intellectual, *a priori* doctrinaire, & "idealist." At least that's what impelled me to the task. Also the helplessness of the "liberals" & of *most* people in the face of naked evil & force. This is a basic weakness in "humanistic psychology" as well & in the Eupsychian network. Just as in McGregor's stuff, there's no systematic place in Theory Y for bastards & sick people & for just plain normal human foolishness, mistakes, stupidity, dopiness, cowardliness, laziness, etc.

One way I said it—as with Harold [Maslow] when he came to visit, as he complained that most of the problems of UCC [Universal

Container Corporation] were bad choices of key personnel who then made some awful mistakes—was that this is what you must expect from fallible human beings, & that *not* getting it is the miracle of good luck. *"Everybody is a nut"* (as well as also saying that everybody has good impulses & metamotivations). Mostly you have to settle for *"pretty* good" or "fair," or half-good/half-bad, whether in business, or science, or marriage, or friends. And yet this is all compatible with the highest metamotivation. But they are aspirations only occasionally reached in most people under good conditions. And yet it's all compatible with liking the human species & having good hopes for it (under good conditions).

Human evils, both experienced & emitted, come not so much from innate depravity or *impulse* to do evil as from ignorance, foolishness, the "stupidity" of the child & of immaturity; i.e., they are mistakes rather than deliberate, willed, & chosen, & are followed by remorse, rejection, or repression rather than by gloating, happiness, or satisfaction with oneself.

I pointed out to the psychiatric residents, to sum it up, that we should change our picture of the devil from a cold, cruel man with a pain-producing pitchfork to a schnook or schlemiel stumbling down the stairs or ineptly falling into a hole or being clumsy & busting things in spite of his good intentions.

Call it overoptimism about human nature, or at least overexpectations about the good effects of being benign, as if this were the *only* way to improve human nature. Was this partly a reaction against the harshness & stubbornness of Freud? Maybe it's one aspect of the *dichotomizing* of psychology 3 against & from psychoanalysis, instead of filling it out, integrating with it, being epi-Freudian rather than anti-Freudian. It's no accident that Bettelheim & one or two other analysts are refusing to become juvenile-worshipers & to take their crap. When I was asked about SA in young people, I reported it to be impossible, if only because of ambivalence toward authority, & other things I put into the preface of the *Motivation and Personality* revision [142].

This attitude fits with the Taoistic way, which requires that we not intrude on children, but also *demands* that we defend *ourselves* against intrusion. Ann made this point—that a great problem with parents of children was their guilt over saying "no," over refusing their children anything. As if total permissiveness, unconditional acceptance of *all* crap, total need-gratifying, masochism, & self-abrogation were the right thing to do. As if this were the definition of love. But where did such a crazy notion come from?

April 28

Basic stress on holism as an axiom in growth-politics—moving toward holism, avoiding splitting, more including, less amity-via-enmity splitting = compassion-respect-responsibility rather than elitism-supe-riority demand for obedience. Good examples in *The Free You*, reporting on violence vs. nonviolence, radicalism & anti-ROTC. Makes no differ-ence about faculty or student votes. Radicals here must have *their* way; i.e., they demand obedience. They are *certain* they are right, so votes & numbers make no difference. All those on the other side are either (1) enemies or (2) benighted, ignorant, malevolent. In either case there is a we-they split, elitism, smugness, righteousness, arrogance, & condescen-sion, very much like the British class system in *The Forsyte Saga* = in-dignation because "they" are not obedient.

The ultimate of this attitude of we-they is paranoia. Speak of "normal paranoia." Example: the Baptist kid on 23rd St. who, shaken by my atheistic arguments, finally got serene again by concluding that I must be of the Devil just *because* my arguments were affecting him. Talk about "Left (or Right) paranoia"? Or, better, *"a priori-ism"?* Dogmatists? How to say they have pre-fixed (preprogrammed?) positions *before* they come to the facts—which, like distorting spectacles, forbid them to see well?

Another axiom of politics 3: the anti-*a priori* empiricism of openness to experiencing, openness to flux & change, not only within oneself but outside too. (Good quote: "A thought or a perception is an experience too.") Otherwise there's no self-correction, no openness to feedback = finally fixed & static positions which predict the future abso-lutely, so that one is unable to change one's position if the future turns out to be *not* as confidently-arrogantly predicted. Quote here the passage in *Motivation and Personality* preface on normative zeal & Taoistic objectivity. Must *trust* future knowledge even before it is born. Against the arrogance of believing the future can teach us nothing, *or* that we *now* know it all & have the final position. Talk of the dangers of absolutes & absolute truth (= hard job to reconcile it with the specieshood absolutes of instinctoid values & metavalues).

If politics 3 is holistic (politics 2 also, because it moves *toward* holism), then the only thing to do with opposition of *any* kind, selfish or unselfish, ignorant or shrewd, greedy or generous, fearful or not, is to be compassionate-brotherly-loving-pitying rather than contemptuous-hostile-dominating-impatient-forcing. (Now I remember my good put-down in John Holt's class at Harvard a year or two ago, to some idiot talking of cops as pigs, trying to get her to see George Wallace as a human being: "How would *you* like to be George Wallace?" It shut her up & made her thoughtful. Thought here: very useful is the "good death with LSD" finding. It impressed tremendously the psychiatric residents in Columbus when I used it as a form of validation for the good person & therefore the good life, i.e., of being & becoming the good person.)

Saying it in another way: if the only, or at least the best, recourse you have with stupid or fearful or misguided opposition is to persuade or educate, i.e., to change his mind rather than to force him or dominate him, then the whole political question changes from "How do you seize power?" or "How do you overpower the opposition?" or "How do you get your way regardless of opposition?" over to "How do you persuade, educate, reassure, remove ignorance, fear, inertia, etc.? How do you win people around to the truth & to acting upon it?" These are all empirical, normative-science, & normative-methodological questions, as for change-agents à la NTL, i.e., methods to do research with.

Make sure to say: this holds even when you *do* have power, or *do* have a majority, or are *able* to have your way! Talk of the Taoistic boss in the same terms as we (Ann & Bertha & I) talked of the Taoistic parent & wife or husband. That is, it includes not only respect for individual differences, but *also* trust in the wisdom of the body & of its impulse-voices & judgments & conclusions. At the CACE panel, I generalized *very* widely from the Clara Davis experiments & from the other appetite, self-choice, & homeostasis researches. Also the testimony of ethnology (& today also ecology & ethology). I wound up with "trust" in the body, the person, the baby, & self-choice in general as (1) very basic to the psychology 3 attitude toward the world & (2) empirically supported, even tho overlooked & not written about much. [*Put this down as a basic job, if I ever get a research staff.*]

April 29

This thought goes back to the 1955 Motivation Symposium at Nebraska with Jim Olds & Dave McClelland. Dave made a good point—that we were each different because we were each struggling to disentangle ourselves (were ambivalent, felt guilty) from some over-whelming teacher or influence, he from Clark Hull & I from Freud. I think I've become postambivalent about Freud well enough & therefore can carry on the good in the Freudian tradition much better than the orthodox & the anti's (with which Riley Gardner agreed at Council Grove, where his contempt & hopelessness for the psychoanalytic orthodox & the "Rapapor-tizing" Talmudism were thick).

But now I've been seeing this in the new realm of the transpersonal & transhuman. Because I have been & am an atheist, I just don't get into any hassle over hidden loyalties & rebellions, as *all* of the God people seem to do, *however* liberal or really religious or sincere they may be. They still feel guilty & ambivalent over the loyalties they've revolted against. I can't think of a *single* person living today talking about "spirituality" or transcendence who doesn't finally show the fatal flaw of transference or countertransference to the past. I can use all the old religious words & concepts, deal with priests & nuns, read theology, etc., & remain cool & unconfused—& certainly untempted. Therefore I can trust myself to be dispassionate about the truth in them & not feel afraid that I might be slipping into temptation—no more than when I am with homosexuals or prostitutes or murderers. [*Try this for B-cognition of the past (embracing one's past).*]

May 2

Why is there a neurotic fear of disillusionment, of looking naive, innocent, gullible, credulous? Why also, then, the universal "joke" of fooling someone, of taking someone in? It's a low form of humor, but very widespread, & can be a put-down, a power play, scoring a dominance point over someone. It can make the (immature) joker feel superior & the (immature) jokee inferior, chagrined, eager to get revenge. I hadn't thought of this angle: it *does* look like hierarchical, baboon-type dominance or pecking order. The mature person doesn't do it, doesn't find it funny either to do or have done to. But it certainly *is* part of immaturity, both chronological & characterological.

Of course, all of this ties in with the Jonah complex also. Work it out. Ultimately this all has to do with the hubris-humility problem. But show the solution to be different at different *levels*! For example, B-humility overcomes fear of one's own greatness because, at the B-level, fear of grandiosity = fear of responsibility of one's own fate, destiny, calling = then *itself* a form of arrogance, a making oneself too big, by refusing to accept one's own destiny. To accept one's own talent or beauty or IQ postambivalently is the solution, at the B-level, of the hubris-humility conflict, à la Spinoza. It is ultimately a *sickish* arrogance to be so afraid of looking naive or undignified or gullible. [*To be so worried about one's dignity = arrogance at D-level.*] What harm does it do to be "fooled," as by a child playing peek-a-boo? A complete protection against all such nonsense is to be honest, authentic, not pompous, not putting up a front, not "dignified"—all of which is a defense against being made to look simple, naive, gullible, credulous. But the best defense is to *be* simple, naive, gullible, & credulous, i.e., to be perfectly willing to take a chance on looking so & to not feel putdown or chagrined by it. Use example: Frank Manuel's trick in interviews of seeing who would be taken in by his talk about nonexistent authors, books, & theories. He told me later I got my job because, when he tried this on me, I just looked naively puzzled & said I'd never heard of "him." Use also current example: I have begun to pick up harmless-looking hitchhikers, hippies, etc., deliberately & consciously taking my chances on the possibility of being held up, etc. *Refusing* a hitchhiker is, afer all, a positive act of mistrust or distaste or rejection. It's an insult & lowers the general level of trust & brotherhood in the air.

Another example: starting long ago at the University of Wisconsin, I remember deciding to lend Lynn Baker fifty cents—a lot of money then—even when I sort of expected he wouldn't repay it = deciding deliberately to give him one chance *before* mistrusting him, i.e., mistrusting him only on the basis of actual deed rather than *a priori* suspicion. And I have always done this since. It's worked out fine for money, but worked out very badly for lending books. *So*, I lend money freely & do *not* lend books, hardly at all (& if I do, I make sure to write it down).

But add: what worked thru this A.M. is the insight that mistrust, cynicism & paranoid suspicion are not in fact "refusing to take a chance" or avoiding a gamble. It is *not* a way of avoiding risk. This is because remorse & regret can come from *both* wrongfully trusting and wrongfully mistrusting. It's like not taking a chance on loving anyone. ("Why should I stick my neck out? I may get hurt!") One *must* take chances. Either choice is a chance. Either lending money or *not* lending money can be a mistake & bring regret & guilt. You do *not* hedge your bets & increase your safety or protect yourself against hurt by assuming everybody is a liar. That assumption, if incorrect, can be very harmful to you, not only by giving up growth, & by winning gambles as well as losing them, but also because it can *decrease* safety by bringing upon oneself hatred & attack & vengeance for insult—as well as cutting off any possibility of love. (Memory: Eddie Gordon refused me a loan, saying that lending money was the best way to lose friends. But by doing it, he lost my friendship forever & earned my contempt.)

Say it this way: what does the cynic, skeptic, mistruster lose by being cynical, etc.? (As well as: what does he gain?)

May 9

At Palace Garden Court restaurant, talking with Harry's friend about student riots, I disagreed with their diagnoses, e.g., of Vietnam, & blamed it mostly on their schmucky teachers, the whole intellectual community & their screwed-up *lack* of a philosophy of life, ethics, morals, values. Value-free science, including physicalistic, social, & psychological sciences; ethical & cultural relativity; lack of a theory of evil & therefore lack of arms against evil, meanness, nastiness, cruelty. Reminds me of Polanyi's "Notes on the Hungarian Revolution," best statement I know on his realization that modern science & philosophy really had nothing to counter Communist cynicism with. *So* it goes over into technologism (do something, *anything*, rigorously), & exactly à la S. S. or, for that matter, most of my APA colleagues & certainly most of my Brandeis departmental colleagues. Not a single real philosopher living in the U. S. today—or anyplace else for that matter. (No, I take that back: Polanyi, Yankelovich & Barrett, Henry Geiger, & lots of the psychology-3 & -4 people, tho none are *major*. I don't really know any of the Europeans—but most of the professionals are busy splitting hairs. Tillich was. Whitehead was.) Skepticism à la Manuel. Anti-U. S. scapegoating. Cynicism. Just plain vengeance & violence. Juvenocracy & Juvenolatry. The *teachers* are without values, so the kids pick it up, & have no limits. Value-uncertainty can't set limits. Since it doesn't know what's wrong, it doesn't know when to get indignant & fight. So the kids are left on their own limited resources & to their immaturities, neuroses, conflicts, & ambivalences. In their *complete* uncertainty, they follow whoever *is* decisive & forceful & definite. The elders, who should be decisive & forceful & definite, are mostly not. So they turn it over to those who are decisive out of sickness & violence & neurosis.

What we need most, therefore, is a system of values, a religion-surrogate, an ethic, a way of life. If we lack metamotivations, we develop metapathologies (not a bad way to describe the present situation).

May 10

Good point in Bronowski: the young are suspicious that success is a sell-out. Can't believe it comes from virtue or that it can be a just reward. Tend to regard it as *automatically* a proof of evil or sell-out. Therefore suspicious of all "successes," which means they must destroy their *own* aspirations, must doom themselves forever to nonsuccess & even to failure in order to remain virtuous. It means the necessity of building into my system all the connections with this: pay & metapay & metamotivations, aggridance as virtuous & deserved, resentment & countervalues. In the good society, "success" *coincides* with virtue. So again comes the political problem of (1) choosing as leaders the aggridants, the superiors, the successful ones, & (2) protecting them against envy & malice & suspicion (including this one belief that the very fact of success & being chosen leader *proves* automatically that they must have sold out & are evil).

It's as if there were implied a deep belief that power, money, status, & success *must* corrupt—that there's no alternative. Must put this in a central place in the theory of evil & of politics.

We can learn about the good leader in many other aspects simply from analyzing the reasons for youth's picking bad leaders almost inevitably—their fake decisiveness, their Oedipal defiance (spit on daddy), their ambivalence about authority, their counterphobic tendencies to respect whoever defies authority most boldly & whoever is most violent & angry. They can't stand to be called "chicken" or "Uncle Tom" or "good boy." They respond immaturely to the 2-valued simplism. They mistrust power, control, authority, money, & success, so *must* reflexively be on the side of the underdog, however evil the underdog might be. (So it's a good manipulative technique: provoke authority to make you look like an underdog.) They are automatically on the side of the weak, as with Israelis first & Arabs now, without respect to right & wrong. The immature find it very difficult to identify with the strong (today, at least—they *used* to do it!). Same with "liberals," with intelligentsia, professors, etc. Why? Why identify automatically with the weak, the failure, the unsuccessful, the rebel? Maybe they're weak, etc., because they're stupid or incapable or evil?

June 5

Puzzle: reading about Kibbutzim & all the self-sacrifice, altruism, hard work, & ego-transcendence for the sake of the collective—more in the early days than now. Problem: how come Theory-X conditions can here produce Theory-Y persons? Could use a hundred other examples throughout history. "War brings out the best in people." Solution is to add to the hierarchical isomorphism between personality & culture the additional concept of the amity-enmity complex; i.e., all these high personality traits come from external threats forcing groups to become a brotherhood, a family, allies.

But then it occurs to me that this is a merely *behavioral* similarity between the altruism, unselfishness, etc., at Theory-X level plus amity-enmity, & the altruism, etc., of Theory-Y people. That is, the latter is characterological & is independent of circumstances; you can count on it. The pseudo-altruism of amity-enmity on the other hand, disappears when external circumstances change & the external enemy disappears (then the group amity & brotherhood disappear). The true Theory-Y altruism comes also out of affluence, leisure, surplus—which is more difficult. Amity-enmity altruism comes from stress, scarcity, & adversary relationships. Also, real altruism *lasts* & pseudo-altruism doesn't. It might be given up with impatience even before the emergency is over.

This answers the old criticism of the need-hierarchy theory, that it doesn't explain martyrs, sacrifice, patriotic self-abnegation, & other homonymous acts where one's own selfish lower needs are transcended for the sake of country, family, church, etc. It may be real (metamotivated) or pseudo (amity-enmity motivated). Call it pseudo-metamotivation?

It can be a source of evil—for instance, as with some college kids today seeking intimacy & group feeling via *creating* artificially any old artificial enemy.

1970

April 29

In continual conflict over whether: (1) to continue writing for the future—pure theory, basic research—passing over the newspapers & the troubles of the day, & resisting the temptation to get caught up in intellectual journalism, polemics, fighting back, seeking for larger audiences; or (2) to take some time out to fight back with my writings against the forces of despair, hopelessness, discouragement. It really comes down to this: I think of myself as embattled & fighting against the forces of evil *either* way. But which is the best way, short-run or long-run or combination?

So far each time I've been tempted to be short-run, I've resisted it & stuck to my last. Even in the prefaces to the *Motivation and Personality* revision [142] & the religion paperback [128], which are certainly credos, i.e., fighting back, I rewrote them to be sober & "academic" in the best sense, even tho quite firm, i.e., the voice of reason, of science, of the advancement of knowledge.

This A.M. read Sidney Hook's *excellent* summary on violence in *Encounter*, April 1970, & was very grateful for it. He speaks for me. And whenever I read stuff like this—lots of it in *Encounter*—I am grateful & am tempted to do the same. But now that I've cooled down a little, I have to admit that it's excellent *polemics*, good debate, but it is *not* advancement of knowledge. It's an excellent summarizing of the *known* arguments against violence. I wish I could send out a million copies of it to every student & professor in the country & in other countries.

My immediate impulse (especially after last night's responses, & all sorts of other unhappy fantasies & angers that woke me up) was to turn to writing all the statements I've been asked to write about this & that, the current scene, & in general to do what I did with my Antioch & Columbus & Palo Alto & Council Grove lectures—to fight back *now* against chaos, nihilism, evil. I've always fantasized that trouble would come of it. But each time no trouble, but rather praise, support, admiration, gratitude for having the courage to say what they all want someone to say but don't have courage enough to.

By the way, I realized after all these lectures—some to large crowds—that I could be casual & easy about them & didn't get tensed up as I did over the precoronary lectures in San Francisco. My analysis is that

I felt the great weight of responsibility & authority on my shoulders, of being pontifical, of responding with tension to the almost-adoration, poems written for me, to the submissiveness & dependence. I had to weigh my words so goddamn carefully—& felt the responsibility of being the authority *so* heavily that it threw me into tension & exhaustion. Like the old business of being *expected* confidently to hit a home run every time at bat, to produce revelations, peak-experiences, conversions, to be a Messiah—& then of course the whole thing introjected so that *I* got to feel the necessity of hitting a home run each time I opened my mouth, of every single time having the biggest ejaculation in the world—in a word, of performing up to *their* expectations, of living up to *their* image. This was made worse when the adoration was greater, the fee higher, the crowd larger, the expectations greater.

May 7

Much turmoil & sadness last few days as the campus situation gets worse & worse—again, with the impulse to get in there & fight. I wrote a letter to ICIS Fellows, but finally put it aside to soak for a while. Again the feeling of always being in a minority—but which has always turned out later to be a majority. Or, better way to say it: since, when I *do* talk up as if I were all alone, I find always some (many?) of the silent ones agreeing with me rather than disagreeing as I had expected, then I seem to get cast in the role of leader & spokesman, i.e., of the courageous one. But I'm just not the leader type! I don't like polemics & debate & personal attack. I am not temperamentally "courageous." My courage is really an *overcoming* of all sorts of inhibitions, politeness, gentleness, timidities—& it always costs me a lot in fatigue, tension, apprehension, bad sleep, etc. Somebody asked me the question at the AHP party, & also Colin Wilson did: How did a timid youngster get transformed into a (seemingly) "courageous" leader & spokesman? How come I was willing to talk up, to take unpopular positions, while most others didn't? My immediate tendency was to say: "Intelligence—just realistic seeing of the facts." But I held that answer back because—alone—it's wrong. "Good will, compassion, *and* intelligence," I finally answered. I think I added that I'd simply *learned* a lot from my self-actualizing subjects & from their way of life, & from their metamotivations, which have now become *mine*. So I respond emotionally to the injustice, the meanness, the lies, the untruths, the hatred & violence, the simplistic answers that run counter to B-comprehensiveness & B-complexity. So I feel cheap & guilty & unmanly when I *don't* talk up. So then, in a sense, I *have* to. If I were really Olympian & long-term, etc., it would be far better to stick to my work & *solve* the problems positively

instead of fighting emergency actions now. So again this A.M. I decided
the obvious. What the kids *and* the intellectuals—& everybody else too—
need is an ethos, a scientific value system & way of life, & humanistic
politics, *with* the theory, the facts, etc., all set forth soberly. What the kids
need is an *alternative* system to the one offered by the stupid hoodlums &
the amoral or antimoral intellectuals. Always I come to this conclusion, &
always it has been effective. I have after all done much of this job already,
& it's already being effective with a sizable group, even if not as sizable as
it should be. So *again* I must say to myself: to work!

Index